THE FAR REACHES

Cultural Memory
 in
 the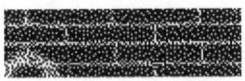
Present

Hent de Vries, Editor

THE FAR REACHES

Phenomenology, Ethics, and Social Renewal in Central Europe

Michael Gubser

STANFORD UNIVERSITY PRESS

STANFORD, CALIFORNIA

Stanford University Press
Stanford, California

© 2014 by the Board of Trustees of the Leland Stanford Junior University. All rights reserved.

No part of this book may be reproduced or transmitted in any form or by any means, electronic or mechanical, including photocopying and recording, or in any information storage or retrieval system without the prior written permission of Stanford University Press.

Printed in the United States of America on acid-free, archival-quality paper

Library of Congress Cataloging-in-Publication Data

Gubser, Michael, author.
   The far reaches : phenomenology, ethics, and social renewal in Central Europe / Michael Gubser.
      pages cm — (Cultural memory in the present)
   Includes bibliographical references and index.
   ISBN 978-0-8047-9065-9 (cloth : alk. paper)
   ISBN 978-0-8047-9252-3 (pbk. : alk. paper)
     1. Ethics—Europe, Central—History—20th century. 2. Phenomenology—History—20th century. 3. Ethics, Modern—20th century. 4. Philosophy, European—20th century. I. Title. II. Series: Cultural memory in the present.
BJ324.P46G83 2014
170—dc23

                                                            2014000494

ISBN 978-0-8047-9260-8 (electronic)

*To those nearest to me—
my wife Elisa
and my children Theo and Mira*

Contents

Acknowledgments　　xi

Introduction　　1

PART I: AUSTRIAN AND GERMAN PHENOMENOLOGY

1 The Solicitude of the Father: Franz Brentano's
   Ethics of Social Renewal　　29

2 A True and Better I: Edmund Husserl's Call
   for Worldly Renewal　　44

3 Phenomenology without Reduction: The Realism
   of the Original Phenomenological Movement　　62

4 The Blueprint of a New Heart: Max Scheler
   and the Order of Love　　80

5 Philosophy *en plein air*: Interwar Social and Ethical
   Phenomenology　　101

   Interlude: Phenomenology and Eastern European Dissidence　　132

PART II: PHENOMENOLOGY IN EASTERN EUROPE

6 The Point of View of Life: Czechoslovak Phenomenology
   through the Prague Spring　　139

7 The Far Reaches: Jan Patočka's Transcendence to the World　　151

8 The Definitive No: Phenomenology and Czechoslovak
Resistance to Impersonal Power   174

9 The Radiation of Humanity: Karol Wojtyła's
Phenomenological Personalism   188

10 The Light of Values: Phenomenological Ramifications
in Polish Dissidence   211

Conclusion: Why Phenomenology Matters
as a Social Philosophy   224

Notes   231

Index   329

Acknowledgments

The history of phenomenology is partly a history of friendships—among the early disciples of Husserl in Munich and Göttingen, among the East European dissidents who joined together against their regimes, and among scholars who study the philosophy today. Fruitful intellectual work requires friendship not only to spark and hone ideas, but also to provide distraction from mental labor. Phenomenology, after all, can be claustrophobic. In the seven years that I have been writing *The Far Reaches*, friends and colleagues from every facet of my life have helped me both to develop and escape my thoughts.

First, the institutional support: the History Department and the College of Arts and Letters at James Madison University (JMU) provided me with funding to attend conferences and present versions of these chapters. More important, I also benefited from a department sabbatical in Spring 2011, to which an American Council of Learned Societies' Ryskamp Grant contributed another invaluable year. That year and a half of dedicated research and writing—supported by the indefatigable efforts of JMU's Interlibrary Loan staff—allowed me to finish the manuscript. I would also like to thank my editors at Stanford University Press, Emily-Jane Cohen and Friederike Sundaram, for showing an early interest in the project and then guiding it through the publication process.

I am also grateful to several journals that published earlier versions of some of my chapters: "A Cozy Little World: Reflections on Context in Austrian Intellectual History," *Austrian History Yearbook* 40 (2009): 202–14; "Franz Brentano's Ethics of Social Renewal," *Philosophical Forum* 40, no. 3 (Fall 2009): 339–66; "An Image of a Higher World: Franz Brentano and Edmund Husserl on Ethics and Renewal [Aukštesniojo pasaulio vaizdunys: Etinis atsinaujinimas pagal Francą Brentano ir Edmundą Husserlį]," *Santalka* 17, no. 3 (2009): 39–49; "The Worldly Ethics of

Edmund Husserl and Jan Patočka," *Analecta Husserliana* 110, pt. 2 (2011): 579–98; and "The Terror and the Hope: Jan Patočka's Transcendence to the World," *Schutzian Research* 3 (2011): 185–202.

Many people have read drafts of all or part of this book. They offered valuable advice, caught countless errors, and made insightful commentary, much of which ended up in these pages. My gratitude goes to (in alphabetical order) Ane F. Aaro, Erika Abrams, Margaret Anderson, Kimberly Baltzer-Jaray, Michael Barber, Ed Baring, Julian Bourg, James Chappel, Ivan Chvatík, Lee Congdon, John Connelly, Nicolas de Warren, Lester Embree, Michael Galgano, Saulius Geniusas, Stefanos Geroulanos, Anne Granberg, Kevin Hardwick, William Hawk, Martin Jay, Erazim Kohák, Piotr Kosicki, Kwok-ying Lau, David Luft, Dermot Moran, Josef Moural, Samuel Moyn, Greg Moynahan, Henry Myers, Thomas Nenon, Thomas Ort, Witold Płotka, Marci Shore, Wojciech Starzyński, Aviezer Tucker, Émilie Tardivel, Lubica Učník, Donald Wallace, and Paul Wilson. The book's strengths are in many cases theirs; its remaining flaws are of course my own. I also thank Witold Płotka for helping me through my struggles with the Polish language.

The Far Reaches would not have been written had I not spent a year teaching in Prague in 1991–92, long before I had heard of phenomenology. I owe much of my subsequent education in Central European history to people over there, and one of the joys of this project has been the chance to return to that time and place. My fellow teachers at Základní Škola Horáčkova extended incredible patience to a green young American who knew no Czech and had no experience in front of a classroom. Though I have lost touch with most them, I am pleased that Dan Janata, who patiently encouraged my first stumbling efforts in Czech language, still counts among my current friends.

My expatriate friends in Prague also laid the groundwork for this project. I did not know what intellectual history was until David Sparandara introduced me to my future career. As a roommate and traveling companion, Stephen Grant taught me about literature and politics. And it is very satisfying to partner with Tim Hetherington once again: I stood next to him in 1991, on the border of Ukraine and Slovakia, when he took the photograph that is now on the cover of this book.

The Far Reaches had other beginnings as well. My graduate advisor Martin Jay devoted the better part of my Ph.D. oral examination to grilling me on the history of phenomenology. In innumerable ways, he set the stage for my scholarly career, and I could ask for no better mentor. The book's second half, on phenomenology in communist Eastern Europe, began in spring 2008 over a Chinese lunch with Jeffrey Herf. Before then, I had planned to limit the project to phenomenological ethics in interwar Germany, citing its influence on East European dissidents only to justify the importance of the topic. Jeffrey's curiosity about this later story convinced me to expand the scope of my book. This enthusiasm was echoed by Samuel Moyn and Saulius Geniusas, who contributed their considerable expertise along the way. To all of these people I owe tremendous gratitude for seeing potential that I did not see myself.

The Far Reaches would also have been impossible without the many close friends and family—too many to name here—who kept me sane by distracting me from it. I want to express particular gratitude to my in-laws, Joann and Han Soo Oh, who allowed me to attend several research-related conferences by visiting the East Coast to help care for their grandchildren in my absence. And without Hasiba Mohammed's loving child care for the past few years, this book certainly would not have been written.

As for Paolo Prandoni, the claustrophobia of book writing would have been unbearable without the escape into song-writing with him. This book took seven years to complete; the friendship and band that Paolo and I have maintained since Berkeley is, by contrast, a lifelong project.

Finally, nothing would have been possible without the infinite gifts given to me by my original family: my parents and sister, Donald and Virginia Gubser and Andrea Tribastone. They will always be the foundation of whatever success I have. And for my new nuclear family, Elisa, Theo, and Mira—to whom this book is dedicated—there is simply too much gratitude to express. Theo was born in 2010, right in the middle of my research; Mira in 2012, one day after I put the concluding period on the manuscript's first draft. While they slowed down the book in some ways, they also provided wonderful reasons for hurrying to completion so that I could spend more time with them.

My wife Elisa Oh has supported me in countless physical, emotional, and intellectual ways. It is above all her patience and encouragement that enabled me finally to complete this book. Like everything I do, it is imbued with her.

THE FAR REACHES

Introduction

When future historians chronicle the twentieth century, they will see phenomenology as one of the preeminent social and ethical philosophies of its age. The philosophical tradition not only produced systematic reflection on common moral concerns such as distinguishing right from wrong and explaining the nature of values; it also called on philosophy to renew European societies facing the crises of the twentieth century, from World War I and interwar totalitarianism to postwar communist dictatorships. Despite this legacy, historians today would find it strange to call phenomenology a social philosophy. In its Husserlian *Urform*, the school has long been discounted as esoteric or solipsistic, the last gasp of a Cartesian dream to base knowledge on the lonely rational mind. Intellectual histories often cite Edmund Husserl's methodological influence on philosophies such as existentialism and deconstruction without considering his school's social or ethical imprint. Even phenomenologists sometimes cast their tradition outside the usual realms of social thought.[1] While a few recent scholars have begun to explore phenomenology's wider social and ethical sway, its image as stubbornly academic still holds.[2]

Central to the tradition from the start, however, was a preoccupation with ethics and social renewal—at times overt, often implicit—that inspired not only second-generation phenomenologists *engagés*, but also the founders. Though phenomenological social and ethical thought took many forms, two broad itineraries can be identified. First, Franz Brentano, Husserl, and their followers used new methods of phenomenological analysis to address standard ethical topics such as how to assess conduct or explain our duty to others. Second—and more crucial to my story—advocates drew phenomenology beyond academic walls into an engagement with the social and political traumas of the century. Both Brentano and Husserl outlined a practical role for philosophy in lending significance to modern life. Their self-appointed mandate to lead a moral-cum-social renewal—a theme evident from the start of Brentano's career and dominant at the end of Husserl's—shaped the tradition's wider arc. From Brentano and Husserl to Jan Patočka and Karol Wojtyła (the future Pope John Paul II), a similar message resounded: that an ethics based on phenomenological insight could spearhead Europe's social and, at times, political rebirth.

Our limited appreciation of this story stems partly from Husserl himself. In early publications such as the *Logical Investigations* (1900–1901; *Logische Untersuchungen*) and *Ideas I* (1913; *Ideen I*), phenomenology's founder heralded the largely theoretical pretensions of his effort to ground empirical science in the data of experience, and at times he even eschewed practical engagement as a second-order concern. Ethics remained in the margins here. Additionally, Husserl's vast output, characteristically prolix and cryptonymic, seems written to repel outsiders and deny broad access. The tortured language of 'phenomenologicalese' grew in part from the demands of a pioneering analysis that abjured ready formulae from past philosophies, but it still makes for extremely arduous reading.[3] Linguistically and philosophically, Husserl appears to shut himself off from the world.

In practice, however, he was not so austere: his courses included regular ethics seminars covering practical matters; he spoke and published on the themes of social crisis and cultural renewal; and he famously ended his career with a call for philosophy to rescue a ruined Europe. Scholars have inked reams of paper interpreting Husserl's last and best-known work, *The Crisis of European Sciences and Transcendental Phenomenology* (1936; *Die Krisis der europäischen Wissenschaften und die transzendentale Phänomenologie*), but neglect of his long-standing social concerns misses a crucial impulse at the origin of phenomenology and allows historians to pigeonhole it as a philosophy of logic and consciousness. Husserl's cohorts, largely forgotten outside specialist circles, were even more explicit in employing phenomenological categories for social and ethical gain. Max Scheler built a name on studies of ethical personalism, absolute values, and philosophical anthropology. Before his death in World War I, Adolf Reinach applied phenomenology to the study of social acts. And Edith Stein developed phenomenological theories of intersubjective empathy and the role of the state. Polish and Czechoslovak dissidents such as Patočka, Wojtyła, and Václav Havel saw in phenomenology a tocsin for depersonalized modern societies, calling their fellow citizens toward fuller humanity. It was in the hands of East European thinkers and activists, the subject of this book's second half, that phenomenology emerged as a full-fledged social philosophy, ranged against both Soviet Bloc communism and Western liberalism. But the critique of modern society was present already at phenomenology's start in fin-de-siècle and interwar Germany, and post–World War II dissidents saw themselves as furthering a tradition that retained the best of modern European culture and thought.

Despite these preoccupations, few histories of contemporary ethics or social theory mention German phenomenology, and those that do tend to echo Jacques Maritain's 1960 dismissal of its contribution as unoriginal.[4] While many scholars have noted the pervasive sense of crisis in interwar Germany and Austria, few have surveyed phenomenological critiques of modernity or proposals for ethical and social renewal. Omens of crisis and programs of reform were, of course, prevalent across interwar Europe, and the omission of phenomenologists from the typical roll call is striking.[5] German phenomenology is a mainspring of twentieth-century Continental thought, and its ethical concerns, both explicit and implicit, helped to define several generations of European philosophers living through the midcentury catastrophe. Those that do consider phenomenology's social impact tend to conclude with the sad tales of Heidegger's Nazism or Sartre's Stalinism. The message is clear: phenomenology was ill-suited to ethical or political judgment.

This book tells a different story, one that is not restricted to interbellum emergencies, but reaches back to Brentano's nineteenth-century pleas for a philosophical renewal of modernity and forward to the momentous struggles of anti-communist dissidents. It focuses on Central Europe, moving from the German and Austrian birthlands of phenomenology to postwar Czechoslovakia and Poland, where the philosophy's social and ethical dividends came to the fore.[6] East European phenomenologists help us to challenge two common charges against the philosophy—one typically lodged against Husserl, the other against Heidegger. The first, made for example by Theodor Adorno, dismisses phenomenology as solely epistemological, even solipsistic.[7] The second contends that as a result of this aloofness, phenomenology was unable to resist the radical politics of being and authenticity embodied in Nazism. Because of its worldly dereliction, in other words, phenomenology led to either meek apoliticism or, worse, the uncritical acceptance of raw power.[8] Patočka and Wojtyła show the philosophy in a very different light. That phenomenology could have such a tremendous impact on the dissident movements of Eastern Europe is a profound challenge to prevailing presentations of it as an abstract epistemological exercise. As we will see in ensuing chapters, the foundations of this social concern were there from the philosophy's start.

Outside of specialist circles, phenomenology's program of social renewal was largely forgotten after World War II. German phenomenological dominance waned after most of its leaders either died or fled the country. In the West, the Paris of Sartre, Merleau-Ponty, and Lévinas became the new hub of phenomenology; and in the United States, exiled phenomenologists trained in Central Europe either adopted new research programs shaped by the midcentury cataclysm (e.g., Arendt) or continued with Husserlian research in a specialist vein. Furthermore, like other prewar monuments of German thought, phenomenology yielded up fascist tendencies to those bent on cleansing Teutonic culture *tout court*. Adorno, as we have noted, condemned Husserl's intuitionism and essentialism for disengaging rational thought. Husserlians Marvin Farber and V. J. McGill attacked Scheler's work as quasi-fascist, demoting him in the ranks of phenomenology and with him the interwar movement's social and ethical profile, which Scheler had done so much to burnish.[9] And of course, phenomenology's political credentials suffered terribly by association with Heidegger. Western phenomenology also lost its initial exuberance as second- and third-generation scions embarked on new programs—structuralist and poststructuralist—that took their phenomenological elders as foils. Though a harbinger of later philosophies, phenomenology came to be seen as a brilliant failure whose Cartesian epistemology and exaggerated subjectivity had been surpassed. The slow but steady publication of Husserl's enormous manuscript library through the Husserliana series has undermined this view among specialists, but beyond a tight circle the scope of his thought remains largely unknown. Still today, he appears as a philosopher's philosopher, the preserve of initiates. Lesser-known phenomenologists, many of them discussed in this book, languish in even greater obscurity. As a result we lack a clear picture of phenomenology's engagement with the mid-twentieth-century world.

I should note at the outset that Heidegger, perhaps the most famous phenomenologist, plays a much smaller part in this book than is typically assigned to him in histories of Husserl's school. While he exercised considerable sway in Central and East European phenomenological circles, his legacy there never overshadowed Husserl's as it did in Paris. Czechoslovak and Polish phenomenologists retained the founder's moral and intellectual stress on responsibility and his calls for social and ethical renewal. Conversely, they worried over Heidegger's dismissal of public engagement and ethical analysis from the ontological realm. As a result, Heidegger plays a secondary role in this book's primary story: the narrative of social and ethical thought within phenomenology. These topics simply were not the focus of his writing. Furthermore, for all the ink spilled over his infamous Nazi foray, it did little to affect the course of Hitler's rule; by contrast, phenomenology had direct political impact through its East European votaries, whose dissident activities weakened their tottering regimes. *The Far Reaches* highlights these lesser-known but more politically consequential trends within Central European phenomenology. Similarly, for reasons of geographic constraint and overexposure, I do not follow those German Heidegger students—Arendt, Marcuse—whose careers flourished in the West, except to note their return influence on the Central European story. Nor is French phenomenological thought, widely examined in other works, canvassed in these pages. Instead, *The Far Reaches* privileges unfamiliar discourses within the movement's Central European pale—thinkers who, unlike in France, guarded the movement's orientation toward essential truth as the latest gem of a besieged European heritage.

Reflections on Phenomenological Social and Ethical Thought

The Far Reaches is not a survey of phenomenology in the manner of Herbert Spiegelberg or Dermot Moran.[10] Instead, it tells the history of Central European phenomenology as a social and ethical philosophy, what I call 'worldly phenomenology' for short. It examines not only the pervasive concern for social and ethical themes in the phenomenological tradition, but also the recourse to phenomenological motifs among non-phenomenologists, especially in late communist Eastern Europe—what we can term, with Peter E. Gordon, the cultural "ramifications" of the philosophy.[11] It is sometimes said that phenomenology is a philosophy of mind shadowed by the threat of solipsism, that thinkers adopting phenomenology's descriptive analytic of consciousness had to turn elsewhere—to socialism, liberalism, or Catholic social thought—for the tools to make it worldly and practical. This was not the case in Central Europe, where phenomenology captured imaginations in great part *because* of its social and ethical vision, not *despite* its purported lack of one. Indeed, the ethical and social—and often the political—were aspects of the same concern for most phenomenologists. Starting with Brentano and Husserl and proceeding through the anti-Soviet dissidents of the 1970s and 1980s, social and political reform was consistently understood to require ethical renewal—achieved by reorientation toward fixed moral values—as a prerequisite. Indeed, the rooting of the social and political in the ethical is one of phenomenology's distinctive features, a source of both its appeal and, as we will see, its weakness.

In arguing the case for phenomenology's worldly outlook, I do not mean to deny its consuming interest in human consciousness. Particularly in Husserl, worldliness was never unambiguous, and it often hid behind other emphases; his oeuvre goes in many directions, enabling critics to find worldless idealism and egological solipsism in some manuscripts, social theses and analyses of human community in others. If the growing body of posthumous publications makes the solipsistic critique less tenable, it is still true that even when phenomenology broached social topics, it tended to do so from an egological or experiential entry point, an angle that was at once a strength—phenomenology offered extraordinarily rich analyses of experience—and a millstone—even at its most worldly, it never broke free of the inward pull. In some sense, we might see in phenomenology an almost desperate quest, taken under the sign of crisis, to connect human beings to the surrounding world, a quest that pulled it in two contradictory directions: on the one hand, it sought a reality beyond the claustrophobia of mind, an assurance of the existence of a world beyond human fabrication; on the other, it celebrated human dignity by elevating man as a transcendent being over other objects and beings. It was, then, both a kind of humanism and a critique of humanist aggrandizement—and the ardor of its claims to essential insight and absolute truth was the converse of persistent doubts about external nature. Indeed, typical of phenomenology was the merger of internal and external, subject and object, person and world—a fusion captured in the original Brentanian seed of intentionality, the reaching forth of all cognition toward objects and beings on the far side of consciousness. Thus, even as phenomenologists defended a non-relative reality, they characteristically turned to analyses of how that reality was humanly encountered and perceived. Yet for all of their focus on experience, they insisted that 'the real' extended beyond human sensory awareness to encompass essential formal and material structures; to believe otherwise was to fall prey to subjectivism and relativism. The crisis of modernity, from Brentano and Husserl forward, lay in the tendency to reduce the world to elemental clay for human molding—to treat it, in other words, as nothing more than a species of experiential irreality. The phenomenological discernment of absolute essences—what Husserl called eidetic intuition, from the Greek term *eidos*, which meant form or essence—was designed in part to rescue this real world from human domination.

But eidetic analysis had a second and inverse payoff as well: the analysis of essences secured human spiritual autonomy by freeing men from the prison house of the factual. Here, Husserl's eidetic method—the imaginative variation of real things undertaken to identify their essential character—was of seismic importance. By systematically imagining the various possible forms of a phenomenon—empathy, for example, to take the case of an early phenomenological preoccupation—a trained phenomenologist claimed to identify its inbuilt characteristics unconstrained by any particular worldly example, to understand the essence of empathetic behavior without being bound to any observed instance of it; we might say he tried educe the ideal type, although for Husserl ideal reality was as real as empirical reality. But one could also take the process in reverse, moving from the *eidos* or essence of empathy to its many possible forms and styles of instantiation. Doing so demonstrates that factual reality (a failed attempt at empathy, for example) is only one worldly possibility, one instance of real being—and that phenomenological reality is vaster than mere circumstance. This recognition constitutes a kind of human freedom over against brute fact, and it had important implications in a century when war and dictatorship estranged men from themselves and enslaved them to technologies of force and power. Against these impersonal dominions, phenomenologists heralded their most cherished ethical aim: the protection and cultivation of man's unique potential.

This aim was not simply a phenomenological parergon, the incidental slough of a chiefly epistemological itinerary. Cultural and ethical renewal was part of phenomenology's original and enduring mandate. As man was an experiential being embedded in the world, phenomenology, in the view of its earliest adepts, was first and foremost an attitude of worldly engagement that Husserl congealed into a descriptive philosophical method. It challenged the neutral and disengaged stance of modern scientific observation, which treated the subject-object division as normative, transformed the earth into a stone, and distanced man from his terrestrial home. Phenomenology, we might say, attempted a kind of reenchantment or resignification of the world.

Husserl did not, I hasten to add, reject empirical science, though he did dispute its epistemological primacy. As he and his followers never tired of saying, science grew from the soil of an original experience in which subject and object, human and world, were already mutually invested. And the phenomenological elaboration of this primordial experience, they believed, would ultimately further the aims of natural science by securing its epistemological foundation and rehumanizing it. Indeed, it was this claim that Brentano introduced with his intentionality thesis, put forth as an epistemological pediment for empiricism. Husserl took it further, contending that intentionality not only stabilized empirical science by rooting its objects in acts of experience, but also—and more fundamentally—opened forth the prospect of examining man's own original world. For despite its claim to the seemingly familiar mantle of science (*Wissenschaft*), Husserl's phenomenological method did not propose a straightforward form of empirical observation but something much more basic: a set of intuitive procedures for uncovering the essential structures and possibilities of man's prescientific experience. This aim was implicit from the start of his career, although, befitting his early mathematical training, Husserl first treated man's engagement with non-sentient ideal objects such as logical forms before turning, later in life, to this-worldly phenomena such as other people, community bonds, and everyday experience. Nonetheless, the latter—the chief focus of this book—was always a pending concern: the epistemological problem of how we know presumed the gnosiological question of where knowledge came from. The world, in its fecundity, was ever-present.

Another striking feature in the history of worldly phenomenology is the steadfastness of certain core themes across radically different social and political milieux. As we will see in subsequent chapters, Central European phenomenologists from the nineteenth-century Franz Brentano to late twentieth-century dissidents shared a personalist anthropology, a commitment to communal solidarity, a belief in moral absolutes, and a staunch critique of both liberal and totalitarian modernity. These tenets took various forms, and they were stronger in some thinkers than others. Yet they lasted as a set of shared convictions throughout a century of social, cultural, and political turmoil—from the crises of relativism in the fin-de-siècle through the destruction of World War I and the postwar German collapse, from Nazi barbarism and the hecatombs of World War II to the desolation of communist East Central Europe. What linked all of these contexts in the minds of phenomenologists—and what underwrote their repeated calls for renewal—was the belief that technocratic modernity had deprived man of purpose and meaning, reducing him to an object of manipulation and force. Each of the century's cataclysms expressed the larger crisis of modern dehumanization, mechanization, and anomie. And while phenomenologists transferred their program from academic print to public exhortation or even political action primarily in the face of disaster—Dietrich von Hildebrand and Aurel Kolnai in the shadow of Nazism, the East European dissidents under communist diktat—their engagements drew explicitly on the tradition's long-standing fears of a pervasive modern nihilism. Central and East European totalitarianism, they warned, was an extreme symptom of a general Western decay.

The metaphorical leitmotif of this book—the human orientational references of distance and closeness, far and near—highlights the focus on modern loss and renewal. Starting with Husserl, phenomenological researchers undertook descriptive investigations of these basic experiential coordinates. As Husserl's assistant Ludwig Landgrebe noted, the categories structured Husserl's latent sociology as well. "The difference between near and far," Landgrebe wrote, is

> important for the elaboration of the fundamental types of life-worlds, as worlds surrounding typical human communities. It is this difference that originally delimits the circle of other people from whose communications and instructions each of us derives his knowledge of the world, so far as they are not immediately accessible to him in his own experience. First of all, in the most immediate sense, this circle is made up of others as fellow-members of the community in which one was born and grew up. These 'others' are marked off from the 'strangers,' the members of a strange and alien community. . . . Thus, the all-pervading difference between near and far, a difference relative to the absolute 'here' of our bodily existence, functions as the basis for a difference between near and far in a transferred sense, namely as a difference relative to our community and its particular surrounding world, which is marked off from the world surrounding any other community. This difference is the ground for a differentiation of the concept of 'world' according to the essential distinction between home-world and alien or foreign world.[12]

The experience of 'far' and 'near' structured political conceptions as well. From Scheler onward, phenomenologists deplored equally the lonely atoms of liberal individualism, distanced from one another, and the totalitarian impulse to fuse anonymous men into a pulsing mass filled with a false sense of intimacy and oneness. Indeed, the former led inexorably to the latter, as people sought escape into the crowd from the meaninglessness of isolation. Accordingly, the phenomenological concern for modern crisis treated the century's many and varied catastrophes as expressions of a single Western anomie furthered by narrow technocratic rationalism. Personalism, community, and morality: for phenomenologists, these antidotes addressed essential human needs unmet in modern times—needs that bound men to their fellows, their world, and, in many cases, their God.

What Is Phenomenology?

That 'phenomenology' is a vexed term is not surprising.[13] The most straightforward definition is that phenomenology is a philosophy focused on the contents of experience. Whether those contents, or *phenomena*, are products of consciousness, as Husserl's transcendental phase suggested, or direct reflections of external reality, as realists believed, is subject to debate; but what they clearly are not is the empirical objects of modern science. Measuring, dissecting, quantifying—these operations turn original experiences, or evidence (*Evidenz*), into objectified data that can be analyzed causally (or genetically, to use the common synonym). Phenomenologists, by contrast, approach experience through fine-grained description, articulating the minute textures of an encounter in order to fathom its essential contours. Accordingly, phenomenology can also be described as a philosophy of essences, understood as the innate necessities of real or ideal things. It reaches beyond the realm of sensory experience to identify phenomena that can only be discerned through rigorous intuitive methods. It was this expansion of reality beyond the confines of empiricism that first made Husserl a philosophical star. Piqued by his defense of essential reality in the *Logical Investigations*, the first phenomenologists sought essences in many domains of the world around them: law, politics, community, art, anthropology, sociology. Unsurprisingly, the temptation to posit an ideal Platonic realm of essences was too much for some to resist: Scheler's and Hartmann's value theory, Reinach's a priori right—these theories revived an ancient pedigree. But phenomenological essentialism did not require such heights. Essences could be seen as worldly objectivities that infused and informed empirical reality, indiscernible to the untrained senses but inseparable from empirical reality all the same. Some interpreters go even further by seeing in phenomenological essentialism primarily a philosophy of meaning and signification.[14] Indeed, Husserl's and Heidegger's extended discussions of language underscored the importance of signification and set the stage for the deconstructive appropriations that followed.

These basic definitions of phenomenology lead readily to its common construal as an anthropology, not in the sense of an empirical study of cultures, but as a descriptive science of human experience. If all conscious encounter, extrapolating from Brentano's and Husserl's cornerstone doctrine, is characterized by the intentional relation to an object or world, then phenomenology, far from locking humans in an experiential cage, reveals an innate human self-transcendence or openness to the surrounding world. As Max Scheler put it, "[t]ranscendence in general is a peculiarity of every conscious intention, for in every one there is present an intending-above-and-beyond its own empirical standpoint, together with the simultaneous awareness that the being of the object reaches out beyond the empirical content of the intention."[15] The emphasis on human openness has two implications: First, it casts phenomenology as a philosophy of human freedom, a philosophy that expands possibilities by recovering the openness of original human encounters. And second, if transcendence leads from the human interior to the ambient world, it can also point further still, beyond terra firma to the divine.

Given this latter implication, it is unsurprising that many Central European phenomenologists inclined toward expressions of faith: Brentano, Wojtyła, and Tischner were Catholic priests; Stein, Scheler, von Hildebrand, and Kolnai, Catholic converts; Reinach and Husserl baptized Protestant; Patočka and Havel, according to several sources, approaching the brink of religious declaration.[16] Attraction could flow in the other direction as well: Wojtyła and Tischner broached phenomenology from Catholic philosophy, not the reverse. Phenomenology shares numerous characteristics with religious belief, including an ethical orientation to fixed values, an emphasis on the nonrelativity of truth, a concern about modern moral and cultural decay, and a desire to embed anomic individuals in communities of purpose. Even the central phenomenological concepts of intention, fulfillment, and transcendence afford ample room for a religious interpretation that finds glimmers of the eternal in the experiences of man, "something transcending the medium of presentation, yet nevertheless apprehended in it."[17] As Hedwig Conrad-Martius put it, citing Peter Wust, a Christian existentialist and follower of Max Scheler, phenomenology tilted its followers toward the "'habitus of Catholic men.'" The "'yearning to return to the objective, to the sanctity of being, to the purity and chastity of things, to the things themselves'"—the yen to "'take the measure [*Maßnehmen*] . . . of authentic [*maßgebenden*] things'"—meant that "all phenomenologists could be called 'catholic,'" whether they professed the faith or not.[18]

Kolnai, Stein, and, later, Karol Wojtyła also sought to link phenomenology with Catholic neo-Thomism. The two schools offered each other reciprocal services: Thomism fortified Husserl's school with a realist ontology and a Church-sanctioned dignification of man, both of which appealed to Schelerian personalists; and phenomenology provided a rich account of human awareness and experience that Thomism lacked, enabling it to engage with modern life and attitudes. Thus, East European phenomenologies of transcendence, such as those of Patočka or Wojtyła, did not have to explode a mind-bound philosophy so much as expand the spiritual scope of a tradition that was "world-open" from the start.[19] While French existential atheism is one of phenomenology's best-known offshoots, loss of faith was by no means inevitable within the movement; the opposite occurred more frequently in Central Europe.[20]

Also noteworthy is that a striking number of phenomenologists—among them Husserl, Reinach, Scheler, Stein, and Kolnai—were originally Jewish. Hildebrand too, though raised Catholic, had a Jewish grandmother. Hildebrand and Kolnai, as we will see, drew on both their religious and philosophical convictions to denounce Nazism and anti-Semitism from neighboring Austria, helping to make pre-*Anschluß* Vienna a center of Catholic anti-fascist activism. Edith Stein as well, herself one of the Nazis' famous victims, called on Pope Pius XI to condemn the Nazi "war of destruction against the Jews." Phenomenology thus contributed to a novel Christian resistance to Nazi rule and to the gradual Catholic acceptance of Jews recently chronicled by John Connelly.[21]

Finally, we can in some sense define phenomenology as a philosophy of Europe and Europeanism. From Brentano onward, its proponents celebrated the ancient Greek bequest of philosophical self-questioning as Europe's defining innovation, and they decried European modernity as an era of perpetual crisis induced by scientific fragmentation, relativism, and subjectivism. The loss of absolute truth and a clear moral beacon left men driftless and alone, unable to find meaning in existence. In the place of ethical purpose, creature comforts and raw power became ends in themselves, with the mass of men sated by consumption while elites competed to dominate the globe and control its resources. The renewal proposed by phenomenologists entailed a return to Europe's Hellenic and Christian inheritance—phenomenologists generally ignored Hebraic and Islamic roots—to an age when philosophy helped to orient humans toward the truth, experience stood as a source of value and insight, and men approached the world with broad humility. Although a few phenomenologists also expressed openness to non-European cultures and insights, most touted Europe's primal heritage—in contrast to its despoiled present—and at times, Eurocentrically, offered it as a model for humanity as a whole.

Since my aim is to trace phenomenology's social and ethical ramifications, I avoid restricting its meaning too narrowly along philosophical lines. Instead, I adopt a broadly historical definition of phenomenology as the movement associated with Husserl's turn "to the things themselves," the rallying cry that won generations of adherents.[22] A narrower denotation would not only fail to account for the variety of phenomenological commitments but would also blind us to the movement's wider precursors and influences. It would, in other words, perpetuate the tendency to restrict phenomenology to initiates. The phenomenological credentials of Max Scheler's final philosophical anthropology, for example, can be disputed according to strict methodological criteria; but that his late work was part of a career-long desire to return to things (and values and persons) themselves—and hence marks a chapter in the ramification of phenomenology—is indisputable. The work of philosophical anthropologists like Helmuth Plessner and Arnold Gehlen affirmed this connection. Similarly, Václav Havel, Jacek Kuroń, and Milan Kundera (in the opening of *The Art of the Novel* [*L'Art du roman*])—none of them self-described philosophers—employed phenomenology only fragmentarily. But the tendency to jerry-build, to simplify, even to misconstrue, does not cancel the highly significant fact that phenomenology, however understood, galvanized thinkers and activists concerned with their modern age. That said, all of the figures to whom I devote extended treatment (as opposed to those whom I mention in passing) either considered themselves phenomenologists or claimed to tap the legacy of phenomenology in some significant way. For this reason, Havel receives greater attention than either Kuroń or Kundera. Historically, these self-definitions are important, for they show that phenomenology was not just an insider affair. In addition to the methodological technicalities that primarily engaged savants, phenomenology engendered a new philosophical zeal that mobilized thinkers to take seriously the social reality they confronted and to justify new ethical and political commitments. As Plessner put it, "the age of open experience had received its philosophy."[23]

Terminology

Phenomenology is a maximalist philosophy; instead of reducing reality to a small set of foundational principles, phenomenologists attempted to honor its infinite expanse—hence, the prolix description and enormous tomes for which it is frequently known. In trying to distinguish among fine shades of experience, phenomenologists invented a technical vocabulary that is notoriously challenging. While many of its terms are best introduced at appropriate points later in the book, some are so pervasive that they must be clarified at the outset. I confine myself here to several key Husserlian terms that remained touchstones for ensuing phenomenological discourse.

Perhaps no term is more basic to phenomenology than *intentionality* (*Intentionalität*), the founding concept revived by Brentano from medieval Scholastic sources. The intentionality doctrine argued that consciousness never existed in isolation; it was always consciousness *of* something, always related to an object. In a single stroke, the doctrine did away with both the singular ego and subjective relativism by insisting that consciousness was essentially bound to real objects. Intentionality in turn became the cornerstone of Husserl's new phenomenology, working in two directions simultaneously: elevating human consciousness as the privileged venue of experience and assuring the reality of the objective world indicated in mental acts. It was a decidedly un-Cartesian basis for a philosophy sometimes accused of Cartesianism.

Where Husserl moved beyond Brentano was in his elaboration of a methodology for intentional analysis. On the face of it, Husserl's *intuition* (*Anschauung*) of *evidence* (*Evidenz*) was similar to the epistemology of empiricism: we know something is true because we verify it through sensory observation and experiment. Evidence fulfills intention, to use phenomenological terms. But like Brentano, Husserl took this premise further than empiricists could sanction, arguing that intuition revealed objects that the senses could not find, even experimentally. Through the imaginative variation of worldly exemplars, phenomenological intuition could uncover real essences unavailable to the eyes and ears but open to trained phenomenologists. It was this intuition of essences that Husserl denominated *eidetic*, a very important theme of his early work that signaled his rejection of the simple empiricism associated with nineteenth-century positive science. Husserlian reality embraced both empirical things verifiable by the senses and ideal forms or essences—absolute logical postulates, for example, or geometric forms—subject only to intuitive affirmation. This essentialism must be sharply distinguished from the idealist philosophies of Kant, Hegel, or Fichte, for the earlier Husserl did not privilege the reality of mind over independent external being. Quite the opposite, he defended the integrity of a vast reality from psychologistic and historicist arguments that appeared to make truth relative to man. Husserl's early essentialism was, he therefore claimed, an expanded realism, secured by the evidence of rigorous intuitive insight.

It was this so-called realist Husserl who inspired the first generation of phenomenologists. In the two breakthrough volumes of *Logical Investigations* in 1900–1901, Husserl outlined a phenomenology that, for disciples, was deeply enmeshed in worldly existence; eidetic intuition could identify a priori essences that imbued the world of experience. But with the *Ideas I* of 1913, the founder announced a new *transcendental* phenomenology privileging the pure ego that supposedly underwrote experience, an ego purged of any unfounded assumptions about worldly reality, of any immediate embeddedness in the world—a turn that most early disciples took as a betrayal of phenomenology as they knew it. For Husserl, by contrast, *constitutional* analysis—the examination of the ways in which the consciousness (*noema*) shaped, or *constituted*, the perception and meaning of its intended objects (*noemata*)—elaborated the project launched in *Logical Investigations*. Reality, he insisted, had both subjective and objective dimensions.[24] To undertake constitutional analyses was not to deny the insights of a 'realist' phenomenology, but to address experience from the other side. In the first half of his career, Husserl examined the objective aspect, or pole, of experience, defending the independent reality of essences from both psychologism, which reduced objects to perceptual figments, and Kantian idealism, which made noumenal reality so inaccessible that it escaped experience. In the second half, by reversing the lens of analysis and examining the subjective contribution to reality, he countered the opposite ill—the tendency to divorce science from human experience altogether.

Husserl's new emphasis, of course, could easily lead to the view that he was reverting to an idealism set aside in his earlier work. Despite attempts of recent interpreters to discredit this accusation, there is little doubt that Husserl's realist legacy is ambiguous. Take the controversial concept of *reduction*: after publishing *Logical Investigations*, Husserl started arguing for the need to suspend the *natural attitude*, the original belief in the reality of the world. He offered two techniques for doing so, both anathema to most of his realist disciples. The *epoché* referred to the bracketing of belief in the natural world, the determination to refrain from judgment regarding its actual existence. It is important to note that while the *epoché* suspended faith in reality, it did not dismiss the experience of reality as did Cartesian doubt; the richness of experience remained, though its independent existence was no longer assumed. From here, Husserl took the further step of 'reducing' this parenthesized experience to what he increasingly deemed its ultimate foundation in the purified ego. The *phenomenological (or transcendental) reduction* uncovered the *pure* (or *transcendental*) *ego* that stood at the base of experience and partially constituted the reality it perceived. For Husserl, as we have seen, this new analytic dimension simply deepened the project he had launched in *Logical Investigations*. For many early disciples, the so-called transcendental turn was nothing short of apostasy. The resulting rift marked the first great schism in phenomenological history.[25]

Ultimately, however, if Husserl seemed to abandon the world with his transcendental turn, he returned to it late in life, although not in a way that appeased his followers. The 'lifeworld' (*Lebenswelt*) analysis made famous in the *Crisis of the European Sciences and Transcendental Phenomenology* (1936) was Husserl's twilight attempt to reconnect science with the everyday world of human experience, what he might earlier have called the world of the natural attitude, from which all experience—including the scientific and phenomenological—arose. The resulting work, one of Husserl's clearest attempts at a socially oriented phenomenology, became his best-known, and the lifeworld remains one of the few Husserlian concepts that non-phenomenologists tap.[26]

Another phenomenological concept, more closely associated with Scheler than with Husserl, also requires opening clarification—namely, the *person*. Phenomenologists sharply distinguished 'persons' from the 'individuals' prized by modern liberalism. A person (*Person*), in their parlance, designated a sentient being of supreme value and with a distinct expressive character—or personality (*Personalität*)—that emerged in mutual engagement with other people. Persons were unique and irreplaceable; individuals were interchangeable. Moreover, personal openness to and 'solidarity' with others—another prevalent term—contrasted with the self-enclosed, isolated modern atoms that phenomenologists understood by the term 'individual.' Persons were communal and responsive to their fellow men; individuals reveled in and foundered on their anomic self-sufficiency.[27] This invidious distinction structured the widespread phenomenological mistrust of the contemporary world: modern crises, in their view, originated in the dehumanization of man, the degeneration of persons into individuals and interpersonal communities into anonymous masses.

While I argue that phenomenologists produced a consistent set of worldly commitments designed to respond to perceived crises in modern life, I do not contend that their notions of worldliness were uniform, univocal, or definitive. Within social and ethical phenomenology, in fact, the range of positions was quite far-reaching, at times even contradictory: anti-psychologist but fascinated with human consciousness; usually religious but occasionally atheist; generally Catholic though sometimes Protestant; mostly anti-Marxist but occasionally Marxist leaning. Indeed, some of the most vigorous challenges to phenomenological efforts at retrieving worldly reality and promoting social renewal came from within the movement itself. Among the intra-phenomenological disputes aired in this book are the interwar realist attacks on Husserl's transcendentalism, Patočka's struggles with Husserl and Heidegger, and Wojtyła's quarrels with Scheler. In almost all cases, accusations against elders by scions circled around charges of insufficient worldliness. This scope and disputatiousness is not unusual for influential social theories—witness the rowdy Marxist and Nietzschean tents—but it nonetheless presents challenges when trying to identify a consistent tradition.

Of course, world*less*ness—in the form of solipsism, transcendentalism, emotionalism, even needless abstruseness—was one of the foremost charges lodged against phenomenology from without, as can be seen in Adorno or, later in these pages, Leszek Kołakowski. It is a central premise of this book that the charge is mistaken. But while phenomenology was a worldly philosophy, it would be wrong to insist that phenomenological worldliness was ever definitive. As we will see, the theme was always under debate as a key aporia—perhaps *the* key aporia—of phenomenological thought. Indeed, it is not too strong to say that access to the real world constituted the red thread of phenomenological evolution, driving younger thinkers to new and more worldly formulations. It is precisely the open-ended quality of this endeavor that makes it so fruitful to engage. I hope to demonstrate the continuity of this interest while noting the varied and at times contrasting positions to which it gave rise.

The Organization of the Book

The first part of *The Far Reaches* traces the emergence of a worldly phenomenology in interwar Germany and Austria. It shows that prior to the well-known ethical turn among French thinkers, Central European phenomenologists had already produced a sustained and innovative set of insights regarding moral responsibility and social renewal that informed the movement's subsequent evolution. An opening chapter on the Austro-German forefather of phenomenology, Franz Brentano (1838–1917), examines the relationship between his empirical psychology, ethics of intuitive certainty, and call for social and moral renewal through scientific philosophy. In his renowned *Psychology from an Empirical Standpoint* (1874; *Psychologie vom empirischen Standpunkt*), Brentano assigned to the nascent discipline of descriptive psychology an ethical mandate that extended far beyond its ostensible task of grounding science in the description of mental phenomena. He saw ethics as the ultimate justification of his pursuit, and expected psychological discoveries to launch a modern moral renascence. His emphasis on intuitive ethical certitudes, his call for philosophy to lead a modern reform, and his demand for scientific responsibility became central themes in the thought of his student Edmund Husserl and the subsequent phenomenological tradition.

Chapter 2 focuses on Husserl (1859–1938), the founder of phenomenology, whose examinations of value, scientific self-responsibility, and philosophy's role in moral and social renewal became touchstones for the school. Husserl's early ethical thought, developed in lecture seminars, attempted to elaborate a formal and practical moral taxonomy based on

Brentanian premises. The carnage of World War I, however, transformed his project. What emerged in subsequent decades was a vision of philosophy that would spearhead European renewal, a call he articulated in articles published in 1923–24, in his 1936 essay *The Crisis of European Sciences and Transcendental Phenomenology*, and in other manuscripts from the mid- to late 1930s. The postwar Husserl's increasing preoccupation with intersubjectivity and his attempt to embed phenomenology in a human lifeworld reflected the wider sense that philosophy needed to reestablish ties with concrete human experience and lead the reform of a modernity in crisis. Thus, he came to see phenomenology not simply in scientific and epistemological terms but also as an ethics—a view implicit from the start of his career, but overt after 1918.

The third chapter considers Husserl's early phenomenological disciples, those galvanized by the publication of the *Logical Investigations* in 1900–1901. It was this coterie, drawn primarily from the students of Munich philosopher and psychologist Theodor Lipps, that first applied Husserlian phenomenology to the analysis of ethical and social depths. Starting in the first decade of the twentieth century, they mounted a strong case for phenomenological realism—the belief that phenomenology opened direct access the external world—against Husserl's burgeoning transcendentalism, which suspended belief in the real world in order to investigate pure consciousness. The phenomenology of Adolf Reinach (1883–1917), perhaps the greatest of this early cohort, pioneered the analysis of social acts and legal right, directing early phenomenologists toward the worldly potential of the new method. The little-known Alexander Pfänder (1870–1941) applied phenomenological analysis to the study of psychological motivation, helping to broaden the Husserlian logical subject into a person equipped with will and emotions. And several of Husserl's followers, foremost among them Roman Ingarden (1893–1970), later the conduit for phenomenology in Poland, launched an ontological defense of the real world against the founder's resurgent idealism. Thus, early phenomenologists expanded both the worldly reach and the anthropological insight of the new philosophy.

The fourth chapter examines the phenomenological ethics of Max Scheler (1874–1928), overlooked since his death but arguably the key figure in cinching phenomenology's early reputation as a social and ethical philosophy.[28] Scheler's work introduced many of the themes that came to characterize phenomenological ethics and social thought in subsequent generations: an emotional intentionality that revealed absolute moral values, a stress on concrete moral personhood, a stringent critique of the "value distortions" that characterized modern civilization. Distressed by the social crises of his day, Scheler enrolled phenomenology in both the diagnosis of a modern decline toward capitalist *ressentiment* and individual anomie and the prescription of a remedy: he called in particular for the recognition of absolute values and the renewal of Christian spirituality. In addition, Scheler is the most dramatic example of the widespread phenomenological turn toward faith and religion. His outspoken Catholicism attracted the young Karol Wojtyła (the later Pope John Paul II), through whom Scheler's thought gained currency in Poland.

The fifth and final chapter of Part 1 addresses lesser-known philosophers who enlisted phenomenology in explicitly ethical, social, and political projects. Influenced by Scheler though not a self-styled phenomenologist, Nicolai Hartmann (1882–1950) wrote a three-part ethics, extolled in its day, that posited a hierarchical realm of absolute values designed to orient human action. Dietrich von Hildebrand (1889–1977) and Aurel Kolnai (1900–1973) used phenomenological value ethics as the basis of a Catholic personalist philosophy that became a springboard for their fervent criticism of National Socialism. Reinach's student and Husserl's assistant Edith Stein (1891–1942) has won attention due to her Catholic conversion and murder at Auschwitz, but in her early career she penned phenomenological tracts on empathy, ethics, and the state. Phenomenology's impact on philosophical anthropology and sociology, notably in the works of Helmuth Plessner (1892–1985), Arnold Gehlen (1904–76), and Alfred Schutz (1899–1959), reveals that it was considered a potent social and ethical philosophy by the end of the interwar period. The chapter concludes with a reflection on Martin Heidegger's subordinate role in the story of phenomenological ethics and social thought.

The second part of *The Far Reaches* follows phenomenology into communist Eastern Europe, where its political implications step to the forefront. The dissident period marked the most public effort to realize a goal embedded in the tradition from the start: the ethical reform of society. The dominant dissident positions of the 1970s and 1980s—Charter

77's rights program, Solidarity's call to moral rebirth, Václav Havel's antipolitics—displayed a similar impulse to trump politics with an ethic of truth. They drew explicitly on calls for social and ethical rebirth issued by the phenomenologists Jan Patočka and Karol Wojtyła, as well as others steeped in the tradition. Patočka and Wojtyła, the two key figures in this section, spent much of their careers interpreting Husserl and Scheler, respectively, and their late renown as dissident and pope built on these philosophical foundations. Czech and Polish dissidence, in other words, could trace a taproot to Husserlian thought.

Chapter 6 considers the early ramifications of phenomenology in Czechoslovakia from the interwar period through the 1960s Prague Spring era. One of its central claims is that phenomenology enjoyed prominence in part because it resonated with other native philosophical schools. Accordingly, many of the figures considered in this section were not phenomenologists, although they played a role in either its pre–World War II ramification or its post-Stalinist rehabilitation. An opening excursus on the philosopher and Czechoslovak president Tomáš Masaryk (1850–1937), lionized by Husserl, argues that his humanism helped to shape the Czech phenomenological reception. The chapter's midsection considers interwar phenomenology, particularly the seminal role of the Cercle philosophique de Prague pour les recherches sur l'entendement humain in disseminating phenomenological ideas and attracting its representatives to Prague. The chapter concludes by examining the importance of reform Marxists, particularly Karel Kosík (1926–2003), in reviving phenomenology during the 1960s.

The philosopher and Charter 77 spokesman Jan Patočka (1907–77), the subject of chapter 7, stands at the crux of Czechoslovak philosophical discussions and in many ways of this book as a whole. Patočka's understanding of phenomenology as a call to freedom and responsibility, an interpretation that combined Husserl's late thought with Heidegger's analysis of Being, shaped his seminal theory of human movement, his vision of a post-European future, and his hope for the renewal of modern society through a retrieval of the ancient practice of care for the soul. Indeed, it may ultimately have informed his political dissidence in the 1970s, an engagement for which he paid with his life.

Chapter 8 concludes the Czechoslovak section by considering the role of phenomenology in the Charter 77 dissident organization. The main figure in this chapter is the most renowned Czechoslovak dissident, the playwright and future president Václav Havel (1936–2011). Drawing on a phenomenological tradition that culminated in Patočka, Charter 77 signatories mounted a critique of Eastern and Western political systems, seeing in the former an extreme version of the rationalist and bureaucratic excesses of the latter. Despite the post-1989 tendency to see Charter 77 as a liberal vanguard, Czechoslovak dissidents sought to forge a new ethical society rather than adopt a ready-made Western mold. Phenomenology, with regional roots and a local humanist cast stretching back to Husserl's *Crisis of European Sciences*, helped to sustain this aspiration by providing both a critique of late modernity and a framework for renewing human autonomy and community. At the same time, as the Patočka student Václav Bělohradsky (b. 1944) saw it, Charter 77 initiated one of the only attempts to enact the social and ethical mandate introduced by Husserl and radicalized by Patočka. If, as the writer and Chartist Eva Kantůrková remarked, phenomenology was Charter 77's "main philosophical trend," we may also say that Charter 77 was one of phenomenology's clearest worldly fulfillments.[29]

The other was the resistance movement in Poland, though here it was the Catholic Church rather than reform Marxists who ushered phenomenology into the public sphere. Accordingly, after a brief history of Polish phenomenology until the 1960s, chapter 9 turns its attention to Karol Wojtyła (1920–2005), Cracow's archbishop and a philosophy professor in Lublin. Wojtyła's journey from priest to pope is legendary, as is the dedication of his early papacy to the liberation of Eastern Europe. Less well known is his intellectual development, especially his effort to model a Catholic ethics on Scheler's personalist premises. Despite an early rejection of phenomenology as ill-suited to a Christian milieu, Wojtyła later produced several explicitly phenomenological treatises designed to reinforce the innovations of Vatican II by updating Church doctrine to fit contemporary life. By the 1970s, his phenomenology of human freedom and spirituality set him at odds with the Polish communist regime, and his surprise appointment to the papacy in 1978 galvanized resistance activity in his homeland. Solidarity, it should be recalled, was a Wojtyłian concept with phenomenological roots before it became a trade union name.

The final chapter of Part 2 concerns the ramifications of phenomenology in Polish resistance of the 1970s and 1980s. Father Józef Tischner

(1931–2000), the chapter's main figure, studied under Ingarden and enjoyed the protection of Archbishop Wojtyła as he developed an unorthodox and anti-Thomistic phenomenology of human encounters with good and evil. Sermons in Cracow and Gdańsk established his reputation as a leading figure in the resistance, and he became closely affiliated with Solidarity as its semi-official chaplain. If Tischner's phenomenological commitments were deep and explicit, other activists articulated similar themes in diluted form. It is this reach that made phenomenology such a potent philosophy of social change in Eastern Europe.

The Far Reaches is primarily a work of historical reconstruction, aimed at reconstituting an overlooked tradition of ethical and social philosophy. The book has two main arguments: (1) that from its birth phenomenology engaged ethical and social questions at the core of its concerns; and (2) that these worldly commitments had significant political and social clout, especially in late communist Eastern Europe. At the same time, a book devoted to explicating a philosophical tradition can hardly avoid the duty of criticism. While I started the project with substantial sympathy for Brentanian and Husserlian efforts to validate the sense of conviction that often accompanies moral commitment, ensuing research somewhat tempered this affinity by raising doubts about certain aspects of the phenomenology's political legacy. In the book's conclusion, I take up these reservations. Here, I anticipate only one of them: Husserl's *Crisis* famously called on philosopher-functionaries to guide the renewal of a fallen mankind. From Brentano through East Europe's philosopher-dissidents, phenomenologists aspired to a distant cultural stewardship based on their claim of insight into absolute truth and goodness. Their model of enlightened guidance contrasted with both invasive totalitarian dictatorship and anomic laissez-faire individualism. But it could also come across as distinctly elitist—condescending toward common minds and average needs, dogmatic in its affirmation of essential verities, conservative in its preference for moral and political hierarchy. While phenomenologists celebrated the plurality and diversity of being, they also demanded a submission to truthful insight that in its own way brooked little dissent. "Truth speaks," Brentano once sermonized, "and whoever is of the truth hears its voice."[30] The catch, of course, was that the phenomenologist was truth's hierophant and preacher, for the truth could not speak itself. In dark times, this moral firmness could take the form of a heroic stand against political evil and cowardice. But in more tempered periods, when the forces of doom are less potent, phenomenological elitism can sound sententious. Again, it is the East European dissidents who best illustrate the fall from anti-totalitarian heroes suffering for their bravery to sermonizing moralists gradually marginalized in a democratic order.

PART I

AUSTRIAN AND GERMAN PHENOMENOLOGY

1

The Solicitude of the Father: Franz Brentano's Ethics of Social Renewal

In the opening of his landmark study *Psychology from an Empirical Standpoint* (1874; *Psychologie vom empirischen Standpunkt*), the young philosopher Franz Brentano (1838–1917) predicted that descriptive psychology would stimulate moral progress to match modernity's political and technological achievement. "How many evils might be remedied," he exclaimed, "by the correct psychological diagnosis, or by knowledge of the laws by which a mental state can be modified!"[1] Brentano compared the potential benefits of his fledgling discipline to the public health boon of nineteenth-century chemistry and physiology. Not only could "the science of the future" impart practical moral guidance; it would also advance principles that might aid in resolving political conflict and healing social disorder.[2] Psychology's ethical mandate outstripped the goals of other disciplines, for even natural science required "a sufficient quantity of ethical knowledge" to become "truly beneficial."[3] As the study of intrinsic and ultimate good, ethics "call[ed] everything into consideration," superseding even the rules of logic. Ethical laws were "absolute," its imperatives "categorical."[4] If psychology was Brentano's first philosophy, ethical insight counted as its greatest promise, and he eagerly anticipated the moral rejuvenation of a modern society beset by skepticism and irrationalism—a hope he passed on to later phenomenologists.[5]

Philosophy incarnate to his students, Brentano had a momentous impact on Central European thought, particularly during his Vienna years from 1874 to 1894, when votaries such as Husserl, Alexius Meinong,

Kazimierz Twardowski, Alois Riegl, and Sigmund Freud followed his seminars.[6] In 1874, when he joined the University of Vienna faculty, the philosophical upstart had already sparked controversy in German academic circles as a staunch Aristotelian, a sharp critic of idealism, and an erstwhile priest who had renounced his vows in protest against the doctrine of papal infallibility. Appearing in the same year, *Psychology from an Empirical Standpoint* secured his professional standing and announced his two most influential doctrines, the intentional (or mental) in-existence (*intentionale Inexistenz*) of objects and the method of inner perception (*innere Wahrnehmung*—literally, inner truth-taking), still half-buried cornerstones of twentieth-century thought. The pathbreaking volume proclaimed Brentano's commitment to psychology as an empirical science, but one based on neither pure sensationalism nor the genetic analyses typical of nineteenth-century positivists.[7] Instead, Brentano charted a discipline whose primary task was to describe mental acts and contents. By clarifying the data of consciousness, psychology, he believed, served as a prerequisite for the nomothetic natural sciences—indeed for all higher human endeavor, including ethical thought.[8]

The Psychology of Inner Perception

Brentano's ethics rested on his psychology of inner perception, a method used to undercut layers of prejudice, tradition, even language and learned behavior in order to arrive at the marrow of experience—perceptual phenomena themselves, the pure data of consciousness.[9] At this core, Brentano famously rejected the division between the mind and its perceived objects, adopting instead the medieval Scholastic notion of intentionality to argue that consciousness was "always and everywhere a certain kind of relation, relating a subject to an object," aimed outward from the cognizant self.[10]

Every mental phenomenon is characterized by what the Scholastics of the Middle Ages called the intentional (or mental) inexistence of an object [*Gegenstand*], and what we might call, though not wholly unambiguously, reference to a content, direction, or toward an object [*Objekt*] (which is not to be understood here as meaning a thing [*Realität*]), or immanent objectivity. Every mental phenomenon includes something as object within itself, although they do not all do so in the same way.[11]

Beyond its linkage of thought and content—a claim that undermined the subject-object discrepancy of post-Cartesian thought—the doctrine of intentional objectivity has elicited little interpretive consensus. Perhaps foreseeing this confusion, Brentano tried to distinguish between mental and physical phenomena: the former comprised *acts* of consciousness such as "hearing a sound, seeing a colored object, feeling warmth or cold, as well as similar states of imagination," whereas the latter were the *perceptual* impressions or objects grasped in these conscious acts: "a landscape which I see, a chord which I hear, . . . odor which I sense; as well as similar images which appear in the imagination."[12] Mental phenomena, in other words, were intentional acts themselves; they always took something as an object. Physical phenomena, by contrast, were the objects of intentional acts, but they did not themselves tend toward anything; they were, in fact, immanent to those acts, not external things.[13] This classification left Brentanian intentionality in an equivocal relation to the external world: conscious acts clearly breached the walls of the solipsistic self, yet they never quite seemed to reach the concrete world of our shared existence.[14] In a philosophical landscape dominated by neo-Kantian idealism and historicist relativism, the prospect of renewed worldliness made Brentano's doctrine appealing to generations of followers. Nevertheless, he never resolved its central ambiguity, handing it instead to the phenomenological movement (and other followers) where it stood at the heart of the realism-transcendentalism dispute between Husserl and his early disciples.

A further quality differentiated mental and physical phenomena. Mental phenomena were available to an inner perception that grasped its objects with immediate certainty, whereas physical phenomena appeared in observations that could never achieve apodictic, or absolute, surety.[15] Brentano's inner perception worked by way of indirection—*en parergo*, as he put it. Unlike inner *observation* (also called introspection), it did not gaze directly at phenomena. Mental acts and states—the phenomena of inner perception—were neither immediately perceived nor utterly distinct from observed entities; one could not isolate them as one could a physical object selected for scientific scrutiny. Instead, mental states were noticed 'on the side' while observing other things.

It is only while our attention is turned toward a different object that we are able to perceive, incidentally, the mental processes which are directed toward that object. Thus, the observation of physical phenomena in external perception, while offering a basis for knowledge of nature, can at the same time become a means of attaining knowledge of the mind. Indeed, turning one's attention to physical phenomena in our imagination is, if not the only source of our knowledge of laws governing the mind, at least the immediate and principal source.[16]

Ever the empiricist, Brentano insisted that only the observation of physical objects could grant us access to mental states. The mind perceived its own activity through engagement with an object-world; indeed, the confirmation of objective in-existence was itself a result of the mind grasping, through inner perception, its own ongoing worldly activity as an immediate, self-evident insight. Though conceptually distinct, perception and observation, mental and physical phenomena, formed poles of a unified consciousness.

We must be careful not to oversimplify this epistemology or assume that it was easily practiced. Although one *could* grasp one's own inner mental states with certainty, most people did not. Noticing immediate inner perceptions and distinguishing them from baseless prejudice took training and effort. A philosopher-psychologist (in Brentano's coinage, a psychognost) learned to notice the oblique states of mind that accompany our awareness of things.[17] Propositions gleaned from these perceptions laid the foundation for empirical knowledge, and only systematic study of mental states could place psychology on secure scientific footing.[18] Thus, inner perception became Brentano's epistemological guarantor, an assured method for achieving a true and original encounter with pure phenomena—and the marker of a scientific elite who alone enjoyed true insight. This subtle denigration of popular attitudes would persist throughout the history of phenomenology.

Given its centrality to his philosophical program, Brentano had to explain his signature doctrine many times. In a March 1889 lecture before the Vienna Philosophical Society, he reminded listeners that "the ultimate and most effective means of elucidation must always consist in an appeal to the individual's intuition, from which all our general criteria are derived."[19] Experiential truth—and all truth ultimately stood on experience—could not be assured on the basis of logical argument alone; instead, it reposed on the evidence of inner perception, which showed the indubitable existence (or nonexistence) of a thing asserted. Truth claims had an existential character: a judgment was true if it correctly asserted the existence of an object, false if it did so incorrectly. Only an act of clear intuition—or secondary reference to it—could affirm this being-in-evidence. "The explanation of a term," he told students in his popular ethics seminar, "is in the last analysis a reference to certain phenomena."[20] Brentano did not deny the power of logical assertions, but he did insist that they offered only second-order verities that lacked a self-grounding ability. Only the inner testimony of objective existence or nonexistence vouchsafed epistemological security. Science, in other words, stood on perceptual foundations, truth on insight. Perceptual psychology, with its sturdy description of mental acts and contents, fortified the rational edifice. It is worth highlighting again the ambiguity at the heart of this argument: the object whose existence truth claims asserted was not necessarily one external to mind. Brentano was never able to resolve the question of how one built from the certain awareness of immanent mental phenomena, or presentations, to the assurance of a transcendental object world, though he was clearly convinced of the reality of both.[21]

Two related assumptions bolstered Brentano's doctrine of inner perception. First, evident insight conferred an immediate cognitive warranty; there was no difference, he insisted, between perceiving an object with evidence and recognizing its veracity. And second, anyone able to train his perceptual faculties could corroborate accurate insights and differentiate clear judgment from blind, truth from verisimilitude. A perceptual analogy can illustrate this claim: if someone says that something blue is red, one cannot logically disprove her. Reason and language fail in this instance. But the false judgment can be *shown* to be wrong in an act of lucid perception: the misperceiver *sees* that what she thought was red is actually blue. She perceives irresistible evidence. That immediate truths are manifested, not rationalized, helps to explain Brentano's abrupt eschewal of argument at crucial turns, his bald assertions of truth by recourse to perceptual intuition and visual analogy, and his appeal to an audience's perspicacity to ratify his claims. Where logic ceased, language could describe the experience of insight and lay out procedures for achieving it, but it could not secure validation. The truth of perceptual claims could be indicated (Lat. *indicare*—to show) by a claimant, but it could be verified only in a similar intuitive act.

Brentano labeled two types of evident judgment: assertoric and apodictic. Assertoric claims derived their force from pure inner perception; they concerned only our own mental states, not broader generalizations, and took the form of verdicts about our consciousness or experience. "I see a horse" or "I feel pain" are assertoric propositions that refer to a particular individual and moment.[22] Apodictic judgments, by contrast, consisted of immediate and certain inductions from a single insight to a general truth.[23] Brentano distinguished this procedure from empirical inductions that rise from individual data to general laws; these were at best probabilistic. Immediate induction, by contrast, recognized absolutely and "in a single stroke" the necessary concept contained in a particular aperçu.[24] The clear picture of a circle, to use one of Brentano chief examples, allowed one to see immediately that no squared circle can exist.[25] A single instance of affliction suffices to demonstrate that pain, in and of itself, is always properly hated.[26] In Roderick Chisholm's account, apodictic verdicts, or "truths of reason," reveal "not merely what does not exist [but] what cannot exist," a definition that foreshadowed the later phenomenological notion of essence.[27] Such insights, per Brentano, allow us additionally to recognize that there are correct and incorrect judgments, and provide us with criteria for assessing the verdicts of others. "[I]f anyone, however arbitrarily, arrives at an opinion which coincides with my evident judgment, then his opinion is correct," he averred, "and if anyone arrives at an opinion that contradicts my evident judgment then his opinion is not correct." Crucially for his ethics, emotions enjoyed a similar clarity. "We know with immediate evidence that certain of our emotive attitudes are correct. And so we are able to compare the objects of these various attitudes and thus to arrive at the general concept of correct emotion."[28] Emotional analogues to assertoric and apodictic judgment occurred in the direct evidence and clear concept of correct feeling affirmed by inner perception. By rooting ethics in emotional clarity, Brentano claimed an empirical basis for moral judgment.

An Ethics of Theory and Practice

Not only did Brentano's ethics hew closely to his descriptive psychology in its methods; it also found a place in his tripartite division of mental acts.²⁹ All cognizance, Brentano contended, began with the *presentation* (*Vorstellung*) of an intentional object. This presentation was simply that—a primordial awareness whose reality had yet to be affirmed. A *judgment* (*Urteil*), in turn, avouched or dismissed the existence of the perceived phenomenon; as we have seen, Brentanian judgments were fundamentally existential. A presentation, in other words, is a primary appearance, the presencing of an object in the mind; a judgment affirms or denies the object as existing, or to use Brentano's post-1905 vocabulary, as a *realia*. In 1907, he explained the difference semantically: the nominative phrase "a green tree" signals an object presentation, whereas the predicative statement "a tree is green" involves the affirmation, or judgment, of a real object. A syntactically explicit version of the latter would read "a green tree exists," which, Brentano noted, is more precise than the account given in ordinary language but wholly synonymous with it.³⁰

In a departure from contemporary ethical schemes that distinguished passive desire from active will, Brentano collapsed emotion and will into his third mode of mental apprehension—known as either *interest* (*Interesse*) or *love and hate* (*Lieben und Hassen*)—which attributed positive or negative value to a presented object. We have already seen that certain types of emotion claimed the same indubitability as evident judgments of truth and falsehood. Invoking a Cartesian faith in clear and evident ideas, Brentano based his ethics on the immediate, intuitive apprehension of the 'rightness' or 'wrongness' of interest in a perceived object. Positive ethical judgments, for example, combined the affirmation of an object's existence with the keen certainty of its rightness, displayed in the immediate awareness of "loving correctly."³¹ There was no distinction, Brentano insisted, between evident feelings of loving correctly and the knowledge of them as right, for "[w]hen something is good in itself, then goodness is tied to its very conception."³² The only difficulty came in noticing one's own insight. It is important to stress that not just any feeling carried the warrant of validity. Only exalted emotions disclosed not just the beloved object, but that which was worthy of love. Higher feelings, in other words, stood as analogues to evident judgments in that both marked a small subset of mental apprehensions that commanded approval.³³ The self-evident insights of exalted emotion formed an empirical basis for the extrapolation of ethical principles and value hierarchies according to a logic of compatibility.

Brentano's lecture seminar on ethics, delivered regularly at the University of Vienna and published as *The Foundation and Construction of Ethics* (*Grundlegung und Aufbau der Ethik*), detailed more fully the relation between feelings and cognition.[34] The emotional basis of moral insight, he conceded, left one to wonder about its reliability. Are not feelings notoriously fickle, bound up with tastes that vary from person to person, culture to culture? Faced with this inconstancy, Brentano made two moves: First, as we have seen, he argued that ethics was not based on just any emotions but on a privileged class of exalted feelings that stood out from others for their distinctive authority. In mapping the contents of emotional experience, descriptive psychology "reveal[ed] directly the distinguishing characteristic of certain acts of love and preference; thus their existence cannot rightly be denied."[35] Second, and more reassuring, Brentano agreed that it was not higher feelings alone but the *cognition* of higher emotion that served to establish ethical dicta. "The principles of ethics, like those of all other sciences [*Wissenschaften*], must be cognitions; they cannot be emotions. If feelings play a part in these principles, it is only as the objects of the cognitions. In other words, feelings are the necessary conditions of ethical principles."[36]

Several points need emphasis here. First, a Brentanian ethical insight contained a double intentionality and a twofold objectivity. At its nucleus was a cognition that took a feeling as its object. But this feeling, in turn, which was itself a mental act, also had an intentional correlate, in this case the inexistent phenomenon valued as good or bad. Thus, the psychological kernel of Brentano's ethics was a cognition of a feeling of an object. It is important to stress the immediacy of this double operation. Value insights did not arise in a catenary sequence of emotional and cognitive acts added up to reach an ethical sum; they occurred "at a single stroke, without any induction from particular cases."[37] An ethical insight immediately certified the cognitive validity of genuine emotional awareness. It revealed further discoveries as well: the concept of correct emotion as a cognitive guarantor and "the goodness of the entire class" of objects affirmed by a single insight.[38] A single instance of pain, as noted earlier, revealed for Brentano that all pain is properly hated. Revelations of moral correctness, in other words, generated a recognizable law of ethical comportment in an intuitive flash. This coincidence of the concept in the percept marked a fundamental distinction between Brentano's and Kant's epistemologies. Whereas Kantian a priori categories denoted inexisting mental structures that shaped experience, Brentanian a priori concepts referred to universal categories of experience itself, embedded in, not prior to, the intentional relationship of a subject and object. Brentano's mind, in other words, was akin to Locke's slate; it was not organized by an innate mental hardware that preexisted experience.[39]

In 1907, persevering against charges of psychologism, Brentano restated his view that correct interest was no mere subjective determination, but found a basis in the experience of "higher feelings" and "exalted way[s] of looking at the world."[40] He once again likened perspicuous emotion to evident judgment, noting that the truths of both were attainable from concepts grasped in direct experience. As exempla of immediate emotional awareness, Brentano cited "contemplation of knowledge [that] causes a love that is experienced as being correct and contemplation of a painful experience—this being an experience which hates itself, so to speak—[that] causes a feeling of hatred that is experienced as being correct."[41] Emotional clarity and its ethical correlate were not separate insights "intertwined" or co-mingled with an object presence, but a concurrent experience of "the concept of the object," discerned in its very presentation: the awareness of love entailed the immediate recognition of its goodness, much as the presentation of a round square manifested its own impossibility.[42] Presentation, judgment, and interest did not, in other words, form a temporal series of acts; they stood instead as the unified and singular basis for ethical truth.

The rapprochement between cognition and emotion allowed Brentano to overcome a classic conundrum for ethicists who based their systems on one mental faculty or the other. A cognitionless ethics tended to founder in emotional subjectivism and yielded no generalizable principles. An ethics without emotion, however, could not prompt action—thus the perceived impotence of Kant's rationalism, which led some successors to replace it with the compelling force of will.[43] Brentano's joint foundation sought to avoid these dangers. The cognitive function enabled him to generalize ethical claims on the basis of rational universality and to escape (so he believed) the danger of emotional solipsism. And an equally fundamental affective premise meant that ethical insights could also move people to act in one way or another. The combination in one faculty of what Kant had split in two—feeling and willing—enabled Brentano to assert the continuity of desire and action.

Consider the following series, for example: sadness—yearning for the absent good—hope that it will be ours—the desire to bring it about—the courage to make the attempt—the decision to act. The one extreme is a feeling, the other an act of will; and they may seem to be quite remote from one another. But if we attend to the intermediate members and compare only the adjacent ones, we find the closest connections and almost imperceptible transitions throughout.[44]

In this regard, ethical practice engaged the whole human person, a view that future phenomenologists would embrace.

Given the stress on immediate intuition, claim verification presented special problems for Brentano's system. The only way to ratify the correctness of an emotional perception—since, as he noted, blind judgments were often "uninfected by doubt"—was to witness directly its appropriateness to the perceived thing. "[I]n those cases where our attitude [*Verhalten*] is correct," Brentano explained, "the emotion [*Gemütsbewegung*] corresponds with the object . . . it is in harmony with the value of the object, and . . . in those cases where our attitude is incorrect, the emotion contradicts the object and is not in harmony with its value."[45] The tautology of this argument—that a love is correct if it recognizes an object's love-worthiness—is obvious, and Brentano felt the need to defend it. "Tautological expressions," he insisted, "may be of considerable use in the task of explication, if one of the two synonymous terms is less subject to misunderstanding than the other."[46] While this clarification does not resolve concern, it does highlight Brentano's refusal of two easy solutions: He did not rely on pre-experiential things in themselves to anchor claims epistemologically, for nothing could be guaranteed outside experience. And he denied the possibility of stepping outside the subject-object relationship to validate truth claims, of achieving a transcendental vantage point exempt from worldly engagement. Absolute truth could only be won through perceptually immanent insight.

In the only ethical tract published during his lifetime, *The Origin of Our Knowledge of Right and Wrong* (*Vom Ursprung sittlicher Erkenntnis*), a reprint of a lecture to the Vienna Law Society on 23 January 1889, Brentano summarized his emotive theory of ethical insight.[47] While acknowledging the difficulty of discriminating evident insight from footless conviction, he nonetheless maintained that the distinction was real and essential.

Many of those blind, instinctive assumptions that arise out of habit are completely uninfected by doubt. Some of them are so firmly rooted that we cannot get rid of them even after we have seen that they have no logical justification. But they are formed under the influence of obscure impulses; they do not have the clarity that is characteristic of the higher form of judgment. If one were to ask, "Why do you really believe that?", it would be impossible to find any rational grounds. Now if one were to raise the same question in connection with a judgment that is immediately evident, here, too, it would be impossible to refer to any grounds. But in this case the clarity of the judgment is such as to enable us to see that the question has no point; indeed the question would be completely ridiculous. Everyone experiences the difference between these two classes of judgment. As is the case of every other concept, the ultimate explication consists only in a reference to this experience.[48]

Blind judgments begged questions and required verification; evident insights mooted all concern for legitimacy. Exalted emotion carried its own warrant that rendered doubt absurd in the light of insight. Pre-logical and pre-linguistic, the evidence of inner perception stood as the purest marker of truth and value, as a perceptual being-in-evidence that could not be otherwise, that could not not-be.[49] The ability to distinguish true insight from bias allowed psychologists to satisfy the epistemological needs of an ethical science.

In its global aspiration, so crucial to the goal of moral renewal, Brentano's ethics embraced naturalistic anthropological premises. "The laws of logic are rules of judging which are naturally valid," he wrote. "We are bound to conform to them, because such conformity ensures certainty in our judgments; if we fail to conform, our judgments become liable to error. In other words, thought processes that conform to these rules are naturally superior to those that do not."[50] The obligation of the 'we' (as opposed to the 'I') presupposed a logical and perceptual absolute that compelled all rational beings, a natural imperative that explained the universal duty to abide by an ethical 'ought.'

Imagine [a] species quite different from ourselves; not only do its members have preferences with respect to sense qualities which are quite different from ourselves; unlike us, they also despise insight and love error for its own sake. So far as the feelings about sense qualities are concerned, we might say that these things are a matter of taste, and *'De gustibus non est disputandum'*. But this is not what we would say of the love of error and the hatred of insight. We would say that such love and hatred are basically perverse and that the members of the species in question hate what is indubitably and intrinsically good and love what is indubitably and intrinsically bad.[51]

As opposed to mere taste or fickle desires, the exalted emotions underpinning ethical certitude were "natural" for all rational species, forming a "higher love that is experienced as being correct."[52] The global claims of this viewpoint allowed Brentano to extract wider social norms and practical guidelines from emotional insight.

Despite his warning that ethics should not treat individual cases so as to avoid slipping into casuistry, it is not surprising that much of Brentano's regular university seminar dealt with the practical matters of social reform and moral behavior, if in rather perfunctory fashion. A broad-minded thinker, Brentano offered his students myriad protocols for worldly endeavor, including a supreme practical maxim, a host of secondary rules, and reflections on free will. He mounted a steady defense of private property, marriage, the family, and the state as necessary instruments for the maintenance of public order and proper socialization.[53] His categorical imperative, the highest dictate of practical ethics, was to choose the best among the ends attainable, the one that would promote the widest possible good.[54] As we will see, this maxim resonated throughout the phenomenological movement, starting with Husserl. What is more crucial for our discussion, however, than Brentano's underdeveloped social program is his sense that societal rules, though useful, could not substitute for the auspices of inner perception. Ethics found its bedrock not in moral strictures but in the demonstrable insights of psychology.[55] An ethical society, therefore, must cultivate among its members—or, practically speaking, among its elite—a respect for higher awareness, the recognition of exalted emotion, and the readiness to acknowledge those who are guided by lucid insight. In other words, Brentano presented a psychologically grounded program for cultivating Aristotelian social virtue, one that he hoped could provide an ethical compass to modern societies adrift in relativism and indeterminacy.

The new psychology, then, would underwrite not only renewed wisdom but also a company of astute psychognosts who would lead the moral reclamation of modernity. Natural scientists were too technically focused to cultivate clear inner perception, modern philosophers had abandoned scientific accuracy, and average men lacked intellectual rigor. Without psychological discipline, Brentano feared, "the solicitude of the father, as well as that of the political leader, remains an awkward groping," as exhibited in the lamentable modern slide to subjectivism. "[B]ecause there has been no systematic application of psychological principles in the political field until now, and even more because the guardians of the people have been, almost without exception, completely ignorant of these principles," he rued, "we can assert along with Plato and with many contemporary thinkers that, no matter how much fame individuals have attained, no truly great statesman has yet appeared in history."[56] Philosophy was a culprit here. Its descent from scientific exactitude through dogmatism, skepticism, and the mysticism embodied in contemporary German idealism deprived men of needed spiritual guidance.[57] Modernity was thus two-sided, demonstrating both an extreme ethical driftlessness and the scientific fortitude to overcome it. Brentano's quasi-redemptive psychology would make good on the modern potential by guiding its moral renewal. Ethics, then, was not simply one aspect of his project; it formed the *terminus ad quem* of the philosophical whole—a view of modern decline and moral revival that he passed on to Edmund Husserl, Tomáš Masaryk, and the phenomenological movement, which transformed the rays of the intentional mind into the radiation of an ethical humanity trained toward absolute good.[58]

Evaluations of Brentano's Ethical Theory

Today's reader cannot help but greet Brentano's ethics with skepticism. Even if we accept that personal conviction can be reasonably assured, how could emotional insight certify universal norms, social legislation, or ethical direction—especially when Brentano's examples of proper emotional interest—loving insight and hating error—remain so general as to seem almost fatuous? As J. N. Findlay remarks, Brentano "presented us with too many unanalyzed ultimates and too many unjustified intuitions."[59] The notion that objective emotional insights could yield global moral laws seems far-fetched. And the ontological ambiguity of

Brentanian values—absolute and global, but also immanent to consciousness like all phenomena—casts doubt on the objective status he assigned to ethical verdicts. Without clear and distinct values, Brentano's axiology relied increasingly on post hoc comparison with similar judgments as a way of validating claims: an emotion was correct not because it corresponded to the purported 'love-worthiness' of a perceived object, but only if it coincided with the insights of an evident judger. The affidavit of ethical correctness, then, became the preferences of those who loved correctly, not values themselves, which were inaccessible to most. Thus, Brentano's ethics drifted toward reliance on a small and well-trained cognoscenti, a set of elite standard-bearers, to discern true judgment and appreciate exalted love. An avowed theism might have reassured Brentano that God provided an ultimate guarantee of judgment and love, a kind of ethical *primum mobile*, but divine reference did not solve the human problem, for one still had to identify those who could interpret heavenly signs.[60]

Brentano's in-built aristocracy of knowledge revealed itself forcefully in the entreaty to take as an ethical beacon not the plebeian judgments of the "great mass of people" but those of the "best among them."[61] As Howard Eaton noticed in 1930, the philosopher favored a kind of elevated normalcy that excluded many values antithetical to his professional and social caste.[62] "Abnormal pleasures," Brentano wrote, "can never be as rich or as complete as those that are normal."[63] Indeed, normality held an exalted worth: After prioritizing the study of "normal phenomena" over "diseased mental states" or "conscious life simpler than our own," Brentano singled out the "great personalities" of history as worthy of special interest, followed by the general if more diffuse tendencies of the ruck.[64] The normal, in other words, stood far above the average, and it is hard to avoid the suspicion that Brentano's universally correct and self-evident preferences bolstered the refined sensibilities of his own estate.

Nonetheless, contemporaries found much to admire in Brentano's ethics. G. E. Moore, the British pioneer of modern ethical thought, praised *The Origin of Our Knowledge of Right and Wrong* as "a far better discussion of the most fundamental principles of Ethics than any others with which I am acquainted,"[65] and remarked on their shared doctrine of 'the good' as an unanalyzable property that brooked no logical proof.[66] Edmund Husserl built his early ethics on Brentanian premises. Indeed, in the incipient phases of an emerging phenomenology, Husserl's chief criticism was that Brentano's theory proffered only an ethics in outline.[67] Max Scheler, too, found things to admire in Brentano, particularly the elevation of emotional insight—love and hate—within ethics; feelings became the basis of his own ethical program.[68]

In the end, though he failed to achieve his *philosophia perennis*, Brentano introduced a unique field of moral investigation distinct from the more familiar programs of Aristotelian virtue, Kantian deontology, and utilitarian calculation. His ethical preoccupations included a stress on immediate insight as the source of moral awareness; an epistemology based on description rather than logical articulation; an emphasis on subject-object co-implication; an openness to worldly calls for ethical engagement; an insistence on substantive rather than formalist or procedural claims of right; the elevation of emotional insight; and, not least, an embrace of Scholastic and theistic categories. Later phenomenological thinkers, such as Husserl, Scheler, Edith Stein, and Karol Wojtyła, inherited all of these concerns as central ethical *topoi*, returning again and again to the problematic interaction between truth and perception in their own moral systems.

Furthermore, Brentano's ethics introduced a founding theme of twentieth-century moral thought. By directing concern toward the perceived world, he not only narrowed the distance between ethical subjects and valued objects, but he also invited concern for the contextual surroundings that embraced them both. By situating ethics within object relations, Brentano raised the prospect of a worldly morality that could be called forth in concrete circumstances. Furthermore, by dignifying the emotional experience of ethical allegiance and appealing to the moral luminosity of firm conviction, Brentano offered a compelling basis for moral engagement and action, one that pointed toward later phenomenological programs of social renewal. His ethics was not simply an academic code; it licensed worldly activity. Above all, despite his scientific commitments, he was not a pure rationalist. Ethical systems could—indeed, must—exhibit logical structures, but their ultimate basis was found in emotional insight that could be intuitively perceived and cognitively affirmed—an argument that induced later thinkers to examine the prelogical convictions that guide our moral impulses. In this sense, the "ghosts of Brentano" haunt the subsequent history of phenomenological ethics.[69]

2

A True and Better I: Edmund Husserl's Call for Worldly Renewal

As incarnate beings, wrote the Czech philosopher Jan Patočka, citing his mentor Edmund Husserl (1859–1938), humans transcend their individual circumstances through freedom; we are, in his words, "beings of the far reaches" (*bytomnosti dálky*), who make higher commitments and bear ethical responsibility as part of our essential being.[1] "We live turned away from ourselves," Patočka explained in the late 1960s, "we have always already transcended ourselves in the direction of the world, of its ever more remote regions."[2] The world and its objects manifest themselves as possibilities, and our freedom, with its concomitant responsibilities, extends beyond closeted self-concern toward the distances of the earth and the depths of other beings. An elliptical phrase, Patočka's "beings of the far reaches" evoked Husserl's phenomenology of the lived body situated in a surrounding world.[3] In *Ideas II*, first drafted in 1912 though printed posthumously, Husserl introduced the body (*Leib*) as the "zero-point" of orientation, from which all concepts of distance and direction, near and far, grow.[4] The 'there' far away is a relative term that pivots on one's near surroundings; distant aspirations redound upon subjective life. Though distances may be bridged and each *Dort* made *Hier*, farness itself hovers as a horizon of effort stretching infinitely ahead. For Patočka, who met Husserl in 1929 and studied with him in 1933—indeed, for Husserl himself after World War I—humanity's distant horizon entailed the ethical overcoming of the turbulent present and the establishment of a world where men could live responsibly, engaged in the far reaches of society and nature that shape our personal and communal destiny.

Husserl's early work, including the seminal volumes that announced phenomenology and attracted its first disciples, gave few clues to the moral and social investments of his later thought. The *Logical Investigations* of 1900–1901 remained steadfastly within the rarefied and seemingly worldless realms of logic. Yet its attack on psychologism and discernment of absolute truths provided the new philosophy with numerous rallying points for an ensuing worldly agenda: First and foremost, *Logical Investigations* denounced all forms of relativism (psychologism, historicism, vitalism) that reduced logic to culture or anthropology and denied the existence of universal, trans-subjective verities. Furthermore, it asserted the existence of absolute essences independent of the minds that perceived them. If this was not exactly an affirmation of concrete worldliness, it certainly amounted to a strong defense of a reality independent of human consciousness. *Logical Investigations* placed intentional objects, which for Brentano, as we have seen, floated ambiguously between the external world and mental immanence, definitively outside the mind in a transcendent reality. The bulk of Husserl's tract employed this revised version of intentionality to show how individual cognitive acts related to real and permanent essences.

Audacious as it was in a university climate dominated by neo-Kantian idealism, this program did not yet suggest the moral and social preoccupations of phenomenology to come. In fact, Husserl was more of a follower than a founder in the realms of worldly phenomenology, although many seeds can be discovered in his early work. The main influence of *Logical Investigations* on our story, as we will see in subsequent chapters, was indirect: it incited a group of eager followers to explore the ethical, social, and political applications of the new and staunchly realist philosophy. All the same, Husserl came to insist in later decades that phenomenology was well equipped to confront the moral and social quandaries of its day, and that these were in effect the proving ground of his philosophy's ultimate relevance.[5] Not only was devotion to truth and rational clarity a moral requisite in itself, but ethics too, as both a philosophical domain and, more important, a social imperative, demanded careful elucidation and dissemination among a wider public.

During the years between the *Logical Investigations* and World War I, Husserl's program remained largely academic: he strove to expound an ethics based on Brentanian premises. His teacher's promise of moral certainty had won a coterie of followers in its time, and if by 1900 Husserl came to reject Brentano's psychologistic premises, he always upheld the call to philosophical clarity and universality, not least in ethics.[6] Husserl also retained the Brentanian tenets that moral insight based on feeling could be universalized through cognition; that this insight, like logical judgment, enjoyed the corroborating evidence of pure perception; and that the chief practical imperative was to choose the best among possible options.[7] There were important deviations: For example, Husserl split Brentano's intentional union of feeling and willing, a move that enabled separate inquiries into motivation and position-taking by phenomenologists such as Alexander Pfänder, Dietrich von Hildebrand, and, later, Karol Wojtyła. Nonetheless, in the prewar years, Husserl's main criticism of Brentano's ethics was that it offered only the outline of a theory—failing, for instance, to distinguish mental judgments from objective value. He would, in his turn, cultivate Brentano's "fruitful seeds" by elaborating a scientific apparatus for ethics to parallel the rational underpinnings of logic.[8] This endeavor, notably advanced in the prewar Göttingen seminars, led to new subfields and coinages encompassing the theoretical and practical technicalities of moral experience: a noetic (mental) theory of ethical acts, an axiology of values, an apophantics linking ethical acts with their objects, and a formal moral praxis. More zealously even than his professor, Husserl espoused an ethics akin to scientific reason.[9]

The prewar seminars, however, already exhibited aporia that pointed toward later ideas. For one, Husserl's ethics revealed a tension between the description of moral phenomena and the prescription of proper conduct. Many early notes were taken up in detailing the subfields of ethical theory or describing the regions and logics appertaining to moral acts and values. At the same time, Husserl endorsed Brentano's practical imperative to do the best that was possible in each situation. Yet the shift from abstract description to a prescriptive 'ought' lacked adequate acknowledgement of the contexts within which ethical directives operate. A further tension arose in the contrary drives to universalize and localize. While Husserl's empirical descriptions and categorical imperative were meant to ground a universal science, his guiding moral principle was not universal in the Kantian sense. Instead, he maintained that a concrete imperative—the call to do the best that is possible—could only be specified in a particular time and place as a local universality: 'anyone in my circumstances should do as I do.' In this form, Husserl's early ethics already presupposed worldly circumstance, a presumption he would deepen as he approached the notion of the lifeworld.[10]

Nonetheless, World War I introduced a new moral urgency to Husserl's project.[11] The war was a personal tragedy for him—taking one son and injuring another—and the postwar years brought him economic hardship and mounting distress over Germany's prostration. The Weimar government, signatory of the humiliating Versailles Treaty, lacked the faith and support of much of the population as it battled paramilitaries on the right and left. Within several years of Germany's defeat, hyperinflation brought further despair, wiping out the savings of many citizens and further eroding confidence in the new government. Husserl channeled much of his dismay over these events into his essays. "The war," he wrote, in a 1922–23 article for the Japanese journal *Kaizo*, "revealed the falsehood and senselessness of this culture," prompting him to seek anew the purpose of his philosophical lifework.[12] In the face of national collapse, the postwar Husserl shifted from his earlier axiological efforts toward a more worldly ethics of intersubjective duty and social renewal. This demarche was not wholly unprecedented: Husserl's influential 1910–11 article for the journal *Logos* offered rigorous philosophy as a basis not just for factual and theoretical science, but also for normative and axiological knowledge, a spiritual balm for a time in need.[13] And his posthumously published *Ideas II*, drafted "in one stroke" in 1912 and emended over the subsequent decade, served as a partial précis of his future ethical concerns.[14] But it was in the postwar years that these aperçus grew into the vision of a philosophy that would spearhead cultural renewal by helping men to transcend political and material differences and nurture transnational ideals.[15] As early as 1917, in three lectures on Fichtean idealism delivered at Freiburg, Husserl declared the wartime crisis "a time of renewal [*Erneuerung*]," and his new ethics prized the recovery of moral idealism, the vision of a new and better world.[16] "The human as human has ideals," he wrote in the early 1920s. "[I]t is his essence, that he must form an ideal for himself as a personal I and for his whole life, indeed a double, both absolute and relative, and strive toward its possible realization." For both individuals and societies, this ideal stood as a "'true' and 'better I,'" an "absolute conception" that encouraged personal and social exertion.[17] More than simply a goal-setting exercise, idealization laid the groundwork for a universal ethic and an individual absolute ought (*absolute Gesollte*).[18] Indeed, the assertion of ideals in the face of the empty scientific facticity was nothing less, in Husserl's view, than the recovery of true humanity.

One can, in fact, identify three distinct formulations of social ethics in Husserl's postwar oeuvre. The best-known, exemplified in the "Fifth Cartesian Meditation" but present as early as *Ideas II*, focused on the *egological* establishment of otherness and intersubjectivity through empathy. Here Husserl waded into a debate about the nature of our awareness of other people whose preeminent positions had been sketched by the philosophers Benno Erdmann and Theodor Lipps, the former arguing that we recognize others through rational analogy between their actions and our own, the latter believing that empathy established an immediate connection with other humans that affirmed their sentience without external analogy. Within phenomenology, Husserl was a latecomer to this debate, preceded by Max Scheler and Edith Stein, whose contributions are discussed in subsequent chapters. Nonetheless, his entry became the most prominent phenomenological treatment of the topic. In *Cartesian Meditations* (1931; *Méditations cartésiennes*), he combined the two positions noted above, erecting an elaborate scaffolding of intersubjective recognition that involved the empathetic experience of another's consciousness through the analogizing appreciation of his living body. This formulation exercised great influence, notably in French philosophy, because of its systematic and public exposition, but it has also invited criticism for its incomplete disentanglement of the other from the solipsistic ego; the other, after all, was still affirmed through corporeal analogy with the self.[19]

Empathy for an isolated other, moreover, fell short of Husserl's growing aspiration for a communal and worldly orientation. Thus, a second *personalist* formulation of Husserlian ethics was not restricted to the lonely ego or preoccupied with the question of the other's existence per se.[20] Instead, it embraced a life motivated by individual but outwardly directed determinations, a life governed by the moral mandates of clarity and purpose. The motivated life had both rational and prerational dimensions, but its focus was the temporal and cultural individual regulated by self-given norms. The personalist ethic, echoing Brentanian and Kantian imperatives, took as its goal a purposive, self-regulated life. With seeds in Husserl's prewar lectures, this vision took shape in the seminars of the early 1920s, and we find it applied to communities—to "personalities of a higher order"—in the *Kaizo* essays on renewal. As James G. Hart has shown, numerous Husserlian manuscripts argue that the 'I' already contains the other within it, that individuals within a community "penetrate one another" in forging a communal personality.[21] "[W]e do not only live next to each other but in one another," Husserl wrote in a typical passage, "determin[ing] one another personally."[22] The other—and the community of others—was already there before any egological proof.

These claims, of course, challenge the adequacy of the philosophical individualism found in *both* the egological and personalist visions, and they point to worldly concerns that increasingly preoccupied Husserl from the 1920s onward. As opposed to the thrust of his younger phenomenology, a third, *worldly* ethic, evident in desultory sketches, took the intersubjective realm, not the unified ego, as man's original experience and fundamental ethical stage. In earlier writings, the mention of social personalities already indicated the possibility of a trans-individual subjectivity, and the postwar introduction of prerational drives, little known beyond Husserl scholars, suggested the precedence of protective, nurturing communities over ego awareness. That Husserl never settled on a final vision of social ethics makes for a perplexing but bountiful foison.

The Ideal of Renewal

It was the *Kaizo* essays of 1923–24 that most clearly announced Husserl's heightened concern for social and ethical renewal. A product of Japan's Western fever, the Tokyo journal *Kaizo* (Renewal), a monthly political and cultural review founded in 1919, secured several prominent European contributors: Bertrand Russell and Heinrich Rickert preceded Husserl in its pages.[23] Although only three of the five *Kaizo* articles appeared in print—and none were published in Europe—the opuscule helped to consummate Husserl's ethical turn by offering his most sustained analysis of social and cultural life prior to the *Crisis* text.[24] His decision to publish on the theme of renewal, a topic prompted by the journal's title, was driven partly by the need to bolster family finances. But the invitation from a former student also afforded the chance to reflect on the post–World War I German debacle and to outline a program of reform led by a philosophy determined to recapture its theoretical-cum-practical authority.

The first article introduced the theme of individual and social renewal and set as a target the establishment of ethical norms for the modern world. "Renewal," announced its opening phrase, "is the general call in our present age of suffering and is heard throughout European culture."[25] The essay moved from these widespread but ill-defined "natural feelings" of community and desire for reform toward a program of social renewal led by philosopher-functionaries.[26] For reforms to succeed, Husserl insisted, philosophy had to be up to the task of leadership. As he had already lamented in his 1910–11 manifesto "Philosophy as Rigorous Science," the human sciences lacked a rationally grounded *Wissenschaft* that could function as mathematics did for natural science. Humanistic methodologies embraced either pure factual empiricism or relativistic worldviews [*Weltanschauungsphilosophie*], neither of which was grounded in true experience or could guide human aspirations.[27] Husserl's missing science would not undertake the theoretical explanation of facts or elaboration of laws, but sought instead to outline an a priori study of norms based on the open possibilities of rational human beings, norms that could guide prudent action and lead a disillusioned mankind toward greater insight and humaneness. Only a science thus embedded in the human world, he insisted, could annul the shameless "political sophistry" and Spenglerian "pessimism" of the age.[28] The motivation that drove Husserl's career from the start—the desire for a foundational rationalism—served here as well, animating the call for a scientific grounding of ethical impulses. The difference, however, was a move from the logic and epistemology of his prewar writings to an outright call for ethics based on the elaboration of human possibilities, a practical "mathesis of the spirit and of humanity" that could guide human betterment.[29] While he retained a lexicon, the enterprise changed.

Husserl's new social and ethical concerns also drew on an earlier methodological vision. The phenomenological technique of eidetic intuition (*Wesensschau*), introduced in *Logical Investigations*, relied on the imagination to vary perceptual objects so as to identify the invariant core or essence that defined them. In the *Kaizo* series, Husserl talked of applying this method to human phenomena in a way that had more direct implications for the social world than mathematics did for natural systems. Calculation, according to Husserl, produced a purely ideal reflection of nature. Each human reality, by contrast, contained a range of pure possibilities that molded and shaped it. Man was distinct from animals because he was greatly defined by these possibilities; he could never be determined by facts or laws alone.[30] Eidetic intuition could identify human possibilities, and in this regard it had clear social implications. Of all beings, only mankind consisted of selves with an "interiority," an inner life that allowed men to reimagine and remake themselves. This mutability meant that humans could not be explained solely by the causal laws of naturalistic psychology. Echoing Kant's renowned distinction between man and nature, the first *Kaizo* essay rehearsed another side of Husserl's familiar critique of psychologism: not only did psychologism conflate logic with psychology; by binding man to factual circumstance, it also voided his distinctive soul, the faculty that granted the ability to differ from oneself, to change, to regenerate, to renew. The opening of the third *Kaizo* issued a call that combined these themes into one: "The renewal of humanity [*Menschheit*]—both individuals and men in society [*vergemeinschafteten Menschheit*]—is the highest theme of all ethics."[31]

Within the framework of renewal, man was both the subject and object of ethics, a free individual capable of judgment and exertion, not bound by the circumstances of the moment or locked in biological reflex. Humans could take a perspective that encompassed past and future, overseeing their lives and forging commitments based on a survey of prospects. In order to promote reform, Husserl called on people to view their actions under the holistic umbrella of their own best possible life, the familiar Brentanian formula.[32] This attitude allowed one to choose a purposive norm as a guide to right and wrong. Indeed, the call to subordinate one's life to a higher ethical goal became for Husserl the expression of a new imperative: "To be truly human, lead a life that you can justify with thorough insight, a life of practical reason."[33] The Kantian vocabulary should not mislead us into seeing a similar project. Husserl's imperative did not lead to a formal concept of universal duty, but to rational responsibility bound by individual circumstances and experiences.

The focus on a "truly human life" was more than simply a methodological posture, adopted or relinquished for theoretical reasons. It was, for Husserl, a multistage transformation whose progress formed the renewal he espoused. The first step required individuals to commit to a calling (*Beruf*) based on a self-conscious review of personal circumstances and possibilities. This effort lifted an individual life from vague yearning for goodness to conscious and guided commitment.[34] But a life regulated by the demands of a calling was not yet fully ethical. While one could judge disparate activities against an overall goal, it was also important to evaluate the goal itself. A life regulated by a calling, in other words, remained pre-ethical as long as it stayed within the confines of a particular profession and did not compare absolute aims against each other or against wider social needs. A calling, Husserl insisted, entailed merely relative value, whereas ethics concerned the absolute. Although the bridge between the pre-ethical and the ethical remained murky, Husserl did suggest one motive for moving from individual devotion toward wider ethical purpose: personal dissatisfaction.[35] If the postwar collapse left people longing for moral direction, individual efforts at reform soon yielded to malaise when they were unable to justify choices according to wider criteria or provoke significant social change. This discontent spurred some persons to redouble their ethical strivings in the attempt to move beyond the dreary "infinity" of possibilities and toward a life focused around freely chosen paragons and defined by "the consciousness of rational responsibility, or the ethical conscience."[36]

Although the ideal ethical life—variously called "the absolute Ought" or "the absolute personal perfection"—was not fully achievable, Husserl suggested procedures for approaching it. It was not feasible to judge one's actions against an exemplar as a matter of everyday practice, but renewal could be engendered through habituation as behaviors launched by conscious effort gradually settled into passive routine. Habituation required a commitment to regular patterns of thought and action, to a consistent program and method of personal betterment.[37] Tireless self-training and gradual regularization could produce an "ethical personality," first as outward expression and then as an inner determination to fuel the ongoing process of renewal.[38]

Achieving individual renewal, however, was but a half-victory, for it ignored our duties to others. A superlative person remained error-prone in an unreformed society, and thus a new "human form" required social as well as individual regeneration and a shared ethical will—reforms extending beyond communities to nations and international humanity.[39] Husserl regularly employed metaphors likening societies to persons: a community was a "personality of a high order," a "many-headed and yet unified subjectivity" that manifested its own distinct character, which in turn determined its moral and cultural outlook.[40] Ultimately, individual and social renewal were mutually implicated. If communities could not simply be reduced to a sum of individuals, it was also the case that "true human societies" could only exist when they had as their members "true individuals."[41]

Husserl also proposed a strategy for transmitting reform. Achieving an integrated culture ultimately fell to dedicated activists who could explain new possibilities and offer a unified vision. He described this activism as a "spiritual Huygens principle," with each reformed individual a node of wider moral renewal. Through writing and speaking, education and persuasion, these advocates would gradually transform society, person by person, from a collection of individuals into a *Willensgemeinschaft*—a community of will—rooted in common values and shared vision.[42] These envoys took on the role of spiritual authorities, and Husserl likened them to mathematicians—rational instigators rather than political leaders—though he noted that cultural and religious dignitaries could also spearhead the "centralization of will."[43] Presaging his famous characterization in the *Crisis of European Sciences*, Husserl designated philosophers as the supreme functionaries of ethical renewal, "the appointed [*berufenen*] representatives of the spirit of reason." Philosophy, in turn, would become a universal science dedicated to the theory and practice of social and ethical revitalization.[44] This transformation would produce societies devoted to the progressive *Technik* of reform, culminating in a rational *Übernation*, even a world imperium governed by ethical ideals.[45] A grandiose and perfectionist vision combining aspects of Aristotelian society with

Platonic philosophical kingship, Husserl's program was not authoritarian, he insisted, because submission to rational authority would be given freely. Philosopher-functionaries would be moral stewards, not political autocrats—a theme that would reappear among Czechoslovak Charter 77 dissidents for whom Husserl's *Crisis* was a touchstone. Husserl did not, of course, consider the goal fully attainable. Renewal entailed living toward a regulative ideal; it was not a final achievement. The ethical increase of mankind was gradual, originating in the individual habitus and communal *ethos* and growing to embrace more and more members of society. As James Hart found in other social and ethical manuscripts, Husserl viewed renewal as an ongoing "movement," an infinite entelechy that approached but never met its aim.[46]

The posthumously published fifth *Kaizo* essay closed Husserl's prospectus with a macrohistorical survey of Western striving for a rational ethical culture. The lengthiest section, it highlighted the interplay between a religious worldview of normative communities and a scientific outlook celebrating individual freedom and rational endeavor. According to Husserl, European thought had launched two essential movements. In the person of Plato, it possessed a cultural forefather who defined philosophy as "rational life practice," a union of theory and practice in one transformative science that foreshadowed the aims of phenomenology.[47] The second, modern movement, epitomized by Galileo and consummated in the Enlightenment, advanced human striving through mathematization and rationalization alone. Cultural renewal would reconnect the two threads—faith and reason, norm and law, theory and practice—which had been severed in contemporary life.

That a Husserlian renewal would have profound political implications is undeniable. Yet Husserl's remarks in this regard are sparse and perfunctory, at times suggesting dirigiste leanings, elsewhere a more egalitarian communalism.[48] One of the fullest sketches of the social import of his renewal came in the well-known 1935 Vienna lecture, among his last public exposés and a prelude to *The Crisis of European Sciences*. The community of philosophical reformers, Husserl averred, was not meant to impose a Platonic hierarchy, but to serve as a model for others to emulate.

Philosophical knowledge of the world creates . . . a human posture which immediately intervenes in the whole remainder of practical life with all its demands and ends . . . A new and intimate community—we could call it a community of purely ideal interests—develops among men, men who live for philosophy, bound together in their devotion to ideas, which not only are useful to all but belong to all identically. Necessarily there develops a communal activity of a particular sort, that of working with one another and for one another, offering one another helpful criticism, through which there arises a pure and unconditioned truth-validity as common property. In addition this interest has a natural tendency to propagate itself through the sympathetic understanding of what is sought and accomplished in it; there is a tendency, then, for more and more still nonphilosophical persons to be drawn into the community of philosophers. . . . The spread . . . occurs as a movement of education, far beyond the vocational sphere.

Of course, state leaders, fearful of losing authority, would react to this popular efflorescence with persecution, but Husserl insisted that truthful ideas would outlast "empirical powers."[49] It is not hard to see why such a program, originally conceived under the shadow of Nazi consolidation, would have inspired Patočka and fellow philosopher-dissidents.

For those familiar with the 1931 *Cartesian Meditations*, the *locus classicus* of Husserlian ethics, a surprising feature of the earlier *Kaizo* series is its lack of concern for the phenomenological problem of intersubjectivity—or more properly, the elision of individual and social ethics.[50] Five years before the *Meditations*, the *Kaizo* articles, as Donn Welton remarks, took it for granted that individuals existed in social relations rather than presuming the need to ground intersubjectivity in a mechanics of empathy.[51] Five years after the *Meditations*, empathy and otherness again played a subordinate role in the *Crisis*, leaving the impression that Husserl viewed intersubjectivity as a technical facet of the wider problem of world apprehension and moral renewal, rather than the crux of an ethics itself.[52] In this light, the call for *Erneuerung* (renewal) was not simply a cul-de-sac of Husserlian moral theory; it reflected a fundamental conviction regarding the centrality of the social world. Like Brentano, Husserl saw ethics as a key to philosophy's social relevance, especially in times of crisis.

The fact that Husserl felt the need to define a philosophical and ethical basis for activism betokened a shift in his earlier phenomenological mandate and the embrace of a world of action that needed philosophical foundation. And the collaboration between phenomenology and social activism promised mutual benefits. If a world without philosophy was ethically directionless, a philosophy divorced from human societies remained nugatory and dry. To be relevant for a troubled age, phenomenology had to become social philosophy. Yet the *Kaizo* essays remained a social philosophy only in brief; they ultimately failed to offer a convincing framework for either ethical duty or practical action. One of their main tensions was between an overt social concern and the persistent Cartesianism of the ethical life reduction. Was the individual or society primary? At this stage in his career, despite metaphorical equations between individuals and personalities of a higher order, Husserl had not yet advanced to the point where a project of renewal could be seen as anything but individually driven. Although he insisted that a society was more than the sum of egos, the greater whole had yet to be explained, and there was no definitive juncture between reformed individuals and higher social forms. Nor did the universality of reason square with the particularity of individual and cultural norms.[53] In a manuscript from 1921, Husserl had introduced communities of joint striving (*Strebensgemeinschaft*) and love (*Liebesgemeinschaft*) in which mutual contact and communication led to a shared ethical motivation that elevated the whole. In these communities of will, "every awakened person (ethically awakened) deliberately sets before himself his ideal I as an 'infinite task.'" The origin of personality lay in empathy and in social acts, in a social world that preexisted and grounded the ego; and ethics grew from communal love and mutual friendship.[54] But these incipient notions made little impression on the *Kaizo* articles. It would require the subsequent decade for Husserl to recognize the superficiality of earlier pronouncements and devote greater care to the phenomenology of intersubjectivity and the dynamics of cultural renewal.[55]

The Crisis

The *Kaizo* essays serve as crucial prehistory to Husserl's final opus, *The Crisis of European Sciences and Transcendental Phenomenology*, published in 1936 in the Yugoslav journal *Philosophia*. Through the years, the *Crisis* has exerted significant fascination among Husserl's followers. Some, such as Alfred Schutz and Aron Gurwitsch, praised its novelty and insight. Others, like Roman Ingarden and Maximilien Beck, felt it simply perpetuated transcendentalism rather than embarking on something new.[56] As we will see, Husserl's late work held particular sway among Czechoslovak dissidents following the Soviet invasion of 1968. Though less socially and ethically explicit than its 1920s precursor, the *Crisis* demonstrated the growing centrality of worldliness and society in Husserl's thought. It was, of course, suffused with the despairs of its time. As in the immediate postwar years, the German depression, coupled with Nazi ascendancy, brought the philosopher renewed professional and personal miseries in the 1930s.[57] Facing straitened family finances, barred from university as a Jew, rejected by his protégé Heidegger, and forced to publish outside Germany, the septuagenarian briefly considered abandoning his homeland for posts in California or Prague.[58] As his workload increased and political life darkened, he avoided newspapers and narrowed his social engagements to pleas on behalf of self and family.[59] Yet somehow, in this atmosphere of gloom and isolation, he launched one of his most feverish bouts of philosophical labor, writing for six or seven hours daily as he elaborated a new account of the social and cultural lifeworld.

The main argument of the resulting work is well known. Modern European humanity faced cultural crisis because of a loss of meaning. Beneath a commercial sheen, men struggled to find significance in fractured lives and conflicting worldviews, and natural science, despite its technical efficiency, failed to provide them with higher purpose. Husserl's was, to paraphrase T. S. Eliot, a hollow age of hollow men. This human emptiness, he believed, took centuries to manifest, though it was inherent even at the Greek inception of philosophy. But a crucial watershed came with the Galilean Renaissance, when natural philosophers disseminated a universal mathematics that disparaged subjective experience as mere opinion, unworthy of scientific concern. The fateful loss of an original actuality became especially acute in the nineteenth century, when the cult of positivist fact reached its apex and industrial advance lost connection with deeper human urges. The disciplines fragmented; scientists became "unphilosophical experts"; and technical rationality, while supplying life's material accoutrements, quenched none of the thirst for greater meaning.[60] The scientific tendency to amputate experience and valorize narrow objectivity produced—to use the orotund phrasing of Husserl's 1935 Vienna Lecture—an "annihilating conflagration of disbelief" that invited extremism of all sorts, a smoldering "despair" and a "great weariness" that gave way—here he echoed Brentano—to either rampant skepticism or wide-eyed mysticism.[61] If, however, a purely calculating reason lay at the root of modern crises, the abandonment of reason was not a proper response. Modern cynicism and irrationalism, both terrifyingly prevalent in Husserl's old age, were symptoms of the scientific abdication of duty, not solutions to it. To counter their appeal, Husserl hoped to rejoin science with subjective experience. The posthumously published third part of the *Crisis* famously propounded the lifeworld—a shared experiential framework characterized by a unifying ethos—as the intersubjective ground of human awareness from which all rational pursuits emerge.[62]

As in the *Kaizo* essays, the desultory concern for empathy is striking for those who know Husserlian ethics from the pages of the "Fifth Cartesian Meditation." The *Crisis* addresses the communal experience of the lifeworld, but largely ignores concerns about the dyadic affirmation of an Other by an ego.[63] By the mid-1930s, Husserl had embedded human beings in a natural and social world that preexisted the intellectual confirmation of self and others. Perhaps acknowledging some of the novelties of the renegade Heidegger as well as recovering his own earlier formulae, Husserl *emeritus* increasingly cast intersubjectivity as a primordial human experience, available without the need of empathetic verification.[64] Perhaps because it was already experienced as multitudinous, the world did not require assurances of Others by lonely egos. Object perception itself, noted Eugen Fink, treated the existence of other humans as given.[65] Strictly speaking, a person could only see profiles of an object, a single side at a time – and yet we always perceived the thing as a whole; we see a chair, not just the side of a chair. This perception of the whole would be impossible without assuming the addition of an infinite number of other possible (the term is compossible) profiles seen from an infinite number of perspectives. To perceive something, in other words, was to presume an all-sided world of co-viewers existing without the need for empathetic demonstration. The singular consciousness of Husserl's transcendental ego came to appear as an abstraction from primal intersubjectivity. And against the binary empathy of a solo subject and its duetted other in worldless *a capella*, the late Husserl posed the phenomenological primordiality of a symphonic whole.

This original world was the forgotten soil of modern mathematization, mechanization, and technicization. For the natural scientist since the Renaissance, geometry and mathematics had become the language of nature, a *mathesis universalis* whose clarification was the infinite labor of modernity. The 'subjective' stylizations of myth, religion, and personal experience were cast aside in favor of precise measurement, and the residues of belief and intuition became the unconquered terrain of future science. For Husserl, this modern Prometheanism threatened to stifle the human experience from which it originated. He took as an example geometry, whose limit shapes he traced back to human practices of surveying and measuring. A precise geometry severed from its original ground could achieve technical mastery, but its feats grew distant from human experience. Indeed, the tools of modern science were so powerful that it was easy to ignore, as Galileo did, the practical and historical traditions from which they arose. The lifeworld was not only overlooked; it was degraded, replaced by an ideal calculus deemed more real than the subjective confusions of daily acquaintance. Only mathematics was real; the human world vanished altogether.[66] It must be stressed that Husserl did not reject modern science or dispute its achievements; in calling for a return to "the naiveté of life" as a way to transcend the "philosophical naiveté" of science, he did not mean to deny the latter its insights.[67] Instead, his project had the sense of a Kantian critique, validating scientific reason by delimiting its sphere of expertise. Yet the emphasis was different, for the aim of Husserl's late thought was to recover experience for a phenomenological science whose methods were not natural scientific. The mistake of modern psychology was that it tried to annex subjective experience to the causal world of genetic science rather than recognizing its innate primacy and unique characteristics.

Husserl's unpublished manuscripts from the 1930s pushed the primordiality of the social world still further. According to one sketch, pre-intellectual drives rooted in parent-child and sexual relations fostered an original sociality that preexisted ego awareness.[68] Another described the earth as a body (*Körper*) and the "ground" of all bodies, suggesting a trans-egological apperception that blurred the self with an encompassing world.[69] The earth was a constant call to activity, a sphere of belonging-together and a "system of perspectives" that affirmed both subjective nearness and the distance of other viewpoints.[70] "What is to be emphasized here is that I can always go farther on my earth-ground and . . . always experience its 'corporeal' being more fully. Its horizon consists of the fact that I walk about on the earth-ground, and going from it and from everything that is found there I can always experience more of it."[71] Indeed, Husserl applied to worldly and thingly awareness a concept he had initially reserved only for the recognition of other conscious beings: empathy.

> The fixed system of sites of all perspectivally accessible external things for me is obviously already constituted through self-propelled walking, and also, that I can carnally bring everything and every object closer (at first directly on the 'face of the earth,' but also indirectly, by means of empathizing with birds I understand flight, and then by idealizing I have before my eyes the ideal possibility of an ability.) . . . I can approach every site and be there, and thus my flesh is also thing, a res extensa, etc., that is mobile.[72]

Empathy not only assured the existence of sentient others; it also opened the world for experience. The ethical valence is hard to miss, whether one interprets it as a responsibility to know and wonder or a duty to acknowledge the being of others and respect the world as such.

To read the writings after 1929, in fact, is to enter unexplored territory. Does a Cartesian phenomenology dismiss worldliness as a naïve assumption in favor of the primacy of ego, whence we restitute the world as a necessary presupposition of our experience? Or is the world pre-given as a constitutive horizon, even the fundamental ground of our being—a direct encounter prior to the constitution of the unified self? On this question, of course, rest some of the great debates of twentieth-century philosophy, and Husserl foreshadowed their direction by tilting toward the latter in his final years. Indeed, Husserl took as his final phenomenological task the project of "initiat[ing] a new age" by reconstituting social and cultural communities on a 'rational' basis. "To be human at all," he wrote, "is essentially to be a human being in a socially and generatively united civilization; and if man is a rational being . . . it is only insofar as his whole civilization is a rational civilization."[73] While this vision of renewal grew from specifically European premises, the rebirth of reason, Husserl believed, promised to ramify across the globe. Echoing the Brentano of yesteryear, Husserl's new philosophy would ground a new humanity.

Husserl never entirely resolved the tension between a privileged self and the far reaches of the world: he clung to the phenomenological ego, the "distancing abstention," until his death.[74] Yet the worldless transcendental

Husserl and the worldly Husserl of the *Crisis* were not wholly incompatible. For it was on the preservation of a subjective moment in worldly experience—of the world there *for me*—that his call for philosophical responsibility rested.[75] From its origins in ancient Greece, the "'philosophical' form of existence" attempted to supplant mythology with theoretical and practical self-mastery that submitted to the rule of "pure reason" and "philosophy." This "superior survey of the world," according to Husserl, offered a "universal knowledge, absolutely free from prejudice, of the world and man . . . [It] frees not only the theorist but any philosophically educated person,"[76] encouraging practical as well as rational autonomy. Modern philosophy had as its foremost tasks the exercise of ethical responsibility and the promotion of social renewal in a decadent age. It sought to recapture what Athens had introduced: the ideal of forming oneself "with insight through free reason. . . . [T]his renewed 'Platonism' . . . means not only that man should be changed ethically [but that] the whole surrounding world, the political and social existence of mankind, must be fashioned anew through free reason, through the insights of a universal philosophy."[77] By reducing thought to problem solving, modern positivist science forgot its ethical mandate and "decapitate[d] philosophy," substituting faddish *philosophies* (in plural) for the quest after a singular theoretical and practical responsibility, the cult of fact for the search for meaning.[78] Through the renewal of philosophy, Husserl sought nothing less than a renascent Europe—or, better, a European culture that could "renew itself radically" by reinvigorating a debased philosophical tradition. In this avant-gardist (and Eurocentric) spirit, Husserl declared philosophers the "functionaries of mankind" who bear "responsibility for the true being" of humanity.[79] This formulation outstripped his earlier program by reconceiving theoretical responsibility as practical world-responsibility, situated in human community. In other words, Husserl came to see phenomenology not primarily as a philosophy of mind, epistemology, logic, or ontology, but as an account of our engagement with the world and those who live in it. He came to see it as an ethics.

3

Phenomenology without Reduction: The Realism of the Original Phenomenological Movement

> To have something as an object in the pure sense, there must be a distance, an absolute detachment from the perceiving subject, it must be grasped and interpreted at the point of its true standing and existence: the ob-ject in the pregnant sense of the word. That is one thing. And the other is that something can only be an absolute object when it enters the perceiving view simply and completely, when it makes the turn from within itself or allows itself without further ado to be given to the perceiving eye, revealed as itself, without losing its position of detached distance. Here is achieved the ideal relationship between knower and known.
> —Hedwig Conrad-Martius, Introduction to Adolf Reinach, *Gesammelte Schriften*, vol. 8

The worldly Husserl of the late works was not the one known by his first disciples. Early phenomenologists instead took their bearings from Husserl's founding text, *Logical Investigations*, which offered a revelatory path to truth and essences through the meticulous description of conscious experience. Especially appealing to them was its attack on psychologism and other forms of relativism and the assertion of absolute and transcendent essences.[1] "Here lies perhaps the principal difference between phenomenology and all philosophical trends of the past," effused Moritz Geiger, an early apprentice. "It is the first attempt to let the given things [*Gegebenheiten*] speak purely as such, in the fullness of their being, extended over all the regions of the world." The "passion of phenomenology" was its devotion to infinity: an infinity of essences to appreciate, an infinity of being to describe, an infinity of philosophical labor.[2] For Geiger and his cohorts, this expanse encompassed what was only implicit in Husserl's early work: a devotion to the world. The importance for our story of the original phenomenological movement—Geiger, Adolf Reinach, Alexander Pfänder, Edith Stein, Max Scheler, and others—is that they turned phenomenology into a social and ethical philosophy years before Husserl's interwar preoccupation with the lifeworld.

The story of the movement usually begins in 1902 with Johannes Daubert's hundred-kilometer bicycle journey from Braunschweig to Göttingen to meet the author of *Logical Investigations*, a book he had experienced as a philosophical tonic bath (*Stahlbad*). A student of Theodor Lipps, Daubert (1877–1947) soon founded the Munich Phenomenological Circle, steering numerous young colleagues, including Geiger, to the new philosophical master. Thus began "the Munich invasion of Göttingen," involving reciprocal visits and the exchange of ideas.[3]

The Munich phenomenologists saw in *Logical Investigations* the blueprint for a realist philosophy that cleared away the phantoms of post-Kantian idealism and returned to the *rizōmata pantōn*, the roots of it all.[4] "All the young phenomenologists," recalled Edith Stein, "were confirmed realists." They felt, in Klaus Held's words, that Husserl had rescued objects from "psychologistic dissolution" and recovered an "objective orientation for philosophy. . . . They understood the philosophy as a 'turn to the object,' an exploration of the essential structure of objects, and they made the maxim 'To the things themselves!' their battle cry."[5] For these converts, phenomenology's recovery of a universe of essences established a new philosophical purpose, whose appeal went far beyond the ostensible goal of providing secure foundations for science. As Rüdiger Safranski notes, they found in Husserl's ideas a novel sense of theoretical and personal responsibility, an "ethos of professional purity and probity," wrote the early disciple Hedwig Conrad-Martius, that "was bound to rub off on a person's attitude, character, and way of life."[6] From the start, phenomenology was seen as both a philosophy and a life practice.

Given this conviction, nascent "Husserlians" were dismayed to find that the philosopher they met in Göttingen "deviated substantially" from the author of *Logical Investigations*.⁷ As early as 1904, they discerned a troubling shift in the master's views away from realism and toward a concern for pure or transcendental consciousness, stripped of worldly connections. The drift became palpable in the 1907 lecture "The Idea of Phenomenology" and undeniable in the first volume of *Ideas* in 1913, which publicly announced Husserl's new transcendental phase. The disappointment of young followers etched a defining split in the movement between realists and idealists, Munich (the base of Husserl's first followers) and Freiburg (where Husserl taught after 1916), the Husserl of the *Logical Investigations* and the Husserl of the transcendental ego. Ironically, 1913 was also the breakout year of social and ethical phenomenology, with the publication of Adolf Reinach's essay "The Apriori Foundations of Civil Law" as well as Max Scheler's *Formalism in Ethics and Non-Formal Ethics of Values* and *The Nature of Sympathy*. Thus, the eve of World War I saw the delineation of two distinct phenomenological trajectories, one aimed at the transcendental purification from consciousness of all traces of the world, the other designed to identify essences *in* the world.

As already noted, many Munich phenomenologists studied under Theodor Lipps, whose psychologism Husserl famously chided in *Logical Investigations*. Both friend and foil of the movement, Lipps himself used the term "phenomenology" to name the pure description of the contents of consciousness, and he understood his work as consonant with the new philosophy coming out of Göttingen.⁸ The student-members of the Akademische Verein für Psychologie, a discussion club formed by Lipps in 1895, however, sided with Husserl in the emergent "Streit um Psychologie und Logik"—the argument over psychology and logic—and disputed their Munich mentor's reduction of the latter to the former.⁹ Yet as Reinhold Smid and Kimberly Baltzer-Jaray contend, the Munich embrace of phenomenology at times bore a Lippsian stamp, for the younger philosophers retained their interest in psychological and social themes that Husserl's logical program ignored.¹⁰ They were fascinated by the human soul, as Geiger remarked of Pfänder.¹¹ Well after the fervor occasioned by Daubert's discovery of Husserl, admirers shuttled between Munich and Göttingen, applying Husserlian methods to Lippsian problems and completing studies under their Munich don. Geiger's dissertation on the psychology of feeling and Reinach's on criminal law, in fact, bore no hint of

Husserl. That their mature phenomenological work, much of it appearing in Husserl's journal, continued to pursue these social and psychological topics—Pfänder on willing, motivation, and directed sentiments; Geiger on empathy, aesthetic enjoyment, and the unconscious will; Reinach on ethics and civil law—shows that the early hybridization became a lifelong merger. Moreover, whereas Husserl emphasized ideal objects and then turned to the mental acts that grasped them, his Munich acolytes, sharing Lipps's interest in psychic processes, tended to start with psychological acts or faculties—the will, empathy, social acts—and proceed from there to the essential correlates. In other words, they took up Reinach's 1914 call to identify "psychic essences," distinct in form and function from Husserl's logical essences.[12] This turn made them worldly from the start, inclined to act as explorers of the widely varied continents of life rather than paladins guarding the purity of an ideal *mathesis*.

Ultimately, this focus required Munich phenomenologists to challenge the intellectualism of Husserl's logic, which treated all mental operations as either objectifying acts—presenting an intentional object—or derivations from them. This delimitation excluded from scrutiny a range of acts, such as questioning, position-taking, empathizing, willing, motivation, or promising, that either took place in the absence of known objects or superadded new functions not strictly reducible to object awareness. Daubert, for example, contended that "a question is complete as a thought, incomplete as a taking cognizance or mode of knowing"; it is the open-ended product of the act of asking, not an operation fulfilled when its object is reached.[13] He further proposed that some states and feelings—such as "being in the mood" or "being in a certain mental state"—were "a new special genus of meaning-bestowing act besides the objectivating ones." Both inward- and outward-directed, they designated a partially pre-reflective awareness of situations, not a logical certainty or object knowledge.[14] Thus, while retaining the commitment to an anti-subjective and anti-reductive analysis of essences, Daubert lifted Husserl's brainchild out of the rationalist "solitary life of the soul" (*einsamen Seelenleben*)[15] and applied it to broader forms of worldly involvement.

As Eberhard Avé-Lallement reminds us, we should not overestimate the split between Husserl and his Munich followers: for decades, disagreements played out primarily in respectful discussions, as master and disciples co-edited Husserl's new house journal, the influential *Jahrbuch für Philosophie und phänomenologische Forschung.*[16] The differences were nonetheless real: Husserl increasingly placed the pure ego, cleansed by the phenomenological reduction of real-world inferences, at the foundation of secure knowledge; and he undertook analyses of the way that objects were created, or 'constituted,' in this purified consciousness. His young followers saw both moves as a return to idealism and an abandonment of phenomenology's original impulse to grasp 'the things themselves.' Adolf Reinach, Alexander Pfänder, Max Scheler, Roman Ingarden, and others feared that the phenomenological (or transcendental) reduction violated Husserl's unique achievement by denying the existence of the world and positing the false indubitability of a purified mind. It now fell to them to carry on the worldly project that Husserl had forsaken, to elaborate a "phenomenology without reduction" from reality.[17] Epistolary exchanges reveal the hardening of positions after 1913, though open dispute erupted only in the 1920s with published attacks on Husserl's new path by erstwhile disciples—the most direct in 1928 by the Latvian Theodor Celms.[18] Husserl's students now worked to rescue valid phenomenological methods (eidetic analysis, the program of intentionality) from invalid (the transcendental reduction and constitutional analysis).[19] For his part, Husserl regretted that his former retinue was stuck in "half-measures" (*Halbheiten*), clinging to an unsubstantiated objectivity in their acceptance of natural reality.[20] Their wide-ranging analyses risked degenerating into a "picture-book phenomenology," a jumble of ill-connected descriptions of an array of different worldly essences, all of which lacked firm transcendental foundation.[21] But complaints by the founder could not dam the new phenomenological currents.

A New Way of Seeing: Adolf Reinach

Among these first phenomenologists, Adolf Reinach (1883–1917), one of Husserl's earliest protégés, led the way.[22] Reinach became a favorite of the founder, and numerous colleagues—Edith Stein, Hedwig-Conrad-Martius, Roman Ingarden, Theodor Conrad, Dietrich von Hildebrand, Alexander Koyré—acknowledged him as their true teacher, a lucid speaker and warm personality compared to the withdrawn and preoccupied Husserl.[23] With Max Scheler, whose renown he might have matched but for his premature death in World War I, Reinach can be credited with pioneering the phenomenology of the social realm.

Reinach's phenomenological innovations were manifold. Like other early phenomenologists, he broadened Husserl's program beyond logical objectification. "[T]he realm of the a priori is incalculably large," he maintained. "All objects known have their 'what,' their 'essence'; and of all essences there hold essence-laws" governing their character and structure.[24] The termini of eidetic analysis were not simply logical forms or inexistent objects; human action, too, had its essential structures. Indeed, for every act-domain, there was a corresponding "family of essences."[25] This belief in the plenitude of the essential realm—embracing not just logical but also social, material, and ethical essences—accounted for much of the excitement surrounding early phenomenology. As Reinach told an audience in Marburg: "Wherever in the world we find ourselves, the doorway to the world of essences and their laws always stands open to us." To enter this world, phenomenology had to cultivate a new "way of seeing."[26]

Reinach illustrated this expansive view in a two-part 1913 article entitled "Die Überlegung" (Deliberation), which distinguished acts of deliberation from objectifying acts by the fact that the former took a position (*Stellungnahme*) on a particular state of affairs (*Sachverhalt*), "situat[ing] us in the phenomenon itself."[27] A worldly act, deliberation drew a person into a project or circumstance; it did not simply orient him toward an intentional object. Reinach identified two types of deliberation: Intellectual deliberation had as its terminus a verdict on the being of a particular state of affairs, a kind of Brentanian agreement or disagreement that such-and-such existed. Practical deliberation, by contrast, engaged the whole person in judging the worth of a project or action; it concerned value, not just existence; commitment, not just verification; the subject's interest as well as the project's merit.[28] It incorporated, in other words, new psychological themes (e.g., interest) and realities (e.g., value, states of affairs) into the phenomenological ambit.

The premier example of Reinach's extension of phenomenology to social analysis was "The Apriori Foundations of Civil Law" ("Die apriorischen Grundlagen des bürgerlichen Rechtes"), published in Husserl's

Jahrbuch in the same year as "Die Überlegung." A high point of prewar phenomenology, the essay posited a new category of act—the 'social act'—which many commentators see as a precursor to J. L. Austin's and John Searle's speech acts. For Reinach, the command was a quintessential example of a social act:

> Commanding is ... an experience all its own, a doing of the subject which according to its nature has in addition to its spontaneity, its intentionality, and its other-directedness, also the need of being heard. What has been shown for commanding also holds for requesting, warning, questioning, informing, answering and for still many other acts. They are all social acts, which, by the one who performs them and in the performance itself, are as it were cast towards another person in order to fasten themselves in his soul.[29]

"[P]erformed in the act of speaking," commands addressed another person; they were not mere externalizations of thought, but had to be heeded to be complete.[30] They were therefore distinct from intellectual or emotional acts that might occur in solitude, and their intentional goals were different from the fixed objects of Husserl's logic. Indeed, the correlates of commands were not timeless objects at all, but essential relations or obligations established in the act of commanding and fulfilled in the act of obeying. Promising was another Reinachian social act. According to its essential structure, a promise generated obligations that, once discharged, ceased to exist. Claim and obligation, then, were not detemporalized Platonic forms, but "entities and structures which are in time, though they do not belong to nature in the usual sense, and which derive from social acts."[31] They were real states of affairs existing in the world, not absolute and permanent eidola in the sense of geometric forms or logical propositions, which persisted whether or not humans perceived them. They came and went wholly as a result of human acts.

These transient essences formed the basis of Reinach's theory of a priori right (*Recht*), which adumbrated essential and necessary relations—such as that between claim and obligation in promises—that formed the pre-legal basis for civil laws. By *Recht*, Reinach meant something like essential legal correctness or even justice, not positive legal codes or human rights.[32] A priori right, he explained, was "independent of human knowledge, independent of the organization of human nature, and above all independent of the factual development of the world."[33] He was careful to distinguish right from morality. Morals, he noted in "Die Überlegung," addressed the value of an object or state of affairs, whereas right concerned essential and necessary relations. The two might conflict. In general, both a priori right and moral duty required that a promise made must be fulfilled. But what if the content of an obligation was morally wrong, as in the promise to commit murder? In such a case, Reinach averred, "it is one's moral duty to fulfill the demand of the higher duty. There is no doubt that in our example one's moral duty would be not to commit the murder. But the essential thing for us in the present and in other ethical contexts is that here too an obligation arises from the promise and remains intact."[34]

The example is an awkward one, since most law codes would discard the promise as well. It is nonetheless easy to imagine a case in which the fulfillment of a legal stipulation would produce morally dubious consequences—the quick, callous foreclosure on a house, for example. Ethics and right, in other words, were not the same domains, though they both dealt with eidetic forms. Furthermore, actual law codes need not always reflect a priori right, though essential relations should guide their conception.

Reinach's analysis extended the worldly reach of phenomenology in another way as well. His concern for social and ethical topics necessitated a broader understanding of the phenomenological subject as a concrete person invested in the world. Reinach's subject, known variously as the ego, the personality (*Persönlichkeit*), or sometimes just the person, was more hale and robust than Husserl's intellectualist cogito. As Karl Schuhmann shows through the reconstruction of a lost 1906 ethics lecture, Reinach viewed moral worth as a quality of persons as well as objects (*Gegenstände*).[35] Social acts, therefore, presumed persons as moral agents. "Claim and obligation," he averred, "presuppose universally and necessarily some bearer, some person to whom the claims and obligations belong." Indeed, he insisted that "only persons can be the holders of rights and obligations."[36] John Crosby and James DuBois are correct to note that Reinach's conception of the person is underdeveloped, but it is nonetheless a tantalizing seed.[37] The ethical concept of personhood would become a prevalent theme for subsequent phenomenologists, particularly in the postwar ethics of Poland's Roman Ingarden and Karol Wojtyła.

Reinach's best-known statement is a lecture on phenomenological method delivered in 1914 in Marburg, home to the rival neo-Kantian school—a speech he jokingly described as missionary activity.[38] Phenomenology, he told his skeptical audience, was an "attitude," not "a system of philosophical propositions and truths"; it was more akin to art than science. Phenomenology cultivated the art of looking at what was hitherto overlooked: essences and ideal objects from which we stand "infinitely far" behind a screen of technical symbols and definitions: "If we aim to grasp the essence of red or of color, then, in the last analysis, we need only to look upon some perceived, imagined, or represented color, and, in what is so presented, lift the essence [*So-Sein*], the whatness [*Was*], of the color away from that which, as singular or accidental, is of no interest to us."[39] Distance was overcome, the essence of a phenomenon revealed, through a clear and intimate act of sight. "If we bring ourselves," he put it, "to the point where, as philosophers, we must bring ourselves—through all signs, definitions, and rules—to the facts themselves [*zu den Sachen selbst*], things will present themselves to us quite differently than is today believed." This effort was "the task of the centuries."[40] For Reinach, then, phenomenological clarification granted access to the world as it was: a manifold of objects and essences, persons and states of affairs. The phenomenologist did not require reductions or purifications, which invariably distanced him from the world. Instead, he cultivated a new way of looking at it. He sought what *is*, the bare truth, without the lenses of theory.[41] For this reason, Reinach tried to convince his audience by illustrating rather than defining his vision—by thrusting them into a realm of essences "lifted off" the world through trained perception. With careful cultivation, he told them, they could verify his insights with their own.

Value and Soul: Alexander Pfänder and Company

Like Reinach, Alexander Pfänder (1870–1941) used phenomenology to demonstrate the existence of a world of essences beyond the logical sphere. Largely forgotten today, Pfänder's studies of human motivation, an impulse he distinguished strongly from external causality when explaining what made things happen, made him an early practitioner, with Scheler, of phenomenological anthropology. Indeed, the distinction between motivation and causality became a phenomenological standard, often invoked without attribution. Under the influence of Lipps's descriptive psychology, Pfänder's pre-phenomenological works already described the human will—which he extricated from the mass of sensations, emotions, and representations into which nineteenth-century psychologists lumped it—as an intending faculty, a "volitional inner-directedness toward something."[42] The encounter with Husserl—Pfänder was never his student—facilitated a deepening interest in anthropology conducted on a phenomenological basis, a focus that culminated in his 1933 book *Die Seele des Menschen* (The Soul of Man).[43] That Pfänder foresaw the psychological and social dividends of the new philosophy was also evident in his studies of characterology and his lectures on life goals, both from the early 1920s.[44]

As part of this anthropological project, Pfänder enlisted phenomenology in the development of a novel though incomplete ethical theory, published posthumously through the efforts of his midcentury champion Herbert Spiegelberg.[45] Fittingly, Pfänder's ethics found the basis for morality not in objects recognized as love-worthy, as per Brentano, but in the human will. Human action—Pfänder's precise term was deliberate or willed behavior (*willentliche Verhalten*)—was "the only thing in the world that can be morally good or bad in and of itself, and thus the only bearer of its own ethical values [*ethische Eigenwerte*]."[46] Man alone had moral value; nonmoral values such as beauty or quality characterized things. Like Scheler, Pfänder condemned what he saw as modern "value-negating" tendencies, the "selfish and brutal ruthlessness and indifference that prevails everywhere today."[47] He deplored the "dirtiness on the streets and sidewalks; the clutter of dirty paper scraps in the countryside, on the streets, in the tramways, railway stations, and trains; the hateful noise and stench of the trucks and passenger cars," and insisted that a belief in values was "the indispensable condition for giving purpose to the spiritual life of man."[48] The *Wertlehre* was meant to reenchant modernity by establishing through phenomenological insight the existence of material values in the ambient world and moral values in free and rational humans. As we will see in the next chapter, Scheler undertook a similar program.

Pfänder's *Wertlehre* was complemented by a truncated *Sollensethik*, whose task it was to explain how particular circumstances could impose ethical demands. Pfänder ascribed to men an innate conscience-perception (*Gewissenswahrnehmung*) that recognized ethical imperatives and certified the sense of duty affixed to certain motives.[49] As his later Aristotelian analyses showed, each person had particular obligations, a kind of individual ought or Brentanian *Lebensziel* to which one was beholden. These personal mandates, in turn, pointed toward objective worldly values—and beyond, to divine creation.[50] In this way, Pfänder's analysis of human value-perception underpinned a rudimentary phenomenology of religion.

Finally, it is important to note one of Pfänder's most significant phenomenological contributions and a quintessential example of the early genre: the two-part study of "directed sentiments" (*Gesinnungen*) such as love or friendliness. These acts, he claimed, were distinguished from mere feeling because they established a direct union (*Einung* or *Einigung*) with—not simply an intentional orientation toward—their object.[51] The vision of direct access to things and beings inspired early protégés such as Gerda Walther to explore the basis for communal identity.

Pfänder's disciples illustrate the range of social and ethical projects drawn from early phenomenology.[52] Maximilian Beck (1886–1950) took up the master's plan for a multivolume metaphysics of value, including a volume on moral or spiritual values.[53] Perhaps his most important contribution was to sunder intentionality from consciousness, arguing that a kind of object-directedness characterized all psychic attitudes, including the unconscious.[54] Without abandoning his phenomenological commitments, he turned toward overtly ethical, political, and religious writings in the 1930s and 1940s, a path also taken by others in the movement.[55] Most telling in this regard were two volumes published in 1938. Surveying Europe on the eve of war, the gloomy Beck echoed Scheler in tracing modern soul-sickness—characterized by individual workaholism and denial of pleasure—to "inadequate intentionality," a failure to feel part of the world.[56] A man freed to fulfill his intentionalities would recognize ethical values and the existence of God; he would know the "essence and reality of the soul." Unfortunately, today's "Faustian-dynamic culture" enslaved men to machines and reduced them to ego and biology. Modern miserliness and nihilism blocked the expansive world of spiritual value and sanctioned war.[57]

More striking is the case of Gerda Walther (1897–1977), who adapted Pfänder's concept of directed sentiment to argue, in a dissertation written under his guidance, that true communities rested on the inner union of their members. Neighbors had to know one another and commit to joint values and purposes; but ultimately, their solidarity rested on a centripetal sense of inner oneness, whose variants Walther described in a 1923 *Jahrbuch* article.[58] Surviving on inheritance from her father, Walther completed the study several years after transforming from a socialist agitator into a student of mysticism, her budding fascination with anagogical experience foreshadowed in her transindividual concept of community.[59] Her most famous work, *Phänomenologie der Mystik* (The Phenomenology of Mysticism), appeared in the same year as her dissertation, but subsequent attempts to apply phenomenological analysis to parapsychology and telepathy left her on the fringes of the movement.[60]

The Existence of the Real World: Roman Ingarden and Company

From the outset, phenomenology was bound up with ontology, the study of being or existence. Husserl's earliest converts effused equally about the methodological access he granted to the realm of essences and his affirmation of the real existence of things. Reinach spoke for many when he praised Husserl's revelation of the necessities of being.[61] Eager young phenomenologists, as we have seen, quickly expanded this ontological certificate to a range of essential social and psychological structures. Unsurprisingly, they understood Husserl's incipient transcendentalism as a retreat not simply from phenomenological methods, but also from previous ontological assurances. Several of them set out to defend phenomenology's inherent realism (as they saw it) from the apostasies of the founder. Some sought to fortify a supposedly authentic phenomenology by limiting the span of its claims—hiving off ontology as a separate field whose task it was to secure the reality of perceived phenomena. Others—Roman Ingarden in particular—acceded somewhat to Husserl's new direction, reserving an epistemological space for transcendental analysis while refuting its ontological implications.

Moritz Geiger (1880–1937) is a useful example of the former. By the late 1920s, he came to doubt phenomenology's universal reach and wondered whether a scientific ontology was needed to affirm the external world.[62] Phenomenology, he wrote "is uninterested in the problem of reality. Only the What of the phenomena, its phenomenality, is of importance to it." Accordingly, Husserl's *epoché*—the bracketing of assumed reality that enabled the pure description of phenomena—was redundant: where reality was not in question, there was no need to set it aside. Simply put, phenomenology was "not yet philosophy," for it lacked an exit to reality.[63]

Hedwig Conrad-Martius (1888–1966), one of several women prominent in the early phenomenological movement, framed the concern differently: phenomenology could identify the *essence* of reality—what she later called "real reality" (*wirklicher Wirklichkeit*)—but it could not establish a corresponding factual reality.[64] The philosophical analysis of reality, she argued in a 1916 essay for Husserl's *Jahrbuch*, proceeded stepwise from the "phenomenal starting material"[65]—sense data purged of external association—through material qualities evident in phenomena and on to an awareness of the "embeddedness of material corporeality in itself." All of this information, she maintained against Kantian noumenalism, was available to phenomenological insight.[66] A transcendent material reality—the "real transcendence" of real things—*could* be discerned in object phenomena. Sense data, she explained in the 1950s, "lead beyond themselves—into what carries and grounds them."[67] Realism, in other words, was phenomenologically verifiable, and it was the task of a phenomenological "ontology of the real" (*Realontologie*; also dubbed "ontological phenomenology") to bring to "explicit view" the *essential* reality of the real.[68] Beyond phenomenology, however, lay the domains of metaphysics (which established the origins and nature of factual reality) and epistemology (which verified the links between essential and factual reality), areas that ultimately verged on the separate field of theology. Although a practicing Christian, Conrad-Martius, unlike many of her colleagues, strictly separated religious from scientific thought. Nonetheless, she exhibited a Thomistic bent typical of her religiously inclined peers.[69]

Nicolai Hartmann (1882–1950), whom we will meet later in his role as a phenomenological ethicist, also restricted phenomenology to bolstering a wider ontological agenda. As J. N. Mohanty remarks, Hartmann used the philosophy primarily as a method for disclosing consciousness. He rebuked Husserl for treating phenomena as mere intentional objects while ignoring their real substrates.⁷⁰ In this, he claimed, the founder of phenomenology fell into the traditional error of reducing Being to one or another principle and thus failed to account for its complexity.⁷¹ Hartmann's "new ontology," launched in his *Grundzüge der Metaphysik der Erkenntnis* (Main Features of the Metaphysics of Knowledge) (1921), treated biology and anthropology, ethics and aesthetics, as facets of a single multilayered reality. In a voluminous oeuvre, he sought to describe "the greatest possible maximum of givenness" that existence afforded the scrupulous investigator, while still acknowledging the ultimate unknowability of a Being that was "overwhelmingly indifferent" to what humans thought of it.⁷² With its exhaustive description and committed realism, phenomenology was an obvious ally. He praised the new philosophy for establishing "a host of important analyses of essences" (*Wesensanalysen*) and shared its anti-Occamite stress on maxima rather than minima.⁷³ But instead of Husserl's latter-day transcendentalism, Hartmann took man's fundamental "epistemological" attitude as the "natural realism" of normal living, in which the independent existence of reality was not doubted, and essence and fact, matter and form, a priori and a posteriori were intimately twined—a position, he maintained, that stood "beyond Idealism and Realism."⁷⁴ To be sure, the ontologist attended more closely to existential inflections than is common in daily life. But by refusing to limit reality to formal confabulations, Hartmann dispensed with false premises that he believed had distorted philosophical history. His ontology, in other words, enlisted phenomenology in a project that extended well beyond its bounds. "One might even say," Michael Landmann writes, "that Hartmann brings phenomenology to maturity" by turning squarely to "the things themselves" without detouring through a subjectivity that simplified reality in order to grasp it.⁷⁵ Hartmann himself made this point: "The phenomenological method tried to free itself from this self-spun web of philosophy. Its solution was: back to the things. But it did not succeed in reaching things. It arrived only at the phenomena of things."⁷⁶

No one, however, devoted himself more steadfastly to healing the rent between consciousness and the world than the Polish philosopher Roman Ingarden (1893–1970). Through a tumultuous career that spanned Poland's tortured midcentury, Ingarden produced an intricate defense of the reality of the world that encompassed ontological tracts, aesthetic analyses, and ethical reflections. In the process, he almost single-handedly established phenomenology in his own country, maintaining it through dark years of war and dictatorship. His writings in the 1920s reveal a thinker agonized over growing disagreements with his mentor and groping to find a philosophical response. The trajectory of his struggle ran from the seminal Idealism Letter of 1918, written to Husserl upon Ingarden's completion of his dissertation, through 1929's "Bemerkungen zum Problem 'Idealismus-Realismus'" (Remarks on the "Idealism-Realism" Problem), the blueprint for his incomplete chef-d'oeuvre, *The Controversy over the Existence of the World* (*Spór o istnienie Świata*), begun in the 1930s and published in 1947–48.[77]

The point of dispute was, of course, Husserl's transcendental turn, which, Ingarden feared, had dangerous ontological ramifications. He cited Husserl's own summary of the new position as cause for alarm: "Reality," Ingarden quoted his advisor as saying, "essentially lacks . . . independence. It is not something absolute itself and binds itself only secondarily to an other; in an absolute sense it is nothing at all, it has no absolute essence, it has the essentiality of something which principally is something intentional, something conscious only."[78] Like his philosophical kith, Ingarden rejected this view for treating the world as merely intentional, a concoction of the mind.[79] Instead, he maintained the "essential heterogeneity between consciousness and reality."[80] But rather than spurning Husserl's transcendentalism altogether, as his peers had done, Ingarden redefined it as the mode of reality that reaches out to experience.[81] In its intentional being, in other words, the real world transcended itself and became perceivable. But it did not thereby become a mere appendage of the perceiving mind, much less a creation 'constituted' by it.[82] In the 1960s, Ingarden traced this error back to the Brentanian "dogma" of *inner* perception, which severed phenomena from reality by isolating a separate mental realm.[83] Husserl's original method of *immanent* perception, by contrast, had uncovered a realm of essences that was not subsumed by consciousness.

In 1921's "Über die Gefahr einer Petitio Principii in der Erkenntnistheorie" (On the Danger of a 'Petitio Principii' in the Theory of Knowledge), Ingarden sketched an alternate epistemology that he believed could secure the knowledge of reality.[84] By "living-through" or "into" (*Durchleben*) an object, we draw it to ourselves, identifying with or inhabiting its real being, recognizing its nature as our own without any chance of falsehood.[85] "In the intuitive living-through of the act the knower is simply identical with the known, and the recognition is in this case a 'grasping-of-oneself.' Because of this identity, any possibility of deception is in principle excluded in the intuition of living-through. Intuitive living-through is an absolute indubitable knowledge. It is absolutely impossible that the thing intuitively lived through can be different from how it is lived."[86] Armed with this claim to certain insight, Ingarden would later defend the importance of epistemology for securing phenomenological assertions.[87] Phenomenology only described being, he wrote; it depended on other sciences of reality for completion.

Ingarden's first full response to Husserl's challenge came in the "Bemerkungen zum Problem Idealismus-Realismus," which outlines the three philosophical domains—ontology, metaphysics, and epistemology—necessary for the verification of an independent real world.[88] Ontology, for Ingarden, was an essentialist and hence phenomenological enterprise that used eidetic intuition to identify the pure possibilities of existence for various regions of being. It was, in turn, divided into three domains: existential ontology examined the various modes of being; formal ontology the possible structures; and material ontology the substantial characteristics that could infuse each form.[89] The first took the majority of his attention. Ingarden identified four modal dichotomies or types of possible being based on degrees of independence.

autonomous	heteronomous
original	derived
separate	non-separate
independent	contingent

A being was *autonomous* when it was complete in itself, *heteronomous* when its existence depended on another. An artwork, for example, had its heteronomous foundation in the intending consciousness of the artist; by mistakenly treating the real world as the heteronomous product of a transcendental mind, Husserl denied its essential autonomy, turning it into "a nothing."[90] A being was *original* when it was not created or destroyed by another, *derived* if the reverse. It was *separate* if it was not simply a part or appendage of another being; *non-separate* if its being required the greater whole. And a separate being was existentially *independent* when its essence did not demand another for continued existence, *contingent* when it did. The separate but contingent husband and wife required each other for their relational being, whereas the man and woman were separate and independent. "If an objectivity is at once existentially autonomous, original, separate, and independent," Ingarden concluded, "it is an absolute being."[91] Defending the absolute status of the real world formed the crux of his life's endeavor.

Although Ingarden devoted the most attention to ontology, its analyses were purely preparatory. Because ontology dealt only with essences and possibilities, it could not reach the core of dispute: the actuality of the world. This theme fell to metaphysics, whose "existential verdicts" pronounced on the world's absolute factual existence.[92] If ontology prevented overly hasty propositions by dictating what *could* exist, metaphysics showed what actually did. This assertion, of course, begged an epistemological question: how do we authenticate metaphysical claims? As Ingarden never reached a planned section on metaphysics, we do not find an adequate answer in his work. But he did discuss the crucial science of epistemology, which served, as he put it later, as a "final check on all reflection."[93] As we have seen, Ingarden already posited immanent intuition—a kind of living through (*Durchleben*) object essences—as an immediate and indubitable form of phenomenological awareness. He put it otherwise in 1929: If consciousness was characterized by transcendence, objects possessed the quality of being available to experience, of "open-being" (*Offen-sein*), a term derived from Geiger. The mutuality of subject intention and object openness ensured that consciousness and world were paired in joint relation.[94] The searching mind could know its objects. Both Kantian noumenalism, which rendered real objects impenetrable, and Husserlian transcendentalism, which made them products of consciousness, were mistaken. All the same, Ingarden maintained a small role for transcendental analysis: the epistemological verification of metaphysical findings had to occur within the transcendental realm to avoid naïve assumptions of actuality. As long as a thinker restricted the phenomenological reduction to this purpose, it had a limited place in the sciences of reality.

Even after this review, Ingarden's importance for this study may not be fully apparent. After all, his career-long defense of the real world did not yield obvious ethical or social positions—at least not until the end of his life when he took up themes of personalism and responsibility, which are examined in chapter 9. But his corpus demonstrates the fervent attempt to authenticate a reality that many fellow phenomenologists simply took for granted, and it thus serves as an important epistemological backdrop for the century's burgeoning social phenomenologies. More than any other follower of Husserl, Ingarden grappled seriously, if somewhat inadequately—it is not clear that his transcendental epistemology ever managed to reach the world it purported to verify—with the apparent apostasies of the founder.[95] And as we will see in a later chapter, he became the primary conduit for phenomenology in Poland, a channel that the young Karol Wojtyła tapped soon after the war.

4

The Blueprint of a New Heart: Max Scheler and the Order of Love

At the height of World War I, Edmund Husserl culminated a speech on Fichte's ethics by calling for a higher morality anchored in the knowledge of persons as "ray[s] in the unfolding of divine being."[1] In that moment, he sounded like Max Scheler (1874–1928). The wartime Husserl could hardly have avoided all agony of influence, especially as it was the Scheler's written outpouring from 1913 that turned phenomenology into a prominent social and ethical philosophy.[2] A magnetic personality in the movement's founding era, Scheler was a visionary whom Martin Heidegger eulogized as "the strongest philosophical power in contemporary Germany, nay, in contemporary Europe—in fact, in all of present-day philosophy."[3] Despite such favor, Scheler's reputation plunged after his death in 1928, a result partly of his own philosophical eclecticism and partly of the victory of Husserlian phenomenology over its Schelerian *Doppelgänger*. The founder of phenomenology viewed Scheler with great suspicion, born perhaps as much from pique at the latter's star power as from disdain for his methodological laxity.[4] A "genius of poses [and] an untrue prophet," Husserl's Scheler misunderstood the transcendental approach and commuted essences into a "rigid ontologism."[5] The two men were temperamental opposites: Husserl—focused, aloof, and agonized in his intellectual struggles; Scheler—erratic, declamatory, preternaturally self-assured, and engrossed in worldly activity. In short, Husserl saw in Scheler a philosophical daredevil, his "antipode."[6]

Subsequent thinkers have generally agreed: Nicolai Hartmann, José Ortega y Gasset, and Dietrich von Hildebrand, admirers all, saw in Scheler a man of galvanizing insight who spent his powers in too many directions and based his claims on flimsy premises. The "Adam of the new [phenomenological] paradise," Scheler grew "drunk on essences," his rampant output buoyed by one conviction after another. Invested with a "blind trust in his subjective impressions," he leaped from idea to idea, unconcerned with contradiction, shortchanging the analysis needed to gird a brilliant insight.[7] And these commentators were his friends; Scheler's critics leveled stiffer charges. Citing the bellicosity of his wartime writings and his tendency to favor intuitive wholeness over rational dissection, some in the anglophone world accused him of proto-fascist leanings.[8] Scheler's restlessness, in other words, cost him in the sober tallies of philosophy, for he has been read out of the ranks of major thinkers. Postwar champions have tried to redeem him, but the rescue effort is still underway.[9]

Yet the posthumous neglect of Scheler overlooks a mighty legacy. While it is hard to ignore his multifariousness, he was more systematic than detractors allow. His steady elaboration of several leitmotifs—the objectivity of values, emotional intentionality, ethical personalism—reveals a patience for conceptual development that belies the case against him. And when considered as a unified plexus, his oeuvre has as its constant and recognizable refrain the moral rejuvenation of a debased modern society. Moreover, Scheler had a considerable, though underappreciated political significance. As James Chappel has recently shown, Scheler's influence, stemming particularly from his years as a sociology professor at the University of Cologne (1919–28), can be seen in (1) the spread of Catholic corporatism in the 1930s, posited as an alternative to both liberalism and totalitarianism; (2) the theory of totalitarianism, most famously articulated in the Cold War writings of Hannah Arendt and Carl Friedrich, that treated fascism and communism as a single phenomenon; and (3) the growth of Rhenish Catholicism, which, in the person of Konrad Adenauer and his Christian Democratic Union as well as the framers of the 1949 West German Basic Law, reshaped German politics after the defeat of Nazism.[10] Ironically, Scheler himself, ever the shape-shifter, turned away late in life from the very Catholicism whose social program he had done so much to form.

The Daylight View

For Max Scheler, phenomenology was not so much a philosophical method as an attitude, a "spiritual seeing" in which one "experiences something which otherwise remains hidden, namely, a realm of facts of a particular kind."[11] In his hands, phenomenological intuition took the form and feel of revelation. The philosophy's theophantic dimension—its ability to disclose divinity—was sensed by many of its proponents, but it was felt with particular fervor by the Jewish-born Catholic convert Scheler, and it stood at the acme of his moral and social vision. Appropriately, he recalled his first encounter with the Husserl—at a 1901 gathering for the influential journal *Kantstudien*—as a kind of conversion experience that set his philosophical trajectory.[12]

Yet Scheler can hardly be described as a Husserlian. Like other realists, he embraced the Husserl of eidetic analysis—the early Husserl of *Logical Investigations*—but he had only contempt for later trends in the Husserliana, especially the turn to transcendental phenomenology, which suffered on two counts in Scheler's eyes: it reduced experience to theoretical life, attenuating the importance of value and ethics; and it tied phenomenology to the abstract ego, a *solus ipsus* that claimed the role of world creator.[13] Little inclined to work under a master's guidance anyway, and lacking a secure academic post, Scheler was, we might say, more *of* Husserl's movement than *in* it—shaped by the founder's discoveries but determined to track his own interests.[14]

For Scheler—and in this he presaged Heidegger—the I was always enmeshed in the world. More urgently than any of the other early phenomenologists, Scheler exploited the sociological and anthropological possibilities of eidetic analysis by elaborating a holistic phenomenology of the human person. "[P]henomenological philosophy," he wrote during the productive prewar years when he laid the groundwork of his ideas, was "the antithesis of all rapidly produced talk philosophy." It reveled in experience, and exhibited "the most intensely vital and most immediate contact with the world itself. . . . The phenomenological philosopher, thirsting for the lived experience of being, will above all seek to drink at the very sources in which the contents of the world reveal themselves. His reflective gaze rests only on that place where lived experience and its object, the world, touch one another."[15]

Freed of the scientific propositions interposed between man and life, the phenomenological philosopher proceeded through a "continual desymbolization of world" to the "radical principle of experience," unveiling a plenum replete with essences, with varied and vibrant being.[16] Mesmerized by this vitality, the phenomenologist "speaks . . . somewhat less, is silent more, and sees more" than other philosophers, striving for a "wide and unrestricted daylight view" of the "prelinguistically given" world.[17] To accommodate this breadth, Scheler expanded the scope of phenomenology to encompass not only the theoretical perception of logical objects but also the emotional perception of absolute values, "brightly on display."[18]

Like other early realists, Scheler advanced a new class of phenomenological or pure facts that stood in contrast to natural and scientific facts. Natural facts formed the regular and largely uninterrogated furniture of our daily living, in which the earth sits flat and stable at the center of our universe. They were oriented to human perception and quotidian routine. Scientific facts were cleansed of this relativity through the reagent of mathematics and the prosthetic of technology, but they nonetheless remained bound to a mechanistic version of life. Pure facts, by contrast, were no longer beholden to life at all; they were spiritual and absolute, existing whether or not they were cloaked in symbols or witnessed by men. In their sundry manifestations, pure facts were the foundation of sensory data, the spiritual essences girding worldly perception, and only phenomenology, with its eidetic procedures, could approach them.[19]

But even trained intuition—and this was one of Scheler's important assertions—could not be made foolproof, as Brentano and Husserl imagined. In a 1911 essay, later expanded, he identified self-delusion as a perceptual fallacy akin to logical error in judgment. Though he acknowledged that genuine essences must be recognizable by all, he found that delusion was a common lapse, especially in the modern age.[20] "There is perhaps no more fundamental obstacle to any kind of knowledge of the psychic world," he expostulated, in reference to his fellow phenomenologists, "than the position of many scientists and philosophers . . . that inner perception, as opposed to external perception of nature, can never deceive, that here the lived experiences themselves coincide with self-evident and adequate knowledge of lived experiences."[21] To take an external example, assuming that a stick that appears split in water is in fact broken confuses perceptual with actual being; it is a misapprehension that occurs in our immediate awareness of the world, a false sense of what is.[22] In order to avoid error, one had to move beyond visual apprehension—beyond the filter of the body—to consider things in their independent objectivity. And what held for outer perception was also true for inner. "[T]hings are 'brought to sight' for embodied humans," Scheler wrote, "but are not dependent on men for their existence."[23]

A further methodological point: Strikingly, Scheler paired phenomenological essentialism with another long-standing commitment, sociological relativism. Essential knowledge, he argued, could affect life only if it were 'realized'—literally, made real—in concrete situations. Absolute insights had to be "functionalized" for use by specific individuals, communities, and cultures. As Scheler laid it out in rather effortful prose, "essential knowledge functionalizes itself [*funktionalisiert sich*] into a law governing the very 'employment' of the intellect with regard to contingent facts; under its guidance the intellect conceives, analyzes, regards, and judges the contingent factual world as 'determined' in 'accordance' with essential relations."[24] Fixed essences met contingent circumstance through a principle of selection whereby each society chose part of an infinitely complex reality for particular focus and development. At this juncture, essential insight was mediated by cultural preferences.[25] The process occurred individually as well: A person's fate—that range of moral possibilities open to a life—was a particular functionalization of the *ordo amoris*, the order of love that the Catholic Scheler identified as the structure of absolute values in the universe.[26] "[O]nly part of the fullness of [God's] mentality should be accessible to any one man, one group, one people," he explained, "since the capacity for spontaneous metaphysical cognition belonging to each of these cognitive subjects is different according to the manner in which they functionalize acquired or traditional essential insights."[27] Since all individuals and cultures perceived essences from a different perspective and integrated them within their own world-experiences, truth demanded cultural diversity and cosmopolitan largeness—a philosophy of intuited absolutes *and* a sociology of their particular historical manifestations. Indeed, Scheler worried about an overweening "Europeanism" that suppressed the insights of other civilizations, and called instead for a "concert of people and ages" allied in the quest for revelation.[28] To be sure, Scheler's cultural relativism—or perspectivalism, as Graham McAleer dubs it—was compromised by his insistence on an absolute value hierarchy, with some cultures and religions expressing values superior to others. For the prewar Scheler, Western Christianity stood above Indian cosmology because the values of love and personalism were more advanced than undifferentiated cosmic unity. It did not follow, however, that the higher superseded or canceled the lower. Indeed, Christian personalism narrowed into a utilitarian individualism without the leavening agent of Indian insight. The higher needed the lower.[29] In this sense, Scheler was, as Jan Patočka later described him, "one of the first thinkers of the planetary phase of mankind."[30]

The Light, the Sun, and the Air

What kind of world did phenomenology disclose? Scheler's seminal work, the monumental *Formalism in Ethics and Non-Formal Ethics of Values* (1913–16; *Der Formalismus in der Ethik und die materiale Wertethik*), published in two parts in Husserl's *Jahrbuch*, virtually created the field of phenomenological ethics, and stands today as the most capacious exposition of three of its primary motifs: the objectivity of values, emotional intentionality, and ethical personalism. Scheler directed his analysis against Kantianism, the dominant ethical philosophy of his day.[31] While he agreed with Kant that morals concerned neither goods nor ends—goodness rested neither on the consequences of actions as utilitarians claimed nor on sensual objects and sympathetic relations as sentimentalists believed—he accused the Königsberg sage of empty ethical formalism that denied the "fullness of the moral world."[32] In reducing the good to the lawful, Kant posited a vacant ethic of rational duty in which our only "moral nourishment" was the "medication of commandments and prohibitions," a punitive rulebook that discounted the readiness of men, when properly induced, to pursue the good freely, to perceive and love absolute values.[33] Scheler further rejected Kant's focus on the transcendental *conditions* of morality rather than on values themselves—on what *could be*, not what *is*. In severing thought from experience, Kant led ethics into the cold stone sanctuary of Protestant stricture. Scheler—born to Jewish and

Protestant parents but drawn from a young age to Catholicism—countered with a value-morality of grace and plenitude. His moral monument was the resplendent cathedral.[34]

Against the categorical imperative, Scheler posited an ethics based on objective moral values available to the emotional intuition, a *logique du cœur*, to use the vivid phrase he acquired from Pascal.[35] Values, he wrote, introducing his chief insight, were "clearly feelable phenomena" that possessed "a determinate order of ranks with respect to 'higher' and 'lower.'"[36] They were given in "an original emotive intentionality" without regard to will, utility, or consequence, in a "punctual moment" of feeling directed at "its own kind of objects, namely, values."[37] The human affective faculty, intentional like Brentanian and Husserlian cognition, disclosed a stratified realm of values shadowing the mundane world, infusing empirical goods but phenomenologically distinct from them.[38] Moral insight emerged through "felt and lived affairs with the world, in performing and rejecting, in loving and hating"—acts in which "values and their order flash before us!"[39] Indeed, "value-ception" (*Wertnehmen*)[40]—Scheler's neologism for the emotive awareness of values—preceded reflective cognition; our initial encounter with things and people was as valued beings, not as objects present-at-hand: "Even prior to the unity of perception, a value signal experienced as coming from things, not from us, announces, as though with a trumpet flourish, that 'Something is up!' This is how the actual things as a rule announce themselves at the threshold of our environment and take their place in it from the far ends of the world."[41] This "annunciation" made "the beauty of the landscape or of a person" a prerequisite for the condition of "being spellbound" by it, preparing the way for experience as such.[42] The task of phenomenology was to strengthen and clarify this innate awareness.

Scheler grouped values into a four echelons: the lowest, values of sense, were epitomized by the pleasant and unpleasant; the vital values were tied to ardor of life and exemplified by nobility and vulgarity; the pure psychic values comprised beauty and ugliness, right and wrong, knowledge in itself; and finally, the spiritual values of holiness disclosed a realm of absolute facts independent of humanity.[43] The good consisted primarily in preferring higher values to lower, an upward "movement" achieved through the vehicle of love.[44] While Scheler insisted that his pyramid was irrefragable to all with phenomenological insight, he warned that clarity did not yield immediate moral certitude, for ethical knowledge had to be culturally integrated—functionalized—for it to influence life. Thus, while he retained, as Lewis Coser notes, an aristocrat's love of hierarchy, he acknowledged the importance of each person's ethos or basic moral tenor, which in turn was shaped by the cultural "milieu."[45] Practical ethics admixed essential insight, social milieu, and personal bearing, joining absolute conviction in the order of values with a relativist's fascination with the standards of other cultures. Far from encouraging contemplative isolation, value absoluteness, Scheler argued, elevated one above the self into the realm of transcendent being, a passage that enriched the paltry experience of each individual life: "[T]he world of values opens up the more [a person] and his comportment are of value. The devout soul always gives thanks for light, sun, and air, and for the existence of his own arms, limbs, and breath; and everything that is 'value-indifferent' to others is populated with values and disvalues."[46] This enchantment set the stage for "[t]he most radical form of renewal" brought on by "the movement of love."[47] Ethics, he wrote, would be capped by "the discovery of the laws of love and hate," for "[o]nly the happy person acts in a morally good way" and "[o]nly the good person is blissful."[48]

The linchpin of Scheler's philosophy was the concept of the person. Kantian formalism, he groused, confined man to the rational will, universalizing and homogenizing him as an "indifferent thoroughfare" for mental activity.[49] For Scheler, by contrast, a person was a "concrete and essential unity" of all experiences and faculties, an "immediately coexperienced unity of experiencing."[50] Several points follow from this. First, a person was not a thing, but rather an act-unity, a being who existed "solely in the execution of intentional acts."[51] The person was not simply an ego or a body, both of which could be reified and fixed for scientific scrutiny; instead, he was always in movement beyond himself, engaged in the "spiritual act of transcending himself."[52] Insofar as humans lived exclusively in their minds and bodies, they were akin to animals, subject to drives and enclosed by the sensory environment. The person's haecceity—that which distinguished him from animals—was a kind of in-gathered spiritual center that established each as an "absolute, always concrete, individual being" who realized himself in outward worldly action.[53] Furthermore, the person's unique character imbued each of his actions, so that it became possible to know someone's moral essence through a single act, carefully observed.[54]

This epistemological potency had particular importance for intersubjective awareness, a theme, as we have seen, that attracted many philosophers in fin-de-siècle Europe. Scheler's personalism allowed him to assert that people understood one another intuitively in and through their acts, without recourse to empathy or analogy.

[E]very moral assessment of another consists in the fact that we measure his actions neither exclusively by universal norms nor by an ideal picture that hovers above us by our own doing, but only by the ideal picture that we form by bringing to their end . . . the basic intentions of the other person which have been obtained through a central understanding of his individual essence and which we unite with the concrete ideal value and picture of the person given only in intuition.[55]

In a variation of Brentano's best possible life, Scheler argued that each person had a "good-in-itself-for-me" that defined his moral purpose, a unique obligation or calling that "whispers 'for you.'"[56] "[E]ach person must comport himself as ethically different and different in value from every other person," he explained, "without violating the universally valid series of norms coming from the idea of the value of the person in general."[57] He went beyond either Brentano or Husserl by describing the individual ought as a personal form of salvation in which universal values were functionalized and situated "for me."[58] Value personalism, therefore, while lodged in the ranks of goodness, also preserved the individuality of each.

At the same time, however, Scheler advanced an inegalitarian principle by encouraging communities to mirror essential hierarchies, a theme that echoed many conservative philosophies of the age. "[T]the ultimate meaning and value of community and history," he maintained, lay in their "providing conditions within which the most valuable persons can come to the fore and freely bring about their effects."[59] Far from parity, this program celebrated hierarchy before God, even an "aristocracy 'in heaven'"—and on earth, leaders who embodied the virtues of life and spirit: heroes, geniuses, saints, expert guides—even epicureans, experts in the talents of living well.[60] Scheler's moral exemplars played a role similar to Husserl's philosophical functionaries: they guided human growth and renewal.

Nonetheless, Scheler deflects easy charges of elitism. His social ethics was not based on a *Führerprinzip*, as some postwar critics might suggest, but rather on the principle of communal solidarity, on an idealized Catholic *Gemeinschaft* in which all persons lived mutually and co-responsibly. "There is no 'I' without a 'we,'" he wrote in 1924, and "[t]he 'we' is filled with contents prior to the 'I.'"[61] Even Robinson Crusoe, Scheler insisted, would experience others as "blanks" in his existence that presupposed the "sphere of the Thou."[62] The ultimate earthly expression of this essential consanguinity was "the unity of independent, spiritual, and individual single persons 'in' an independent, spiritual and individual collective person [*Gesamtperson*]," best exemplified by ancient Christian communities.[63] Like individuals, *Gesamtpersonen* were defined by a sovereign "spiritual act-center" shared among mutually sympathetic community members.

The glue of communal solidarity was this capacity for sympathy, a topic to which Scheler devoted another long work during his prolific 1913. *The Nature of Sympathy* (*Wesen und Formen der Sympathie;* originally published as *Zur Phänomenologie und Theorie der Sympathiegefühle und von Liebe und Hass*) marks the first extended phenomenological entry into debates over intersubjectivity that later attracted Husserl and Edith Stein. Scheler, as we have seen, disputed both the theory of analogy, which claimed that we recognize other people by comparing their bodily gestures with our own, and the theory of empathy, which supposed that we know others by feeling into their bodily expressions directly. Both theories, he argued, relied too heavily on bodily individuation, taking for granted that humans existed first as corporeal units for whom others were necessarily foreign and strange. He felt, by contrast, that men understood each other only by transcending the self, a prospect ignored in the modern celebration of individual experience and physical pleasure. The body, he warned, "condition[ed]" the inner reception of an experience, but it did not determine experience as such. Only by escaping the physical shell could one access the mental life of others.[64]

Bolder still, Scheler argued that we can directly and immediately witness other people's experiences "as a sort of primary 'perception'" through their expressions. "It is in the blush that we perceive shame, in the laughter joy."⁶⁵ A "universal grammar of expression" assured the direct grasp of another's "state of mind . . . without any sort of projective empathy."⁶⁶ But facial grammar alone, linking sign to sentiment, did not explain this transparency. Our awareness of one another grew from a primordial experiential unity. Prior to individuation, Scheler speculated, there must be an "immediate flow of experiences undifferentiated as between mine and thine, which actually contains both our own and others' experiences intermingled and without distinction from one another. Within this flow there is a gradual formation of ever more stable vortices, which slowly attract further elements of the stream into their orbits and thereby become successively and very gradually identified with distinct elements."⁶⁷

A startling mixture of stream-of-consciousness metaphors found in William James, Henri Bergson, and Buddhism, Scheler's cosmic experiential flow supplanted Husserl's egocentricity as the *Ur*-existential state, nullifying the customary division between internal and external experience. While our own inner perception was not as limpid as Brentano assumed, neither was everyone else's experience so closed. One could directly perceive the experience of both self and others by tapping a primordial wholeness that preexisted the distinction of you and me, inner and outer.⁶⁸

A's act of internal perception embraces not only his own mental processes, but has both the power and the right to take in the whole existing realm of minds—initially as a still unorganized stream of experiences. And just as we start by apprehending our present self against the background of our whole temporal experience, and do not manufacture it by a synthesis of our present self with earlier remembered states of itself, so too do we always apprehend our own self against the background of an ever-vaguer all-embracing consciousness in which our own existence and the experiences of everyone else are presented, in principle, as included together.⁶⁹

The intersubjective analogy was reversed. We do not know others through inference from ourselves; rather, we live in others before ourselves and know ourselves by knowing them—directly, intuitively. The ethical experiences of love and sympathy, then, were so potent because they recalled an original union that would only be renewed in the kingdom of the divine.⁷⁰

This a priori oneness suggested the direction of moral renewal: the movement from lower to higher preferences, from isolation to solidarity, mirrored on earth the unity Scheler saw in heaven. The ultimate fuel of this movement was love, an affirmative emotion far more puissant than sympathy. Through love, "every concrete individual object that possesses value achieves the highest value compatible with its nature and ideal vocation."[71] Love was a personal relationship in two ways: it allowed man not only to know others sympathetically, but also to urge them toward the higher good intrinsic to their nature, toward "the light streaming from . . . the person's essence onto all of his empirical experiences"; it afforded the "likeliest chance for the qualitative betterment of mankind."[72] Both knowledge and love entailed active participation of the knower in the known, yielding, like Ingarden's later notion of *Durchleben*, understanding in direct and personal terms—an epistemology that would find echoes among religiously inclined phenomenologists, in part because it dovetailed with their neo-Thomistic interests.[73] Younger thinkers also appreciated Scheler's vision of loving co-activity as "[t]he most radical form of renewal," implicating all in the joint pursuit of fulfillment. This individual-cum-communal enlargement was love's ultimate success, for it encouraged the "solidarity of all moral beings"—an idea that would resonate in the works of Dietrich von Hildebrand, Aurel Kolnai, and, ultimately, Karol Wojtyła, who drew it in postwar Polish phenomenology.[74]

Living in our Stomachs

Scheler's vision of love and solidarity stood in profound contrast to the social morass he observed in the contemporary West. Treading in the footsteps of Ferdinand Tönnies, Oswald Spengler, and others, he censured modern capitalism for cultivating isolated individuals with base material values.[75] The primary psychosis of Scheler's modernity was one familiar to readers of Nietzsche: *ressentiment*, obsessive rancor and animus. This psychological state became the title of a short volume, published in 1912 just prior to *Formalism in Ethics* and *The Nature of Sympathy*, that applied eidetic analysis to a single unit of experience and offered one of the sharpest early examples of phenomenology as social commentary. "Ressentiment," Scheler explained, was a "self-poisoning of the mind" caused by "the systematic repression of certain emotions and affects which, as such, are normal components of human nature. Their repression leads to the constant tendency to indulge in certain kinds of value delusion and corresponding value judgments. The emotions and affects primarily concerned are revenge, hatred, malice, envy, the impulse to detract, and spite."[76] Where he diverged from Nietzsche was in the source of this modern malady. Nietzsche famously asserted that Christianity cultivated a slave morality bent on undercutting noble and vital values and replacing them with the craven, the jealous, and the meek. The Catholic Scheler rejected this view, tracing the origin of spite to bourgeois society, "where approximately equal rights . . . go hand in hand with wide factual differences in power, property, and education. While each has the 'right' to compare himself with everyone else, he cannot do so in fact. . . . A potent charge of ressentiment is here accumulated by the very structure of society."[77]

Though *ressentiment* took several forms, its hallmark was the assessment of value by comparison with others, rather than in absolute terms: "A is affirmed, valued and praised not for its own intrinsic quality, but with the unverbalized intention of denying, devaluating, and denigrating B."[78] This invidious sensibility overturned the natural order of values by elevating lower to higher.[79] Modern hedonism, for example, equated value with desire; utilitarianism promoted usefulness over vital, psychic, and spiritual worth. Market exchange institutionalized this value relativity, excluding all absolute credentials of quality. These distortions reduced humans to a kind of biological functionalism, cocooned in physical bodies, chasing after material comfort rather than aspiring to greater good. Modern men "lived 'in their stomachs,'" Scheler vituperated, using a phrase from St. Paul; they were engulfed in hatred, starved of value and goodness.[80] Contemporary philosophy encouraged this debasement by privileging doubt and critique over intuitive evidence, reflective consciousness over lived experience.[81] And since false valuation violated a deeply felt sense of rectitude, modern society gave rise to the crippling feeling of living in a "sham world."[82] As Merleau-Ponty put it, Scheler aimed "to restore to consciousness the variety and the diverse intentionalities which *ressentiment* has removed"—a variety with distinctly aristocratic ranks.[83]

One of the more fascinating instances of modern *ressentiment* was the popular fad for humanitarianism. A misplaced love, Scheler's humanitarianism elevated homogenizing biological needs over the personal spirit, treating humans as suffering animals in need of aid. Humanitarians did not value "the personal act of love from man to man"—the only true love, according to Scheler—but favored instead "the impersonal 'institution' of welfare" directed at the human "sum," or mass.[84] They lifted primal pleasure over higher spiritual values; privileged institutional management over interpersonal sympathy; and dissolved cultural diversity into species uniformity—cultivating pity rather than "exuberance of life."[85] Paradoxically, while belittling individual people, humanitarians aggrandized humankind as a whole, placing it, blasphemously, in the position of God as that which commanded moral attention.[86] In all this, humanitarian 'love' revealed itself as disguised hatred that assailed noble values and glorified self-justificatory pain.[87]

For all his concurrence with Nietzsche regarding this modern disorder, Scheler balked at his attack on Christianity. Nietzsche had missed the religion's free sacrificial impulse, he argued, its ability to counter modern skepticism and distrust.[88] In a voluntary reversal of the ascendancy of love, Scheler's Christian "knight" inclined from higher to lower, sacrificing himself in a heroic act of noblesse oblige in order to lift up the suffering and cultivate their virtues.[89] "There is not a trace a ressentiment in all this," contended Scheler. "Nothing but a blissful ability to stoop, born from an abundance of force and nobility."[90] How different it was, he believed, from the modern fetish for sickness and poverty as occasions for pity or charity. The Christian combated these ills without relishing them.[91] He faced misery in order to elevate the world, while the modern realist wallowed in it. In this revised doctrine, the Gospel took on a severe concern for "the salvation and being of the soul" rather than the amelioration of suffering for its own sake.[92]

At the same time, a Christian ethic drew men into the world of human solidarity, where the co-responsibility of all, rather than narrow self-centeredness, bound them in joint endeavor. It is no surprise that Scheler reserved the highest tier in his scale of social forms for an idealized vision of early Christian communities, described as "the unity of independent, spiritual, and individual single persons 'in' an independent, spiritual, and individual collective person."[93] They were, to use Stefanos Geroulanos's term, "communit[ies] based on communion" with God and other men.[94] The lower tiers of human association included the unconscious mass bereft of self-possession and the modern society of autonomous individuals who lacked solidarity and mutuality. The spiritual community of persons, by contrast, sought to fulfill the supreme values of holiness without regard for individual achievement, ultimately preparing its members for revelations denied in modern life. Despite contemporary mundanity, the religious ideal grew with humanity's vital spirit, "develop[ing] incessantly in its form and direction, thrusting out again and again into an infinite universe which flows around 'nature' . . . as the things we 'divine' surround the horizon of our eye—like the sailor and explorer who sails out courageously into maritime regions never yet mapped by geographers."[95] Indeed, God, for Scheler, was the premier *Gesamtperson*, the infinite and all-embracing whole.[96]

Castles of the Soul

Until now we have considered works written on the eve of World War I. But it was the war that made Scheler famous. Most commentators either condemn or ignore the war writings—even Scheler later disavowed them—but if one pushes beyond their jingoism, it becomes clear that they mark a pivot in his career.[97] Scheler dashed off his most bellicose tract in the months just after the conflict began.[98] Despite appearances, *Der Genius des Krieges und der Deutsche Krieg* (*The Genius of War and the German War*) did not overturn his earlier tracts on love, value, and the fallenness of modernity; instead, it characterized war as a "metaphysical awakening out of the dull state of a leaden sleep," a fulfillment of the creative drive of life and spirit that prepared the way for higher community.[99] The battle, he might say, pitted ideals against idols: Germany embodied the "historically proven cultural ideas" of spirit and solidarity in combat against both Russian hordes and English materialists.[100] By late 1915, however, as the grisly war stretched beyond all expectation, Scheler began to doubt its moral uplift, and cast his hopes increasingly for European renewal in general rather than German victory alone:

This war is either the beginning of the rebirth of Europe from the morass of its capitalist swamp, or it is the beginning of its dissolution and the start of a world epoch in which it will become the servant of the rest of the world, first the

Russians, then next the Orientals [*der Gelben*], sinking from the inspired genius of human culture to a worker in its civilizational cellar.[101]

Scheler later revised this apocalyptic vision of non-European ascendancy, viewing the prospect more positively as a supersession of capitalist materialism and the demise of a stifling Europeanism. By 1916, in fact, he believed that calm and repentance, not the ongoing slaughter, would actuate change: "In the coming peace, there must come a time of powerful repentance and atonement, and from this disposition a richer and more serious effort at moral construction." Central Europe remained "the source of this new Europe-saving spirit," but he looked to its Catholics in particular to spearhead the transformation.[102] The war seems to have fed his Catholic ardor, turning religion into the agent of continental recovery and reunion.

Two essays written in 1917 reflect this hope. The Christian, Scheler admonished, would "have to regard the European anarchy of this war . . . as resting on a collective original sin of the last few centuries of European history."[103] Modern bourgeois culture had wrought hyperrationalism, materialism, social fragmentation, solipsistic individualism, national idolatry, and baleful militarism—all stations on the path to war. Only when a religious ethos once again infused European life would the continent experience a cultural and social renascence. Man's existence, Scheler informed readers, was *"ab origine* . . . an outward-conscious, co-responsible, communal reality," and the religious urge felt by many war-weary Europeans required widespread social interaction and communion, not simply spiritual inwardness.[104] He anticipated a "positive age of belief" after the war that would humanize modernity and cultivate "a new and lasting dwelling-house for human society."[105] The change required personal and social transformation: a "whole, fully active man," a new moral bearing, a rebirth of the "Christian idea of corporation" and solidarity.[106] Scheler further advocated a European federation (and ultimately, a world body) of decentralized communities made up of spiritual men.[107] He dubbed this vision "spiritual cosmopolitanism" and distinguished it starkly from the internationalism of his day, which offered global uniformity rather than corporate plurality.[108] This moral upsurge demanded collective repentance, and a Christian love that would replace contemporary "world-hostility" with an eagerness for social participation.[109]

A second essay, published in the Munich periodical *Hochland*, reiterated the moral and social dimensions of renewal and underscored the distance Scheler had traveled from his earlier warmongering:

A cultural reconstruction is only possible if an increasingly large proportion of the European population learns to look upon this cataclysm as resulting from a collective guilt of the European peoples, . . . as, therefore, a guilty evil which can only (if ever) be removed and inwardly conquered by common expiation, common repentance, and common sacrifice, and which can only be replaced with the positive blessings of cultural community by dint of co-operative construction, mutual assistance, joint action consequent on solidary responsibility.[110]

As a prerequisite for "cultural reconstruction," Europe would have to pass from "common guilt through common repentance and expiation to the mutual respect of every European nation and cultural minority, thence finally to the solidary will to build anew." This interdependence extended beyond Europe as well: greater parity with Asia could only benefit an Occident that needed "repose and dignity."[111] Thus, the war became not just a sign of Europe's collapse, but a sacrifice portending new birth. Indeed, Scheler abjured his earlier war boosterism, condemning it as algophilia, or love of suffering for its own sake—the same ill that, in different form, had animated his prewar humanitarians. In its new spiritualized sense, suffering allowed one "to enter the deeper 'castles of the soul' and remain there for the reception of a higher world of spiritual powers."[112]

This line of thought peaked in the 1921 essay collection *On the Eternal in Man* (*Vom Ewigen im Menschen*), the apex of Scheler's Catholic phase. Modern spiritual deformities introduced by Luther and exacerbated by the pantheistic reduction of divinity to nature had ultimately led to the dissolution of God into scientific rationality and the "veering currents of history."[113] In place of modern atheism, Scheler called for a return to earlier religiosity, joining Augustine's theological philosophy with Francis of Assisi's panentheistic love for God's Creation in a new program for contemporary rehabilitation.[114] The "self-healing of the soul," Scheler wrote, "is in fact the only way of regaining its lost powers. And in religion it is something more: it is the natural function with which God endowed the soul, in order that the soul might return to him whenever it strayed."[115] Repentance led to "moral rejuvenation" by "cast[ing] down" past transgressions, "thrust[ing] them out of the totality of the personal Self."[116] It was, in short, a violent self-reformation that disclosed "the blueprint of a new heart" and formed "a new man out of the 'old Adam,'" readying humankind for collective renewal just as "early Christianity renewed the outgoing world of antiquity."[117]

The war prompted the necessary "revulsion" to spur change.[118] The hypertrophy of bourgeois individualism and materialism and the prewar idolatry of nation and empire had been "blown away" (*hinweggeweht*)[119] by the conflagration, and a new moral and religious hunger stirred in their place. Phenomenological philosophy could serve as a handmaid to this spiritual yearning, outlining the experiential conditions of faith, promoting the transcendence of mere life, and pointing toward the threshold of faith. But only revelation could grant genuine renewal.[120] Put another way, philosophy could outline the nature of religious acts and the forms of revelation—"the manner and principles" of religious reason—but only grace could fulfill human spiritual needs.[121] Religion redeemed knowledge by completing it.[122]

This claim should not be taken to mean that religious encounter lacked phenomenological structure. Quite the contrary, experience of the divine afflatus was perhaps Scheler's quintessential phenomenological encounter, the purest discernment of the transcendence that characterized conscious intent. Every intentional act, Scheler wrote, points "above-and-beyond its own empirical standpoint" and contains the awareness "that the being of the object reaches out beyond the empirical content of the intention."[123] Or, as he rhapsodized: "The soul's design points infinitely beyond this life, [and] of its nature it participates in a supersensual realm of being and value whose contents and objects cannot stem from the experience of finite things."[124] A religious encounter occurred when the thing transcended was "the world as a whole (including the subject's own person)," and revelation was simply the manner by which divine fulfillment was given to man.[125] Thus, religion came to mark the ultimate fulfillment of phenomenological personhood, and Scheler summarized the match between man's transcendental longing and his divine *telos* with an aching maxim from Augustine: "Inquietum cor nostrum, donec requiescat in te" (Our hearts are restless until they rest in you).[126] For Scheler, all humans had faith as an inherent constituent of their being. "You cannot choose," he asseverated, "between having and not having a good of this kind. You can only choose whether your absolute sphere will be inhabited by God, as the one good commensurate with the religious act, or by an idol," such as Mammon or Reason or the positive Nothingness of atheists.[127]

Transcendence led not only to spirit, however, but also to the world. For to "every positive religion [there belongs] a positive idea of community," and religious knowledge had as an "essential" correlate "the community of love and salvation."[128] Faith was not only a vehicle for personal redemption, but a prerequisite for the organization of anomic societies into communities of purpose. Scheler said little, of course, about the all-important topics of state structure and political administration. But while his communitarian hope betrayed a kind of romantic medievalism, it also echoed modern thinkers such as Saint-Simon, Kant, and Tocqueville in espousing a vision of European federalism.

Planetary Thought

In 1922–23, Scheler experienced a crisis of faith, possibly connected with the collapse of his second marriage, and he abandoned the Catholicism he had so ardently professed.[129] The personal crisis coincided with an increased focus on philosophical anthropology.[130] Scheler's renunciation of positive religion, it must be stressed, did not mean the relinquishment of spirituality as an abiding concern. On the contrary, he placed the knowledge of salvation at the crown of his 1925 typology of human knowledge. *Herrschaftswissen*, or knowledge of control, yielded authority over the natural world, with Western science its apex. *Bildungswissen*, or knowledge of culture, exemplified by Husserlian phenomenology, offered insight into essences. And *Heilswissen*, or knowledge of grace and salvation, revealed the holy. If the first enabled instrumental manipulation and the second essential insight, the third was received from above.[131] Historically, Europe sought knowledge to control external nature whereas Asia cultivated spiritual awareness to manage subjective drives.[132]

In light of what he perceived as a gradual convergence of cultures and spiritualities, Scheler described the interwar era as an age of adjustment (*Ausgleich*). The Western confinement of experience to individualism and rationalism led to a blindness or delusion in which material values were touted and spiritual truths denied. The process of adjustment would correct this imbalance by recognizing the fullness of being and preparing the salvation of humanity. Outside of a Catholic framework, it was no longer clear what salvation meant in concrete terms, though it certainly involved a spiritual elevation that linked man with absolute being. Yet Scheler's harmonious premonition was also earthly, righting many inequities that plagued the present world: vitality would leaven over-intellectualization; capitalism and socialism, culture and technology would merge in a humane synthesis; divergent cultures would enjoy the protection of a new federalism; nationalism and colonialism would retreat, and racialism abate; even gender poles would come together in a newly united mankind.[133] The Occident would "re-sublimate" its Apollonian reason in a natural equilibrium, cultivating the total man who would see value in the "old wisdom of the East."[134] For all its headiness, this vision showed more continuity with Scheler's earlier phenomenology than many commentators allow.

Particularly striking in light of his former religious commitment was Scheler's disparagement of Christian myopia. Judeo-Christian anthropology, he now asserted, endorsing the Nietzschean critique he had abjured in *Ressentiment*, "fixedly opposes man" by lifting him out of the "total structure of life . . . and the natural cosmos." In fact, the Christian ideal of the spontaneous sacrificial spirit now become an ideology of the upper class, set against an equally one-sided lower-class socialism and naturalism.[135] What seemed to unify all of these distortions—rationalism, nationalism, scientism, humanitarianism—was their embodiment in the hegemonic Europeanism of the day. Yet the loss of European cultural and imperial dominance was imminent, for "not only have the old trans-oceanic, agrarian countries, Russia, and even Eastern cultures under Japan's leadership, learned from Europe the methods and arts for building industries based upon technical and positive science—they have also progressed in this so considerably by themselves that the time is not far away when they say to Europe: 'The Moor has served his purpose, and the Moor can now go!'"[136] In a striking turnaround of the dramatic line from Friedrich Schiller's play *Fiesco, or the Genoese Conspiracy* (*Die Verschwörung des Fiesco zu Genua*), Europe appeared in the role of the dark Moor whose shadow life was famously traced by Edward Said. Schiller's theatrical dismissal (actually a self-dismissal in the play) now stood as an epitaph for the Western era when Europe played an "engineer controlling world civilization," and a signpost for the new planetary age when European energies would focus on spiritual knowledge and scholarship rather than power politics and foreign conquest. In this role, a humbled Europe could share its insights with the globe. Little surprise, then, that Scheler forecast a different renewal from his earlier calls: the decline of European hegemony and the rise of non-Western influence. As Scheler's appreciation for Eastern thought grew after the war, so too did his hopes for a positive post-European epoch.

The sociology of adjustment arose from the larger and better-known concern of Scheler's late years: man as a philosophical project. Continuous with his earlier Christian anthropology, Scheler saw man as the plastic "movement of the universe," whose essence was "the open decision."[137] In a brief but seminal essay, *The Human Place in the Cosmos* (1928; *Die Stellung des Menschen im Kosmos*), an outline for a longer study cut short by his death, Scheler described the human being as the intersection of "impotent spirit" and blind "demonic impulsion."[138] Although it was the spirit that separated man from animals, Scheler reversed his earlier theism by arguing that life energy moved "from below upward."[139] In a peculiarly post-theistic theology, God needed men to realize himself: he was a "God-in-Becoming," in and through man's effort.[140] Despite his new disbelief in Christian grace, Scheler's description of man as "world-open" rather than trapped in his environment like a snail in its shell still echoed earlier themes.[141] And whether or not he was right in declaring that modern humanity had suddenly become enigmatic to itself, Scheler continued to see the renewal of man—this "microtheos," or small god—as the goal of the lost art of ethical and virtuous living.[142]

5

Philosophy *en plein air*: Interwar Social and Ethical Phenomenology

In 1980, Husserl's student Helmuth Plessner, one of philosophical anthropology's first luminaries, lauded the founder of phenomenology for his revolutionary "work style." The "dismantling of philosophical theories and 'isms', standpoints and principles, the renunciation of systematic frugality, devotion to small things, patience with fragments, self-restraint before the immeasurable, these traits enchanted two generations," he recalled.

Here was a way to incorporate philosophy into the modern work world, to overcome historicization and relativization, the writing of books about books in philosophy, and to break through to the things themselves. Here it appeared that the age of open experience had received its philosophy: philosophy as a subject among subjects, as work in an open horizon.[1]

Plessner was captivated by phenomenology's "childlike wonder," which "only artists" had hitherto enjoyed.[2] Husserl had drawn philosophy back to being, to the immediacy of first experience.[3] He had recovered the natural world in its freshness and originality, and Plessner likened the influence of this renewal to the effect of painting *en plein air* on nineteenth-century French art.[4]

But if Husserl indicated a path to the outside, it was Scheler who first blazed it. His career-long effort at developing a philosophy of man made him a pioneer of worldly phenomenology and the font of philosophical anthropology.[5] In this sense, all those who applied phenomenological analyses to social and ethical fields were Scheler's children as much as Husserl's. This chapter examines four interwar thinkers—Nicolai Hartmann, Dietrich von Hildebrand, Aurel Kolnai, and Edith Stein—who stemmed from this genealogy. Not only did they attempt to employ eidetic methods for ethical gain, but they also advanced transformative social programs for a supposedly blighted modern world. Hildebrand and Kolnai went further still, tapping phenomenological insights in the struggle against Nazism. By the end of the interwar period, philosophical anthropologists and sociologists such as Plessner, Arnold Gehlen, and Alfred Schutz were introducing Husserlian methods into social scientific analyses. Phenomenology had become, in other words, an established social philosophy. The chapter concludes by considering why Heidegger holds a secondary position in this tale.

A Firmament of Stars: Nicolai Hartmann

Nicolai Hartmann (1882–1950), whose realist ontology we have already considered, was born in imperial Russian Riga, schooled in St. Petersburg, and trained under the neo-Kantians Hermann Cohen and Paul Natorp. That his best known work, the three-volume *Ethics*, is also his most phenomenological—Hartmann was always more of a fellow traveler than a movement member—attests to Scheler's success at enlisting the new philosophy for wider ethical purposes. In Hartmann's estimation, it was Scheler who reopened "the gates to the kingdom of values."[6]

Hartmann was explicitly Platonic in his vision of an ideal value realm.[7] Yet he saw values as "unactualized masses" that, unlike geometric principles, for example, did not necessarily correlate with worldly reality; indeed, they often stood outside it, in need of worldly realization.[8] This fact did not mean that values were nonexistent: there was, Hartmann maintained, "a pure valuational a priori" that "lends to everything . . . the mark of value or anti-value."[9] But values needed man's intervention to cross over from ideal to real existence; human acknowledgement was "the annunciation of their Being."[10] Moral acts, accordingly, infused the world with values that otherwise stood "on the further side of reality," and the duty to enact value was a human practical imperative—in Hartmann's terms, an Ought-to-Be that prompted an Ought-to-do.[11] Like Scheler, Hartmann embraced ethical personalism; persons were necessary agents for realizing values, which entered consciousness through axiological intuition and exited "in the deed." But men did not, *pace* Nietzsche, create value as such. The free, acting person was just "a point on its journey" from unreality to reality, the "unresting point of the world," a kind of ethical disequilibrator.[12] Values, not persons, were the primary agents—the "first movers" and the source of "creative energy."[13] And "only through the intrusion of values as determining powers into his actional sphere does the subject become that which he morally is, a person."[14]

Hartmann's axiology replicated the internal hierarchies of his ontology, noted earlier. Amid the "incurable pluralism" of ethical values, Hartmann drew, with Scheler, two discriminating vectors: height and strength.[15] As a general rule, he wrote, higher values were "more complex" and "more valuable," the lower more "elemental." But in strength "the elemental is always the superior"—and it is less violable. Life alone, for example, possessed limited worth—merely to live was not a moral achievement—but murder was among the gravest crimes.[16]

Hartmann identified four stratified value groups or "series." The most basic encompassed the field of primary antinomies that condition all higher values: collectivity versus individuality, activity versus inertia, harmony versus conflict—each pole a value that contradicted its opposite.[17]

If these were not strictly moral values, they did set up the tragic circumstance that values necessarily conflict, that every value fulfillment was at once the violation of another, every merit a conjoined guilt. For Hartmann, there was no heaven of moral harmony.[18]

The second series, which Hartmann called "values that condition contents," embraced a collection of nonmoral values—life, consciousness, freedom, power—that conditioned or grounded higher virtues. Life, for example, though not a great value in itself, was necessary for the achievement of others. It was characteristic of values in the second series that they could be used for good or ill.

Hartmann's third and fourth value sets were specifically moral, that is, they concerned human conduct. The third comprised "fundamental moral values" found in all ethical systems, those that formed the "logic of the heart."[19] Its members included nobility, richness of experience, purity, and goodness as such.

Hartmann's Four Value Groups

Categories	Examples
The most general antitheses	Collectivity versus individuality; harmony versus conflict
Values that condition contents	Life, power, freedom
Fundamental moral values	Goodness, purity
Special moral values	Ancient, Christian, modern

The most interesting category, however, was the fourth, the tripartite "special moral values" specific to historical eras. The ancient virtues included justice, wisdom, courage, and self-control; the Christian, brotherly love, truthfulness, trust, faith, and modesty; and the modern or post-Christian, love of the remote, personality, and personal love. While these were variously honored in each age, their existence, per Hartmann, was independent of human esteem. What varied was not the values themselves, but human recognition of them—their functionalization, we might say, using Scheler's term. And some of the special values conflicted. The Christian call to love one's neighbor—*Nächstenliebe*—for instance, could interfere with the more icy modern *Fernstenliebe*, or love of the remote, which might sacrifice personal sympathy for the progressive gain of the whole. In turn, the modern quest for personality and self-expression could clash with the ancient and medieval emphasis on justice and brotherly love, which aligned individuals to the community and the law.[20] Hartmann seems to have preferred the modern set. "So act," ran his personalist imperative, "that the maxim of thy will could never become the principle of a universal legislation without a remainder." In other words, have your own moral calling.[21]

Hartmann's most crucial divergence from Scheler was his explicitly secular, at times starkly atheist ethical framework. His was an anthropodicy, vindicating man as the realizer of values, not a theodicy of God's creation.[22] Indeed, he saw in the religious sublimation of value an annulment of man's freedom and an abdication of his purpose. Guilt was inherent to moral autonomy in an antinomial world, and the attempt at divine purification was a "sign of inner bankruptcy."[23] Ultimately, Hartmann entirely divorced his ethics from religion, an immunity that set him at odds with most phenomenologists.

What contemporary significance did Hartmann ascribe to axiology? Human improvement, he believed, demanded progress along the varied and infinite ranks of moral values, a stuttering effort defined by failure and recovery, surrender and advance.[24] It required men to train a searchlight, in Eva Hauel Cadwallader's pithy phrase, over the vast "Yonder of values," though they could never see the "whole firmament of stars."[25] Prefatory to this work was the renunciation of Kant's moral asceticism, a move that once again recalled Scheler. "An ethics exclusively of the Ought," wrote the erstwhile Kantian Hartmann, "is a blindness to the value of the actual. No wonder that, historically, pessimism follows in its track. In a world stripped of values and profaned, no one could tolerate life."[26] Instead, Hartmann hoped to restore vision to a blinkered humanity through the revelation of the infinite value realm—to bring man "into conscious possession of his 'moral faculty,'" to open him to the world.[27] Life's greatest disappointment, he warned, was to "go empty away."[28]

Dietrich von Hildebrand

Hartmann's ethics echoed the wide-ranging phenomenological call for the renewal of modern man and society. But like Brentano, Husserl, and Scheler, he remained page-bound, tied to a theoretical apparatus that offered little practical guidance for ethical life. Not so Dietrich von Hildebrand (1889–1977). To this point, we have seen that phenomenological interest in ethical and social themes coincided with the birth of the movement itself. Outside of the war writings of Scheler and Husserl, however, this interest was largely academic, accompanied by regular but largely impotent hand-wringing about modern despair. When it came to practical concerns like choosing values or acting morally in a world of ethical disharmony—not to mention political action—phenomenology came up short of guidance; it was, in other words, better at describing moral circumstances than at prescribing appropriate stands. Hildebrand was the first really to mobilize it in the service of activism. As a young philosopher, he was inspired by Husserl's trailblazing, though Scheler and Reinach, with their worldly concerns and rejection of transcendentalism, proved to be his more direct phenomenological forebears.[29] The son of a famous sculptor, Hildebrand is best-known as an interwar personalist who took up cudgels against National Socialism. Less familiar was his membership in the early phenomenological movement—and the influence of phenomenology on both his personalism and his anti-Nazism.[30]

Hildebrand first learned of phenomenology at the University of Munich, where he met Lipps, Pfänder, Geiger, Scheler, and Reinach—the latter particularly influential as a friend and teacher.[31] His first adumbration of an act-oriented moral theory came in a 1912 dissertation on ethical action, lauded by Husserl and later published in the *Jahrbuch*.[32] It offered a three-part anatomy of ethical acts. The first step was conscious engagement (*Kenntnisnahme*) with a particular object or state of affairs. From this investment, a person spontaneously took a position (*Stellungnahme*) regarding the object or situation based on an emotional reaction to the value with which it was laden.[33] "The soul of every morally good attitude is abandonment to that which is objectively important, is interest in a thing because it has value," Hildebrand explained in 1933.[34] This value response (*Wertantwort*) was Hildebrand's signature addition to phenomenological ethics.[35] Each value had its own proper emotional response, which in turn stirred action—the third step—aimed at realizing the value in a new and better state of affairs.[36]

Several points bear noting. First, while Hildebrand indicated, like Scheler, that values attach to objects, ethics applied properly only to situations relating persons to objects and values, 'states of affairs' (*Sachverhalte*) such as an action designed to realize good in the world or a stance regarding a particular right or wrong. The concept of states of affairs, introduced by Carl Stumpf and expanded by subsequent thinkers, including Reinach, provided an important correction to Brentano's objectivism. Ethics now involved not simply the proper judgment regarding an object's love-worthiness, but the complex situational relation between persons, objects, and values—a relationship of judgment and action aimed at realizing good. This conceptual growth helped phenomenology better to confront real worldly circumstances.[37]

Hildebrand also shared Scheler's commitment to the whole spiritual person, not simply the mind, body, or ego—a position that Edith

Stein, Roman Ingarden, and Karol Wojtyła would later echo. "Every experience," Hildebrand wrote, "is the experience of a person. . . . [and a] relation to the person always takes place whenever an experience is the bearer of moral value."[38] Like other phenomenologists, the Protestant Hildebrand converted to Catholicism in 1914, adopting a religious faith that became the hub of his thought and fed his personalist vision. In a postconversion essay on the recognition of value, Hildebrand located virtue in a person's "basic moral attitude" (*sittliche Grundhaltung*).[39] Personal goodness, he averred, sprouted from a "single root . . . a spirit that is in all of us."[40] Hildebrand also shared with other Schelerians a preoccupation with Christian virtues—and especially, like Kolnai and Wojtyła after him, sexuality. Volumes on virginity and marriage appeared in 1927 and 1928, respectively, examining in worldly, embodied forms the interpersonal love that Scheler had exalted philosophically.[41]

Hildebrand's personalist conviction carried forward into the 1930 book *Die Metaphysik der Gemeinschaft* (*The Metaphysics of Community*), in which he asserted that every affirmation of another person's worth was "morally positive" and every rejection "negative."[42] In a Schelerian critique that foreshadowed Hildebrand's denunciation of Nazism, he decried modern relativism and vitalism as value distortions and insisted that authentic community arose only from "devotion to God and one's neighbor." In the contemporary world, however,

> man falls into the misconception that the ethos in which the individual feels simply a momentary part of the whole relieves one from the spasms of the I [*Ichkrampf*], lets one leave the egocentric position of the modern age. In this one forgets that there is also a descent under one's own life, a descent into a merely vitalist "social consciousness" whereby the individual relinquishes any spiritual attitude to which, as a personality, he is not only entitled but positively obliged.[43]

Devotion to values and love of others, by contrast, allowed one to escape egotism and establish communal ties; indeed, personality—and here he presaged Wojtyła—grew from self-transcendence rather than self-possession. Values themselves had a socially unifying effect—a *virtus unitiva*— that helped to forge communities of purpose; this *virtus* was, in fact, "the key to understanding the objective structure of society."[44] Communities came about, Hildebrand believed, through a process of *incorporation*: the incorporation of values by persons, of persons into wider communities, and of persons and communities into the value realm. The res publica—the true community—emerged in shared openness to the value hierarchy and recognition of the "primacy of the individual person" as the dearest creation.[45] Hildebrand's *Metaphysik der Gemeinschaft* concludes with an attack on the "dangerous mistake" of state or social exemptions from morality, an obvious critique of the left and right moral relativism of Bolsheviks and National Socialists and a bridge to his anti-totalitarian activism. In 1933, he espoused instead a Christian corporatism that embedded persons in hierarchical 'natural' communities—family, church, nation, and only latterly, the state.[46] Within a year, he found a contemporary model of this vision in neighboring Austria.

With the Nazi ascension, Hildebrand, a vocal adversary since before the Beer Hall Putsch of 1923, made the difficult decision to leave his beloved Munich, passing first through his birth city of Florence and then on to Austria, where he championed Chancellor Engelbert Dollfuß's conservative Christian policies.[47] Dollfuß has not fared well with historians: In the effort to overcome internal fragmentation and rising Nazi threats, he adjourned the Austrian parliament in March 1933 and imposed authoritarian rule—dubbed 'Austro-Fascist' by its critics—based on Christian corporatist principles. In line with recent papal doctrine, he sought to reorganize Austrian society into supra-partisan estates that would quell social disorder and promote loyalty to Church and government. This effort prompted a strike in early 1934, which Dollfuß crushed in a bloody civil war that led to the abolition of the Social Democratic Party. The artillery bombardment of the Karl-Marx Hof, a low-income tenement block in Vienna's outskirts and a symbol of the city's progressive tradition, became an emblem of the chancellor's heavy-handedness. Claiming to defend Austria against Nazism, critics charge, he marched it halfway there.

Nonetheless, Dollfuß had his advocates. The essayist Karl Kraus came to respect his defiance of Hitler and defense of Austrian independence against Nazi calls for annexation. And the newly exiled Hildebrand not only viewed the chancellor's measures as necessary in the face of internal and external Nazi threats; he also saw them as midwives of a more devotional society that would finally reject the anomie of liberal modernity. In this regard, Dollfuß's authoritarianism did not contradict Hildebrand's vision of communal reciprocity; as James Chappel has shown, Hildebrand was one of the premier representatives of a conservative Catholic anti-Nazism that saw in hierarchical and illiberal corporatism a defense of the human person, threatened not only by totalitarianisms of the right and left, but also by liberal individualism.[48] Whereas both liberalism and totalitarianism stripped men of spiritual qualities and subsumed them in the amorphous mass, corporatism dignified each person by embedding him in communities of love and meaning, overseen and secured by the corporate state.

Upon arrival in Vienna, Hildebrand was recruited to edit the regime's mouthpiece journal *Der christliche Ständestaat* (*The Christian Corporate State*), funded by Dollfuß himself.[49] In that capacity, he attracted around himself "perhaps the central group of Catholic-conservative resistance against Nazism outside of Germany."[50] In Dollfuß's vision of a corporate state organized around Christian communities and social estates, Hildebrand saw both a compelling alternative to totalitarian absolutism and a worthy response to the forlorn individualism and godlessness of liberalism. Indeed, modern antipersonalism, embodied in the rise of the mass man and state leviathan, was liberalism's miscarried child—and it led, Hildebrand believed, directly to fascist nihilism. Austria's Catholic mission, he declared in 1933, was "to give the correct answer to the weighty mistakes of liberalism, which have undermined Europe for centuries, to show the correct way for the German people in a time of boundless confusion, in which the bankruptcy of individualistic liberalism has led to two new and far more terrible mistakes that threaten to destroy the whole of Western culture at its roots: Bolshevism and National Socialism."[51] In the face of this existential threat, corporatism afforded the chance to rebuild organic community around "solidary togetherness," to recognize that a person's responsibility to his ethos, family, church, and humanity preceded his duties as citizen and needed state protection.[52] Such a social and spiritual rehabilitation required affirmation of the human "as a being [*Wesen*] with an immortal soul and a calling to eternal community with God"—an integralist message that persisted throughout Hildebrand's Austrian years.[53]

While their focus was cultural and political, Hildebrand's essays in *Der christliche Ständestaat* rested on his phenomenological analyses of yesteryear. Most obviously, he defended the existence of a Christian-cum-Schelerian "hierarchy of goods" that National Socialists rejected in favor of "blood materialism." The Nazi "heresy" elevated the vital over the spiritual, degrading the person to a "mere function of blood and race" and denying the value-richness that phenomenology revealed.[54]

In 1938, Hildebrand was once again forced to flee the Nazis when they annexed Austria, going first to Switzerland, then to France. Finally, in 1940, he became an émigré in America. Nazism and Bolshevism, he declared the following year, reflected an antipersonalist "slave uprising against the spirit," a tragic preemption of higher intellectual and spiritual values by the agents of blood and might.[55] While this claim echoed Scheler's assault on modern *ressentiment*, Hildebrand also drew on another realist forebear, Reinach: The discovery of social acts presupposed the orientation of free persons to the independent world of values, a stance that Nazis and Bolsheviks—and liberals before them—denied.[56] Much of Hildebrand's critique was stock phenomenologicalese:

In today's chaos, in which the idolatry of the vital sphere has led to an antipersonalism and a revolt against the spirit, we must not see a corrective for rationalism, but a terrible aberration that simply draws its consequences from rationalism and makes for us the compelling task, now more than ever, to elaborate clearly the true nobility of the realm of the spirit and the spiritual person.[57]

Like Husserl, Hildebrand blamed an overweening rationalism for crippling human understanding and prompting a crisis of meaning and spirit. Only by acknowledging the infinite worth of persons and the objective hierarchy of values—realities disclosed by phenomenologists—could we hope to "rehabilitat[e] the spirit."[58] This conviction fueled his forceful condemnation of Nazi racism in a 1937 talk, "Jews and the Christian West," in which he rejected anti-Semitism on personalist grounds and celebrated Jews as a root of the Christian faith, a privileged people in God's eyes.[59] Hildebrand spent the second half of his life—a Christian philosopher at Fordham University in New York—dedicated to the social and spiritual renewal he had adumbrated in his European years.

Aurel Kolnai

Hildebrand was not the only student of phenomenology to target Nazi dictatorship and European anti-Semitism. The list of contributors to *Der christliche Ständestaat* included several Jews-turned-Catholic with phenomenological backgrounds. Hildebrand called on Annie Kraus, an erstwhile Husserl student and a colleague of several interwar phenomenologists, to pen a 1934 critique of "religious anti-Semitism." Kraus, who would not convert until 1942, insisted that Catholic appreciation for the Old Testament bound its believers to recognize Jewish contributions to their confession; the widespread Catholic anti-Semitism of the day was therefore a violation of the faith, even "an anti-Christianism."[60] And Waldemar Gurian, who had studied with both Scheler and Hildebrand, pioneered what later became totalitarianism theory, linking Bolshevism and Nazism, putative enemies, under a unified term of opprobrium.[61] In neither of these cases, however, is there a clear connection between earlier phenomenological studies and later resistance writings, though the common background is suggestive.

For Hildebrand's friend and colleague Aurel Kolnai (1900–73), by contrast, the link between phenomenology and activism was direct—or at least he aimed to make it so. Despite admiration for Hildebrand as a philosopher, Kolnai differed vehemently from his elder colleague's views on Austria. The Hungarian Kolnai, whose experience under Béla Kun's Bolshevik Republic inspired a lifelong antipathy toward dictatorship, deemed his confederate's embrace of Dollfuß naïve and contemptible. "So great a philosopher, and no character, no backbone at all," he fulminated in 1934.[62] Hildebrand's phenomenology was

> directed against the pseudo-world of constructivisms, snobbisms, philosophies of ressentiment and of power-seeking spiritual supermen—intended to overcome the professional feeble-mindedness of thinking in formulae. . . . What a shame he is a toady of Austrofascism. . . . There is no philosophical thinker whose thought I am so close to (I've known that for years!)—and yet I shudder to shake hands with him when I think of his vomit-making Regime-salon Thursday evenings and his apotheosis of Dollfuß![63]

Kolnai's revulsion at Hildebrand's political alliance illustrates in stark relief a fixation of his wider oeuvre: the failure of philosophers to translate ethical principles into effective moral practice. He did agree, however—disgust notwithstanding—to contribute several articles to Hildebrand's journal under the moniker 'Van Helsing,' cribbed from Bram Stoker's warrior against spiritual evil.[64]

Born to a liberal Jewish family, Kolnai fled Budapest for Vienna near the end of Kun's regime to avoid right-wing anti-Semitic reprisals.[65] Working as an independent writer, he first took interest in phenomenology when he enrolled at the University of Vienna in 1922.[66] Not only was the philosophy, he later wrote, the "glorious movement of a new realism, the most important departure in philosophy since Socrates and Aristotle"; in its Schelerian form, phenomenology spurred Kolnai's budding interest in Catholicism, to which he would convert in 1926.[67] The phenomenological method, said Kolnai in his Hildebrand-influenced 1930 book on sexual ethics, offered "the most penetrating analysis" of spiritual and mental essence available to philosophers, revealing "what is really meant . . . in a spiritual act" and dispensing with scientific "'inferences' and 'inductions'" in order to "attain a 'direct view' of the objects or their spiritual structure."[68] His conversions to phenomenology and Catholicism were clearly of a piece.

In later life, Kolnai was fond of saying that his 1925–26 dissertation on ethical value contained the seeds of all his subsequent thought.[69] It is certainly true that the essay suggested the lines of his 1930s critique of Nazism. Its express purpose was to "complete the phenomenology of moral values" pioneered by Brentano, Husserl, Scheler, and Hildebrand, borrowing the Thomist affirmation of objective ends and moral rules—a pairing that presaged Stein and Wojtyła—in order to bind ideas with practical reality.[70] Phenomenological ethicists, Kolnai averred, had left their task incomplete, confirming the existence of absolute values but failing to enlist them for moral practice. He would "design the bridges which lead to a morally valuable reality."[71] This engineering feat required him to span the chasms between absolute values, everyday circumstance, and contemporary norms, to "bring about an ethically desirable state of things . . . on the basis of existent moral needs and powers."[72]

The key to achieving this goal was recognizing that no single group of values should monopolize decision-making. The firmament of values, to use Hartmann's term, was infinite and kaleidoscopic, and men needed a rubric to map it. To that end, Kolnai introduced the concepts of value limitation and gradation. Every value, he wrote, had "limits of appropriateness" and applicability, and at the margins it verged on the domains of others.[73] In addition, values were graded, each implying other values that had a "watered down and . . . peripheral presence" in the precinct of the first.[74] In other words, values interpenetrated, one or two emphatic in any given situation, others muted but present. As circumstances changed, new emphases arose.

Kolnai further specified four types of value experience. The most common ethical encounter was the struggle against vice—what Kolnai called value exclusion. So crucial was this police work that Kolnai dedicated much of his career to combating the evils of materialism and totalitarianism. But he also identified three further forms of value experience, these inclusive rather than exclusive: coordination, by which features of reality were related with compatible values; incorporation, through which one embraced and absorbed the values of a loved one; and directness, which indentured one to God and the good. The latter two in particular broached the heights of moral "rapture," through which a person transcended herself by affirming the being of another while still preserving the "distance" essential to personal dignity and autonomy.[75]

Like his contemporary Hartmann, and like Wojtyła after them, Kolnai resisted the rigorist tendency to impose an austere moral yardstick on complicated human realities, a monomania typical of absolutism. Practical ethics abjured purity: responsible decisions required a survey of "the entire range of ethical value" appropriate to a situation.[76] Duty ethics, vitalism, utilitarianism, and especially totalitarian planning—all of these attitudes disregarded the value conflicts intrinsic to moral life, yielding at times to "blatant immoralism" in the name of ethical absolutes. Communism in particular promoted a "moratorium on values" in its pursuit of false utopia, a bearing that betrayed deep "contempt for Mankind."[77] Like Scheler and Hildebrand, Kolnai traced these ills to totalitarianism's liberal precursor—to the "atomistic individualism" that had laid waste to human community. As correctives in the quest for ethical renewal, he embraced Catholicism and democracy, the latter a "movement for social liberation and construction in the most serious and responsible sense."[78]

Like other Catholic phenomenologists, Kolnai saw the human person as an ultimate value.[79] Accordingly, he preferred reform—what he celebrated as the "[m]eliorism of the ethics of moral-mindedness"— to revolution because it respected the "precious value" of each person.[80] Genuine reform, Kolnai insisted, required "the actual presence of ethical need, the availability of moral energy in the circles concerned, and respect for emphatic and consideration for unemphatic constants."[81] At times, reform could even entail drastic action: the renewal of a materialist society, for example, demanded "extensive transformation" that involved "working, inventive, free and promising engagement for the cause of good in the business of the world."[82] Yet it always respected real circumstances and genuine needs rather than sacrificing men to beautiful utopias.

Phenomenology, it seemed to Kolnai, provided the best philosophical prop for this ethical vision. Its appreciation of moral plenitude, its orientation toward objective values—what he called its value-intentionality—became the marks of ethical probity and good will.[83] "The moral seriousness which most quickly leads us to intuit the idea of a finite concrete world is itself closely related to that reverence for the world which prevents us from inspecting and dissecting it as though it were a 'globe' we could roll about in the palms of our hands."[84] By contrast, "[t]he pursuit of distant . . . ends" led revolutionaries to override present needs. Men had to resist "the dreary imperious demand to confine the motives of conduct within materially simple, indeed uniform bounds," an attitude driven by "ice-cold pride." Kolnai's own resistance to this form of politics increased in the 1930s.[85]

The German and Austrian high press, with its sophisticated mixture of cultural analysis and political commentary, was an ideal venue for Kolnai's philosophically oriented social essays, and he was able, like Hildebrand, to adapt the technical and granular analyses of phenomenology to the more colloquial flair of local feuilletons. Throughout the late 1920s, he penned a series of 'essential' analyses—presenting phenomena "according to [their] essence," not as a factual catalog of surface traits—of political and ideological movements on the radical fringes, the left and right extremists who threatened personal sanctity and distorted value hierarchies.[86]

Although Kolnai joined the Social Democratic Party, his editorials displayed a deepening conservatism. Liberal ideology came in for particular attack, a view echoed across the phenomenological spectrum. In two articles from 1927, Kolnai condemned liberalism's utilitarian conception of progress. Although they were right to emphasize the gradual amelioration of want over revolutionary fervor, liberals reduced men to material contingencies, making them animalesque and poor.[87] Rooted in naturalism, liberal ideology denied the spirit and turned subjects into anonymous mass men who exemplified the scientific meaninglessness Husserl later diagnosed and incubated crises that extremists could exploit.[88] Alas, the overcoming of liberalism took pathological form. In 1927, Kolnai declared Bolshevism a graver threat than fascism because it was more seductive: as he put it colorfully, "it stood at once nearer to God and the devil."[89] By 1931, however, he was coming to see the Nazi threat as the more urgent—a quintessential counterrevolution distinguished from conservative anticommunism by its embrace of revolutionary violence, terror, and deception.[90] In 1933's "Der Inhalt der Politik" (The Content of Politics), Kolnai assailed the right-wing jurist Carl Schmitt's vision of politics as an external relation of friend or foe. War, in Schmitt's view, was an intimate partner of the politics of existential survival. Kolnai countered by stressing the primacy of domestic political disputes and "the coexistence of opponents" in a common society. Political discussion, not mortal combat, was the "essential mark" of politics, its proper content debates over the "fashioning" of a shared destiny.[91]

In the face of Austria's increasing brutality, Kolnai continued to endorse the vision of a Europe of spiritual persons limned in his earlier phenomenological treatises.[92] Indeed, his first clear statement of the pragmatic conservatism for which he became known in the West appeared in the 1930s:

Conservatism, of the culture-, law-, person- and continuity-affirming sort, can only effectively take up its struggle against the anarcho-naturalistic extreme right if it is aware of being conservative with a very specific character and aims, which has distinct bridges to the left and takes over from it certain responsibilities, but otherwise occupies a middle point, from which it strikes the actual enemy, the right-totalitarian and mythical variety, beating it on its own territory and hitting it partly with its own weapons.[93]

Here he echoed the earlier call for a Christian, democratic personalist order: Whereas "[f]ree democracy means the personalistic life of man in society, fascist dictatorship means the person-denying rule of the masses."[94] No doubt it was for this reason that Kolnai deplored Hildebrand's truck with Dollfuß, for he saw in the Austrian strongman not a bastion against Hitler but an agent in the suppression of personal freedom and political liberty.[95]

In posthumously published memoirs, Kolnai reflected back on the relation between his phenomenological and political interests. While acknowledging the danger of abstraction from reality, he ventured that Husserl's brainchild had a democratic-conservative slant. "[I]t bases philosophy on the broad pediment of 'current experience' and develops it in keeping with the categories and valuations of ordinary man," Kolnai wrote. But this bias did not pander to base popular will or delirious visions of national unity:

> The phenomenological attitude reveals . . . a 'democratic' slant in the sense of thinking 'in correspondence with' the thinking of the 'people,' not in the sense of any sanctification of 'the people's will.' It has a natural affinity to 'government with the people' rather than 'by the people.' It is aligned to the conservative-democratic idea of popular participation in government as opposed to the national-democratic and totalitarian formula of an 'identity between the rulers and the ruled.'[96]

This democratic-conservatism, already emergent in the 1930s, became Kolnai's hallmark during his second career, after he fled Central Europe in 1937, settling ultimately in England where was hailed by philosophers such as David Wiggins, Bernard Williams, and Pierre Manent.[97] As we have seen, it drew expressly on phenomenological convictions little-known in the English-speaking world but shared by many of his Central European compatriots.

Edith Stein

In 1916, a year before his battlefield death, Adolf Reinach wrote the following missive to his wife Anna from the Belgian front of World War I:

> My plan is clear to me before my eyes—it is of course quite modest. I want to proceed from the experience of God, the experience of being sheltered in God, and do nothing more than show that one cannot object to it from the perspective of 'objective science.' I want to explain what is included in the sense of those

experiences, to what degree it can claim 'objectivity'—even if it presents itself as knowledge in a particular, albeit real sense—and finally to draw conclusions from this. Such a presentation can certainly not grant true piety. But it can bolster the weak that have wavered due to the objections of science, and urge those along for whom these objections have blocked the way to God. I believe that to undertake this work in all humility is today the most important thing, much more important than fighting in this war.[98]

This letter, along with other epistles and related project fragments, eventually came to Reinach's students in the postwar years.[99] Edith Stein (1891–1942), who became one of Nazism's most renowned victims, was deeply moved by their piety—the Jewish Reinach and his wife were baptized Protestant while he was on leave in 1916—and by his widow's equanimity in the face of her husband's death. By Stein's account, their "experience of God" spurred her on the path toward her own religious conversion.[100]

Many themes evident in the circle of early phenomenologists came together in Stein's savagely truncated career: an interest in the ethical and social dividends of phenomenology; a concern for contemporary crisis and the activist role of the philosopher; and a concerted effort to join phenomenology and ontology in a way that was sensitive to personal experience. Stein's story is well known: born into a devout Jewish family in Silesia, she lost her faith as a teenager, studied psychology under the personalist Wilhelm Stern, transferred to Göttingen to work under Husserl and Reinach, converted to Catholicism in 1922, took the habit a decade later, and was finally slain as a Jew in Auschwitz in 1942.[101] Pope John Paul II canonized her as St. Teresa Benedicta in 1988.[102]

Stein shared with her Göttingen cohort a belief that phenomenology was a realist enterprise. But unlike many of them, she was fluent in Husserl's transcendental thought and inclined at times to its nomenclature. The greater sympathy accrued from 1916 to 1918, when she served as Husserl's Freiburg assistant and took on the arduous task of editing the hundreds of loose, cryptic pages that would become *Ideas II*.[103] Like Ingarden, she adapted some of Husserl's new language to her own phenomenology, embracing constitutional analysis in particular, minus the transcendental assumptions. In other words, she accepted certain methodological innovations of Husserl's later thought, although she balked at its putative idealism.

Stein's 1916 dissertation on empathy, praised by Husserl, already displayed some of this openness. From the outset, she placed her analysis within the phenomenological reduction and determined to reveal, through an accounting of experience, the existence of other persons, which many realists simply took for granted.[104] Stein had encountered the theme of empathy (*Einfühlung*)—the recognition of another as a conscious subject and not an object—on numerous occasions in phenomenological literature: in Lipps, of course, as well as in Husserl's early flirtation with Lipps's model; in Adolf Reinach's 1913 seminar, "Einleitung in die Philosophie" (Introduction to Philosophy);[105] and in Scheler's prewar texts, especially his book on sympathy. Yet the experience of it was poorly explained. Stein tried to clarify it with a two-sided account: empathy was "primordial as present experience," yet "non-primordial in content."[106] In other words, in affirming other people as such, empathy was immediate and assured, but their thoughts and feelings could never be directly encountered.

Contra Scheler and his pre-individuated stream of experience, Stein insisted that "empathy was not a feeling of oneness," that the pure I remained an indissoluble "zero point of orientation."[107] The spiritual person, who joined together a soul or "conscious unity of an 'I'" with a physical "living body," became the centerpiece of her ensuing thought.[108] Yet Stein's subject was not solipsistic; though Husserl's egology left an imprint on her thinking, she did not accept its transcendental loneliness. The subject's worldliness, she insisted, was secured by empathetic experience, which allowed one to recognize the outer realm as separate and distinct from consciousness.[109] Moreover, in offering reflective self-awareness through the eyes of others, empathy assured a unified sense of self oriented around particular qualities and values. "Person and world (more exactly, value world)" were so "completely correlated" that any philosophy of the person required "a value doctrine [from which] the person can be obtained. . . . The ideal person with all his values in a suitable hierarchy and having adequate feelings would correspond to the entire realm of value levels."[110] The spiritual subject, the empathic Other, and the world they shared—all were shown in phenomenological awareness. And like so many of her peers, Stein's phenomenology led her to call for a study of religious consciousness, long before she converted to Catholicism.[111]

Three years later, in an ill-starred *Habilitationsschrift* that never found a university taker, Stein built a complex model of the relation between individual and community.[112] Adopting Ferdinand Tönnies's famous sociological duo, she examined the person-to-person interactions presumed in human *Gemeinschaft* (community) and *Gesellschaft* (here translated as association).[113] Community, she proposed, entailed solidarity among its members, the recognition of mutual spiritual persons engaged in a common purpose and oriented to higher values. Unlike Husserl, who saw in communities a kind of *Gesamtperson*, Stein insisted that they were not metaphorical individuals with souls or egos; instead, true community rested on the cultivation in each person of a sense of shared experience and joint affective links that bound together neighbors and friends.[114] This communal sense was not merely an experiential aggregate of individual wills, but a meaningful whole in which each member participated. "[N]ot only do communal experiences . . . mesh together motivantly [that is, share common motivations] and form complex unities," she wrote, "but all stirrings of life of the community stand in manifold connections according to the community's sense and grow toward unity."[115] Recalling Pfänder's differentiation of internal human motivation from external natural causality, she argued that individual members motivated one another to spiritual growth and ethical achievement, leading to a kind of joint purpose and "collective experiencing."[116] In associations (*Gesellschaften*), by contrast, individuals treated each other as objects, instruments used in the pursuit of individual goals. In reality, of course, the types mixed; associational interaction could not exist without a modicum of communal trust, and communities needed some instrumental routine.

Yet the distinction was critical. Communities nurtured active, thinking leaders—functionaries, in Husserl's later usage—who could spearhead ethical and spiritual growth; associations yielded managers (at best) or demagogues (at worst).[117] In proper *Gemeinschaften*, a spiritual elite not only generated ideas; it also helped to channel the communal "lifepower" that stirred residents to act. This living energy "coalesces from the power of single [members]," emboldening everyone toward higher aspiration.[118] As Stein later put it, communities "renew" themselves "out of the soul of individuals" who remain spiritually open to values and empathically to other persons.[119] "Where the individuals are 'open' to one another, where the attitudes of one don't bounce off of the other but rather penetrate him and deploy their efficacy, there a communal life subsists, there the two are members of one whole; and without such a reciprocal relationship community isn't possible."[120] Persons, and hence interpersonal communities, were "value-tropic"—they tended or grew toward values. "[W]e see what the person is," she explained, "when we see which world of value she lives in, which values she is responsive to, and what achievements she may be creating, prompted by values."[121] Influenced by Conrad-Martius's "Gespräch von der Seele" (Conversation about the Soul), Stein described the person's durable core as the soul, that which "took up the world into itself" and expressed one's axiological uniqueness.[122] "Having a soul means carrying your being's center of gravity inside of yourself," she wrote, even as the individual spirit moved outward to other subjects and the world they shared.[123] Husserl's pure ego was nothing but a "radiation point of experiencing"; Stein's soul thickened it by joining mind and body in a communal and value-laden person.[124]

Stein's 1925 contribution to Husserl's *Jahrbuch* continued these efforts by examining the institution of the state, whose essential property she identified as sovereignty: all state "actions and laws," she wrote, "originate from itself and not from any community standing under, beside, or above it."[125] Accordingly, a state's paramount purposes—the essential expressions of its sovereignty—were legislating and governing.[126] Echoing her earlier analysis of *Gemeinschaften*, Stein acknowledged that states were generally dominated by elites who served as "carriers" of the life of the community.[127] But she tried to mitigate any autocratic intimations by arguing that lawmaking and governance were Reinachian social acts requiring "the recognition of those to whom the claim is directed in order to become 'legally binding.'"[128] Law was doubly binding in another sense as well, obligating adherence from both citizen *and* state—a characteristic later exploited by East European dissidents.[129]

Stein also distinguished the state from those executives who acted in its name. Just as her mentor Reinach's pure law formed a legal a priori to which all worldly law referred, so the state itself possessed absolute claims on its subjects that did not accrue to individual leaders.[130] This caveat hedged worldly authority in two ways. First, legislators were supposed to adhere as closely as possible to the dictates of *pure law*; the legitimacy of their civic statutes (or *positive law*) depended in part on concurrence with the essential rules of right and wrong that preexisted any earthly code.[131] More important, despite the state's title as sovereign commander, its leaders and policies required the "sanction" of the governed.[132] States evolved for the sake of free communities; they were not organic entities or natural executives in their own right. Instead, sovereign control and state legislation needed citizen acceptance, the "*placet* of those who are to be represented."[133] Any state whose laws violated the conscience of its subjects "lost the basis of its existence."[134] And though the state managed the legal realm, it barely touched the ethical. Even its juridical function of punishing crime to ensure public safety could not supplant conscience or allay personal "sin." Again echoing Scheler, Stein wrote on the eve of her Catholic conversion that the ethical renewal of modern humanity could only come about through large-scale, earnest personal repentance.[135]

With the completion of her three extended essays and her newfound religious commitment, Stein seemed to feel that she had pushed phenomenology to its limit and needed further philosophical tools to develop her ideas. Her writing slowed during the 1920s while she taught at a girls' high school, picking up again at the decade's end as she made a last fruitless attempt to secure an academic post. From then on, Stein focused her writing on the complex relationship between phenomenology and Catholic philosophy, a project she shared with Scheler, Hildebrand, and Kolnai. Recalling in the 1930s the impact of Husserl's *Logical Investigations*, Stein now described phenomenology as a "'new scholasticism' [that] turned attention away from the 'subject' and toward 'things' themselves."[136] It helped, of course, that Husserl's cornerstone was Brentano's revived Scholastic doctrine. Even the founder's transcendentalism provided some service in her new effort: Stein coopted it away from Husserl's pure I and redirected it to an absolute non-I (God, being), with phenomenology now supporting a kind of *parousia*, or full spiritual disclosure—the fulfillment of the highest human intentionality.[137] These moves would find later echoes in Karol Wojtyła.

Despite the concern of friends, Stein never foreswore phenomenology even as she turned to the translation and exposition of Aquinas.[138] Instead, she described "an inner need" to bring the two philosophies together.[139] Her first attempt at joining a phenomenological analysis of consciousness with Aquinas's realist ontology was a contribution to Husserl's seventieth-birthday *Festschrift*—a comparison, in dialogue, of Husserl and Aquinas.[140] Both philosophers, she said, attacked a common ill in the lack of spiritual meaning and purpose: "Ours is a time that is no longer content with methodological deliberations. People have nothing to hold on to and are looking for purchase. They want a truth to cling to, a meaning for their lives; they want a 'philosophy for life.'"[141] Husserl partially addressed this need by cultivating a unique receptivity to the external world, thereby overcoming modern schools of subjective and even scientific thought. But in the end he failed to recognize that the "immediate beholding of eternal truths" was "reserved for the blessed spirits, and indeed . . . for God himself."[142] Thomas moved beyond Husserl's transcendentalism to find renewal in spiritual faith and attention to worldly reality.

Though unpublished in her lifetime, Stein's two summae—*Potency and Act* (*Potenz und Akt*) and *Finite and Eternal Being* (*Endliches und ewiges Sein*)—represent her most heroic efforts at using the Scholastic-cum-phenomenological notion of intentionality to cast Thomistic ideas in an experiential vein: "Spiritual life," she wrote in the first, entailed an integral and living subject transcending itself toward the absolute.[143] *Finite and Eternal Being*, written after her 1933 entry into the sisterhood of Discalced Carmelites, attempted a similar merger: "[P]henomenology," it announced, was an entryway into "the majestic temple of scholastic thought," for its discussion of consciousness achieved access to the world of being.[144] Stein the Carmelite, as we can see, turned to God on experiential pathways blazed by Stein the phenomenologist.

Scheler's Children: Philosophical Anthropology

The headiness described by Helmuth Plessner (1892–1985), quoted at the start of this chapter, gives a deeper clue to the significance of phenomenology for the human sciences. Even if the classic philosophical anthropologies of Plessner and Arnold Gehlen drifted far from a phenomenological itinerary, their inherited commitments to natural experience and descriptive analysis became standard tools of their scholarly trade.[145] Several further phenomenological structures remained in place as well: philosophical anthropologists transposed the object intentionality of consciousness into the "essential correlation" of the human person and the surrounding world.¹⁴⁶ At the same time, man existed as a kind of living *epoché*, excerpted from the world even as he engaged it. Plessner's ex-centric man lived beyond himself in society, yet always guarded an inner core—acting into the world, then retreating from it to the haven of self. Tied to the "here-now" realm of daily life, man was also able "to distance himself from himself, to draw a cleft between himself and his experiences," and to exist on both sides of the abyss. "[B]ound in body, bound in soul, and yet nowhere, placeless without any connection in space and time—and thus it is human," Plessner wrote elegiacally.¹⁴⁷ As Axel Honneth and Hans Joas put it, using Husserlian terms, man "brackets" himself from himself.¹⁴⁸

As unrealized creatures caught between transcendence and interiority, Plessner's humans needed a world where they could both reveal and hide themselves. The craving for private shelter *and* public prestige—for staging a confident image while burying an insecure core—provided the anthropological framework for Plessner's surprising defense of modern *impersonal* society over the traditional communities that attracted so much contemporary nostalgia. "The idol of the age," he warned, "is community," understood as social unit that overcame modern atomization through interpersonal transparency and intimacy.¹⁴⁹ The radical German yearning for "social renewal" ignored the crucial human need for distance and performance.¹⁵⁰ The artificiality of image, the drama of masks—these had their place in the anthropology of self-affirmation; show was as necessary for man's well-being as authenticity. Ultimately, Plessner's human action was rooted in irrationality, for reason, he argued (*pace* Husserl), could not manage the urgencies of life. Instead, men resorted again and again to intuitive decisions. Nor could state power be rationally grounded, even though strong leadership was needed to police the boundaries between public and private space. Indeed, Plessner reserved his insights into anthropological drives and human social order for a minority elite of "ruler[s] and leader[s]" alone, who could use them to bolster authority and maintain social peace. The majority "remains unconscious and should so remain; they only should remain useful."¹⁵¹ Paradoxically then, Plessner espoused authoritarian rule in order to resist the totalitarian threats of communal excess.¹⁵²

Phenomenology's catalytic charge likewise energized Arnold Gehlen (1904–76), whose early direction reversed Plessner's: instead of attacking totalitarian cultural trends only to promote an authoritarian balance, he joined the Nazi Party as a young academic only to drift away from it by the late 1930s, when he published his classic work *Man: His Nature and Place in the World* (1940; *Der Mensch: Seine Natur und seine Stellung in der Welt*) without mentioning the racial distinctions favored by the regime.[153] Like Plessner, Gehlen acknowledged the "invigorating and beneficial" effect of Husserl's thought: "[P]henomenology, by its authority, enabled many young thinkers to regain a sense of immediacy and the ingenuousness to adopt a direct approach to philosophical problems."[154] Of particular importance for him were his teachers Nicolai Hartmann and Max Scheler. From Hartmann, Gehlen took a realist ontology; from Scheler, the anthropological thematic and the characterization of humans as "world-open." Gehlen's men were also deficient beings, driven to outward action by their incompleteness in order to secure a position and realize themselves.[155] Flooded with stimuli, innately ill at ease, humans restlessly reshaped their environment in order to inhabit it, imposing meaning as a bulwark against a strange and formless world. Naturally unnatural, men fashioned culture in order to survive, using their imagination to plan the future and live into the distance. World-openness was a consequence of world alienation, meaning a response to meaninglessness.

Gehlen ultimately drifted from any clear phenomenological allegiance. While he accepted the descriptive approach, he complained that phenomenology's grandiose notions of consciousness disabled scientific observation and thwarted an adequate conceptualization of man. This was perhaps nowhere clearer than in his constructivist anti-essentialism: knowledge and truth, he came to insist, were human institutions designed to master a threatening world, a vision very far indeed from the convictions of phenomenologists.[156] That they were nonetheless genealogically linked suggests the startling reach of Husserl's brainchild in interwar German social thought.

Husserl's Children: Phenomenological Sociology

Alfred Schutz's phenomenological sociology presents a striking contrast to the salvific hopes of philosophical anthropologists. For Schutz (1899–1959), phenomenology was a scientific tool, not a visionary program—and his appropriation of it was Husserlian rather than Schelerian, methodological not redemptive. Though Schutz became the most famous phenomenological sociologist, he was not the first. As Ilja Srubar shows, phenomenology's appeal for sociologists was similar to that for other *Geisteswissenschaftler*: it overcame the epistemological deadlock between advocates of formal analysis (neo-Kantians, logical positivists) and proponents of lived experience (Nietzsche, Bergson, Dilthey) by contextualizing logic and ideas in lived experience.[157] Reason and experience were reconciled, to quote Quentin Lauer, "since reason itself [was] a kind of experience, and experience itself [was] rational."[158] Phenomenology enabled new analyses of the intentional lifeworlds of social action and institutional structure, and starting in the 1920s, a clutch of thinkers—Alfred Vierkandt, Theodor Litt, Siegfried Kracauer, Fritz Schreier, Tomoo Otaka, and Gerhart Husserl (the founder's son)—applied its categories to the study of society.[159]

Schutz's prominence owes much to his long postwar career in the United States. But his most famous work remains 1932's *The Phenomenology of the Social World* (*Der sinnhafte Aufbau der sozialen Welt*), which sought to gird Weberian sociology with "the philosophical foundation which it has hitherto lacked." As is well known, Schutz was not concerned to demonstrate the *possibility* of intersubjective experience: he assumed the world of self and others as a fact given in lived experience. And while he carried out studies within the phenomenological reduction, he applied their insights to the 'naïve' social world, undertaking, as he put it, "a constitutive phenomenology of the natural standpoint."[160] He was, by admission, not the first phenomenologist to make this bridge. Stein, Scheler, and other realists had applied eidetic analysis to concrete social problems, but their work was, he opined, vitiated by unexamined prejudices about the apodictic and a priori essence of social phenomena. Husserl, too, Schutz noted years later, applied his insights to the concrete *Lebenswelt*.[161]

But of course Schutz wrote his *Phenomenology* without the benefit of the *Crisis*, and he credited as primary inspiration the scourge of many early followers: Husserl's transcendentalism, particularly the analysis of time-consciousness and meaning-constitution. The main conundrum of social science, Schutz explained, was that it tried to construct an objective understanding of social actions understood by participants in subjective terms. Because its goal was to clarify "what is thought about the social world by those living in it," social science had to make "objective" meaning out of "subjective meaning-contexts."[162] To do so, the researcher had to understand how subjective meaning was constituted in relation to the social world of friends and contemporaries (the *Mitwelt*, or "with-world"), predecessors (the *Vorwelt*, or "preceding-world"), and successors (the *Folgewelt*, or "world to follow"), all possessing their own unique contexts and perception. To make sense of this temporal meaning-flow, Schutz distinguished two key motives for social action: the because-of motive and the in-order-to motive. Because-of motives derived their aims and strategies from past experience—"I do B because of experience A in the past"—whereas in-order-to motives anticipated some future project—"I choose A in order to realize B in the future." Of course, these motivations intertwined in reality: past experience informed the choice of strategies for achieving desired future results. But for Schutz, grasping the matrix of social action required an appreciation of the role played by these phenomenological distinctions in subjective meaning-constitution.

Equally important was Schutz's recognition of the limits of objective social understanding. "In the face-to-face situation the partners are constantly revising and enlarging their knowledge of each other," an impossibility in the "They-relationship" of scientific analysis, where one rarely knows the object of study.[163] Sociological analysis had to accept ideal-typical knowledge that was "not concerned with the other person in his given concrete immediacy, but in what he is, in the characteristics he has in common with others."[164] The adequacy of this Weberian typological knowledge depended on its predictive power. But it could never be complete, for ideal types were essentially limited by the human freedom to buck patterns—by the fact, in other words, that men were "type-transcendent."[165] Social scientific understanding was, as a result, always only approximate.

Two related thinkers also deserve mention. In three works published between 1922 and 1936, Schutz's friend and fellow Viennese Felix Kaufmann (1895–1949) used Husserlian phenomenology to outline a methodological *Grundwissenschaft* for jurisprudence, one in which normative claims rested on essential insight rather than contingent fact.[166] The test of all theoretical statements in law, Kaufmann averred, was their essential "meaning-content" (*Bedeutungsgehalt*), not their empirical correlation.[167] Like Schutz, he accepted Husserl's transcendental insights and used them to illuminate the constitution of legal norms in conscious action. The law's core concepts—the "concept of the human, which we will designate in its legal apriority as the person, the concept of behavior [*Verhalten*] and finally the concept of the 'ought'"—were only certified, he contended, through eidetic analysis, a belief that cast his project as a kind of jurisprudential 'logical investigation,' an effort to ground the law in disciplinary essences and free it from faulty scientific analogies.[168] Kaufmann also echoed Brentano's ethical theory by claiming that legal norms were rooted in a sense of the rightness of facts or states of affairs— what he called a natural right (*Naturrecht*). A good legal order, he wrote, echoing Stein, was one that its subjects viewed as right (*richtig*).[169] Ultimately, Kaufmann's introduction of a phenomenological epistemology in legal studies allowed him to reduce "the realm of the 'ought' (the norm) to the realm of the 'is' (the underlying human behavior)" and to expound normative criteria "based upon human conduct."[170]

Still another variant of phenomenological sociology can be found in Moritz Geiger's student Aron Gurwitsch (1901–73), whose 1932 *Habilitationsschrift*, *Human Encounters in the Social World* (*Die mitmenschlichen Begegnungen in der Milieuwelt*), broke new methodological ground by combining insights from phenomenology and Gestalt psychology. Gurwitsch rejected the equation of the natural world with the observed physical world and repudiated theories of intersubjectivity based on analogy or empathy for treating others as objects whose mental life required a plan of access—views he partly associated, pre-*Crisis*, with Husserl. Adopting Scheler's notion of the milieu-world as a natural intuition and Heidegger's primacy of engagement over contemplation, Gurwitsch contended that "we live in [the world] rather than stand over against it," and the world includes other persons as well as things.[171] His book canvassed three modes of human social encounter: partnership among individuals in society; shared membership in a joint community; and emotional fusion in a charismatically bound group.

Why Heidegger Plays a Supporting Role in this Story

Here at the conclusion of Part 1, it is worth addressing a thinker who takes center stage in most accounts of German phenomenology. The absence thus far of Martin Heidegger (1889–1976) will be conspicuous to many readers. His enormous influence on phenomenological history cannot of course be gainsaid. Nor can his impact on East European philosophers such as Jan Patočka or Józef Tischner, discussed in subsequent chapters. But it is one of the contentions of this book that Husserlian phenomenology was not simply the flawed predecessor of later philosophies but a potent and living school for much of the twentieth century, capable of renewal from original sources precisely because of its social and ethical investments. Phenomenology's Central European history is not the same as the French experience, where Heidegger's influence overshadowed that of the founder.[172] Among Central European thinkers who applied phenomenology to worldly concerns, Husserl remained Heidegger's equal.

Of course, Heidegger introduced many insights that phenomenologists employed for social and ethical gain. First and foremost, he placed human beings—*Dasein*, to use the term of art—squarely in a world that could not be suspended or bracketed; *Dasein* was always and essentially worldbound. Heidegger captured this involvement in a simple but poignant term with wide appeal: care. *Dasein* did not contemplate the world indifferently as a thesis; he engaged with it, cared about it, and this care structured his being. This claim had several corollaries. First, consciousness did not precede being, and original experience did not entail detached reflection—*theoria*—on a distant world. Instead, *Dasein* was always thrown into the world, engaging with it practically, confronting it. The rational and contemplative ego prized by Husserl was a derivation from *Dasein*'s original worldly involvement.[173] Furthermore, being-in-the-world was always a being with others, a *Mitsein*. And because other beings fundamentally shaped *Dasein*, there was no need to prove their existence reflectively; one of the more fractious problems of Husserlian thought simply vanished. That Heidegger muddied this insight with his famous condemnation of the fallen publicness of *Das Man*, lost in inauthentic conformity, should not, as Ethan Kleinberg observes, blind us to the intersubjectivity inherent to *Dasein*'s makeup.[174] Even in the isolated quest for his ownmost possibilities, man was always a being with others. Finally, countering the Western metaphysical (and at times his own phenomenological) tradition with its millennial efforts to distill a timeless human soul or rational essence, Heidegger emphasized the radical finitude and temporality of human existence. All being was, in his account, historical, stretched between a beginning and an end. These insights issued from *Being and Time* (1927; *Sein und Zeit*), but Heidegger's later writings on ontology also won an appreciative Central European audience. Most obviously, his attack on the technological enframing of the world struck a chord with Soviet Bloc phenomenologists already sensitized by Husserl's critique of scientific reason. And the question of Being appealed to dissidents like Patočka and Havel, who read it as a call to transcendence that lent meaning to human life and weight to ethical rumination.

Heidegger, however, would not have followed their course. Unlike Husserl, Scheler, and others, he resisted elaborating an ethical or social philosophy; indeed, after his turn to fundamental ontology, he dismissed these domains as chapters in the forgetfulness of Being that led to modern man's anomie and despair. I do not mean here to discount the many interpreters who have tried to draw an ethics from Heidegger's thought—only that, to paraphrase one of them, weaving an ethics from Heideggerian ontology requires one to rescue elements that Heidegger himself diverted to other purposes.[175] Heidegger was particularly fallow when it came to the humanistic preoccupations of many later phenomenologists. Of course, *Dasein* could be attacked as *too* humanistic for a world in which man's hubris had wrought ecological and imperial disaster; Patočka issued just such a charge. Still, fundamental ontology provided little assistance in the recuperation of concrete personhood and interpersonal solidarity, an important project for midcentury phenomenologists. And while the *Daseinsanalytik* offered key anthropological insights, they were couched in a philosophical vessel lacking any concrete historical anchorage.

Furthermore, Heidegger foreswore the absolute values and truths that many phenomenologists cherished in their calls for human responsibility. All of these were symptoms of a philosophical trajectory that turned away from humanity, an abdication that worried many phenomenologists set on defending human experience against totalitarianism. For the burgeoning social and ethical preoccupations of Central European phenomenology, Husserl offered more philosophical ammunition than Heidegger.

As a final aside, it is worth noting that my discussion of phenomenological social thought places the ever-present question of Heidegger's Nazism in a new historical light.[176] The typical approach to this problem is to ask whether there is a link between Heidegger's politics and his philosophy, particularly *Being and Time*. Most analyses, in other words, remain fixated on Heidegger's thought alone, without seeking for traces of his political views in the phenomenology from which he emerged. As we have seen in the cases of Husserl, Scheler, Hildebrand, and Kolnai, while many phenomenologists prior to Heidegger had opposed Nazism, they generally favored elite conceptions of social and political hierarchy as the proper framework for moral and cultural renewal, a leaning that at times sanctioned authoritarian governance. To note this is not to accuse phenomenology of crypto-Nazism; conservative phenomenologists such as Hildebrand tapped the philosophy for the express purpose of condemning totalitarian radicalism, even if they supported autocratic rule as an alternative. Yet it is important to recognize that Heidegger's political conservatism could find some sympathetic, if less dark, anticipations in his own philosophical milieu.

The phenomenological concern for ethics and social thought in interwar Central Europe also provides an important backdrop for mid-century French phenomenology, which, in the persons Emmanuel Lévinas, Jean-Paul Sartre, and Maurice Merleau-Ponty, is often credited with inserting ethics into the phenomenological itinerary. Sartre's rejection of the transcendental ego in favor of the worldly phenomenology of existentialism and Lévinas's concern for the primacy of ethics over ontology had important precursors, as we have seen, in the German phenomenology that inspired both men.[177] And it has long been known, if insufficiently amplified, that French phenomenology found a tremendous number of its leading lights among East European émigrés who studied in Germany before settling further west, a trajectory of some importance for tracing the origins of phenomenology's ethical enterprise.[178] Although French phenomenology is beyond the scope of this book, it is important to note that the worldly fixations of the philosophy's French phase may be less Gallic in origin than is commonly supposed.

Finis

Adolf Reinach, the soldier-philosopher, fell in Flanders in November 1917, almost eight months to the day after Franz Brentano expired. Ten years later, Max Scheler died suddenly at the young age of fifty-four. A decade after that (almost to the month), Husserl passed as well, isolated and beleaguered in the Nazi state. Aurel Kolnai and Dietrich von Hildebrand fled Central Europe in 1937 and 1938, respectively; Alfred Schutz in 1939. In 1942, Edith Stein was gassed at Auschwitz. Heidegger of course remained in Germany, but his reputation was sullied by Nazi involvement even as he drifted from phenomenology toward the question of Being. In the short span of a decade, German phenomenology lost its leading lights and the school its German locus. It is now hard to recall the social and ethical hopes invested in interwar phenomenology, as these were largely destroyed by the Nazis and ignored in postwar summaries. The view of Husserlian thought as a profitable but failed transcendentalism was perpetuated not only by critics, but also by Western disciples hoping to surpass the founder. The legacy looks markedly different from Eastern Europe.

Interlude: Phenomenology and Eastern European Dissidence

In 1986, Milan Kundera opened his essay cycle *The Art of the Novel* with a gloss on Edmund Husserl's *Crisis*, by then a fifty-year-old philosophical tract.[1] For Kundera, Husserl's swan song was a quintessential performance of Central Europe's tragic outlook. The modern dominion of science, as Kundera paraphrased it, brought on the loss of a meaningful lifeworld and, turning from Husserl to Heidegger, the forgetting of Being. The dark ironies of modern enlightenment—moral decline despite technical progress, spiritual enslavement despite material freedom—were particularly apparent in the communist half of *Mitteleuropa*. Yet despite the impingement of Soviet tyranny and modern technocracy, only Kundera's East Central Europe still clung to Europe's humanist tradition.[2] Kundera was not unique in placing Husserl at the head of an endangered European culture. By the 1970s, phenomenology was widely seen by East European literati as a philosophical diagnosis of the modern crisis facing both Soviet and Western Bloc countries. But it was also more than that, offering a vision of personal freedom and transcendence that stood in stark contrast to the stultifying realities of late communism. While it is true that Czechoslovak and Polish dissidents drew on Western liberal thought in their critique of 'real socialism,' as pundits argued soon after the Cold War, their debt to the native phenomenological tradition was far greater.[3]

Phenomenology was the philosophical soil of many widely recognized dissident themes: antipolitics, moral politics, social renewal, and critique of technocracy. Nonetheless, scholars of Eastern European politics acknowledge it mostly in passing, partly because of phenomenology's mischaracterization as an epistemological and apolitical enterprise. Yet the roots of dissident thought cannot be fully appreciated without an awareness of this influence and without knowledge of phenomenology's long-standing concern for modern social and ethical decline, a concern that resonated widely in the dissident circles of Prague and Cracow. Moreover, the East European reception of Husserl, Heidegger, and Scheler broadens our sense of the social investments of phenomenology by demonstrating the political importance of a philosophy too often dismissed as academic.

We have already seen that East Europeans played a significant role in the original phenomenological movement based in Göttingen, Munich, and Freiburg. The Pole Roman Ingarden and the Hungarian Aurel Kolnai were important figures in the early development of worldly phenomenology, as was the Riga-born and St. Petersburg-educated Nicolai Hartmann. Russian Latvia also produced Theodor Celms and Kurt Stavenhagen, the former prominent among challengers of Husserl's transcendentalism. And Alexander Koyré, later a renowned French philosopher of science, came from southern Russia via Paris before joining the band of young phenomenologists in Göttingen. Phenomenology spread eastward as well in these early years. In Russia, it appeared before the First World War, especially in the works of Gustav Shpet, who spent a year in Husserl's Göttingen. Starting in the 1910s, Shpet argued—against the founder's pure ego—that consciousness originated in communal or collective activity. Of particular note are his 1920s writings on language, which crossed eidetic analysis with dialectics to argue that poetic language, in addition to having a structural essence, pointed outward to the culture that received it. Although non-Marxist philosophies were persecuted in Stalin's Soviet Union, phenomenology once again attracted interest starting in the 1960s.[4]

The philosophy's reach among post–World War II East European dissidents was also extensive—and it often complemented Marxism, despite the mistaken impression that socialism and dissidence were antithetical.[5] In Hungary, the young and philosophically voracious György Lukács (1885–1971) had taken an interest in the phenomenology before the war. As the more sober doyen of the reform Marxist Budapest School from the 1960s onward, Lukács turned to Nicolai Hartmann's realist ontology in an effort to enrich the theory of society offered under institutional Marxism.[6] Lukács's interest in Hartmann was apparently prompted by the East German Marxist Wolfgang Harich (1923–95), who was imprisoned as a humanist critic of the regime in 1956 and emerged in 1964 more hardline than the Party itself and opposed to modernist experimentation. Harich spent a lifetime trying to enlist his teacher Hartmann's realism as an ontological underpinning for Marxism.[7] His case is particularly intriguing because he encountered Hartmann's ontology coevally with his reading of Lenin and found the two amenable.[8]

The more typical fusion of phenomenology and Marxism was so-called phenomenological Marxism, cultivated by Western and Eastern thinkers alike in order to humanize the rigid ideology of institutional communism.[9] Associated in the West with the young Herbert Marcuse, Trần Đức Thảo, Maurice Merleau-Ponty, Enzo Paci, and Paul Piccone, phenomenological Marxism also enticed an East European cohort that included Karel Kosík (discussed in the next section) and Mihály Vajda. Starting with his dissertation, Vajda (b. 1935) launched the most concerted Hungarian effort to heal Eastern Bloc Marxism with the tonic of Husserlian phenomenology. Though known primarily for political articles, he published several books and essays on the crisis of modern rationalism and the dangers of anti-humanism, which he saw embodied in Soviet-style communism.[10] In Yugoslavia, Gajo Petrović (1927–93), a spokesman for the journal *Praxis*, engaged Heideggerian philosophy, inter alia, in the effort to rethink the Marxist categories of man and alienation.[11] The Dubrovnik-based Phenomenology and Marxism workshop, which ran annually from 1975 to 1978, also provided a forum for the dissemination of phenomenology across Eastern Europe.[12] Even in Stalinist Romania, where independent thought could only exist in hiding, phenomenology had its agents. Neither Constantin Noica (1909–87) nor Alexandru Dragomir (1916–2002), the latter a Heidegger student, produced a specifically dissident philosophy, but they did introduce a generation of students to non-Marxist thought.[13] Nowhere, however, did phenomenology plant roots as deeply and have such dramatic political effects as in Czechoslovakia and Poland, to which we turn in the ensuing chapters.

One note before proceeding: up to this point, we have considered only systematic philosophers whose elaboration of worldly phenomenology took place primarily—though not exclusively—through written exposition. In Eastern Europe, we encounter a different sort of phenomenological ramification in the activist or dissident. To be sure, many of the Czech and Polish thinkers discussed below—Jan Patočka, Karol Wojtyła, Józef Tischner—were philosophers with a professional commitment to phenomenological exegesis. There were, however, others in the loose and varied dissident community of the 1970s and 1980s who drew on phenomenology not chiefly to elaborate a social philosophy, but rather to reinforce and articulate what Jonathan Bolton has called an everyday "practice of dissent."[14] Phenomenological formulae stood for them as a set of existential commitments invoked to mark out an alternative to the drab oppressiveness of late communist society, and as a code for communicating current dissatisfactions and future hopes with one another and the wider world. As Václav Havel put it, most dissidents were drawn to the "atmosphere" of phenomenology rather than to its "particular theses, concepts, conclusions."[15] It is tempting to see this embrace as motivated primarily by the fact that phenomenology was *not* official Marxism-Leninism. It is certainly true that philosophies outside the legally sanctioned orbit—whether phenomenology, existentialism, liberalism, conservatism, or even reform Marxism—were appealing for the very reason that they liberated thought. It helped, of course, that Czech and Polish phenomenology could boast revered spokesmen—Patočka, Ingarden, Wojtyła—who were admired for both their philosophical prowess and their personal charisma and moral fortitude. And by Soviet times, phenomenology had native roots in both Czechoslovakia and Poland that increased its appeal as an alternative to official doctrine. But one the major premises of this book is that phenomenology captured dissident attention not simply for what it was not, but for the positive social resources and emancipatory promise it contained—resources that could be both sharpened by further exegesis and simplified for wider mobilization. While one can challenge these simplifications philosophically, it is hard to deny that dissident mobilizers enhanced the social and political prestige of phenomenology.

PART II

PHENOMENOLOGY IN EASTERN EUROPE

6

The Point of View of Life: Czechoslovak Phenomenology through the Prague Spring

In April 1948, three years after the end of World War II and two months after the communist takeover in Prague, the phenomenologist Jan Patočka, who would become Czechoslovakia's leading postwar philosopher, declared humanism "the most important element in modern Czech thought."[1] It was primarily as a humanism—a philosophy, that is, that celebrated human value—that phenomenology took hold in Czech philosophical discourse. A concern for anthropology and ethics, as we have seen, had preoccupied phenomenologists since Husserl and Scheler. Yet phenomenological humanism did not, as in humanisms past, ensconce man at the foundation of knowledge or elevate him above the world as an observer and surveyor. Husserl's attack on psychologism had done much to demolish that sort of anthropocentrism. Instead, while phenomenological personalism prized human dignity and experience, it embedded men in an independent reality that extended beyond them. In Czechoslovakia, this moderate, "antifoundational" humanism resonated with national philosophical traditions, placing phenomenology in a position to support Marxist reform in the 1960s and bolster resistance to Soviet occupation in the 1970s.[2] That the school achieved such standing testifies in great part to the brilliance of Patočka, its premier Czech advocate. But its appeal also grew from the fact that phenomenology shared with the Czech humanist tradition a preoccupation with the defense of human meaning and culture in a coldly technocratic world. By the second half of the century, phenomenology became a philosophical lingua franca for Czech dissident literati, not so much by replacing predecessors such as Masarykian humanism and reform Marxism as by elaborating their concerns in new garb. Czech phenomenology, in other words, joined with indigenous schools of thought in ways that raised its prominence and buttressed its humanist credentials.

Tomáš Masaryk's Spirit of International Humanity

One of these philosophical predecessors was Masarykian humanism. The philosopher and Czechoslovak president Tomáš Masaryk (1850–1937) has long held a small but luminous position in the prehistory of phenomenology. Masaryk befriended the young Edmund Husserl in Leipzig and mentored his earliest philosophical efforts, ultimately steering the novice mathematician to his former master Franz Brentano in Vienna. At the end of his life, the Jewish-born Husserl considered emigrating to safety in Masaryk's Czechoslovakia, allowing several Prague-based colleagues (Emil Utitz, J. B. Kozák, and Ludwig Landgrebe) to arrange a post for him that he ultimately declined. The despair of a man hounded in his own land may explain some of the flattery Husserl lavished on Masaryk in letters from those years: my "much revered Masaryk" who embodied "the spirit of international humanity" and awoke in me "the ethical conception of the world and life that governed my philosophy in all respects."[3] The elderly Husserl attributed to the friend of his youth political and social hopes that played an increasing role in his own late work. "Let your old ideal of national-ethical being be fulfilled in the kingdom at whose head Providence had the genius to place you," he wrote in a 1935 letter.

A single citizenry [*Staatsvolk*] united by the love of its common home and the unity of the country's history—A citizenry that is not divided by its different languages but enriched and elevated through reciprocal participation in the linguistically shaped cultural achievements. You brought me to this ideal already in Leipzig! Through such political and ethical ennoblement, may the republic become the ethical foundation for the renewal of a European culture seriously endangered by nationalist degeneracy.[4]

The encomium echoed the *Kaizo* essays from 1923–24, another period when the two men resumed correspondence after a decade of silence.

Indeed, Husserl's 1921–22 letters to the new president anticipated the *Crisis of the European Sciences* by outlining hopes for a social renewal (*Wiedererneuerung*) led by philosophers. One must awaken "the sense of philosophy as a rigorous science," he insisted:

> One can win over the youth to it, if it is only made clear that truly scientific philosophy aims not at theoretical specializations, but at the last and highest goals of all theoretical and also practical human striving. . . . The youth that I see before me want to bravely build a new life, and their will is deep and serious. They are starved for ideas with which to live, for ideas to which adherence makes it worthwhile to live [*denen gemäss zu leben es ein Leben eben lohnt*]. I am thus certain that a new spiritual Germany is in the making, gradually perhaps, but definitely, that will not prove unworthy of the great forefathers and will bring the world new blessings.[5]

While these expressions demonstrate no substantive philosophical influence from Masaryk, they do suggest a shared vision of Europe's moral renewal as well as the iconic power of the president's statesmanship in times of distress.

In 1938, Aurel Kolnai, too, "pause[d] in front of T. G. Masaryk and the nation bearing the stamp of his royal spirit." The recently deceased leader knew only "'ethical' ideals," Kolnai eulogized; "all his long life he had been at bay fighting 'Titanism', the 'Superman' ideology of all descriptions, the unsound mythologies of national conceit. . . . [T]he new-born Czechoslovak nation reveals heartening, perhaps even exuberant, vitality; all this, however, without a trace of 'Life' religion. Enlightened democracy and progress as well as peaceable pursuit of her normal self-interest, are her only creed."[6] A champion of European virtue confronting the forces of racism and war, Masaryk received the last word in Kolnai's anti-Nazi tome. Though fulsome, Kolnai's praise shows considerable familiarity with Masaryk's tenets both as thinker and as statesman: his ethical commitment, his critique of "titanism," his embrace of progressive democracy, his attack on nationalist vendetta. A philosopher-politician, after all, is a rare thing. As Patočka later noted, "Philosophers were so far building a state in their minds only. To build one through a genuine political action was given to one thinker only in all of history—namely to Masaryk."[7]

It is tempting to overstate Masaryk's role in phenomenology in order to boost the movement's profile. There is, however, scant evidence that his thought directly shaped that of Husserl or his followers, despite shared Brentanian roots.[8] Instead, Masaryk's most formative role seems to have been as a kind of avatar of the movement's political ideals: he was a philosophically informed statesman, rather than an original philosopher. With the noteworthy exception of Masaryk's late conversations with Karel Čapek, it is not clear that Husserl even read his friend's work.[9] Indeed, he seems to have accepted Brentano's opinion that Masaryk was primarily a man of action, not a top-tier thinker—a view echoed by Patočka.[10] But even if it was the favor of politics rather than rigor of thought that recommended Masaryk to phenomenologists, their admiration is notable for its sense of self-recognition. What distinguished phenomenological affection for Masaryk from his wider public veneration was the assumption that he was almost one of their own and that he shared their project of employing philosophy to renew a decadent Europe. In their eyes, he was the preeminent Husserlian functionary.

Masaryk's thought did broach many of the concerns of interwar phenomenologists.[11] Like Husserl, he was a thinker of European crisis and renewal, a theme he inherited from Brentano and Comte long before his younger friend discovered the topic. Masaryk's *Habitationsschrift*, accepted by Brentano and published in 1881, traced the nineteenth-century increase in European suicides to a pervasive modern subjectivism, an analysis reiterated throughout his career.[12] Contemporary "half-education," he warned, supplied men with dilettantish range but no unified worldview to replace their loss of faith. "The soul of the modern man disperses itself in all directions, into all corners of the earth—[but] there is no solid substance to it, it has no kernel, no core."[13] Contemporaries succumbed to what Masaryk called, citing the French writer Alfred de Musset (1810–57), the disease of the century: "total skepticism and hopelessness." In "the century of the despairing Titan," man suffers from "intellectual and moral disquietude"; he is "unready, inconsistent, half-finished . . . wearied, nervous, irritable from the struggle."[14] This agitation led to greater ills—suicide or militarism, each a kind of "titanism" that supplanted God's prerogative with man's own. Masaryk called for the humbling of humanist pretensions that placed man at the pinnacle of creation.

Like phenomenologists, Masaryk proposed to solve this malaise through a reorientation toward truth and ethics. Rejecting the dominant positivism of Czech philosophy, which, he believed, could not resolve spiritual crises, Masaryk followed Brentano in turning to psychology, conscience, and something very much like inner intuition. Indeed, as Ján Pavlík argues, his belief in the immediate certainty of basic ethical principles such as the value of sympathy or charity for one's fellow humans echoed Brentano's apodictic moral awareness and foreshadowed phenomenological insight; doubt itself was a sign of contemporary waywardness.[15] The anticipations of the *Crisis* are clear as both Masaryk and Husserl waged a common battle against relativism and cynicism.

To counter modern despair, Masaryk sought a moral-cum-religious renewal rooted in the appreciation of "humanity." The ambiguity of this pseudo-concept mattered less than its plangent ring: appeals for neighborly alliance among men and nations; dedication to the "small-scale work" (*drobné práce*) that builds society; and, not least, restored faith in God. Like Brentano and many interwar phenomenologists, Masaryk combined a stringent commitment to scientific philosophy with ardent religious belief. A Protestant convert from Catholicism, he saw in his new faith both a threat and a promise. By disturbing the medieval religious synthesis, the Protestant Reformation had contributed to the modern crisis of truth and meaning. Moreover, by encouraging human self-assertion, it nurtured the misguided aspiration for complete knowledge and environmental control.[16] Yet Protestantism also held out the prospect of a unified worldview based on "free investigation" and human striving, rather than the ready-made and hierarchical vision of Catholics. And though the imperfect Protestant suffered more deeply than the errant Catholic, Protestantism "gives everyone true freedom, makes everyone independent and yet binds all in one beautiful whole."[17] Masaryk preferred the faith rooted in reason and moral sentiment.[18]

Masaryk's 'humanity' had a political leaning as well. As Andrea Orzoff reminds us, Masaryk's conception of democracy was more moralistic than legalistic; it aligned with limited parliamentarianism, constrained political parties, and an elite hierarchy that provided "enlightened political instruction" for the masses.[19] Nonetheless, his paeans to democratic work in the name of social reform contrasted with both dictatorship and revolution.[20] The scientific method was his ideal: "The democratic character of modern science consists mainly in its use of the scientific method as contrasted with the theocratic method.... Consistent and energetic observation, the search for and discovery of new ... scientific details and systems ... is utterly different from the cherishing of ready-made and reputedly superhuman items of knowledge based upon direct revelation."[21] The man of science—the humanistic philosopher and sociologist—was a model of progressive social reform and a tutelary embodiment of the democratic "aspiration towards a new life."[22]

As should be apparent, Masaryk's program dealt in grand concepts: humanity embraced science and democracy, which in turn cultivated a neighborly morality based on small-scale work and reform. "[W]orld-humanity," he declared during the war, "is another name for the inborn striving of men for general friendship and union," an ambition that embraced democracy, science, ethics, and religion—each a face of the same humanity—in progressive social renewal rooted in the "human person."[23] Such sweeping rhetoric seems far from the scrupulous distinctions of phenomenology. Yet the visionary equation of science, truth, morality, and humanity—all organized and activated by philosophical functionaries—prefigured Husserlian motifs. Nor would the younger Husserl, himself given to bouts of German patriotism, have balked at Masaryk's claim that humanism "can find practical expression only through labour on behalf of one's own people."[24] By the 1930s, of course, when Husserl sought Masaryk's aid one last time, German nationalism had taken a virulently anti-humanist turn.

The Truth Has Us: Interwar Czech Phenomenology

Husserl's connection to Prague was not limited to Masaryk. While it is somewhat disingenuous to claim the founder of phenomenology for Czech philosophy due to his Moravian birth, Prague did serve as a springboard for the launch and dissemination of the *Crisis of European Sciences*.[25] And it was, of course, during Husserl's final period that Patočka knew and worked with him.[26] Through the Czech disciple's initiative, the *Crisis* project was introduced by a letter read at the Eighth International Congress of Philosophy, held in Prague in September 1934.[27] The establishment that autumn of the Cercle philosophique de Prague pour les recherches sur l'entendement humain, under the joint chairmanship of Emil Utitz (German) and Jan Blahoslav Kozák (Czech)—with Ludwig Landgrebe and Jan Patočka as secretaries—assured the continued influence of phenomenology in Bohemia. It was the Cercle that sponsored Husserl's November 1935 Prague lecture and the ensuing publication in a Belgrade journal of the first parts of the *Crisis*. Husserl's local profile was further elevated by his former assistant Landgrebe, who moved to Prague in 1933 to complete his habilitation. At the German University in Prague, he occupied himself with collecting and editing Husserl's pieces on transcendental logic, published in 1939 and immediately whisked underground away from the invading Nazis.[28] Cercle members were also involved in the effort to ferry Husserl's manuscripts to safety in Leuven, Belgium.[29]

But Czech phenomenologists did not simply disseminate Husserl. Both Cercle chairmen, for example, were touched by the school. In the 1930s, J. B. Kozák (1888–1974) drew on Husserl's and Scheler's analyses of intentionality and value experience to deepen his own ethical theories, even as he turned toward resistance against fascism and defense of democracy. A similar combination of besieged Masarykian humanism and phenomenological forebodings can be felt in Emil Utitz's 1935 *Die Sendung der Philosophie in unserer Zeit* (The Mission of Philosophy in Our Time), which presents the philosopher's life as an "experiment, . . . test and model" of his thought, a worldly "self-realization" that may demand "spiritual heroism" and "sacrifice."[30] In 1939, as the Nazis dismembered his country, the Charles University philosopher Ladislav Rieger (1890–1958) sought to rescue his discipline's cultural authority from a modern "scientism" that valorized physical over spiritual power. Rieger's book *Idea filosofie* (The Idea of Philosophy) traced the evolution of philosophical self-awareness—what he called its radical noetic self-clarification, constitution, and systematization—from early mythic stages through the heightened self-reflectiveness of Kant, Husserl, and Heidegger, who, Rieger hoped, might guide rational and moral human improvement.[31] While the gathering concern of Kozák, Utitz, and Rieger for the social function of philosophy could do little to stave off disaster, it did help to establish phenomenology as a lasting resource for Czechoslovak cultural and social critique.

Although Kozák, Utitz, and Rieger were not phenomenologists, their engagements with the philosophy attest to its influence beyond an inner circle. The most suggestive illustration of this reach, however, and the most extreme voice of Czech midcentury despair, was Masaryk's disciple Emanuel Rádl (1873–1942), whom the Protestant theologian J. L. Hromádka called the "Don Quixote of Czech philosophy."[32] Rádl's *cri de coeur*, *Útěcha z filosofie* (The Consolation of Philosophy), written in the dark years of 1941–42, constituted an important bridge from the late president's humanism and the phenomenological analysis of crisis to postwar reformers and dissidents. Like Husserl, Rádl blamed Galileo for casting off ancient and medieval reverence in favor of blank technical science and mechanism, leading to the modern world's denial of truth and morality.[33] Inevitably, technocracy undercut moral life, and the original human experience of worldly wonder was overtaken by fantasies of anthropocentric control. Modern philosophy, too, broke with its ancient heritage by divorcing itself from experience and embracing historical relativism and biological vitalism.[34] Against these trends, Rádl proclaimed the dominion of absolute moral laws. "[W]e do not have the truth," he exclaimed, "[T]he truth has us."[35] His deathbed hope was for a renewed appreciation of absolute morality and transcendent truth. The echoes of phenomenology's founders are unmistakable.

The Question of Praxis: Phenomenology and the Prague Spring

In 1948, the year when Jan Patočka declared humanism to be the pedestal of Czech thought, any lingering democratic hopes for the small country collapsed in the face of a Stalinist coup. In Klement Gottwald's Czechoslovakia, philosophies other than Marxism-Leninism fled into hiding, with Masaryk now the symbol of the bad old days.[36] During his decade-long banishment, Patočka worked as an isolated scribe at the Masaryk Institute and the Academy of Science, an internal exile from which he escaped finally in 1958 during the slow thaw of the post-Stalinist era. At the Institute of Philosophy, where he remained for a decade, Patočka found shelter for his phenomenological research and colleagues, both Marxist and non-Marxist, who took interest in his work.[37]

Indeed, in the 1960s, as Czechoslovaks gradually emerged from their Stalinist underworld, phenomenology's preoccupation with ethics, community, and human experience placed it at the forefront of an incipient reformist agenda. It was ushered back into the public sphere not by anticommunists—as one might think from an exclusive focus on the post-1968 era—but by reform Marxists, Karel Kosík above all. This rehabilitation, which helped phenomenology become *the* dissident philosophy of the subsequent decade, occurred because of the joint interest of both schools in human praxis—man's creative and productive activity. For Marxism, as is widely known, praxis forms the basis of our ability to transform the world. Phenomenology, too, despite its common characterization as esoteric, was deeply concerned with the category. As Patočka told Josef Zumr in 1967, phenomenology "leaned increasingly toward the question of praxis as an original approach to the world. The way to the problem begins in Husserl's *Ideas II*, where it was developed in connection with the theme of the body, of our corporeal activities and the potentialities they raised; *Experience and Judgment* (*Erfahrung und Urteil*) spoke further about the world of human praxis; in the *Crisis*, finally, the experiences of measurement and of quantity in general serve to show concretely that the 'lifeworld' is at the origin of the practical world."[38] Husserl's philosophy thus emerged as an ally in the battle against Soviet Marxism's vulgarized pretensions to science. Not only did it help to recover and elaborate Marx's own early concern for human experience; it also provided an avenue for reintroducing man's free will and creativity—in a word, humanism—into an official ideology that treated men as byproducts of historical forces.

In the 1960s, reform Marxist thinkers across Eastern Europe countered official ideology with calls for democratization, personal freedom, and political responsibility. Under the spell of Marx's early humanist essays, which were rediscovered in the 1920s and 1930s, they assailed bureaucratic impersonality for crushing man's creative impulses. Patočka's Charles University colleague Karel Kosík (1926–2003), a recovering Stalinist who became a key proponent of internal Party reform, was quick to see the links with his friend's philosophy. Kosík's 1963 fusion of humanistic Marxism with phenomenological anthropology became a philosophical touchstone of the Prague Spring era, its preoccupations echoing the technological concerns of Husserl and Heidegger and anticipating the fears of later Czech dissidents.[39]

Contemporary man, announced Kosík's *Dialectics of the Concrete* (1963; *Dialektika konkrétního*), lived in a "pseudoconcrete" world of alienated forms that failed to reflect his experience. Only a vigorous dialectical method could recover the concrete reality behind the ideological façade, for dialectics, he wrote, fusing Marxist methodology with phenomenological aspiration, was after "the 'thing itself'"—which "does not appear to man immediately." Only through praxis—that is, human activity or work—could one penetrate "the chiaroscuro of truth and deceit." The task of philosophy was to do just that—to uncover "the essence of things, the structure of reality, the 'thing itself,' the being of existents." Like Husserl and Heidegger, Kosík blamed positive science for substituting an "image of reality for reality itself."[40] The rationalism inaugurated by Galileo's mathematics cleaved reality in two: a quantifiable domain of objective data confronted an irrational nimbus of subjective experience. With subjectivity demoted, man became an object and the world a lifeless stone.[41] The phenomenological category of intentionality, when recast in materialist terms as a world-shaping praxis, could help to retrieve the original experience of worldliness lost to modern image-mongers. And dialectics, in turn, defined the movement of phenomenological insight, spiraling from "the abstract to the concrete" in its "infinite process" of "humanizing man."[42]

Human practice, Kosík argued, adopting the Heideggerian position, was rooted in the structures of care—practical worldly involvement conceived from a personal standpoint.[43] Marxist dialectics retained phenomenology's experiential focus while replacing its vague appeals to intuition with a rigorous analytic method. For the thing itself was no mystical *eidos*: "actually it is not a thing at all. The 'thing itself' that philosophy deals with is man and his place in the universe."[44] By breaking with the fetishism of false categories, phenomenological Marxism promoted an "existential modification" in which "the individual liberates himself from inauthentic existence and chooses an authentic one among others, by considering"—and here he echoed Husserl and Heidegger—"the everyday *sub specie mortis*."[45] A transformed attitude toward self and society led to active criticism of the regnant ideology. For Kosík, then, there was no doubt about phenomenology's social and political immediacy. In a Czechoslovakia barely altered from Stalinist days, the philosophy provided crucial assets for renewing social engagement and political critique.

"Our current crisis," Kosík warned five years later, in the full bloom of the Prague Spring, reflected above all

a conflict regarding the meaning of the people and of human existence: have we sunk to the level of anonymous masses, for whom conscience, human dignity, the meaning of truth and justice, honor, civilized behavior, and courage are unnecessary ballast which only hinders us in the scramble for apparent or real comfort? Or, are we capable of coming to our senses and of resolving existing economic, political, and other issues in harmony with the demands of human existence and of the existence of the nation?[46]

Technicization and bureaucratization, whose apotheosis he recalled in Stalinism, allowed men to "transform not only the earth, but gradually even the entire universe, into a perfectly operating laboratory, into a gigantic, inexhaustible storehouse of energy and raw materials, designed to serve for the comfort of mortals." But the human cost of this dominion was deplorable: The highest values disappeared, reduced to the sole standards of "measurability, comparability, and adjustability"; man's life withered into meaninglessness and indifference.[47] The Prague Spring sought to allay Kosík's fears by recovering an original human experience along with the values it dignified. Indeed, the philosopher saw his little Czechoslovakia as the vanguard of a humanist socialism that would replace "both capitalism and Stalinism" and set "technical reason in a framework of meaning."[48] It was the front line of a modern battle for humanity, community, and morality.[49]

Kosík was not the only Czech Marxist to laud phenomenology. In the spirit of theoretical openness that infused 1960s reformism, socialist thinkers tapped a Husserlian tradition with strong national roots and a history of ethical and anthropological examination. Following Kosík's retrieval of phenomenology, his colleague Ivan Sviták (1925–94) called on Marxists to engage with its vision of man as a creative and "open being," rather than the materialist creature of Soviet "Panzer-Marxism."[50] Robert Kalivoda (1923–89), integrating the Frankfurt School philosophy of Herbert Marcuse and Erich Fromm, noted the stimulus of phenomenology in

Marxist aesthetics.⁵¹ And Antonín Mokrejš, in *Fenomenologie a problém intersubjektivity* (Phenomenology and the Problem of Intersubjectivity), found in Husserl valuable dividends for Marxist social thought.⁵²

Patočka himself, clearly now the country's leading phenomenologist, enjoyed new favor during the Prague Spring era, a revival capped by his brief return to university teaching and by a commemorative issue of *Filosofický časopis*, the official philosophical journal of the Czechoslovak Academy of Science. The 1967 installment, issued on the occasion of his sixtieth birthday, included a retrospective interview with Patočka; essays by Jaroslav Kohout, Radim Palouš, and Ladislav Major; and a celebratory review by Ivan Dubský of Patočka's thirty-year-old book *Přirozený svět jako filosofický problém* (The Natural World as a Philosophical Problem).⁵³ As we will see in his reflection on the post-European future, Patočka reciprocated the interest of reform Marxists, acknowledging Marx's relevance to his own concern with modern crisis. As Erazim Kohák notes, in the late 1960s Patočka reclaimed humanistic socialism for Czech national philosophy, identifying man's liberation as the original core of both traditions.⁵⁴ Thus, while Patočka never compromised with the Party, neither was he anti-Marxist. Instead, like others, he found in socialism and phenomenology a common humanist concern, one that enabled a 1960s alliance that would persist under the umbrella of post–Prague Spring dissidence.

7

The Far Reaches: Jan Patočka's Transcendence to the World

At the height of Czechoslovak normalization and after a lifetime of professional isolation, the septuagenarian philosopher Jan Patočka (1907–77) was asked by the playwright Václav Havel and the former Prague Spring foreign minister Jiří Hajek to serve as co-spokesman for the new dissident organization Charter 77. Despite his initial hesitance, the invitation must have occasioned some excitement: Perhaps he even espied the potential for a political act to consummate his philosophical thought. While we should beware of binding the final act too tightly to earlier scripts, Patočka seems to have felt that the ethical impulses contained in his philosophy demanded engagement with the worldly crises of his day.[1] Ultimately, the commitment may have cost him his life. In March 1977, he succumbed to heart attack in the days following an eleven-hour police interrogation, a death that was soon cast as a Socratic ending for a reluctant dissident.[2]

For Patočka, phenomenology was *the* moral philosophy of its age, albeit one that needed reorientation to correct the deficiencies of its founders.[3] The purview of specialists prior to 1989, Patočka's thought has won growing appreciation since the communist collapse, due in no small part to eulogies from celebrities such as Paul Ricœur, Jacques Derrida, and Václav Havel.[4] Although he is still outshone by more prominent phenomenologists and dissidents, scholars have begun to locate him in several historical narratives, most obviously the story of regime resistance in Eastern

Europe, but also the history of the philosophy and phenomenology he cherished.[5]

Patočka's lifelong commitment to the renewal of technocratic modernity drew direct inspiration from Husserl and Heidegger. He met Husserl during a 1929 student year in Paris, and accepted an invitation to work under him in Freiburg four years later.[6] Soon he became Husserl's liaison for the 1934 Prague Philosophical Congress, transmitting the letter that first adumbrated the *Crisis* project. But Patočka was also a stringent critic of his mentor, often taking Heidegger's side in disputes between founder and heir. The remnants of Cartesianism, he complained, led Husserl to an overly theoretical outlook that isolated individual phenomena rather than exploring the dynamic interplay of subject and world.[7] This error grew from Husserl's cardinal sin: an overdeveloped subjectivism that excluded the world from the egological mind. While Patočka celebrated the *epoché*—the suspension of faith in perceived reality—as an act of freedom that emancipated men from the tyranny of objective circumstance and allowed them to transcend their narrow worldly situations, he condemned the phenomenological *reduction* of experience to the transcendental mind for turning the world into a distanced and reflective object-presence rather than a field of engaged activity.[8] The error was twofold: Not only did the move sever the subject from his surroundings; it also turned the world into a mere thesis of consciousness, denying its independence.

These charges, of course, echo the complaints of early realists. For Patočka, however, it was Heidegger who most emphatically exposed Husserl's flaws. Heidegger's Being-in-the-World highlighted the priority of our practical engagement with things over our theoretical contemplation of them. The world was not, as Heidegger knew, a thesis that could be suspended. Its objects were always *zuhanden* (ready-to-hand) before they were *vorhanden* (present-at-hand), to use his well-known coinages. And yet Heidegger too, according to Patočka, shortchanged the promise of phenomenology when he turned away from human worldliness in the quest for personal authenticity, rejecting others as the anonymous 'they' and retreating into anxious solitude. "Perhaps one can say," Patočka confided late in life to the Polish philosopher Krzysztof Michalski, "that Heidegger's philosophy suffers from the reverse ailment of Husserl's. The latter suffers from unclearness regarding the ontological, and attempts to dissect an array of ontic phenomena . . . [while the former] rediscovered the ontological, but did not find the way back to anthropology."[9] If Husserl's worldiness was blocked by Cartesian suppositions, Heidegger reneged on the very world that he had done so much to demonstrate. One can put the difference in moral terms: whereas the founder of phenomenology held out hope for an ethical renewal of modern humanity, his wayward heir forsook ethics altogether as a vestige of the worldly day-to-dayness that drew *Dasein* away from Being. In this regard, despite Patočka's Heideggerian concern with finitude and death, he was ultimately a philosopher of life lived at the limits, even unto sacrifice, and he followed Husserl's worldbound responsibility more closely than Heidegger's lonely authenticity. Yet only by joining—and finally surpassing—the insights of both could a satisfactory phenomenology be achieved.

Phenomenology as a Philosophy of Freedom

Over the course of a tumultuous life with only a handful of years in his chosen teaching profession, Patočka developed a unique phenomenology of freedom admixing Husserlian, Heideggerian, and Platonic themes. Indeed, he read a commitment to human autonomy back into the origins of the school. When Husserl died in 1938, his Czech disciple eulogized him as a philosopher of freedom:

The conviction that a human is free for the idea, free for truth, free to determine his own life, to the final objectives that he has the ability to reach, and is in no way subordinated to mere nature, is not simply an index of relations and fates—in this view Husserl fits within the great streams of thought who find their sources in Greek philosophy. . . . And to the belief in this luminosity of human history, which calls us finally to the wide power of the work of ideas over all of life, it is to this that the works of Edmund Husserl commits us.[10]

Thirty years later, in a *samizdat* text from the Prague Spring era, Patočka again commended his mentor's work as "nothing less than a striving for freedom and complete autonomy for humankind."[11] These statements illustrate a theme for which Patočka is now becoming known: the notion of freedom that entails rejecting the bonds of objectivity. Self-responsibility, he maintained, keeping a Husserlian formula but incorporating a

Heideggerian thematic, could transform modern men from mere objects or technical resources into free beings with a renewed purpose and interest in the world, calling them from a life of "equilibrium" to a life of "amplitude."[12]

The phenomenological itinerary was a philosophical expression of this transcendence. And as its most important prospect, phenomenological intuition revealed "the mutual interlocking and interdependence of humans and the world, interdependence which will not let us consider the world without taking humans into account, or humans without taking into account the world."[13] For Patočka, Husserl was the quintessential thinker of this 'natural world' of human experience, which he distinguished from the dead world of scientific laws. It seems fitting, therefore, that Patočka launched his most productive decade with a detailed *Introduction to Husserl's Phenomenology* (1965–66; *Úvod do Husserlovy fenomenologie*). The title, as Kohák notes, was excessively modest, for Patočka in fact offered a novel reinterpretation of Husserlian phenomenology that highlighted its social and ethical significance.[14] In his Czech disciple's hands, Husserl became an activist thinker, a philosopher of free human responsibility, not simply a theorist of direct intuition; the founder's work, Patočka wrote, was "a concurrent reflection about the meaning of things and about the meaning of human life."[15] And while Husserl fell into Cartesian pitfalls, his philosophical approach nonetheless held emancipatory potential, for it liberated historically situated human beings from both scientific facticity and blank circumstance. Phenomenology recalled humans to the world as a meaningful set of relations, a project in the making that preexisted the technical sphere.[16]

Husserl's earliest liberatory move, his break with objectivizing science, involved the split from Brentano and the embrace of an intuitive method for discovering essences, acts, and laws beyond empirical fact.[17] But it was the *epoché*—and in this Patočka differed from the early realists—that finally liberated man from the tyranny of circumstance, opening the prospect of transcendence from within the world. The emancipation of man from the mundane presumption of an immutable reality broke the hold of mere things, mere biological need—rendering the world as an ever new set of open horizons and possibilities.

The uncovering and the revealing of the world and of things in the world remains irreducible to the objective aspect of the world. This means that incarnate being is free with respect to the world, that it is not forced to accept it as finished, as it presents itself, but can also become aware how immensely it transcends everything given in that extreme distance which Husserl elaborated in his *epoché*. For the *epoché* is nothing other than the discovery of the freedom of the subject which is manifested in all transcendence.[18]

To be sure, Patočka accused Husserl of reducing the *epoché* to a methodological operation—even worse, of treating it as the gateway to the purified aerie of the disinterested observer. Husserl exacerbated this error when, in rejecting objectivism, he fell prey to the counter ill of dismissing the world from the transcendent 'I,' now an outsized Fichtean subjectivity.[19] Nevertheless, the *epoché* stood for Patočka as a supreme refusal to submit to the lawbound realm of scientific reality and a determination instead to preserve man's free aspiration.

Patočka rejected what he saw as the false transcendence of Husserl's pure ego—subject-centered, world-exempting—by recasting the *epoché* as an anthropological-cum-ethical movement of human freedom *within* the world—transcendence to the world rather than from it—that allowed one to move beyond quotidian immediacy to an open horizon of being. In Patočka's hands, the *epoché* helped men escape facticity and turn toward vistas of prospect and action that lay beyond the current self. Freedom is a "distance," he wrote in the 1953 essay "Negative Platonism"; it is a "remove" from all objectivities, a beyond from which the whole world becomes evident.[20] As he put it in his introduction to Husserl, the subject's "freedom is manifested in that, within its dependence and no less for it, it is capable of truth."[21] Man was not imprisoned by his surroundings or by the formulae of modern science. For in outward, *ekstatic* movements, humans could approach truths that stood beyond them. And the world, newly conjured in Patočka's thought, stood beyond all things as their permanent experiential horizon, irreducible to either subject or object.[22] Despite Husserl, then, the *epoché* was not simply a technique or method, but a seismic historical event. Indeed, as we will see below, it could be called history itself.

Patočka found other bases for freedom in Husserl as well. Through the incarnate body, the "point zero" of experience, man received the world, touching the near and seeing the far. As the corporeal basis of "the 'I can,'" bodily kinesthesia offered the "consciousness of freedom."[23] We make our first, intensely poetic acquaintance with worldly phenomena through our bodies: the "merciless blue of the sky above" rather than the physics of light and color.[24] But the solitary human, embedded in and straitened by bodily circumstance, was not Patočka's ultimate source of freedom. For men could not reach a wider trans-subjective world except through the recognition and affirmation of others. "[W]hat else is the intersubjective reduction," Patočka asked rhetorically, "than the reassurance that anything that calls itself 'I' cannot be wholly alien, that, for all that separates it, it is not hopeless to attempt to approach another, to address one another, to understand one another? . . . In principle, no I stands outside the possibility of communication, no I is isolated, each is in its own way an inflection of all others as all others are inflections of its own."[25]

The point is crucial for moral awareness. An ethical society must combine the recognition of distant truths worth striving for with the essential nearness of community and home. And freedom, Patočka insisted, did not mean "only life *for oneself* alone," but also "from oneself," oriented toward a higher responsibility through participation in social life and historical community.[26] Philosophy, he cited Husserl as saying, prepared this transformation by "making possible humankind's development into personal autonomy and into an all-encompassing autonomy for humankind—the idea which represents the driving force of life for the highest stage of humanity."[27]

The World as Light

None of Patočka's phenomenological assessments make sense unless we clarify his distinctive concept of the world. In an essay written just after the Second World War, he exploited the etymological link between the Czech words *svět* (world) and *světlo* (light) to argue that "the fundamental phenomenon of the world is nothing other than the light."[28] The primordial world of human experience was neither an armillary globe girded in latitude and longitude nor a mere assemblage of things; nor was it simply the social and environmental ligature of individual lives. Instead, Patočka told an audience in Warsaw in 1971, "the 'natural' world of our life" was that to which our "*ou heneka* ['for the sake of which,' or ultimate purpose]" pointed. "[I]t is not the concrete context, structured by our active life, that merits the name, as much as that about the very foundations of our actual life that makes such a structuring possible—the worldhood of the world toward which the human *Dasein* transcends himself."[29] As the light metaphor suggests, Patočka's Heideggerian world was not something fixed or objective, but a kind of clearing in which things appeared, an open horizon of human encounter and activity. In this primordial glade, lifeworlds and then science worlds emerged, coalescing into fixed and measurable forms. Even Husserl's lifeworld, Patočka remarked elsewhere, was a secondary concept that at times obscured the more primary natural world beyond it.[30] The world in its experiential originality preceded and outstripped these frameworks.

The "natural" world, in fact, launched Patočka's philosophical career. Inspired by the lifeworld problematic of Husserl's late work, Patočka's 1936 *Habilitationsschrift*, *Přirozený svět jako filosofický problém* (The Natural World as a Philosophical Problem), focused on man's primordial experience of the earth. Its key aim: to confront objective science and metaphysics, which treated the world as dead matter subject to force and mastery, with the prevenient and meaningful world as experienced by men but banned from modern positivity. Phenomenology, Patočka ventured, offered a method for mending the split between man and his world by recovering first encounters. Blending Husserl and Heidegger, Patočka laid out the vision of a common being-in-the-world extending from center or "domicile" to "indeterminate depths."[31] Encounters with strangers were an emphatic reminder of the dynamic interaction of home and foreign. The world, Patočka insisted, was just this encounter, this "totality of experience."[32] It was not "the object of position, it was not a thesis, not an attitude that one could adopt or from which one could subtract to replace it with another—it is, by contrast, the position of possibility of all clarity and of the consciousness in general."[33] Modern science and metaphysics depended upon this a priori natural world even as they suppressed it.[34]

Patočka's most nuanced reflection on the human relation to the world came in lectures delivered during his final professorship at the Charles University in 1968–69, just before his ouster on political grounds. His mature sense of the world as set of interpenetrating movements—including, paradoxically, a transcendence from and to the world—appears in the book that resulted from these lectures, *Body, Community, Language, World* (*Tělo, společenství, jazyk, svět*). The modern division of world into subject and object, Patočka warned, already obscured its primary wholeness and motility. The body inserted humans into the world as a "null-point" of orientation, a personal "moment in an impersonal situation"; but it did not circumscribe an inviolable "thing" called "I."[35] Instead, because of the situated body, "humans are not only the beings of distance, but also the beings of proximity, rooted beings, not only innerworldly beings but also beings in the world."[36] Objects, too, were worldly phenomena, "a continuum of references that [led] from one experiential moment to another," pathways "to the rest of the world" and hence "partners" in worldly possibility and actualization.[37] In movement, Patočka saw the ontological fundament of being: his world was not encountered in pure consciousness, but through activity, engagement, reflection. Subject and object shared a joint mobility that bound them together in one common clearing.[38]

Patočka elaborated this vision into his signature theory of the three movements of human existence.[39] The first movement of sinking roots anchored us in the world instinctively, affectively, naturally—a process exemplified in the upbringing of a child. The second movement of self-sustenance maintained and perpetuated life, primarily through work. Recalling Hannah Arendt, Patočka characterized the original project of labor as the "bondage of life to itself."[40] These two earthbound movements, based in the rhythms of biological existence, contrasted with Patočka's third and crowning movement of transcendence. In this mode, humans directed themselves from below to above in an effort to "break through our earthliness," to end "the bondage of life to its self-consumption."[41] Trapped in mundanity, humans strove toward the eternal, the permanent, the transcendent—trying to reach the sky from earth.[42] As Rodolphe Gasché puts it, the movement of freedom marked the human resistance to perpetual decline and mortality.[43]

Here as elsewhere, Patočka's exemplar was Greek. In order to confront man's "damnation," Hellenic philosophy offered a "plan for life" and "greatness" that modern men missed.[44] Overcoming the tyranny of fact, the Greeks realized that "it is not necessary to fear death," for humans possessed a soul that, through care, could be gathered up to achieve a kind of mortal immortality, a transcendence in time that was quantitatively but not essentially different from that of the gods.[45] Truth and justice were the scales of this "infinite task," their achievement man's ultimate aim.[46] If timorous resignation led to the forfeiture of freedom, transcendence—the recognition of goods for which even life might be sacrificed—sanctified the world and men in it. The desperate relevance of this hope in "normalized" Czechoslovakia, where the regime raised consumer standards in exchange for popular quiescence, could hardly have been missed by Patočka's listeners.

Transcendence, however, was not simply an individual quest, a personal escape from worldly imprisonment. Heeding Husserl's "drive to responsibility," Patočka ventured that humans exist primordially as "an empathy of a kind," a harmony between self and world that encompassed both things and others.[47] The human distinction was that we alone related to being, singling ourselves "out of the whole in an explicit relation to it."[48] As Patočka told his students: "Humans are the only beings which . . . can live in truth [*žít v pravdě*]"—a phrase that would take on enormous significance in the dissident decade of the 1970s.[49] Yet even in transcendence, "harmony with the world" remained.[50] Freedom was not metaphysical escape into a Platonic empyrean, but a transcendence *to* the world aimed at elevating human beings beyond mere life by exposing their truthful potential.

And the move had a distinctly social dimension. "Responsibility," Patočka wrote in 1939, "means: it is not only for me, it is also for the other [*pro druhé*] and it has to be for the other, I don't work for myself, I am not free in relation to myself alone, rather I am free in relation to all, I am free for the society which supports me."[51] Modernity's exaggerated individualism neglected social responsibility in favor of autonomic control. Yet there was a difference, Patočka insisted, between the world as "what is in our power" and "what opens itself to us of itself."[52] By privileging the latter, phenomenology countered arrogance and rooted what was torn up, placing men back in the world.[53]

Patočka's anthropology of openness, we should note, ill-accords with the self-possessed subject of liberal rights that he defended in his Charter 77 pronouncements. The self of the earlier Patočka was not composed and collected, but always in a "pilgrim state, ever on the way from somewhere to somewhere."⁵⁴ As he wrote with particular piquancy: "We live turned away from ourselves, we have always already transcended ourselves in the direction of the world, of its ever more remote regions. . . . The projection into the world never ceases, we never live in ourselves, we always live among things, there where our work is, living in horizons outside ourselves, not within."⁵⁵ But this centrifugal motion also entailed the centripetal. A person remained localized and situated even as she "thrust toward the world," rooted and reflexive, always returning to self.⁵⁶ The recoil of "self-retrieval" remained part of the wider project of "seek[ing] and constitut[ing] ourselves, los[ing] ourselves, and find[ing] ourselves again."⁵⁷ In short, "[l]ife's drive into the world . . . makes us what we are," whether we embrace possibilities or sink into redundant banality.⁵⁸

Ethics for a Post-European World

"Europe has disappeared, probably forever," announced a morose Patočka in 1974 from the netherworld of 'normalized' Czechoslovakia after the Soviet invasion. It was destroyed by a hyperrationalism that squelched open inquiry, fueled overseas expansion, and fired wars at home.⁵⁹ Even in the thaw before the Prague Spring, Patočka had anticipated a dawning post-European age in which non-Western cultures would become the civilizational avant garde, overcoming the strictures of European scientism and imperialism. Yet his devotion to Europe's fraught legacy was too great for him simply to write its epitaph. By the 1970s, despite a characteristically dour outlook, Patočka advanced a desperate hope for European renewal, spearheaded by those few who rose above the continent's recent catastrophes.

Patočka's striking philosophy of history served as a backdrop for his phenomenology of human existence. Although it remains less well-known than his theory of human movements, the two were intertwined; in fact, the fear of Europe's demise may have fueled his determination to articulate a redemptive phenomenology of freedom. Philosophy of history had attracted Patočka since young adulthood. In 1934, as a twenty-seven-year-old, he had declared that "history is incompatible with indifference"⁶⁰ because it concerned what it meant to be human, to be free in the world. As the realm of anthropological self-comprehension, historical understanding helped men to avert humdrum routine in favor of "a new life" of liberty.[61] A year later, Patočka distinguished between a superficial history concerned with straight facts and a philosophically informed history that grasped the innate "ensemble of possibilities" forming each age.[62] Starting in the 1950s and growing into the heady days of Czechoslovak reform, Patočka cultivated these seeds into a verdant historical philosophy of truth and insight.

It was precisely 'world openness,' Patočka asserted, that had established Europe as a cultural and spiritual entity in ancient times, with Greek politics and philosophy its herald. The Greeks recognized the inherent problematicity of the world—the notion that it was not a fixed presence but an open question—and venerated human inquiry, establishing insight and responsibility as moral standards. This recognition launched the historical age, for history was nothing else, according to Patočka, but an openness to being and a questing for truth. "History arises," he wrote in 1976, "when people in a certain insignificant region of the earth cease to live for life and begin to live in order to conquer, for themselves and those who share their will, the space for their recognition, the space for freedom. That is politics in its original definition: life from freedom and for freedom."[63] Social life in prehistoric societies had taken the form of a giant household, exhausting its members in labor for monarch and kin. Mythic societies spurred the move from prehistory to history by lifting man's attention above life's drudgery and fixing it beyond the world of things. But mythic peoples still merely accepted external truths. History only began in earnest when men—in Patočka's account, ancient Greeks—started questioning received axioms and embraced the inherent change and uncertainty of their world, giving joint birth to the polis and philosophy. The city-state demanded risk-takers who rose above mere life-sustaining labor—Patočka credited Arendt with this insight—and embraced action and inquiry instead.[64] At that moment, "[n]othing of the earlier life of acceptance remains in peace," Patočka declared. "All the pillars of the community, traditions, and myths are equally shaken. . . . In the moment when life renews itself, everything is cast in a new light."[65] Rejecting the "will to tradition," the Greeks "reach[ed] forth" toward the "unsheltered life . . . [toward] a world that opens itself" to action and quest.[66]

Modern man, by contrast, played it safe, affirming freedom as his highest ideal but enslaving himself to objective rules and patterns. The contemporary West, according to Patočka, produced the first universal or metacivilization [*nadcivilizace*], overcoming through rationalism the particularist cultures and religions of earlier epochs.[67] Yet this ecumenism, which afforded Western civilization a worldwide reach, engendered sharp internal and external contradictions. For modern technocracy, by eroding cultural and religious allegiances, maintained only a superficial moral and emotional hold on men. Recognizing the motivational shortcomings of a calculating ethos, modern rationalists of the revolutionary era embraced the liberalism of rights and virtues as a heroic bulwark against irrationalist retrenchment, an ally that could stir the passions where sober rationalism only piqued the intellect.[68] But this was ultimately a partnership of convenience forged to defend the gains of rationality. And like most opportunisms, the alliance could be broken.

Modern civilization took two forms in Patočka's eyes: an original, moderate, liberal technocracy and a radical countermodel that pushed rationality to an extreme. In its moderate form, parliamentary liberalism institutionalized political freedom, but it also fostered a kind of "moral somnolence,"[69] even nihilism, intensified by an increasingly heavy-handed scientism that rendered life in terms of manipulable forces. Rather than asserting their own spiritual potency, liberal technocracies offered their members only an anodyne, agnostic, superficial faith that rejected particularism and banished the divine.[70] Yet empty liberty and instrumental proceduralism could not feed the moral imagination or fuel the quest for wider purpose. As Patočka rued in 1966, modern man had a natural and a scientific world but no longer an ethical one.[71] A shrunken, atomized humanity faced a world voided of meaning.[72]

This spiritual emptiness was exacerbated by economic and political hypocrisy. In a startling reference from the 1950s, Patočka praised Marx and Lenin—notwithstanding recent Stalinist excesses in his country—for their insights into modern social exploitation. The sordid inequities of capitalism, the grave privation suffered by many across the planet—these were harrowing injustices that modern civilization seemed unable to redress despite its egalitarian promises.[73] Nowhere was this flagrant deceit more apparent than under Western imperialism, which Patočka saw, again echoing Lenin, as a late nineteenth-century "crisis of expansion" that transferred European inequities around the world.[74] It was hard to imagine a starker betrayal of liberal norms than the brutal hierarchies of empire.

These contradictions prompted a radical reaction *internal to* Western civilization, one that rejected liberal cant and pushed egalitarian rationality to the brink. But the grim ratiocinations of Jacobinism and Marxism—Patočka's examples of metacivilizational radicalism—exacerbated rather than curbed the central error of modernity, for they suppressed human morality in the name of banausic control and planned dominion.[75] Soviet communism marked the apotheosis—the Frankenstein—of radical technocratic dominion. But in the end both bourgeois and socialist—moderate and radical—brands of modernity provoked metacivilizational decline.[76] The carnivorous clashes of Patočka's day—World Wars I and II and the Cold War—were the dying spasms of a broken order, fought by alter egos. At their root lay an overweening rationalism that substituted scientific mechanism for the intuited world and dissolved human responsibility into neutral forces.[77] Universal rationalism, Patočka lamented in the early 1970s, turned the world into a "gigantic inorganic body."[78]

This danger, it should be noted, was not new; like Husserl's ancient rational *Urstiftung*, technocratic excess was a Hellenic seed that came to modern fruition. At its origins in the Greek polis, the European *ratio* carried with it an impulse to dominate and expand—expressed potently in the *Imperium Romanum* but already evident in the Attic decline of Socrates' day—that progressively reduced truth to mastery and worldliness to conquest. Initially, this impulse was leavened by a sense of ethical responsibility for others and a soulful relation to being and truth. But technocratic enticements multiplied with the advent of Renaissance humanism, when rationalist subjectivism and technical instrumentalism were increasingly conscripted in the service of war. This mutation—from the ancient sense of *aletheia* as world-openness to a modern controlling rationality—impelled the tragic Western surrender to science that turned humanity into molding clay.[79] Even Husserl was a sinner in that his subjectivism had swung too far inward in the effort to counter the objectivist threat.[80] Seeking to free phenomenology from the errors of its master,

Patočka called for a new relation to the world and others, for the moral renewal of a modernity dulled to materialist indifference.

Continued Western "titanism" posed particular trouble for relations among peoples, because Europeans no longer understood cultural difference once they cast human interaction in a mechanical frame.[81] Understanding gave way to technical expedience, and European arrogance, subject-centered and blindly rationalistic, widened the gulf with others.[82] The failure of intercultural dialogue was inevitable as non-Westerners tried to preserve their traditions in the teeth of European hegemony, a cause for which Patočka felt some sympathy.[83] In this regard, he made a strong distinction between the (originally European) principle of insight, which he would soon label "care for the soul," and Europe as a geopolitical entity disfigured by the cult of domination.[84] Europe's noblest vision—the ideal of a society based on constant seeking after insight and responsibility—led a fugitive existence in the continent's actual history, regularly suppressed, often forgotten, occasionally renewed.[85] The post-European world, Patočka hoped, might revive this legacy while rejecting its "decadent culture of subjectivism" and "over-technicization." For "[o]nly when post-European peoples understand not to fall back into the errors of Europe will they achieve the prospect of solving their problems."[86]

But Patočka was not sanguine in believing that non-Westerners could resist the seductions of technology. Writing in the aftermath of the Prague Spring, he saw the history of socialism as a cautionary tale of how movements based on justified demands—Patočka decried the gulf between "the blessed haves and those who are dying of hunger on a planet rich in energy," as well as the way that modern economies mobilized workers at "the crack of the whip"—could succumb to the siren call of technocracy.[87] Despite the mid-1960s hope that Czechoslovakia might birth a humane socialism, Patočka came to see Marxism exhibiting the same technocratic fixity that poisoned modern rationality *tout court*; indeed, socialism intensified rational dominance in its effort to cure the ill of inequality—but more toxin had sickened not healed the patient.[88]

Yet Patočka's hope for a renewal led by non-Europeans was not entirely in vain. He appreciated the persistence of cultural variety across the globe, a richness that sprang partly from the strength of mythic faiths. If East Asian leaders such as Mao cloaked themselves in Marxist garb, their vision, Patočka maintained, was distinctly local, reaching back to a tradition that Europe had never extinguished. Non-Europeans, he anticipated, might yet learn to trust their customary moral (*sittliche*) resources.[89] And prerational mythologies, while phenomenologically naïve, provided an opening to transcendence that could temper technocratic 'omniscience.'[90] Indeed, it was ultimately a European conceit to believe in a single mankind united under the hegemony of reason. Other peoples retained continuous religious and cultural worldviews, but only Europeans—since the days when Greeks disparaged barbarians—had insisted on measuring all men against themselves.[91]

Nonetheless, the ancient Greek principle of insight retained value for Patočka as a human possibility, though not as a European property. For it could transcend the geographies of its birth and encourage others to cultivate their particular worlds, regardless of the violations committed in Europe's name.[92] There were, in this sense, two Europes: a positive principle of insight available beyond the borders of the continent; and a negative history of domination associated with its actual past and present. The latter Europe had destroyed itself; the former could be passed to someone else.

Care for the Soul

According to ancient myth, Patočka asserted in a 1973 lecture series that was subsequently published under the title *Plato and Europe* (*Platón a Evropa*), "man is the being that dares to penetrate into the domain that is not his."[93] Ancient Attica, he said, had elevated this daring to a standard of human excellence: its greatest legacy was having cast life as a free response to the cosmos, an ongoing engagement that preserved problematicity and privileged insight. This narrative, as we can see, historicized the phenomenological *epoché*—Husserl's abstention from faith in perceived reality—in the Hellenic moment when naïve acceptance of the existing world gave way to the broad horizon of philosophical inquiry and political activity. The modern Husserl, in this regard, had not so much discovered something new as revived an ideal from the Athens that both he and his disciple cherished. And perversely, in the turn to Cartesian subjectivism, Husserl also replayed the key betrayal of European history: the abandonment of an original Greek insight that Patočka called "care for the soul" (*péče o duši* in Czech; *tēs psuchēs epimeleia* in Greek) in favor of the idol of rational mastery.[94] Socrates first decried this heresy as the Peloponnesian city-states slipped from being communities dedicated to ethical self-transcendence into factions seeking dominance over others. As if in echo, Husserl diverged from his own epochal insight toward a pure transcendental ego designed to secure for itself an absolute knowledge.

To make sense of Patočka's "care for the soul"—the premier concept of his late career—we must first note his endorsement of a novel midcentury interpretation of Plato associated with Tübingen School classicists, who claimed that the most significant aspects of the philosopher's teaching were found in the 'unwritten doctrine,' especially the lost lecture "On the Good."[95] In both the *Phaedrus* and the *Seventh Letter*, Plato worried that written teachings would be misconstrued by an unschooled public, that ultimate lessons should not be inscribed for wide dissemination but shared only with the sharpest pupils, those "capable of discovering the truth for themselves with a little guidance."[96] Recorded clues to these teachings, along with references from several students, including Aristotle, led some interpreters to speculate that Plato's real opinions did not appear in the written dialogues. Patočka endorsed this view, arguing that the master's true beliefs differed from the positive metaphysics found in *The Republic* and typically associated with his name. Plato, said his Czech admirer, recognized that being and the Good were finally one, that there was not a heaven of fixed forms, and that ideas instead were "first relations" set between "indeterminacy and unity."[97]

In keeping with this rendition, Patočka's 1953 essay "Negative Platonism" ("Negativní platonismus") characterized human freedom not in terms of the elevated contemplation of ideal permanence, but as a distance from all objectivities. Here he highlighted a philosophical quandary found in Plato commentaries: How, interpreters wondered, could permanent ideas determine a shifting human world when there was such a gap between the physical and metaphysical realms? For Patočka, this *chōrismos*, or gap, between the Ideas and human reality was not a problem demanding resolution but the very condition of human liberty, the key to Plato's emancipatory insight. In resisting the closure of positive answers, the *chōrismos* designated the space of free inquiry and open possibility.

The mystery of the *chōrismos* is like the experience of freedom, an experience of a distance with respect to real things, of a meaning independent of the objective and the sensory which we read by inverting the original, 'natural' orientation of life, an experience of a rebirth, of a second birth, intrinsic to all spiritual life, familiar to the religious, to the initiates of the arts, and, not least, to philosophers.[98]

Both scientific facticity and positive Platonism bound men to fixed metaphysical forms. Plato's Ideas, by contrast, had a "deobjectifying power," allowing humans to overcome circumstantial realities through inspired aspiration.[99]

Yet Patočka's emphasis on negativity, his refusal to foreclose possibility and surrender to fixed forms, did not mean that truth was insignificant. On the contrary, the yearning for truth reflected "the pure asubjective call of transcendence," the attraction of the far reaches that drew men into the open.[100] Without a relation to truth—however unconsummated—humans would acquiesce to fatalism and nihilism. Contra Nietzsche, the "hopeless adventure" of life could steer by a glimmer of eternity even if it never reached port.[101]

An increasingly Heideggerian Patočka put these claims differently in the 1970s: the world, he now said, was not characterized by metaphysical presence, but by a constant exchange between presence and absence played out in the manifestation of things. "All our life takes place within the very showing of things and in our orientation among them," he explained.[102] Phenomenology alone, as the science of pure appearance, elucidated this situation; indeed, there was no science of manifestation until Husserl retrieved an ancient theme.[103] This revelation gave rise to Patočka's project of an asubjective phenomenology, expressed primarily in two essays from 1970 and 1971 that have drawn significant scholarly interest.[104] The project grew from earlier premises: If the ego only realized itself through actions in the world, then surely phenomenology could only investigate the subject by observing worldly phenomena, rather than turning inward to consciousness. Descartes's cogito, Brentano's psychic phenomena, Husserl's transcendent subject, even Heidegger's *Dasein*—all were misdirected.[105] In privileging the 'I' rather than treating it as one phenomenon among others, subject-centered philosophies prompted, in dialectic counterpoint, an excessive objectivism as well. Thus, Patočka's stress on *showing* rather than *the thing shown* not only weakened the subject-centered "integral humanism" (*integrální humanismu*) that led to world domination, but also helped to de-objectivize philosophy, undermining the tendency to posit a fixed world of things as absolute reality.[106] The 1971 essay went further: the true aim of phenomenological reduction was not to reveal the subject per se, but to uncover the world *as it appeared*. Manifestation, not man, was phenomenology's paramount concern.

Much of this analysis came from the later Heidegger, particularly from the anti-humanism exemplified in his "Letter on Humanism" (1949). Like Heidegger, Patočka's late work insisted, against earlier humanisms, that man was not the basis of knowledge or the pinnacle of creation, but instead a being enveloped in the world and distinguished chiefly by his ability to reflect on that predicament. If this "negative anthropology" did not obliterate man altogether, it certainly demoted him from ranks to which he had earlier aspired. No longer was man the master of the globe.[107] But of course, the Czech humanist tradition in which Patočka participated had long warned against 'titanism,' man's striving for empire and control. And if Patočka's condemnation—with Husserl, Heidegger, and even Masaryk—of modern technocratic rationalism was a clear indictment of humanistic hubris, it also invoked man's ability—his *responsibility*—to escape the scaffolding of the objective world. In this sense, Patočka never relinquished his commitment to human exertion and aspiration. This point may also be made in the language of his phenomenology of manifestation. Even though the world shows itself independently, the showing tends toward subjects who witness appearance and recognize unity. The dialectic of self and world remains, because manifestation, or "light in the world," singles out man "from all else."

> [A]nd is not the consequence of this manifesting, which is after all in a certain sense the human privilege, something that also places duties before man? Care of the soul is fundamentally care that follows from the proximity of man to manifesting, to the phenomenon as such, to the manifesting of the world as a whole, that occurs within man, with man.[108]

Thus, lowering "the subject in its appearance [to] a 'happening' like everything else" did not dissolve it completely within the show.[109] Man is, as Gasché puts it, "the addressee of everything that manifests itself."[110] Humbled before the scene of the world, persons could adopt an ethical stance by opening themselves toward truth and toward others in care and concern.

In a manuscript from the late 1960s, Patočka had already characterized the soul as the moral spirit of man—"that for which good and bad have sense."[111] In 1973, he described it as that which was "capable of truth in man," that which turned toward the eternal and the transcendent.[112] As ever, Patočka traced the origins of soulfulness to the pagan Greeks, who had understood it, he claimed, as openness to truth, rather than the Christian immortal anima. Like Patočka's human movements, care for the soul had three currents: Ontocosmological care concerned one's relationship with the whole beyond the stream of factical life. Social care drew men from solo pursuits into community with others—and ultimately with the whole society of man. The third current nurtured the inner self to whom the world was manifested.[113] Each demanded cultivation.

Equally ancient was Patočka's likening of soulcraft to statecraft.[114] The soul of a community derived from the movements of its members, and the outer pursuit of justice expressed the inner aspiration for truth, the "fitness of the soul."[115] Under certain circumstances, "man could make at least the human world a world of truth and justice," an omega that formed "the very subject of care for the soul."[116] The ideal demos—and Patočka's intentions were clearly democratic, as opposed to the ambiguous Husserl and the egregious Heidegger—overcame the tyrannies of solitary ignorance and routine mundanity by striving toward a just community.[117] But forging such a community of excellence, in which duty bound men together and drew them outward into the world, required citizens to make a choice: A man could either "capitulate and degenerate into mere existence" or "realize himself as a being of truth.[118] If normalized Czechoslovakia exhibited the former propensity to extreme, Patočka rehabilitated the antique ideal of a society dedicated to higher goals.

Patočka's Husserlian aim was "complete responsibility, in thought as much as in practical life."[119] Of course, the aim was unfulfillable. Indeed, the philosophical key to Patočka's care for the soul was the preservation of "problematicity," of an ongoing *chōrismos* or *epoché* that resisted closure and cast the subject as a living question within the play of manifestation.[120] But this inconclusiveness was not cause for despair. For "[w]hen we think about what can be directly given to me in this way, in a certain sense, it is everything as long as I get to it, as long as I get there, as long as it is at all physically possible for me."[121] The world is unending, but the human reach is far. And the philosopher's concern, Patočka asserted, here drawing on Aristotle rather than Plato, was not the ascent to heaven but return to life in the cave.[122]

Leaning out of the World

What conditions might revive the ancient ideal of care for the soul in a parlous modern world? Patočka's final long work, *The Heretical Essays on the Philosophy of History* (*Kacířské eseje o filosofii dějin*), written in 1975 and treated today as a kind of *summa*, was his most apocalyptic, but it also attempted an answer to the question above that differed from the notion of a post-European renewal of a decade earlier.[123] In recalling Athenian achievement once again, Patočka now discerned the possibility of a *European* rebirth. Although a life of unexamined complacency was more comfortable than anxious incertitude, it was in moments of great terror, when all familiar meaning collapsed, that politics and philosophy could reassert their claim as domains of transcendent human action. In the "shaken situation" of conflict or war—Patočka employed Heraclitus's term *polemos*—humans could embrace "new possibilities of life" and accept their role as free creators.

History arises and can arise only insofar as there is *areté*, the excellence of humans who no longer simply live to live but who make room for their justification by looking into the nature of things and acting in harmony with what they see—by building a polis on the basis of the law of the world, which is *polemos*, by speaking that which they see as revealing itself to a free, exposed yet undaunted human (philosophy).[124]

This dauntless history became the deep content of Patočka's phenomenology, revealing the conditions of human conversion, or *metanoia*, in the "shaking of accepted meaning" and the "transcendence of humans toward the world, to the whole of what is brought to light."[125] Ecstatically, humans "lean out of the world" and must "call within and towards it."[126] This *ekstasis* was not only—perhaps not primarily—a solitary act.

It is not only individual life which, if it passes through the experience of the loss of meaning and if it derives from it the possibility and need for a wholly different self-relation to all that is, comes to a point of global "conversion." Perhaps the inmost nature of that rupture . . . lies in that shaking of the naïve certainty which governs the life of humankind up to that specific transformation—and in a more profound sense really unitary—origin of politics and philosophy.[127]

Modern rational science denied these ecstasies, individual and collective, transforming men from beings open to the world into material for manipulation and control.

The core of the *Heretical Essays* was a "history of the soul"[128] from ancient Greece to the modern era that highlighted the struggle to transcend creaturely life. Patočka's soulful exemplar was Socrates, whose maieutic questing was appropriated and revised by phenomenology in the eidetic method. Yet Socrates lived and died at a moment when the Greek polis was strife-ridden and failing. The Hellenism and Romanism that replaced it spread Greek idols across Eurasia, demonstrating the schism at the heart of the Attic experience. While Mediterranean empires fostered a spiritual impulse, their unity took the form of political conquest, and the fealty they demanded was no longer that of free citizens accepting an ideal but of subjects bending to a mighty state. Athenian care for the soul split into the duality of dominance and obeisance. And while the ensuing Neoplatonism preserved a human relation to the *mysterium*, it also set the stage for the progressive withdrawal of goodness and responsibility from the human realm. Christianity affirmed this departure. If, on the one hand, Christian care called the soul to higher responsibility, it also cast the source of goodness—God—wholly outside the world and threw individuals back on themselves alone, not as citizens realizing the good in consortium. Indeed, the world and the society of men were denigrated as temptations drawing one from divine regard. But it was only in the modern age that this dialectic gave way utterly to domination. Modern technoscience, for all its marvels, inaugurated an age of meaninglessness, when man grew "estranged from any personal and moral vocation."[129] A "cult of the mechanical" replaced care for the soul, and man became a force majeure, not a free moral agent, savagely deployed in two world wars where Europe died along with its millions.

Yet Patočka found a desperate glimmer in this battlefield demise. For the loss of all sense, the devastation of life and thought, shook some people from torpor and led them to protest the rule of death and join in the effort to renew man's ethical vocation. This "solidarity of the shaken" (*solidarita otřesených*) allowed some to understand "what life and death are all about."[130] And here Patočka's narrative returned to its start. For the modern age, in effect, threw men back into prehistory, into a situation in which truths were externally imposed and man accepted alien forces rather than embrace his true vocation to question and co-create the world. History had ceased, but it might yet start again. Phenomenology became an agent of this renewal, a new philosophy of "living in truth," to invoke the Patočkan formula that Havel later made famous.[131] As in ancient times, humanity needed a rebirth of truth and meaning, one that would come from men prepared to face the open world and sacrifice themselves in the name of transcendent truth—the final expression of freedom from the tyranny of mere survival and a rejection of the status of object. The act of sacrifice would shake others as well, bringing them face to face with human freedom and possibility. It could, in other words, relaunch history by rededicating men to "the shaken certitude of pre-given meaning."[132] Like Marx, Patočka turned Hegel on his head: rather than the end of history, he called for history's return.

Conclusion

"We always take hold of liberty," wrote Patočka in 1934, "in a historical situation, while becoming what we are, unshakable, stronger than the world."[133] In 1977, after a career thwarted by communist Czechoslovakia's praetorian guards, he made the fateful decision to defend "moral sentiment" and "human rights" against a regime that preached justice and practiced violence. In two manifestoes, Patočka proclaimed the significance of Charter 77 as a kind of public tribunal born of private conviction.[134] Human rights, for him, entailed the confidence that even states and societies must "recognize something unconditional that is higher than they are, something that is binding even on them, sacred, inviolable, and that in their power to establish and maintain a rule of law they seek to express this recognition."[135] Their invocation, however, stood in some tension to his open-ended advocacy of freedom: a commitment to the new human rights "utopia," with its minimalist but fixed metaphysics of human essence, seems to limit transcendental problematicity.[136] Or perhaps the tension comes only with our current understanding of rights, for Patočka may have sought nothing more by exalting them than to safeguard negative metaphysical openness against an overreaching totalitarian state, whereas we understand rights as part of a positive liberal and individualist program. At any rate, if the letter of human rights theory ill-accords with an open phenomenology, the act of protest surely fit Patočka's philosophy in spirit: Among a community of dissidents determined to resist the abasement of their fellows, he sacrificed his safety to goad a moral response among citizens, acknowledging by his example that humans might transcend any historical moment.

8

The Definitive No: Phenomenology and Czechoslovak Resistance to Impersonal Power

The story of Charter 77 is well known.[1] In response to the trial by Gustav Husák's regime of several underground musicians associated with the rock band Plastic People of the Universe, Václav Havel, Jiří Hajek, Jan Patočka, and other prominent political and cultural figures drew up a petition protesting the widespread denial of rights guaranteed in Czechoslovak law. The declaration, published in early January 1977 with an initial 243 signatures and circulated in the underground samizdat press, on Radio Free Europe, and in émigré papers, announced the establishment of a new citizen watchdog group that would monitor government activity and draw attention to illegal violations of rights. Unlike the Marxist revisionists of the 1960s, Chartists claimed no political platform; they were not a political party and did not seek office. A loose collection of individual 'dissidents'—they generally rejected that name—from across the political spectrum, Charter members shared only a moral and 'antipolitical' commitment to hold the government to its legal obligations, notably the guarantee of human rights articulated in the 1975 Helsinki Accords, to which the country adhered. In the weeks following the Charter's announcement, state potentates boosted its profile by launching a scurrilous attack campaign, including a televised gala in which celebrities and cultural icons publicly declared their party loyalty and signed on to the so-called Anti-Charter. More threatening were the regular police detentions of Charter spokesmen, one of which led to Patočka's extended interrogation, collapse, and death. Despite (or perhaps because of) this onslaught, Charter 77 succeeded in drawing attention to regime abuses, and its growing prominence allowed it to persist through the remaining years of communist rule and eventually form the core, with other groups, of the Občanské Fórum (Civic Forum) that took power after the 1989 collapse of the communist regime .

The significance of phenomenology among Charter 77's founders has also been remarked, albeit recently and selectively.[2] Yet without wider appreciation of the long-standing social concerns of the Central European philosophical school, its full importance for the Chartists cannot be grasped; nor can one understand why such a putatively esoteric philosophy should have enjoyed such regard among the diverse array of writers, scholars, and religious leaders who comprised the Charter membership. For while the story of phenomenology and dissidence in 1970s Czechoslovakia centers on Jan Patočka, it does not end there. And while Václav Havel became Patočka's most renowned admirer, he did not exhaust the reception. Lesser-known Chartists also felt the influence of a philosophy whose texts some claimed to know only cursorily. That an assorted community of dissidents who were mostly nonphilosophers converged around similar phenomenological themes illustrates the school's social and cultural reach.[3]

Part of this convergence undoubtedly had to do with Patočka. His role as Charter 77's intellectual and moral "binding agent" is widely attested.[4] Havel, of course, cited him liberally and praised his formative influence. "I don't know what the Charter would have become," he told Karel Hvížďala in the 1980s, "had Patočka not illuminated its beginnings with the clarity of his great personality."[5] The two manifestoes that Patočka released in January and March 1977 gave intellectual clout to the movement's antipolitical focus, justifying its defense of human rights and personal morality against the imperialistic claims of communist technocratic control. The Charter, he hoped, would "educate" people about free citizenship and community purpose.[6]

Eulogies for the felled Patočka echoed this collective esteem. For the Catholic philosopher Václav Benda (1946–99), whose 1978 essay "The

Parallel 'Polis'"⁶ questioned the effectiveness of the Charter's early moral strategy, Patočka was the *spiritus movens* of the original movement. His passing, combined with waning regime persecution, marked the end of an era when a single paragon could unite dissidents of myriad political stripes.⁷ The philosopher Ladislav Hejdánek (b. 1927), a postwar student of Patočka and Kozák, saw his teacher's sacrifice as emblematic of his words and convictions—"the definitive No," in Ludvík Vaculík's apt phrase.⁸ Even Patočka's rare critics recognized his imprint: the political scientist Emanuel Mandler (1932–2009) chided Patočka for depoliticizing the Charter and turning it into a moral platform for elite resistance.⁹ Likewise, Milan Šimečka (1930–90)—a Czech writer in Bratislava—worried over the elitist legacy that Havel drew from his sage.¹⁰ And the flamboyant revolutionary Petr Uhl (b. 1941) bemoaned the "ghettoization" of the movement around 'vulgarized' concepts of Patočka.¹¹ Nonetheless, while the philosopher's influence provoked occasional contention, it was uniformly acknowledged.

Part of Patočka's posthumous appeal, of course, was that his sacrifice voiced a distinct yes to a particular view of human aspiration. For his student Václav Bělohradský (b. 1944), safe in Italian exile, Patočka bequeathed to Charter 77 the epochal mission of waging a struggle against impersonal power. According to Bělohradský's 1982 *Krize eschatologie neosobnosti* (The Crisis of the Eschatology of the Impersonal), a book that influenced Havel, it was Patočka's criticism of modern technocracy and the dissident activism it inspired that brought Husserlian lifeworld analysis to full maturity as a social and political agenda. This activism, he wrote, pitted the values of subjectivity, community, and morality against the mechanization and banalization of modern life. Bělohradský's impersonal power operated along four vectors: (1) the transformation of an experiential lifeworld into a fixed world of technical and scientific precision; (2) the passage from politics as an expression of civic life to the state as a political end in itself;¹² (3) the demotion of subjective and communal experience to mere opinion and its replacement by dry legality;¹³ and (4) the shift from a view of liberty as personal space free from external intervention to one circumscribed by participation in state functions.¹⁴ Most insidious, impersonal systems of power, law, and economy maintained a halo of innocence and impartiality even as they denuded life of meaning. In the face of this desertification,

Husserl revived, Patočka radicalized, and Charter 77 enacted a European ethical and humanist tradition—now captured in the concept of rights as the defense of persons—to counteract a sere modern "political rationality based on the imperative of impersonality."[15] What is easy to forget in the post–Cold War era is that Bělohradský, along with many Czechoslovak dissidents, saw their country as the front line of a struggle that extended across the industrial world, East and West. Soviet communism showed in extremis the tendencies found in its Cold War foe as well.

But phenomenology's impregnation of Czech dissidence—and this is a crucial point—cannot simply be attributed to Patočka's intellectual and personal appeal. Decades of scholarly attention—we have seen the inroads phenomenology made in the 1930s, the prominence it regained in the 1960s—made it a respected non-Marxist philosophy that shared thematic interests with other native schools. By the 1970s, phenomenology was widely acknowledged among Czech literati, its basic ideas affirmed *in nuce* even by those who claimed no familiarity with its works. Indeed, many phenomenological preoccupations dating back to Husserl and Brentano appeared in the mimeographs and "unbooks" of Czechoslovak samizdat, sometimes with, but often without genealogical attribution—sometimes even without apparent awareness of the lineage.[16]

Husserl's crisis motif is the premier example. Updating reform Marxist attacks on Soviet bureaucratization, 1970s dissidents shared broad agreement that the totalitarian menace reflected a crisis of hubristic modern science, not simply of Eastern dictatorship—and that it posed the gravest threat to human freedom and culture. "The natural sciences," warned the Protestant Hejdánek, an early Charter spokesman, "have divided among themselves a 'world' . . . impoverished and depleted without even noticing that they were dividing only a pile of objects that had long ceased to be the universe, the unified world, reality as a whole."[17] Like Patočka, Hejdánek saw socialist autocracy as an "offspring of liberal-democratic traditions" whose human roots needed resuscitation, in part through alliance with Christianity.[18] As Václav Havel's scientist brother Ivan (b. 1938) explained, "[b]y striking out the subject, modern science also struck out the personal experience and enjoyment to be gained from cognition, and even more so any cognizance derived from personal lived experience. . . . Modern science has forgotten to breathe!"[19] Scientific omnipotence took a devastating political toll as well. The Catholic priest and Charter spokesman Václav Malý (b. 1950) decried the metastasization of "depersonalized power" with its consequent social uniformity, as did his counterpart Václav Benda, who feared a "worldwide crisis of politics" that only independent civic activism could meet.[20] "We will have to defend ourselves against the leveling process," urged the priest and theologian Josef Zvěřina (1913–90), best known for pushing Prague's cautious archbishop to adopt a pro-opposition line, the "coordination by the state of all aspects of culture [zglajchšaltování], a changing of gears by one side and not the other, manipulation, the crushing greyness of life, the stifling fog, the endless boredom, cruelty and perversity. These are the fruits of violating freedom of the spirit."[21] The worldwide domination of societies by states had to be resisted.

Among those who most vilified technocratic power were distraught socialists. For Rudolf Battěk (1924–2013), a 1960s affiliate with Patočka and Kosík of the Academy of Sciences, the modern political crisis elevated consumerism over spiritual and moral values. "To build and direct one's life exclusively in terms of consumer values leads to 'microcosmic tragedy,' to 'a loss of humanity,'" he warned. "Spiritual orientation is the only possible goal that satisfies the meaning of humanity in ways that are accessible to human beings."[22] Across the globe, technological civilization had wrought "intersocietal and inter-human devastation unknown to earlier history."[23] For Petr Uhl, both capitalism and Stalinism fostered "the reification of labour, the manipulation of those who carry out that labour and of the entire society, the political and economic expropriation of workers and the feeling of alienation."[24] If his Trotskyist call for an anti-bureaucratic revolution placed him on the dissident fringes, his joint critique of Western capitalism and Eastern 'real socialism' was hardly unusual. Not only did Charter 77 include many socialists, but even those like Patočka or Havel who lacked Party affiliation were influenced by Marxist thought in ways that reinforced their phenomenological critique of modernity.[25] In this regard if not in others, the 1960s partnership of phenomenology and Marxism continued into the dissident era.[26]

Many regime critics also found phenomenology far-sighted in its crisis remedies. For Tomáš Halík (b. 1948), a Catholic theologian who would later work with Pope John Paul II, Husserl's philosophy "led us out of the 'reason-cobweb'" by recovering lived human experience.[27] The concept of intentionality revived by Brentano and Husserl, noted Hejdánek, enabled the return to experiential wellsprings, to moral and spiritual sources.[28] Likewise, for Martin Palouš (b. 1950), Husserlian thought recovered genuine human experience:

> Phenomenology . . . attempts to reveal the structures by which in its individual acts the I relates to the world, to explain how in its consciousness the I constitutes object-meaning as a correlate of these acts . . . Only mindful elucidation of man's original relations to his own existence, only an incessant 'exercise' in transcendence, that is, in transition from self to world and world to self, establishes the possibility of human knowledge, of science in that rigorous sense that Husserl calls for.[29]

"[U]nequivocally personal," Husserl's philosophy also broached political activity in its original sense.[30] In Josef Zvěřina's view, Patočka and Heidegger offered a "therapy for hate," an antidote to the "ressentiment" bred by imprisonment in the status quo.[31]

The dissident obsession with renewal—of independent culture, of moral concern, of free communities, of human experience—was regularly cast in Patočkan terms. The writer Ivan Jirous, artistic director of the Plastic People of the Universe, urged a revival of community relations and human solidarity, a return to the meaning of things.[32] Josef Zvěřina called for a "constant *metanoia*—a transformation in outlook" that would start to "take man, culture and society seriously."[33] And the literary critic Václav Černý (1905–87), once considered an alternative to Patočka as Charter spokesman, aspired to a "movement for renewal."[34] The Charter itself, reported the historian Vilém Prečan (b. 1933) in 1977, was meant to catalyze "a new national and democratic revival" echoing the national rebirth of the Czech nineteenth century.[35] Calls for the renewal of a latent cultural tradition also meant a return to the Europe from which Czechoslovakia had been barred since 1948—and an elegy, à la Kundera, for a West that had abandoned its heritage for consumer allures. This lament, as we have seen, had deep roots in phenomenological thought.

To most dissidents, renewal also meant the rebirth of responsibility understood as a turn away from material goals and toward transcendent values, variously defined. At its most generic, this transformation might entail a renewed focus on life's purpose, broadly understood, rather than on simple quantitative measures of comfort or accomplishment.

Hejdánek, Zvěřina, Malý and others demanded new respect for "solid ethical values"—truth, justice, law—and for the sense that some things were more important than personal advantage.[36] Radim Palouš (b. 1924), an early Patočka student, elaborated this view into a new philosophy of responsibility, a science of goodness—he called it "care for the soul"—that would lead one from self-centeredness to a super-personal, transcendent orientation.[37] One must grasp "the essence of things," added the writer Eva Kantůrková (b. 1930). "Not ends, but meaning: this might stand as a slogan for our activities."[38] Though the phenomenology of Husserl, Heidegger, and Patočka went unmentioned in most of these offprints, the chorus of essences, transcendence, and responsibility—of a return to Europe's Hellenic bequest and a battle against technocratic indifference—meant that its presence hardly needed naming.

If all this was appealing to some, it was also vague. It is hardly surprising, therefore, that numerous dissidents followed a path trod by so many earlier phenomenologists: they interpreted 'higher values' as a call to religious revival. In their elevation of Christian values to a position of civic importance, dissident priests, theologians, and believers—Catholics and Protestants alike—such as Václav Malý, Josef Zvěřina, and Ladislav Hejdánek recast in devotional terms the "spiritual horizon" that Patočka, Husserl, and Heidegger had rendered philosophically.[39] Indeed, some dissidents credited Patočka with enabling a Christian revival. According to Tomáš Halík, the deceased philosopher had led a return to divine and even Christian thought.[40] Václav Benda, inspired by the new Polish pope as well as Patočka, saw the need for a theology of faith to sustain his alternative polis.[41] A group of Czech pastors concurred:. In a statement welcoming Charter 77 as a new civic initiative, they praised the philosopher's idea "that above the conscience of individuals and above the world of politics, there exists a supreme moral and spiritual authority. We understand this in the light of Jesus Christ's witness before the representatives of political power . . . and we accept the supremacy of truth over ourselves."[42] As Eva Kantůrková remarked, if Charter 77 took its philosophy from Patočka, "it derive[d] its ethics from Christianity."[43]

And what of politics? What has been said so far qualifies the dissident appropriation of phenomenology as a distinct social program calling for a reorientation of humans away from technocratic subservience and toward renewed ethical and communal exertion. But politics understood as a program of governance was absent from this vision—and deliberately so. As Patočka put it, Charter signatories aimed "to subordinate politics to justice, not vice versa."[44] The 'antipolitical' label vaunted by many East European dissidents entailed the rejection of state politics as an apparatus of control standing over and against independent human initiative. Normalized Czechoslovakia exhibited the totalitarian excesses of this domination, but it also evinced features similar to those found in the West, where party machines and state bureaucracies stood increasingly aloof from apathetic electorates. The central message of Havel and György Konrád (George Konrad), the two most famous spokesmen for antipolitics, was that the crisis of politics was global.[45]

But dissident political views did not end in pure negativity. In considering how an orientation to truth and goodness might shape the administration of society, the Chartists intimated an aloof and guiding role for an intellectual elite that harked back to Husserl's philosopher-functionaries. An ethically informed politics, they proposed, should foster social and cultural development, but not dominate it. Philosophers could steward the process of national reform, explained Radim Palouš, by stepping back from state affairs in order to comment on them.[46] Hejdánek agreed: philosophy had a duty to observe politics "from a distance" in order to see it in the light of the whole.[47] In this spirit, the Hungarian György Konrád called for an "international intellectual aristocracy" to combat the MAD (Mutual Assured Destruction) ideologies of both East and West—a striking contrast to his earlier condemnation of Soviet socialism for imposing a class of intellectuals as rulers over an exploited working class.[48] Gil Eyal has argued that dissident thinkers renounced political power for what he calls pastoral or cultural power, the privilege of guiding demoralized citizens "from afar" rather than imposing their will through policy.[49] That this attitude might be seen as disdain for the majority—"Only citizens with a weakened moral and spiritual background," wrote Ladislav Hejdánek in 1978, "only soft and corrupted citizens, only fearful men and those for whom nothing would justify their personal sacrifice and deprivation, can become willing objects and instruments of absolute power"—was a fact that Charter members demurred but could not entirely debunk.[50] Indeed, the Slovak philosopher Miroslav Kusý (b. 1931) worried that the Charter's moral emphasis restricted protest to "an exclusive community of personalities"—mostly Czech rather than Slovak, it should be noted—and failed to "inspire the public to . . . mass actions."[51] As Jiřína Šiklová put it, the invocation of truth, ethics, and personal sacrifice fortified the besieged dissident confidence, assuring Chartists of the right in a world of evil and indifference.[52] Unsurprisingly, charges of misplaced heroism dogged them into the postcommunist years.

For That Which Gives Life Meaning: Václav Havel's Antipolitical Politics

Czechoslovakia's most renowned dissident was Václav Havel (1936–2011).[53] As a writer and organizer, he helped to mobilize Czechoslovak resistance activity through both informal gatherings, in Prague and at his cottage in Hrádeček, and written essays, particularly "The Power of the Powerless," which galvanized Polish as well as native dissidence.[54] Like Patočka, the bourgeois scion never joined the Communist Party, a distinction that boosted his reputation after 1989. A celebrated playwright by the late 1970s, Havel has attracted considerable popular and scholarly attention, though many shy away from the denser philosophical passages in his work. This reticence may grow partly from Havel's own demurrals: He freely admitted that he was not a systematic philosopher, phenomenologist or otherwise.[55] But his writings nonetheless showcase prominent phenomenological themes—Husserlian, Heideggerian, Lévinasian, and Arendtian—all filtered through the ideas of his mentor Patočka. Havel himself credited Patočka's *The Natural World as a Philosophical Problem*, which he read in the 1950s, with shaping his social and political vision.[56]

The clearest evidence of a phenomenological debt appears in *Letters to Olga* (*Dopisy Olze*), the epistolary volume Havel penned between 1979 and 1983 while languishing in jail. Writing to his wife Olga under extreme constraints—one letter weekly, four pages only, no drafts allowed, no library resources, and of course heavy censorship—Havel stitched a philosophy from phenomenological and existential threads, evoking, as he put it, the school's "atmosphere" rather than "particular theses, concepts, conclusions."[57] Amid Patočkan and Heideggerian calls for openness to transcendent Being and a Lévinasian turn to the absolute other, Havel christened his own philosophical notions: the memory of Being, which recalled every human act, however small; the moral conscience turned toward an absolute and mysterious horizon; the call for a "renewal of all forms of 'interexistentiality,'" relating self to others in meaningful community.[58] "[I]t is only in the responsibility of human existence for what it has been, is, and will be," Havel told his wife, "that its identity dwells. . . . [I]f human identity is the irreplaceable locus of the 'I' in the context of the 'non-I,' then human responsibility is what determines that locus: the relationship of the former to the latter."[59] Without this relation, human beings fall into crisis, trudging mechanically through existence as mere corpora, manipulating others and manipulated by them: they become "lump[s] of mud."[60] Only an interexistential tropism, the sense of responsibility to something other than me, explains why men are good—why, he wrote in a famous illustration, we pay our tram fare even when we ride alone.[61] The conscience that urges us to do so "might be described as the experience of 'counterpoint' between the 'voice of Being' in the 'I' . . . and the 'voice of Being' in the 'non-I' (in the world). . . . It is in this counterpoint that it first seems possible . . . to hear a suggestion or an echo of the as yet unfamiliar theme from the symphony of Being."[62] The channel of this counterpoint is conscience, which the moral person, as someone who "has fallen out of Being and . . . continually reaches toward it,"[63] allows to regulate her worldly activity. Paradoxically, it was in the relation to an absolute other-cum-Being—here Havel blurred Heidegger's ontology with Lévinas's ethics—that man renewed his responsibility for his earthly fellows as well; in higher purpose man found his fellow feeling.[64] Alas, Havel feared, our age had turned from Being, replacing it with the worship of technology and material products; men were captive to their "consumer instincts," sequestered from one another, devoid of real community.[65]

There was of course little that is expressly political in Havel's prison epistles, because the censor would have disallowed it. We find clearer statements in other essays, such as 1984's "Politics and Conscience" ("Politika a svědomí"), written soon after his release. There, Havel matched the image of a conductorless streetcar with a new one of a young boy in the Bohemian countryside watching a smokestack pollute the sky. If the former highlighted man's moral potential, the latter demonstrated his destructive hubris. Whereas *Letters to Olga* shows Havel at his most Heideggerian, "Politics and Conscience," written under the influence of Bělohradský, returns to Patočka's Husserlian concern for the crisis of rationalism. The smokestack reflected disdain for man's "lived experience" of the "natural world"; it marked "an arrogant, megalomaniac, and brutal invasion by an impersonal and objective science." Modern technologies of power, such as machinelike states or totalitarian ideologies, showed "the inevitable consequences of rationalism, a grotesquely magnified image of its own deep tendencies, an extreme offshoot of its development and product of its own expansion."[66] They endangered the whole of Western civilization, not simply the unfortunate citizens of its communist fringe. To combat this tendency, men must

> reconstitut[e] the natural world as the true terrain of politics, rehabilitating the personal experience of human beings as the initial measure of things, placing morality above politics and responsibility above our desires in making human community meaningful, in returning content to human speech, in reconstituting, as the focus of all social action, the autonomous, integral, and dignified human 'I,' responsible for ourselves because we are bound to something higher, and capable of sacrificing something, in extreme cases even everything . . . for the sake of that which gives life meaning.[67]

Following Patočka's lead, Havel rejected modern governmental machinery as a cybernetic "technology of power and manipulation" and called instead for a return to the Greek ideal of politics as a way of "seeking and achieving meaningful lives," a "humanly measured care for our fellow humans." Within the community of the shaken forged at the Eastern "ramparts of dehumanized power," politics became a "practical morality." Havel dubbed it "antipolitical politics."[68]

This recognizably phenomenological formula served as backdrop to the famous greengrocer allegory in "The Power of the Powerless" (1978; "Moc bezmocných") It is tempting to prune away the philosophical thickets that ensnare Havel's *malý český člověk*—small Czech man—in this signature piece, but to do so misses the point of the essay.[69] In hanging a "Workers of the World, Unite!" banner in the window of his shop, Havel's fruiterer exemplified an existential dilemma that phenomenologists had long adumbrated. He acted thoughtlessly, in a habituated gesture of obedience whose social implications he barely noticed. But in doing so, he contributed to what Havel called "the panorama of everyday life," the ubiquitous daily scenery whose details fade away but whose implicit messages shape social bearings and facilitate political control.[70] The unconsidered meaning of his automatic act was conveyed tacitly to fellow citizens and authorities: "I conform to social expectations and I expect others to do so as well." The greengrocer was thus both a victim and a constituent of "post-totalitarian power."[71] His behavior joined in the "social auto-totality"[72] of modern society, which entangled citizens in a self-perpetuating mechanism built of consumer rewards, an exculpatory ideology, and rituals of loyalty and participation. The system functioned smoothly as long as citizens "live[d] in a lie" by accepting everyday appearances, neither shirking their assigned roles nor distinguishing themselves unduly—as long as they certified what Miroslav Kusý called the ideology of "as if" by acting 'as if' they believed the fabrications.[73] The cost was paid in personal alienation and social anomie. The greengrocer's dutiful conformity, his willing blindness, his unconcern for the reverberations of his apparently minor acts—all of these attitudes contributed to the political and moral impasse of modern societies, where persons existed to serve the system and where obedience verged on enslavement. In this regard, as Havel insisted from the outset of his classic essay, post-totalitarian countries manifested an extreme "form of the consumer and industrial society" prevalent in the West, "with all its concomitant social, intellectual, and psychological consequences."[74]

"The Power of the Powerless" exhumed the ethical and existential bases of political life—what Havel called its prepolitical soil—in order to reconstitute society on new ground. What happened, Havel asked, if the greengrocer awoke one day and decided to do what he believed was right and honest? The blank space in his window where the banner had once hung would glare at passersby, the act of integrity a silent accusation revealing the falseness of the surrounding façade and the complicity of fellow citizens. Punishment would be swift: he would lose his job, his vacations would be revoked, his family denied valuable privileges. Because politics subsumed everything in Eastern Bloc countries, all individual acts were ideologically charged, either reinforcing or undermining the status quo. But ubiquitous politicization brought with it an ever-present threat to the system—not of violent overthrow, but of the revelation of hidden consciences. Whereas normalized Czechoslovakia demanded that citizens hide their scruples behind a façade of conformity, Havel urged them to address the world openly, to "live in truth."⁷⁵

Havel did not call for democratization along Western lines, and it is a mistake to view him as a political liberal. Despite his rejection of 1968 reformist ideals, he never disavowed socialism and at times spoke favorably of its egalitarian premises.⁷⁶ And while he espoused elections, opposition parties, and selective privatization, he did not believe these nostrums cured the ills of modern social and political alienation:

> People who live in the post-totalitarian system know only too well that the question of whether one or several political parties are in power, and how those parties define and label themselves, is of far less importance than the question of whether or not it is possible to live like a human being. To shed the burden of traditional political categories and habits and open oneself up fully to the world of human existence and then to draw political conclusions only after having analyzed it: this is not only politically more realistic but at the same time . . . politically more promising as well.⁷⁷

No single "organizational measure," including the instatement of parliamentary rule, could humanize politics by itself; rather, state and economic models had to emerge from the "moral reconstitution of society," a phrase with more concrete significance among dissident communities, concerned about the political compromises made by fellow citizens in order to secure a quiet life, than it does in today's postcommunist world.⁷⁸ Practically, this prescription meant defending persons, especially the unjustly persecuted, from state overreach and supporting initiatives that contributed to independent social, political, and spiritual life: individual creativity plus communal sentiment, Ivan Jirous's second culture plus Benda's parallel structures.⁷⁹ Havel advocated the replacement of state-corporations with economic self-management, and formal party structures with local and often ephemeral community groups committed to cooperative politics based on "solidarity and fraternity."⁸⁰ His program, then, entailed not just the vaunted defense of human rights, but a communitarian revival as well. While he explicitly likened this ideal to the dissidents' own open circle, it also echoed the romance of community found in many phenomenological texts. And if his call for a leadership based on personal authority rather than administrative capacity did not precisely equate to Husserl's functionary, it nonetheless privileged spiritual-cum-intellectual charisma over the grey bureaucrat of Husák's Czechoslovakia, a leaning that might be considered at once emancipatory and paternalistic.[81]

Havel emphasized the existential far more than Patočka—and certainly more than Husserl or Heidegger. And unlike them, he turned primarily toward his own concrete reality—toward practical life and present engagement.[82] Little wonder, then, that he understood the "relation to Being" as primarily a call to worldly responsibility.[83] Despite these modifications, Havel belongs in any history of East European phenomenology, for he popularized an ethical and social analysis with deep roots in phenomenological history, disseminating it to a wider contemporary audience as well as to many subsequent admirers. As Havel and his dissident colleagues demonstrate, phenomenology in communist Czechoslovakia did not remain a philosopher's philosophy, but spread within elite cultural circles in ways that had profound political effect. As the Chartist and novelist Eva Kantůrková remarked, "it is no accident that the main philosophical trend in [Charter 77] is phenomenology."[84]

9

The Radiation of Humanity: Karol Wojtyła's Phenomenological Personalism

In 1976, on the eve of his appointment to Catholicism's highest office, the Polish archbishop Karol Wojtyła (1920–2005) characterized his decades-long philosophical labor as a phenomenological enterprise.[1] This identification capped a steady reversal in his view of the school, which he had staunchly criticized twenty-five years earlier in the *Habilitationsschrift* that launched his professorial career. After dismissing Max Scheler's ethics in 1953 as an inadequate basis for Christian moral thought, Wojtyła spent the subsequent quarter-century rehabilitating it for anthropological analysis.

Wojtyła's thought owed much to the tradition of phenomenology in Poland, and his scholarship and advocacy helped to transform it from an academic subfield into a timely social philosophy that infused 1970s resistance to communist rule. During the interwar years, Polish phenomenology was chiefly the preserve of one man, Roman Ingarden, who labored obscurely in an academic culture dominated by the analytic philosophy of the Lvov-Warsaw school. Ingarden, as we have seen, played a pivotal role in the original German movement as the most dedicated foot soldier of the realist retrenchment. Taking the *Logical Investigations* as his *locus classicus*, he mounted a career-long assault on Husserl's transcendentalism, stressing the givenness of real essences over the reality-constituting mind.

He also became the primary conduit for phenomenology in his own country, a channel the aspiring Wojtyła tapped soon after the war.[2] Yet for all his criticism of the master, Ingarden remained Husserl's wayward disciple; Wojtyła, by contrast, was really Scheler's child, and through his writings late twentieth-century Polish phenomenology adopted an anthropological cast that was distinct from Charter 77's preoccupation with Husserlian crisis.

Wojtyła became, of course, the prominent and controversial Pope John Paul II, a freedom fighter to some, but a conservative stalwart to others. It is not my intention here to enter, except in a very limited fashion, the substantial debates regarding the impact of his papacy. My analysis focuses instead on his pre-papal career and then briefly on his engagement with Eastern Europe during his first decade in the Vatican. In this context, he appears as an influential and even radical agent in undermining East Europe's communist autocracies and defending personal freedom. By emphasizing this role, I do not mean to deny the conservatism of some of his engagements in other regions of the globe, such as his suppression of Latin American Liberation Theology, his unwavering stance against contraception, or his refusal to consider the ordainment of women. A reformer of Church tradition in some ways, Wojtyła stood as a bastion of orthodoxy in others. While I limit my focus to his transformative impact on the Soviet Bloc, the reader who is aware of his more conservative policies may find some of their filiations in the writings discussed here.

Between God and Nature: Polish Phenomenology under Ingarden

As in Czechoslovakia, phenomenology gained appeal in Poland partly because it resonated with other native philosophies. The country's dominant analytic school, founded by Kazimierz Twardowski (1866–1938), an early scion of Franz Brentano, took the descriptive psychologist's thought toward logical empiricism and formal ontology. Twardowski, the so-called father of Polish philosophy, earns regular citation in phenomenological history for distinguishing the content, or mental image, of a conscious act from its object, or external referent, a move that clarified one of the core ambiguities of Brentanian doctrine.[3] The analysis led his student Ingarden to dub Twardowski's "the first consistently constructed theory of objects manifesting a certain theoretical unity since the times of scholasticism and of the 'ontology' of Christian Wolff."[4] Other adherents of Twardowski's school also took explicit interest in phenomenology: Kazimierz Ajdukiewicz attended Husserl's seminars during a prewar study year in Göttingen; and both Jan Łukasiewicz and Władysław Tatarkiewicz published early briefs on Husserl's thought.[5] These remained, however, minor feints in the march of a school whose analytic focus dominated twentieth-century non-Marxist philosophy in Poland.[6]

Neo-Thomism also flourished in interwar Poland, its Catholic circles fertilized by contact with French thinkers such as Jacques Maritain and Étienne Gilson. The Odrodzenie (Renaissance or Renewal) group, which included Wojtyła's Lublin colleague Stefan Swieżawski and the future Polish primate Stefan Wyszyński, became a particular conduit for French neo-Scholasticism.[7] So too did Wojtyła's future employer, the Catholic University of Lublin (KUL), founded in 1918 as the new country's third tertiary institution. As we have noted, Catholicism had particular appeal for phenomenologists after Scheler's example, and several of them, notably Edith Stein, tried to blend phenomenology with Thomism. This disposition eased its passage into Poland.

Nonetheless, compared to analytic philosophy and neo-Thomism, phenomenology had few interwar adherents and little clout.[8] If it shared with Twardowski a common Brentanian genealogy, Husserl's school followed a different trajectory, as suggested by his remark in *Ideas* that the Polish master's distinction between mental content and objects remained "phenomenologically obscure."[9] The same can be said of Thomism, with which interwar phenomenology shared a penchant for objective values and personalist convictions. In both cases the seeds of possible alliance went largely uncultivated before Wojtyła.

Postwar Stalinism, of course, devastated Polish faculties, with non-Marxist professors subject to intimidation, dismissal, and public reproof.[10] Ingarden was ousted from Jagiellonian University in 1949 on charges of "idealism," an accusation with particular sting for the longtime critic of Husserlian idealism. Perhaps the most shocking attack came from the philosopher Tadeusz Kroński (1907–58), whose evolution from impassioned young philosopher to obedient Stalinist the poet Czesław Miłosz recounted in the wistful final chapters of his autobiography.[11] "Tiger"—the nickname by which Kroński was widely known—is remembered today chiefly as a Hegel scholar, but in his youth he was drawn to phenomenology and wrote a review of Jan Patočka's first book in which he affirmed the phenomenological recovery of the natural (or naïve) world (*świat naiwny*) as an assertion of human freedom against the tyranny of objectivist forces. Scientific theories offered valuable hypotheses, but they become dangerous when they stood in for reality itself, when man came to think of his world as simply "a ball and a cloud of dust," rather than the ever-changing backdrop of his life. "It is harmful when a human being defines himself as a part of nature, governed by absolute laws, and when he doubts his freedom. The naïve world demands its own laws."[12] Although he acknowledged this effort to defend the human world, a frustrated and sometimes sardonic Kroński warned that Patočka fell short because he reduced its existence solely to the prior dimension of time. The real world itself remained elusive.

This concern about phenomenology's shortcomings, expressed philosophically in 1939, turned ideological a decade later, when Kroński joined the ranks of Poland's Stalinists. In a broadside against Ingarden that appeared in *Myśl filozoficzna*, the Party's philosophical mouthpiece, Kroński accused the Polish philosopher's mentor Husserl of moving from objective to subjective idealism, not, as his Polish disciple would have it, from realism to idealism. It followed that in defending the objective against the subjective, the 'secessionist' Ingarden was wholly an idealist ("*en plein idéalisme*").[13] Phenomenology, Kroński charged, could only reveal intentional phenomena, not actual reality; it therefore served as an intellectual weapon in the "war against materialism" and the proletariat. "The absurd and painful record of phenomenological paralysis of the will and intellect, bequeathed by Husserl," he vociferated, "even led one of his disciples to announce in an article before the war—the phenomenological description of the 'phenomenon' of 'being forced by Hitler's regime to leave his homeland.'"[14] Ultimately, the Husserlian tradition helped to "weaken German society morally, to disarm it at a time when it needed to go on the attack" against a "bourgeois dictatorship" launching an "imperial war." As if on cue, Max Scheler's 1915 warmongering enters Kroński's review to cinch the assassination: "'To arms and to victory!'" cheered the Teutonic Scheler in a panegyric from *Der deutsche Krieg* that for Kroński encapsulated phenomenology's latent intent.[15] Thus, Ingarden's *Controversy over the Existence of the World* (*Spór o istnienie Świata*), although a "poorly conceived and badly edited" book, was the least of phenomenology's sins. A political naïf, the hapless Ingarden had no sense of the wider implications of his school. Despite his claim to defend reality against its Husserlian dissolution, the *Controversy* was a thoroughly "idealistic book . . . [and] a glaring example of the sterility, degeneracy and bankruptcy of contemporary bourgeois philosophy."[16] Kroński's credentials helped the accusation to stick.[17]

The death of the hardline Bolesław Bierut in 1956 and the ensuing political relaxation did not bring an immediate rebirth of phenomenological fortunes. Given the long-running prominence of the Lvov-Warsaw school and the stature of second-generation affiliates such as Władysław Tatarkiewicz, Kazimierz Ajdukiewicz, Tadeusz Kotarbiński, and Tadeusz Czeżowski, it is not surprising that the first post-Stalinist philosophical renewal cultivated primarily analytic roots. Nevertheless, Ingarden's influence grew after his 1957 reinstatement, when he found himself in a vibrant circle of Cracow philosophers, including Wojtyła, who were increasingly taken with the axiological and anthropological dividends of phenomenology.[18]

It was in this context that Ingarden delivered a highly regarded ethics seminar in 1961 that marked his turn to anthropology.[19] Its themes were later distilled into two small volumes: the Polish *Książeczka o człowieku* (*Little Book on Man*) and the German *Über die Verantwortung* (*On Responsibility*).[20] Man, wrote Ingarden, had both a natural and a human essence, but his distinctiveness lay in the "incessant effort" to develop the latter by cultivating ethical value and cultural meaning.[21] Unique among creatures, he established "an entirely new reality" suited to the creative, ethical, and spiritual qualities of his makeup, attaining "his genuine stature" only because

> he creates a reality which manifests or embodies in itself the values of goodness, beauty, truth and law; because in his life . . . he remains in the service of realizing values within the reality he has created; only then does he attain to the mission that tells of his humanity: he becomes a man who mediates between what is merely 'nature' and what he can divine only crudely, as if in a reflection, through the values he has disclosed and embodied.[22]

He became, in short, an "acting person" with a unified personality, oriented toward the bright world of values, trying to infuse man's world with light.[23] Ethical responsibility, in turn, was a fundamental element of man's nature whose anthropological preconditions needed unveiling. Ingarden identified three premises—ontic foundations, he called them—that were necessary to account for the fact of responsibility: the existence of rank-ordered positive and negative values; a world structured as a multiplicity of linked systems that could be causally influenced; and the self-identical person who could transcend her own experiences and shape reality through action—all postulates rooted in the phenomenological realism of Ingarden's interwar cohort.[24]

Uncoincidentally, Ingarden's analysis echoed Wojtyła's contemporaneous masterwork, imprecisely translated as *The Acting Person* (1969; *Osoba i czyn*).[25] Once a reader on Wojtyła's *Habilitationsschrift*, Ingarden now participated in the archbishop's Thursday night gatherings throughout the decade and presented some of his evolving ideas there.[26] By the 1960s, Wojtyła, the head of this circle, was cultivating his own distinct but affiliated phenomenological genealogy that turned squarely to anthropological and theological priorities. Largely gone was Ingarden's preoccupation with defending realist ontology and exploring aesthetic objects. Wojtyła's 1969 volume, discussed below, drew considerable attention to the merger of Thomist and phenomenological personalism and to Scheler's brand of philosophical anthropology.[27] Unwittingly, it also pointed toward future political trends: Solidarity, we should recall, was a Wojtyłian concept with Catholic and phenomenological roots *before* it became a trade union name; its papal invocation facilitated the translation of an obscure technical term with a long history into a mobilizing slogan with worldwide appeal.[28]

Karol Wojtyła's Existential Personalism

Wojtyła might have remained a marginal philosopher had he not been called to St. Peter's chair. As it is, he is surely the most renowned figure in this study. Before his anointment on 16 October 1978, Wojtyła served as both Cracow's archbishop and a professor at the Catholic University of

Lublin, nearly three hundred kilometers from his archdiocese. Yet within the vast literature on this storied pontiff, only a handful of books examines the philosophy that informed his papal message.[29] Wojtyła's "existential personalism," as it has been dubbed, had many sources, though it bore little resemblance to the homonymous French philosophy.[30] Most obviously, Sartrean existentialism condemned man to godless solitude, emblematizing the modern crisis that Catholic philosophers decried. Echoing Scheler, Wojtyła confronted his *horror vacui* by arguing that atheism misconstrued metaphysical reality and human experience, both of which demonstrated a plenitudinous spiritual world. And to the Sartrean aphorism that "existence precedes essence," Wojtyła countered with the Latin *operari sequitur esse*—action follows being. Humans were *in essence* beings of ethical action and higher truth, not creatures who acted in a derelict, meaningless void.

Personalism, of course, received its most prominent articulation when Pope Pius XI made it an alternative to 1930s left and right totalitarianism.[31] For his personalism, Wojtyła drew more heavily on Gallic sources: Jacques Maritain and Étienne Gilson, who interpreted essence *as* existence rather than a separate form or substance and measured goodness in degrees of being. God's virtue, in this rendition, was synonymous with the plenum of being, and worldly creatures enjoyed merit insofar as they participated in its fullness. Thomism, in effect, ordained the goodness of existence.[32] Furthermore, Maritain's "integral humanism" celebrated religious experience as part of the personalist whole.[33] Rocco Buttiglione speculates that Wojtyła may have learned of these doctrines during a 1947 summer visit to France.[34] He certainly encountered them in his doctoral years at the Pontifical University of St. Thomas Aquinas (known as the Angelicum) in Rome, where Maritain served as French ambassador to the Vatican at the time of Wojtyła's matriculation. And as we have already noted, French neo-Thomism enjoyed a substantial following in Poland, where Wojtyła's mentor and colleague Stefan Swieżawski was one of its spokesmen.

But Wojtyła's biography reveals still other sources for his personalism, phenomenology chief among them. The young philosopher devoted years to the study and translation of Scheler's writing, and his views on it divide rather neatly in the mid-1960s. He spent much of the preceding decade discounting phenomenology as unsuitable for Christian ethics. The verdict was not wholly censorious: In itself, Wojtyła's selection of Scheler for extended scrutiny reflected a noteworthy openness to modern philosophical trends. It is nonetheless true that the early Wojtyła, as we will see below, emphasized Scheler's shortcomings and used them to illustrate the wider inability of contemporary philosophy to escape consciousness and grasp objective reality.

The experience of Vatican II, however, marked a watershed for the philosopher-priest, who strongly espoused the Council's call for greater lay involvement in Church affairs and greater Church attention to contemporary experience. Perhaps unsurprisingly, he also learned to appreciate some of the insights of *nouvelle théologie*, a controversial francophone movement that used historical scholarship to criticize the accretions of recent Church tradition. Indeed, Wojtyła started to dose his own language with an academic and political vocabulary that spoke to modern dilemmas. He sought to advance Church teaching by adapting the Catholic *philosophia perennis* to the needs of a traumatized modernity—restoring faith in an age of secularism, reinvigorating a humanity wracked by doubt and conflict. Implicit in this renewal was the "creative continuation," or updating, of the Catholic Magisterium in light of contemporary philosophy.[35] Wojtyła captured this goal in a favorite adage of Leo XIII, the pope who inaugurated the modern Church: "vetera novis augere"—promote the old through the new.[36]

In the post-Conciliar years, Wojtyła sought to elucidate the human experience that girded what he saw as Vatican II's main message. In a striking case of philosophical reappraisal, the prelate enlisted Schelerian insights he had once dismissed in order to cast human action as an orientation to truth and morality; he then joined a phenomenological anthropology with a Church metaphysics of real human substance and absolute norms. In other words, the post-Vatican Wojtyła affirmed phenomenology as a valuable, even necessary complement to Scholastic teachings, a startling shift for a man who had once disputed its credentials and a move that revealed earnest doubts about the ability of Church Thomism to address modern needs.[37] The Angelic Doctor, Wojtyła came to believe, presupposed subjective experience without developing the tools to explore it. Phenomenology, by contrast, offered a philosophical instrumentarium that could detail the riches of consciousness, enabling thinkers to "visualize" or "reveal" (*unaocznienie*) human action from the inside. It even provided a method for describing the experience of revelation, though it could not—this much remained from his earlier critique—serve as a complete religious philosophy for it lacked an adequate metaphysics and ontology.[38] What phenomenology could demonstrate—and here Wojtyła altered his 1950s position—was the anthropological orientation to truth, ethics, and spirituality. Rather than imprisoning men in consciousness, as the young Father Wojtyła had believed, phenomenological analysis led men back toward eternal truths in a more personal and meaningful way than the mere recitation of doctrine; it disclosed the lived encounter with grace that Scholastics understood but could not detail. Phenomenology and Thomism, in other words, were complementary.

To appreciate this rapprochement, it is important to trace the course of Wojtyła's thought and the diverse vocabularies it employed. His lifelong philosophical and pastoral interest centered on the lived experience of faith and ethical action, a concern heightened by his experience of Poland's traumatic midcentury. To remain relevant in a crisis-ridden age when religions competed for loyalty with secular and materialist ideologies, the Church had to address the specific needs of modern men by grounding its doctrine in a rigorous engagement with contemporary life. Consequently, Wojtyła's writing employed vernaculars designed to reach multiple audiences: the religious language of Scripture; a latinate Scholasticism; a phenomenological idiom of consciousness and experience; and a political phraseology of community, justice, and rights. These intertwined scripts served not only the purpose of ethical and anthropological elucidation but also as outreach to a diverse laity navigating the modern maelstrom.

The Failure of Phenomenological Ethics

Ordained in 1946, Wojtyła began his restorative philosophical quest in Rome under the unlikely tutelage of the Dominican and arch-Scholastic Reginald Garrigou-Lagrange, his dissertation supervisor and the scourge of Catholic modernists. A neo-Thomist in the Leonine (from Pope Leo XIII) tradition, Garrigou-Lagrange attacked what he saw as the postwar revival of modernism in *nouvelle théologie*.[39] Wojtyła imbibed a deep respect for official doctrine from this stalwart of the faith, but his dissertation, on the safely conservative topic of Counter-Reformation mysticism, already revealed unorthodox leanings: his focus on the "subjective" experience of St. John of the Cross—a figure, we recall, who also attracted Edith Stein—earned a skeptical note from his mentor.[40]

Upon returning to Poland, Wojtyła embarked on a second doctorate in philosophy. It is not certain how he arrived at the topic of Max Scheler's phenomenology, but the choice reflected a noteworthy liberality: one need only recall that the Church, with Garrigou-Lagrange in the conservative vanguard, had recently renewed its attacks on theological modernism. Buttiglione cites Ingarden as the "decisive factor" behind Wojtyła's choice, whereas George Hunston Williams credits the theologian Ignacy Różycki for drawing attention to Scheler's influence on interwar Catholic thought.[41] Wojtyła himself recalled that the Dominican Jacek Woroniecki (1878–1949), an early rector and ethical philosopher at the Catholic University of Lublin, displayed interest in Scheler's axiology.[42] Regardless, a concern for Christian ethics and Catholic mysticism would have undoubtedly exposed Wojtyła to Edith Stein (whom he later canonized) if not to Scheler himself.[43] Simply put, for a young theologian and ethical philosopher in Cracow, an engagement with Schelerian thought was in many ways preordained.

Wojtyła's *Habilitationsschrift*, completed in 1953 and published in 1959, acknowledged the value of phenomenology as a tool for investigating human experience from the inside. In contrast to other modern philosophies, Scheler's school, Wojtyła opined, combined a richness of analysis with an openness to intuition, including the religious; it was the best instrument offered by modern thought for plumbing human depths.[44] Phenomenology also shared with Church doctrine a common root, through Brentano, in the Scholastic tradition.[45] And it could hardly have hurt that numerous phenomenologists had become staunch Catholics.

Despite these concessions, however, the young Wojtyła evaluated Scheler's ethics quite harshly. Not only did it provide no basis for a *Christian* ethics; it offered no basis for a functioning ethics at all. At best, the German philosopher laid out an insightful psychology of value that never escaped the cage of modern consciousness, despite its promise to reconnect experience with objective good in a post-Kantian age. This deficiency stemmed from both basic phenomenological postulates and Scheler's idiosyncratic employment of them.

Wojtyła's analysis began from premises intrinsic to his faith and reinforced by doctoral study: the truth of the Christian ideal and of Church metaphysics. The Gospels and the Catholic Magisterium offered benchmarks for evaluating the sufficiency of modern thought, and Wojtyła broached Scheler's phenomenology through scriptural comparison. But he also assessed it according to the demands of ethical practice. On both counts, it fell short, its primary flaw an orientation away from absolute truth in favor of intentional consciousness. Here, Wojtyła pinpointed an ambiguity that had troubled phenomenology from the start. Did intentionality truly escape the Kantian mental barrier and connect with external reality, as its proponents contended? For Wojtyła the answer was no. Instead, the fixation on intentionality trapped Scheler and company in value *experiences* that could not cross over to genuine goods or practical actions. As a result, phenomenological ethics remained a theoretical construct, not an applicable program.[46] Rich and analytic as it was, phenomenology ultimately remained confined to the mind; and the concept of intentionality, Wojtyła remarked in a swipe at the Brentano, was but a "timid reference" to the dynamic Aristotelian and Scholastic structure of act and potency (*actus et potentia*).[47]

To this general phenomenological limitation, Scheler added a flaw of his own: emotionalism.[48] Wojtyła agreed that feelings were crucial elements of human moral experience, too often ignored by rationalist philosophers. And he sympathized with the project of an emotional axiology as opposed to crude utilitarianism or the mealy sentiment of Scottish moral philosophy. But he accused Scheler of pushing a good insight too far: his emotional reductivism narrowed ethical encounters to feeling alone. Lacking any rational entailment, Schelerian values could not be defined or classified. As a result, it was nearly impossible to speak of moral truth in a meaningful way, and one was simply left with firm conviction as a guide to ethical judgment. As Wojtyła put it, "phenomenology . . . allow[ed] us to speak only of a hierarchy of values [subjectively experienced] and not of a hierarchy of [objective] goods."[49]

Additionally, emotionalism had severe consequences for the understanding of human agency. By reducing ethical experience to affective receptivity, Scheler denied persons moral efficacy, the ability to affect and improve the surrounding world. He tied values "so radically and so exclusively to the emotional sphere in the person's life, and he divided this sphere so fundamentally from the will's power of causality that the person cannot be their causal origin."[50] Without the power of assertion, persons could gain no traction in the world; they lost all dynamism, turning into acquiescent emotional receptors with a passive catalogue of experiences.[51] Clearly, an emotive-experiential ethics did not compass the human breadth witnessed in life or acknowledged by Thomism. Nor could it comprehend moral action once love and feeling were severed from willpower.[52] Action, in other words, fell outside Scheler's ethical ken, and his moral homunculus could not realize practical goals or willed values.[53] Wojtyła privileged instead an ethical agency incorporating will and reason as well as emotion.

Furthermore, without access to a "permanent, 'finished' world of objective goods," Scheler succumbed to ethical perspectivalism, reducing ethics to mundane cultural 'ethos,' a term that Wojtyła saw as a *mot clé* of his thought.[54] The phenomenological ethicist was left with no way to judge apparent goodness except by comparing it to the various worldly value orders, the various ethoi culturally but not rationally affirmed as the courts of highest appeal.[55] This conviction, he feared, reduced morality to moral experience, inviting subjectivism, relativism, and passivity. A moral relativist *malgré lui*, Scheler even insisted that good and bad—the most basic value categories—came only "on the backs" of activities directed at other (material) values, rather than standing as goals in their own right.[56] There was, then, no such thing as genuine moral striving, for seeking goodness directly, rather than becoming good in the achievement of other values, was for Scheler a brand of pharisaism.[57] His good, defined only as movement from lower to higher values, not as the relation to an absolute, was solely a relative phenomenon.[58] Wojtyła's critique, of course, struck at the core of phenomenology's mantra of truth-as-evidence: that moral truths could be revealed but not logically proven. In Christian ethics, by contrast, "the good is a specific personal, objective value," one that required metaphysical justification, not simply emotive or intuitive vindication.[59]

Perhaps Wojtyła's gravest reservation about Scheler's "hypertrophy of the ethos" concerned its religious implications.[60] By reducing moral truth to experience, phenomenology treated the Gospel as simply the ethos of Christ, and Jesus became solely a moral exemplar, not a teacher of truth. Furthermore, in the effort to distance his ethics of "pure ethos" from Kantian deontology, Scheler rejected all types of moral command and discarded "every form of *normative ought*."[61] This prohibition on "negativity," however, eroded even the biblical commandment to love and the promise of reward or punishment.[62] While Wojtyła agreed that ethics should express freedom rather than obedience, liberty presupposed a relationship to truth and to God that was experienced as an inner command. "In an ethics without an ought," he warned, "there can be no talk of the realization of values" or of man's moral power. Only a fathomless redemption could renew or purify humanity.[63] In the end, therefore, Scheler's phenomenology failed to establish a relationship with God despite its Catholic allegiances. It granted access only to the idea of God, the "god-like" in man, not to God himself; Scheler's Augustinian talk of participation in divinity betokened a mere phantom.[64] And because perfection was only intentional, rooted in felt values, there was no perfect model—no earthly Savior—in the system, only more or less feeble men. Contra Thomas and the Gospels, phenomenological ethics offered no prop for Christian faith, and theologians who tried to merge the two were mistaken.[65]

Phenomenology Renewed

After such an indictment, how did Wojtyła come to reconsider phenomenology? His condemnation, of course, was never complete: we have seen that he appreciated the philosophy's resources for experiential analysis even as he doubted its ability to escape the modern trap of consciousness. And he acknowledged that phenomenology had tools for apprehending willpower that Scheler had ignored.[66] The 1960 volume *Love and Responsibility* (*Miłość i odpowiedzialność*), Wojtyła's first extended treatment of interpersonal ethics, gave an early suggestion of his coming reappraisal.[67] The theme, as we have noted, had already drawn interest from the phenomenologists Dietrich von Hildebrand and Aurel Kolnai. Wojtyła's

Church Thomism was obvious in the understanding of sexuality as a natural metaphysics of act and potency, objective purpose (reproduction) and final end (a new human life). Yet it was joined in the book by a novel phenomenological stress on the experience of pleasure and the attention to otherness. Embracing Kant's maxim that one must not employ another as means to an end, Wojtyła insisted that nonexploitative sexuality required the gift of the self to a lover in order to ensure reciprocal affection, even a kind of "membership" (*przynależność*) in each other. Without this grant, intercourse degenerated into mutual masturbation; with it, sex became the basis for love and "'altero-centrism'"—the seed of community. Echoing Scheler (and the late Husserl), Wojtyłian love evinced the "law of *ekstasis*," through which a person found a fuller self in others.[68] An experiential language of self-fulfillment and loving intention, in other words, enhanced a traditionally Scholastic take on the natural purposes of the sexual act.

The pivot of Wojtyła's career was the Second Vatican Council (1962–65), called unexpectedly by the new Pope John XXIII. The little-known Polish prelate, who was elevated to archbishop partway through its proceedings, avidly endorsed the Council's pastoral mandate to prioritize Church-parishioner relations over the promulgation of dogma, and he came to believe that the central calling of the modern Church was to accommodate the lived experience of contemporary men and women. From the multivolume *Acta Synodalia*, we know quite precisely where Wojtyła intervened in Council sessions, calling on clergymen to modernize and unify Church teaching, strengthen engagement with the lay apostolate, embrace a robust religious freedom from both state and Church, and reject political interference in Church management—the latter aimed at communist meddling with the Polish See.[69] The Council's focus on pastoral concerns and the needs of the modern world—what official documents called "signs of the times" (Matt. 16:3)—galvanized Wojtyła to develop a richer understanding of contemporary experience. Indeed, his subsequent output can be read as lengthy commentary on a statement from the most characteristic Conciliar proclamation, *Gaudium et Spes* (The Pastoral Constitution on the Church in the Modern World), that "the human person deserves to be preserved, [and] human society deserves to be renewed."[70] As Wojtyła wrote a decade later: "It may be said without exaggeration that the whole work of Vatican II sprang from a particular sense of responsibility towards man and his fate in this world and the next. It is here that we must seek the basic measure of all Christian responsibility: man is, so to speak, the central value to which that responsibility is referred in every sphere."⁷¹ This message formed the core of his later philosophy.

A bit player at Vatican II, Wojtyła became one of the Council's most avid latter-day spokespersons. His pastoral commitment was most obvious in *Sources of Renewal* (1972; *U podstaw odnowy*), a *vade mecum* on Council texts written for the Cracow Synod he convened from 1971 to 1979. Its titular theme—renewal—Wojtyła defined in alternately existential, ethical, and spiritual terms as a "restoration of man's value" (*dowartościowanie człowieka*), a "redemption of the world," and an "enrichment of faith."⁷² For a cleric, of course, redemption had clear other-worldly significance, but Wojtyła intended the promotion of worldly justice as well. Earthly redemption necessarily accompanied heavenly, with the human person the cynosure of both. The book also stressed existential concerns of the Christian "lifestyle," even introducing Schelerian nomenclature by embracing the "perennial truth of human ethos."⁷³ Wojtyła's new theology was in part, therefore, a social program cast in churchly terms.

But it was in Wojtyła's most important work, *The Acting Person* (1969), written as an anthropological underpinning for Vatican II teachings, that the echoes of phenomenology sounded most clearly.⁷⁴ He presented the volume as an elucidation of Church personalism from an experiential point of view, but it was not evidently sectarian or theological; instead Wojtyła crafted a largely philosophical tract, devoid of missionary purpose, a kind of *praeambula fidei* that responded to the modern retreat from ethics, loss of philosophical unity, and erosion of respect for man.⁷⁵ As he confided to the *nouvelle théologien* Henri de Lubac, Wojtyła viewed as the foremost "evil of our times" a "degradation, indeed a pulverization, of the fundamental uniqueness of each human person," a calamity "planned at times by atheistic ideologies" to which "we must oppose, rather than sterile polemics, a kind of 'recapitulation' of the inviolable mystery of the person."⁷⁶ His book would wage this fight. Its analysis grew from the claim that action entailed both an outward movement into the world and a reflexive self-apprehension, a moment of heightened awareness available for descriptive illumination. Wojtyła viewed action as the privileged mode of human ethical being, revealing and molding a person, rendering her good or bad. The "dynamic totality of 'man-acts' [*człowiek działa*]" became his primary analytic node.⁷⁷

In this effort, Wojtyła made extensive use of phenomenological description in order to analyze consciousness and clarify worldly action, reversing his earlier opinion that the philosophy was incapable of appreciating human agency or escaping the prison of the mind. To be sure, his new phenomenology revised many of the tradition's typical categories. In particular, he rejected the assertion that all consciousness was intentional, restricting that classic trait to objectivizing cognition alone. Broader consciousness instead related to external reality through reflection (*odbicie*), mirroring (*odzwierciedlenie*) the world but not reaching toward or constituting it—a revision that reinforced Wojtyła's phenomenological realism.⁷⁸ Underneath intentional cognition, in other words, lay an experiential substrate, a person, embedded in the world, living through his engagements, reflecting reality as it was.

If intention formed such a small facet of human mental activity, how could the broader subtending consciousness become known? In the same spirit of emending phenomenological categories for a new anthropology, Wojtyła introduced a novel methodological reduction designed to 'objectivize' human conscious experience for cognitive scrutiny. Rather than the typical suspension of naïveté, Wojtyła's reduction brought to cognition what was previously only passively conscious, explained what was only vaguely pre-understood. To use Eugen Fink's distinction, Wojtyła's reduction made thematic what was previously only operational.⁷⁹ This reduction was possible because consciousness was internally reflexive (*refleksywna*) as well as externally reflective (*refleksyjna*); it could both subjectivize (*upodmiotowienie*) objective experience—bringing the external world into consciousness—and objectivize (*uprzedmiotowienie*) subjective experience—lifting simple conscious awareness into cognition for greater scrutiny. These twin operations contributed to the integration (*integracja*) of the subjective and objective person as a unified whole.⁸⁰ Ultimately, experience revealed—though only metaphysical analysis could confirm—that man was not simply a concentration of sense data as sensualists would have it, but an independent being of supreme value—a *suppositum* in Scholastic terminology.

In addition, Wojtyła highlighted the *moral* modality of human action by revising the phenomenological technique of bracketing. Whereas Husserl parenthesized naturalist assumptions in order to suspend faith in reality, Wojtyła bracketed out (*wyłączenie przed nawias*) ethics in order to *elevate* its importance in his anthropology of action, much as an overarching algebraic function stands outside the parentheses of the variables it affects.[81] Wojtyłian action took place under the sign of ethical judgment—or, as he wrote in a supplementary essay of the same year, "morality 'defines itself' through the sheer fact that it is given in experience."[82] If phenomenological analysis could not grasp essential ethical truth, it could at least recognize the anthropological penchant for morality from clues granted in experience. In this sense, Wojtyła now felt that phenomenology could provide an experiential groundwork for ethics. It was precisely in human action, he wrote,

> that moral good and evil are realized; it is here that they take on real, existential form. In actions, this moral good or evil—or, to put it differently, this moral value—becomes a reality in human beings. . . . Beyond human beings we do not find moral value anywhere. When we ask about the content of morality as given to us in experience, we are trying to objectify that which constitutes the essential structure of the moral fact.[83]

And *pace* Scheler, human experience pointed further still—to guiding ethical norms that were "more profound and fundamental" even than values. Ultimately, norms alone, with their mandates and strictures, established the distinction between good and evil: the norm of truthfulness—and not simply the intrinsic value of truth—allowed men to appraise truth-telling over lies.[84] Human beings were indeed rule-bound, and though normative reality fell beyond the domain of experience, its clues could be found, phenomenologically, therein.

Wojtyła made a further distinction between what happened to man (*się dzieje*) and his deliberate acts (*działa*). While human animation ranged from vegetative activity to conscious agency, it was the self-constituting quality of deliberate acts, rooted in free will, that made them quintessentially human and ethical.[85] The moment of "I may but I need not" (*mogę—nie muszę*) stood at the threshold of autonomy and agency, for it supposed an integral self-governance (*samo-panowanie*) that could choose to follow ethical norms—or as he put it more technically, relinquish freely the horizontal (*transcencja piozoma*) concern with worldly objects in favor of a vertical or transcendent (*transcencja pionowa*) appeal to higher verities. In this sense, truth guaranteed personal freedom by securing independence from intended things.[86] To use a later Wojtyłian preposition, transcendence placed persons *above* their self-contained acts.[87]

In fact, Wojtyłian action entailed a double transcendence: upward toward freedom in the truth and value, and outward to the world of objects and other persons—a joint spirituality and worldliness that echoed Patočka's transcendence to and from the world. In its worldly sense, action formed the basis for human agency, or efficacy (*sprawność*), the capacity to engage with and transform the circumambient world. A dynamism of will and conscious choice, human action enabled both the realization of a forward goal and a back-bending "self-determination" (*samostanowienie*).[88] Like the duality of consciousness, a willed action had both transitive (*przechodniość*) and intransitive (*nieprzechodniość*) effects; it was at once an outward performance and an inner self-fulfillment (*spełnienie*).[89] In its reflexive role, action built moral qualities back into the person, turning him into "'somebody'" who was good or bad. "Human actions perdure in men," Wojtyła explained, "thanks to their moral value, which constitutes an objective reality closely linked with the person."[90] This "autodeterminism"—the self-formative moment of willing for or against moral good—distinguished human action from animal behavior.[91]

With this analysis of human dynamism and transcendence, Wojtyła introduced a novel spiritual form of intentionality: In relation to objects of intentional cognition, he wrote, man preserved "a specific ascendancy through the truth," a "'superiority' [*wyższość*] connected with a certain distance."[92] At the same time, a moral person had to surrender—Wojtyła's term was *uzależnienie*: literally, to become addicted—to the "unconditionality" of values.[93] Ethical judgment, or conscience, transformed a value acknowledged as true into an obligatory norm that governed behavior; and ethical acts tried to render that norm in the world. Echoing arguments made sixty years earlier by the Catholic Max Scheler and the atheist Nicolai Hartmann, Wojtyła made man the gateway between absolute values and their earthly instantiation. "In each of his actions," he contended, refuting Hume's famous dictum, "the human person is eyewitness to the transition from the 'is' to the 'should'—the transition from 'X is truly good' to 'I should do X.'"[94]

Yet Wojtyła's "conscience was no lawmaker"; it simply discovered moral truths that existed outside it. And "the tension arising between the subjective order of norms and the inner freedom of the subject-person" could only be relieved by a belief in the "truthfulness of the good."[95] Here one reached the brink of what phenomenology could intuit, the border where it must cede to metaphysics. St. Paul's *rationabile obsequium* met its highest obligation, per Wojtyła, in the commandment to love.[96] Acts of conscience motivated by love allowed a person to stand "above the world" and "above society" in an intimate and humble relation to truth and goodness.[97] Phenomenology could sketch this "drama" in a particularly expressive manner, but it could not verify the unique wholeness of the spiritual person or the divine firmament of truth and love.[98] Józef Tischner, as we will see, would later elaborate this human drama of good and evil at the experiential brink.

Integrating Brentano's immediate moral judgment with Scheler's axiology of values and Kant's normative duty, Wojtyła's formula for arriving through experience at an understanding of the moral act exhibited both an appreciation for and diffidence toward the phenomenological standard. On the one hand, phenomenology offered exquisite detail regarding the subjective experience of human agency. Yet its exclusive commitment to consciousness blocked a full understanding of the reality of the human person and the transcendence to absolute truth. While neither of these conditions was devoid of experiential markers, phenomenology was not equipped to recognize their objective sources. A novel phenomenology of transcendence could broach these limit-experiences, but even a methodological expansion did not preclude the need for metaphysical analysis and religious faith. Wojtyła spoke repeatedly of an objective and a subjective dimension to action, each available to different forms of comprehension; phenomenology could address only the latter. What it disclosed through the analysis of experience was that the human person, confronted with the ascendency of truth and the puzzle of existence, was necessarily a transcendent and spiritual being. But it could not plumb the nature of this reality.

Wojtyła devoted the final chapter of his chef d'oeuvre to human intersubjectivity and sociality.[99] For a morality based on personal self-possession and transcendence, the need for—even the possibility of—community was not immediately evident. But Wojtyła insisted on its necessity, even as he argued vigorously that social norms must not violate the ethical core of personhood. To avert this threat, he adapted the Platonic-Augustinian notion of participation (*uczestnictwo*), originally coined to describe man's involvement in the divine essence, to a social framework: through participation, man "retains ... the personalistic value of his own action and at the same time shares in the realization and the results of communal acting."[100] In 1975, Wojtyła described participation as "the ability to exist and act together with others in such a way that ... we remain ourselves and actualize ourselves."[101] The participatory community involved joint individual actions directed toward a common good that not only guided social projects toward an agreed goal but served reflexively to integrate community members as "neighbors" (*bliźni*).[102] Like the lovers of *Love and Responsibility*, neighbors shared in each other's "humanness," a reciprocity built on joint engagement with truth and morality.[103] "Man's alienation from other men," Wojtyła explained, "stems from a disregard for, a neglect of, that real depth of participation which is indicated in the word *neighbor* and by the related notion of interrelation and intersubordination of men in their humanness, that most fundamental principle of any real community."[104]

To be sure, the archbishop of Cracow, who was often at loggerheads with the communist authorities, knew the danger of repression in comradely societies dedicated rhetorically to the greater human good. And he was quick to distinguish his personalist order from both the totalist and individualist systems that marred the respective Cold War foes. Whereas totalism sacrificed persons to the social whole, individualism alienated them from the communal participation needed for self-fulfillment. Both systems were "'impersonalistic'—or 'antipersonalistic.'"[105] Social participation, for Wojtyła, had both authentic and inauthentic forms: Solidarity and opposition involved full and virtuous engagement in communal life; their opposites, conformism or avoidance, exemplified withdrawal from others and disdain for fellow men.

The social dimension of Wojtyła's anthropology remained underdeveloped in *The Acting Person*, but it became the keynote of increasingly phenomenological articles written during the 1970s, while the busy archbishop was implementing Vatican II.[106] Whereas the earlier Wojtyła had emphasized the metaphysical ground of human being, the mature prelate feared a crisis of receding self-awareness, of the inability of "metaphysical subjectivity [to] manifest itself as personal subjectivity." After all, he insisted, "being a subject (a *suppositum*) and experiencing oneself as a subject occur on two entirely different dimensions."[107] In today's world, the human being itself was in question, he warned, repeating Scheler's apothegm, an existential dilemma that stood at the center of Polish ideological debates during the turbulent 1970s. The challenge was not simply to appreciate the person as "an acting subject," but to reveal him to himself—after years in which he was treated as mere matter—"as a subject experiencing its acts and inner happenings, and with them its own subjectivity."[108] The personalist philosopher became man's coach and guardian, and phenomenological anthropology was integral to the defense, for it allowed philosophers to "pause cognitively at lived experience."[109] Indeed, Wojtyła credited Scheler, his former nemesis, for leading him to "that specific experience which lies at the basis of the concept 'actus humanus.' . . . The entire exposition of mine is . . . a certain attempt at identification of this experience. Is this identification phenomenological? I believe that it is."[110] The decisions of conscience, Wojtyła now wrote, "reveal us as persons who fulfill ourselves by going beyond ourselves toward values accepted in truth and realized . . . with a deep sense of responsibility"— beings in other words, who realize themselves by reaching toward the good.[111] Moral acts were self-constitutive as well as socially efficacious, for without transcendence "I as a person, I as a personal subject, in a sense am not myself."[112] Communal life also achieved ethical values in the production of culture and the dedication to work, activities that made "the nonhuman reality outside ourselves more human." Although these domains were colonized and exploited in communist Poland, Wojtyła hoped to rescue them as essential "radiation[s] of humanity."[113]

Drawing out a distinction from earlier works, Wojtyła described community as the co-existence of people "as if from the perspective of the personal subjectivity of each," whereas society was forged through joint commitment to common values and aims.¹¹⁴ The ideal communion combined both characteristics—the communal "I-Thou" and the societal "we"—in an interpersonal harmony analogous to the *communio personarum*. The common good, while ensuring unity in transcendence, had also to preserve personal dignity, a safeguard best maintained in the interpersonal familiarity of local communities and guaranteed by state commitments to human rights and autonomy—hence Wojtyła's endorsement of political subsidiarity, the modern Catholic teaching that government offices should be decentralized and political functions exercised by the lowest competent authority.¹¹⁵ Anticipating his papal directives, Archbishop Wojtyła was already moving in the 1970s from the language of philosophical personalism and transcendence to an idiom of rights and politics.

Epilogue

John Paul II was not the first pope to link personalism with an overt political and social agenda. The anticommunist platform of his early papacy, along with his persistent critique of liberal individualism, referred back to Leo XIII's denunciation of capitalist excess and Pius XI's introduction of personalism as an antitotalitarian program. His defense of human work in the encyclical *Laborem Exercens* amplified messages from *Rerum Novarum* in the 1890s, *Quadragesimo Anno* in the 1930s, and Vatican II's *Gaudium et Spes*. And his appeals to human rights as a defense of personal dignity echoed John XXIII's famous call in *Pacem in Terris*. But John Paul II gave more consistent attention to this agenda than his predecessors, making it the cornerstone of his early papacy and tapping new philosophical traditions in the effort to update Church doctrine and practice.

In his first encyclical, the new pope issued a call, familiar to his Polish brethren, to penetrate "the depth of human consciousness" and "enter [man's] 'heart.'"¹¹⁶ Only there could the Church lead the modern redemption so desperately needed. He enlisted his own concept of solidarity as an antidote to the general "moral disorder" of the age, a goad to the development of political and economic institutions that would relieve human subjugation and a celebration of social interdependence based on joint responsibility, global equity, and neighborliness.¹¹⁷ These commitments would, he noted in the 1987 encyclical *Sollicitudo Rei Socialis*, guard against the degradation of labor by recognizing work's "dignity," a plea whose timeliness could hardly be missed in light of the worker mobilization and suppression in his homeland. The self-actualization and cultural productivity of work—aspects that came clearest "in the subjective dimension"—needed protection from both communist and capitalist exploitation—a message that his Polish confrere Józef Tischner, discussed in the next chapter, had recently articulated as well.[118] If socialism was a particularly egregious response to the modern dilemma, John Paul II affirmed after 1989, its primary error was a materialist anthropology mirrored in the capitalist West. In fact, he was quick to issue a warning made by many East European dissidents: the socialist demand for economic equity perverted what was at root a just concern for capitalist derelictions. If Western societies laudably embraced political freedom, they often supplanted the natural orientation to justice with an "unbridled affirmation of self-interest."[119] As we have seen, this fear had deep roots in twentieth-century phenomenology.

One further aspect of John Paul II's pontificate deserves mention as well, for it too reflects a widespread tendency of phenomenological social thought: The archbishop who had once stood for greater lay involvement in Church affairs became a pope who, by most accounts, tolerated little dissent. It is impossible to know how other phenomenologists might have wielded the power granted to Wojtyła, but the tradition, as we have seen, had long sought to elevate philosophers to positions of social and cultural authority. Thus, while phenomenological thinking helped to undermine the dogmatic Marxism of Cold War Poland and Czechoslovakia, it may have also have bolstered the spiritual eminence and self-certainty of the pope who dominated the twentieth century's end.

10

The Light of Values: Phenomenological Ramifications in Polish Dissidence

Pope John Paul II's return to his home country on June 2–10, 1979 marked a watershed in Poland's recent past. The preceding decade had been a turbulent one. In 1970, the new Party Secretary Edvard Gierek effectively ended countrywide labor strikes by agreeing to rescind the price hikes that had sparked them and promising greater worker involvement in future decisions. Though successful at restoring order, Gierek's strategy of negotiating with workers established a new and explosive political dynamic. The regime's tacit commitment to increase living standards in exchange for calm meant more loans and mounting debt, especially after the oil spikes of the early 1970s. And it did not always ensure popular favor: In 1975, facing pressure from Church and intelligentsia, the Party dropped clauses from a new constitution referring to its leading political role and to Soviet-Polish friendship. When in 1976 Gierek again proposed price increases, he faced violent resistance from workers and intellectuals flush with confidence in their recent ability to sway policy. Again the regime backed down. The protesters' success grew in part from the new union of intellectuals and factory workers, who had struck and acquiesced separately in 1968 and 1970, respectively, but now joined their opposition efforts. The most prominent product of this partnership was the Workers' Defense Committee (KOR), an independent organization founded in 1976 by intellectuals such as the veteran radical Jacek Kuroń to assist arrested strikers and their families. Uniquely in Eastern Europe, the Polish Church had also long provided an independent source of authority and loyalty; in the 1970s, it too grew bolder in its support for citizen activism. Wojtyła's synod, based in the cultural center of Cracow, was particularly important in this regard, though it is easy to exaggerate his 'dissidence' retrospectively.[1]

The papal homecoming, in other words, capped a decade in which social discontent and political resentment fueled a groundswell of independent civic activity aimed at curbing the power of a capricious regime. John Paul II helped to gather these initiatives around a unified vision and clear slogans. While his homilies were thin on political substance, their message was plain: Polish struggles were a priority to Western Christendom and the world supported them. Endorsements of the "human person" and the renewal of "natural social bonds" showed that Father Wojtyła had not resigned himself to the recent Vatican *Ostpolitik* that accepted Soviet authority as an international fixture.[2] Instead, this "most fantastic pilgrimage in the history of contemporary Europe" served, according to Adam Michnik, as "a lesson in dignity" for a restive population confronting a grey dictatorship.[3]

In addition to nationwide enthusiasm for his ministry of hope, John Paul II could count on the local cultural elite to appreciate some of its philosophical anchorage. By the 1960s, as we have seen, phenomenological fortunes had improved in Poland, with Roman Ingarden, reappointed at Jagiellonian University, grooming a circle of students who would expand the reach of his school. Though many of these pursued relatively nonpolitical research in logic and aesthetics, some joined Wojtyła and the later Ingarden in undertaking more socially provocative analyses of anthropology and ethics.[4] The archbishop-philosopher, a phenomenologist at Lublin's Catholic University (KUL) since 1954, extended intellectual encouragement and institutional protection to many free thinkers in Ingarden's circle. Through his efforts, as well as those of Antoni Bazyli Stępień (b. 1931), KUL became an important center for the fusion of Thomism and phenomenology from the late 1950s on. As Stanisław Judycki notes, phenomenology's commitment to classical notions of absolute truth and objective value appealed to Thomists confronting the philosophical desert of Marxist materialism and analytic formalism. Both Stępień and Wojtyła incorporated phenomenology into their respective seminars on epistemology and ethics.[5] Indeed, it was the Church—and not reform socialists as in neighboring Czechoslovakia—who ushered phenomenology back into the Polish public sphere after its moral dividends became apparent with Ingarden's 1961 ethics seminar at Jagiellonian University. Within a half decade, Wojtyła's Lublin colleague Jerzy Kalinowski (1916–2000), a lay auditor at Vatican II, identified phenomenology as one of the major modern schools of moral thought. Despite its inadequacies in his eyes—a failure to acknowledge moral law, the reduction of axiology to emotions, an underappreciation of man's need for God—"the moral philosophy of the phenomenologists is of all original contemporary moral philosophies the most developed," Kalinowski claimed, an assertion that would have been as surprising in Poland before the 1960s as it is today in the West.[6] Over the next couple decades, translations and interpretations of Husserl, Heidegger, and Scheler appeared regularly in Poland.[7]

Greater attention, of course, came with increased criticism. Kalinowski's fellow Lubliner Mieczysław Krąpiec (1921–2008), KUL's rector in the 1970s and a neo-Thomist like Swieżawski, commended Husserl for illuminating the intentional character of consciousness but complained that his philosophy did not pierce through to metaphysical reality, as its advocates seemed to suppose.[8] With this charge, Krąpiec paradoxically approached his ideological opposite, Leszek Kołakowski (1927–2009), once Poland's premier Marxist philosopher but by the 1970s an exiled skeptic of the communist project. Kołakowski confronted Husserl's school on several occasions. While he credited phenomenology with demolishing several epistemological fancies, he chided it for erecting others—in particular, the myth of the transcendental consciousness as a realm of pure objects and values.[9] In the end, Kołakowski told a Yale audience in 1975, the phenomenological project showed the inevitable frustration of any quest for certitude and all attempts at overcoming moral conflict, "the logical hopelessness of all philosophical endeavors which start from subjectivity and try to restore the path toward the common world."[10] Other Marxists were more favorable, notably Ingarden's student Jan Szewczyk (1930–75), a Communist Party member and author of a volume interpreting phenomenology through Marxist categories.[11] For both Thomist and Marxist thinkers, then, phenomenology offered analyses of consciousness that could augment, though not supplant, their own philosophical commitments.

By the 1970s, phenomenology had also penetrated Polish sociological circles, notably in Warsaw, where particular note should be made of the philosopher Krzysztof Michalski (1948–2013), whose Husserl seminars drew prominent foreign speakers and who assisted in founding the influential Institute for the Human Sciences (IWM) in Vienna.[12] While writing a dissertation on Heidegger, the Catholic Michalski was introduced to Jan Patočka by Tadeusz Kroński's widow, the philosopher Irena Krońska, and he later managed to print one of the Czech philosopher's *Heretical Essays*—unpublished in Czechoslovakia—in the journal *Znak*.[13] Later, as director of the IWM, Michalski was instrumental in promoting Patočka's work and in organizing talks by leading intellectuals at John Paul II's summer residence of Castel Gandolfo. He became thereby a crucial conduit for communication between Eastern and Western European phenomenology.

Dissident leaders too evoked phenomenological themes. Marci Shore has shown the drift among Warsaw literati, inspired by Kołakowski, from a 1950s Marxist commitment to people and systems to a 1970s defense of persons and subjectivity.[14] The ethical protection of human initiative, the renewal of communal solidarity—these phenomenological-cum-Catholic premises became mandatory touchstones for opposition organizers, though not every invocation should be traced to philosophical sources.[15] Whereas Charter 77 was a bona fide community of intellectuals, Solidarity and its predecessors, such as KOR and the Movement for the Defense of Human and Civic Rights (ROPCiO), forged alliances among workers, peasants, thinkers, and priests, for many of whom philosophical musing had limited interest.[16] The intellectual's role in these coalitions, Adam Michnik acknowledged in 1976, was not theoretical but strategic: "to formulate alternative programs and defend the basic principles." As a result, Polish resistance leaders did not expatiate on modern crisis like their Czechoslovak counterparts.[17] Dissident organizers such as Michnik and Kuroń embedded statements of collective aspiration in more tactical accounts of the ways to unify historically segregated social groups and apply pressure to a reeling regime. In this sense, Solidarity fulfilled Vaclav Benda's dream of an active parallel polis better than anything in his native Czechoslovakia.

Nonetheless, dissident tracts articulated *grosso modo* many of the themes that Polish phenomenologists had pushed since the 1960s. While

Adam Michnik's determination to "live in truth"—to regain "belief in the autonomous value of truth and human solidarity"—owed more to his rapprochement with Church teachings than to a particular academic philosophy, his 1977 appeal for Church-Left solidarity embraced the phraseology of Wojtyłian personalism by acknowledging the human need for "transcendence" and "internal moral order."[18] Entranced like other Poles by the pontiff's visit, Michnik (b. 1946) clearly recognized its message as part of a burgeoning antipolitics of moral values and human rights.[19]

Michnik's phrases did not necessarily indicate familiarity with phenomenology, for Church dissemination had placed its themes in wide currency. Jacek Kuroń (1934–2004), by contrast, was explicit in his debt. In the 1960s, Kuroń burst to prominence as co-writer of an "Open Letter to Communist Party Members" advocating proletarian revolution against a technocratic and state-capitalist bureaucracy.[20] During his ensuing prison stints, he shed his incendiary Marxism and developed instead a new theory of action based upon readings that encompassed Husserl as well as many others.[21] Kuroń's prison-spun philosophy joined a dialectic of self-overcoming—perhaps a Hegelian residue of his Marxist youth—with a Catholic phenomenological aspiration to realize values and meaning against the horizon of the eternal. Human action, he maintained, both oriented experience toward ultimate ends and enabled the recognition of others.[22] It followed that the "light of values" shone only in society, for only as part of a culture and tradition, among co-citizens joined in shared endeavor, could one learn the moral norms necessary for love and cooperation.[23] Crude Marxism, alas, reduced humans to their material existence, amputating the transcendent values that Kuroń now placed at the nub of human life.[24] The transformation from radical revolutionary to spiritual humanist, reinforced through discussions with Wojtyła and Tischner, led Kuroń to appreciate the importance of religious insight.[25]

Yet Kuroń never entirely lost his youthful enthusiasm for Marx, a fact attested by a 1975 essay that tried to bridge Marxism with phenomenology. While he praised Husserl for recovering an original awareness of the encounter with being (*byt*), the erstwhile revolutionary nonetheless affirmed the more "fundamental" Marxist formula that humans engaged in the world through action—what he described, fusing the two philosophies, as "intentional acts that affect what is external"—and in turn became aware of themselves.[26] Although phenomenology valorized lived experience and the innate human relation to "external" persons, objects, and values—a stance shared by Poland's Church as well—it did not supplant the Marxist call to action as far as Kuroń was concerned.

Józef Tischner and the Ethics of Solidarity

But it was Father Józef Tischner (1931–2000), more than anyone else, who found in phenomenology the theoretical basis for Solidarity and resistance to the communist regime. Whereas John Paul II's phenomenologically informed defense of the human person provided "an expressive master frame"[27] for opposition, Tischner enlisted phenomenology directly in the struggle. After taking his vows in 1955, the young priest studied philosophy in Warsaw and Cracow, where he fell under the influence of Ingarden at the time of his pathbreaking ethics course and anthropological explorations. Under Ingarden's direction, Tischner completed a dissertation on Husserl's transcendental ego in 1963; a *Habilitationsschrift* on the phenomenology of consciousness followed a decade later. The latter in particular revealed an independent streak in its defense of Husserlian idealism against Ingarden's long-standing charges.[28] Tischner was thus steeped in phenomenology by the time he embarked on anti-regime activity in the 1970s. Based in Cracow and writing for the liberal Catholic journals *Znak* and *Tygodnik Powszechny*, he made his first foray as a public intellectual with a controversial article condemning Church Thomism.[29] There he met the like-minded Archbishop Wojtyła, who, though less skeptical than Tischner, also felt that Thomism lacked the philosophical tools to address modern needs. Their friendship shielded Tischner from Church and regime retaliation throughout the 1970s, allowing him to steer an independent philosophical course.[30] During the Solidarity years starting in 1980, Tischner attracted a substantial following with sermons in Cracow and Gdańsk, and he subsequently became a regular participant in John Paul II's annual Castel Gandolfo lecture series.[31]

In the 1970s, Tischner concentrated on working out his own distinctively spiritual and sociological phenomenology designed to confront modernity's "deep crisis of hope"—a project that drew heavily on Husserl,

Heidegger, Scheler, and Ingarden.[32] Even Husserlian transcendentalism, Tischner wrote, taught the valuable lesson that the existing world is not the only one possible—a realization needed to prompt change and renewal.[33] Tischner's philosophical labors bore fruit in two original treatises.[34] Published in the late 1990s but comprising essays written over the preceding decades, *Filozofia dramatu* (The Philosophy of Drama) and *Spór o istnienie człowieka* (The Dispute over the Existence of Man) depict human existence as a drama of men caught between a revealed good that they strive to achieve and a positive evil that tempts and menaces them. The stagecraft is not monologic: People live and work in concert, engaging and challenging each other in a Manichean moral theater. Drawing on Emmanuel Lévinas, Tischner redirected intentionality away from 'things themselves' and toward other people witnessed in face-to-face encounters that show each human being as a kind of battleground between good and evil, a revelation that Tischner dubbed "agathological," from the Greek *agathon*, or good. Accompanying the unique possibilities of every existence was a distinctive "evil which threatens it, . . . [a] suffering with which it threatens others, [and a] good it has to fight for and which it has to demand of others."[35] A person won her true value in the personal struggle with angels and demons, aspiring to hope but courting ruin in the battle to stave off iniquity. People were constituted, in other words, by their agathological force field.

For Tischner, the main nerve of philosophy was not the question of being, but the nature of man—a clear echo of Wojtyła and Scheler.[36] Like them, he affirmed absolute values set in an axiological hierarchy.[37] When a person oriented her life toward a particular value, she engaged in a process that Tischner termed "solidarization," integrating the value in a way that defined her character and allowed her to participate in the good; the process can be compared with Scheler's "functionalization," discussed earlier.[38] However, while axiological orientation was a "projecting experience"—aimed at realizing projects and values—the agathological was a "revealing experience," disclosing the face-to-face encounters missed by earlier phenomenologists.[39] Human existence, agathology showed, evolved under the threat of tragedy imposed by evil; and "thinking in values," to use Tischner's watchword and the Polish title of one of his books in the early 1980s, was an effort to avoid this tragedy through concerted orientation toward the good and toward other people.[40]

As the discussion above suggests, Tischner followed Wojtyła's practice of adapting traditional phenomenological categories to new social and ethical purposes—in particular, a novel form of intentionality. Understood as part of the axiological I—that is, the I oriented to values—the object-directed 'toward' intentionality of Husserlian consciousness became in Tischner's hands an other-directed 'for' intentionality, a being-for-someone that culminated in the agathological recognition of their unique worth.[41] Ultimately, in fact, Tischner's persons found themselves only through one another, in reciprocal concern for each other's inherent good and looming tragedy.[42] Phenomenology, he felt, was particularly suited to analyzing this existential pathos.[43] But the human drama was only partly explained by an intentionality tied to individual consciousness. For Tischner, like Wojtyła, men realized good not simply through orientation to another, but in association with them, in community. His philosophy was intrinsically dialogical, opening with the face of the other and proceeding to a theory of communality. Even the thinking subject, contra Descartes, "seeks a community with others and is certified by the community."[44] By traversing the between-space that separated men from one another, persons joined in the collective project of world-realization. Since "the common world of objects can only be perceived as common by those subjects who perceive it from the same standpoint," the struggle for joint perspective and shared identity "represents a particularly dramatic motif of interpersonal action."[45] Only through dialogue could it be achieved; dialogue, not truth, "returns us to the origin of the world hierarchy," and dialogue was governed by responsibility, not intentionality.[46] Both Husserl and Heidegger, Tischner warned, promoted "monological thinking" that led to abstract termini (the transcendental ego, *Dasein*) rather than concrete persons in communal solidarity.

Dialogical collaboration entailed both proximity and distance: the closeness of personal cooperation, the remove that preserved autonomy. In this "dance" of spaces, achieved through and with others, Tischner's freedom appeared.[47] A dramatic category, freedom "sketches the space between me and the other. It is the space of distancing oneself and coming close, the space of being beside, above, under the other."[48] Aided by others, man liberated himself for the good, oriented himself toward the world—and here Tischner employed Patočka's metaphor—as a "field of light."[49] But in dialogue, malice too arose in a reverse desolidarization as men fled from one another and shunned values, hiding from "the reach of intentional experience."[50] Without openness to transcendent good and to other persons, evil entered as a kind of phantom or apparition (*zjawa*), haunting the between-space that truth and mutual concern might have held.[51]

Evil for Tischner—and this is an important point—was essentially intra-human and dialogical, perpetrated by man against man in the senseless imposition of pain. It could also take the form of a flight from solidarity and a surrender to despair, an abdication that left the public proscenium to doomsayers.[52] Or it could take the aggressive shape of exploitation, dictatorship, murder. Only an authentic human revelation, Tischner wrote, echoing Havel and other dissidents, a turn toward others in shared dialogue, could exorcise its falsifications. Modern men faced a crisis of hope, a breakdown of community, and a loss of truth and value. In its original sense, Tischner explained, politics was "the science of projects, reasonable projects for sacrifices by human beings at this stage in history."[53] But in place of a dialogic politics of joint commitment and acceptable sacrifice, men today "danced to the false music" of totalitarianism and followed an "evil genius" into a "new hell."[54] Tischner's Solidarity-era writings urged the reestablishment of communities of joint moral endeavor, and he called on citizens to engage in open and honest discussion, to practice an original politics.[55]

Tischner differed from many dissidents in attacking not only the 'real socialism' of the Eastern Bloc, but Marxism *tout court*. According to him, Poles embraced Marxist thought primarily for its ethical proclamations, though in this they were sorely disappointed, for it simply added "new forms of exploitation" that were "'moral' in nature."[56] Tischner, in other words, saw Marxism's ultimate error as ethical: it performed "drastic surgery on human hopes," limiting them to "rule over the earth, its natural forces, and the social forces of production. . . . The ethical horizon of Marxism," he remonstrated, "is an earthbound, terraistic horizon and the hope of socialization is terraistic."[57] He reminded readers of the human despair wrought by the shared capitalist and Marxist project of domination, quipping that "[t]erraistic philosophy at a certain point becomes terroristic philosophy."[58] Materialist and scientistic, Marx reduced men to raw material, fostered the sham solidarity of collective work, and trumpeted the false ethics of political expediency. Authentic persons withdrew into hiding, while mistrust and conflict pervaded public life. Ultimately, Marxism became a "neopaganism," without sanctity or love. Only by reversing this maleficence at the individual and social level—drawing people out of their hiding places, nurturing communities of genuine concern, renewing the commitment to absolute value—could the peril be fought. That Christianity adopted such a comprehensive program made it, in Tischner's assessment, the most constant opponent of twentieth-century totalitarianism.

For Tischner as for Wojtyła, the slogans of opposition activity—solidarity, work, freedom—were experiential concepts employed as names and rallying cries. In a slender 1981 volume titled *The Spirit of Solidarity* (*Etyka solidarności*), which includes a sermon delivered at Solidarity's first national convention in October 1980, Tischner set out to elucidate their deeper phenomenological significance.[59] To the false collectivism of class warfare, he counterposed a vision of moral solidarity rooted in interpersonal concern and shared cultural identity.[60] Solidarity entailed "a closeness" with those who suffered at the hands of others, "a brotherly feeling for those who have been struck down."[61] In the context of a burgeoning trade union, it took the form of a "communion of working people who strive to free human work from the hardships and suffering caused by other human beings, that is, from hardships that are not inherent in the process of converting raw materials into a product."[62] And to express solidarity with workers demanded more than sympathy; it required one "to carry the[ir] burden."[63]

A central aim of *The Spirit of Solidarity* was to prise the category of work away from official Marxist ideology and recast it as a fundamental element of dialogic solidarity. The Catholic Church, of course, had long taken an interest in the social and anthropological significance of modern work. Ever since worldly concern for exploitation was placed on the Church itinerary by Leo XIII, Catholic officials had condemned the ills of capitalist modernity, notably infringements against the workplace and human labor. And despite a clear stance against communism in the 1920s and 1930s, worker exploitation remained at the core of the Church's message, a point sharpened by John Paul II in *Laborem exercens*—issued the same year as Tischner's brief—when he condemned both capitalist and communist abuses. In the 1970s, Poland's Primate Wyszyński had described Marxism as a "rebirth of capitalism [that made] man an appendage of the productive system and condemn[ed] him once more to slavery"—an analysis captured in the widespread characterization of Soviet-bloc communism as 'state capitalism.'[64] Catholic resistance to the Polish regime clearly should not be misread as an endorsement of Western economic modernity.

Tischner shared this native interest in *homo laborans*. At its best, he believed, work was a creative and solidaristic activity that joined men in common pursuit of valuable projects. But too often in today's world it degenerated into oppression and "moral pain."[65] "Polish work is sick," he railed, sick from fraud and exploitation that sapped the dignity of laborers.[66] Its rehabilitation required a revolution of the spirit—the non-Catholic Havel might have prescribed an "existential revolution"—that would establish a new ethical foundation in trust and dialogue.[67] The essence of work, in fact, *was* dialogue: "an interpersonal conversation" in labor and products designed to "sustain and develop human life"; it was a type of original politics, as Tischner understood it.[68] As a "service to humankind," work required people to be "in the truth"—to exhibit openness and genuineness rather than the transparent lies of erroneous statistics, glowing production reports, or the false satisfaction of quotas.[69] Authentic work expressed a moral commonality reflected in shared fruitfulness.[70] As a practical program, Tischner, like Michnik, sought dialogue among workers and intellectuals, students and Church leaders—groups that were historically separated—aimed at restoring a true appreciation of human labor and a shared understanding of interdependency. The plight of Polish labor, he hastened to add, should not be taken as an endorsement of capitalist property relations, with their inherent exploitation.[71] Reiterating Wyszyński and Wojtyła, Tischner warned that the metaphysical illusion of property infected both East and West. Private capitalism and "state capitalism" treated labor as a possession to control, not a divine gift whose fruit assured human survival.[72]

Reiterating Catholic and phenomenological priorities, Tischner reversed the Marxist order of social change. "Socialism," he explained

suggests that one should begin [creating brotherhood] by ordering the relationship of human beings to the riches of this earth, since objective reality precedes what is subjective.... Christianity proclaims that one should begin differently; one must start by putting in order the relationship of one human being to another, by introducing the harmony of love. Subjective reality comes before what is objective. Justice is a fruit of love.[73]

Human freedom, rooted in the ability to make moral choices, always operates in a world of others, in a historical community that "awakens human consciences and ... defines an ethos that fits the emerging needs. Ethos is first. Ethos acts on people so that they might speak and act according to [it]."[74] What Wojtyła disparaged in the early 1950s—the moral significance of Scheler's cultural ethos—his younger confrere redeemed two decades later. While Tischner owed much to Husserl—the mutuality of conscience and responsibility, the solidarity of mission directed at the good, the primordial sociality of ethical pursuit—we hear primarily the echoes of Scheler in his objections to the *ressentiment* of senseless work, the hope for a renewed solidarity through Christian love, the call for reorientation to absolute values, and the elevation of ethical-cum-cultural community.[75]

"[T]he world in which we live is not the kind of world that can and ought to be," Tischner rued in 1978, but man could work to improve it.[76] For this, of course, both physical labor and intellectual guidance were needed. Historically, Church leaders had guided their parishioners while maintaining a majestic distance. In late communist Poland, however, Tischner, Wojtyła, and others sought to join with those below, validating the experience of everyday Poles, urging face-to-face dialogue over dogmatic proclamation. By allying the modern clergy with laypeople and opening a conduit to everyday lived experience, the post-Conciliar Church encouraged greater ecclesiastical outreach and fellowship, including the embrace of modern schools of thought—a path taken most dramatically in Poland.[77] But if solidarity was a closeness, what became of spiritual fathers? Polish resistance was undoubtedly more broad-based and popular—and hence more inclusive—than its Czechoslovak counterpart, the charge of elitism less potent on the Vistula than on the Moldau. Nonetheless, the work of mentoring remained. A good mentor, like a good parent, instructs and encourages the apprentice, leaving her free to pursue a personal course but standing ready with advice and guidance. In the post-Vatican Church, the pope aspired primarily, in Michnik's words, to be "the greatest teacher of human values and obligations" rather than the keeper of dogma—an antipolitical avatar, not a potentate, though still someone who shepherded the flock. The modern state, Michnik felt, should take note of this stewardship; it too should remain distant from citizen's lives, guarding their safety but not managing their interactions.[78] A similar aspiration to distant mentorship and refined management also guided the intellectual leaders of Polish dissidence. It is notable that Lech Wałesa, initially inclined toward a decentralized Solidarity as a network of semi-autonomous unions, took a more centrist and executive posture in the months after he initiated direct contact with the Polish pope. Wałesa first met John Paul II in January 1981 and received his praise for Solidarity's commitment to the "moral good of society."[79] Two months later, the pontiff urged trade union leaders to rein in rank-and-file agitation for mass strikes in the northern city of Bydgoszcz. Wałesa's cancellation of the strike left many union members angry and resentful. While the decision was taken chiefly for tactical reasons related to the fear of Soviet intervention, it surely also reflected Wojtyła's urging, reinforced perhaps by a preference for elite-led reform over popular upheaval. "[T]he ethics of solidarity," as Father Tischner put it succinctly, was an "ethics of awakening—awakening to being a parent according to hope."[80]

Conclusion: Why Phenomenology Matters as a Social Philosophy

Soon after the 1989 revolutions that toppled communism, many Western commentators classified dissident movements under the familiar label of liberalism, with its emphasis on limited government, popular elections, free market economy, and rights-based individualism.[1] The year 1989, we should recall, brought Francis Fukuyama's widely discussed article "The End of History?" which crowned liberalism the winner of the twentieth-century war of ideologies. Its controversial thesis, later elaborated in a book, remained prominent in political debates throughout the next decade and helped shape Western understanding of the East European revolutions.[2] East European revolutionaries were, of course, aware of the liberal agenda, and many were sympathetic to some of its principles. And there were certainly eager liberals behind the Iron Curtain, just as there were staunch conservatives and hidebound Marxists.[3] However, the region's leading regime critics, as we have seen, generally rejected the equation of their goals with those of Western-style markets and party democracies. The tendency to see liberalism in Eastern resistance, therefore, reflected the West's own political myopia more than accurate reportage.

Instead, the tradition most germane to the views of prominent East European dissidents—the one with which they directly identified—was not Western liberalism but native Central European phenomenology. Over the course of a century, Husserl's school produced a body of social and ethical thought whose itinerary was distinct from (if influenced by) other philosophical traditions. It emphasized the rescue of a modernity whose fixation on technological advance had gradually led to moral drift, individual anomie, and bureaucratic impersonality—the reenchantment of a dry rational worldview and the renewal of concrete ethical personhood. Phenomenologists stressed the need for a double transcendence: horizontally toward fellow men and communities, and vertically toward absolute values. Indeed, it was this twin move that joined their ethical and social programs in a relatively united vision, one in which true community and authentic relations with others grew from the intersubjective commitment to a shared good. Since the time of Brentano and Husserl's best possible life reduction—and explicitly in Scheler's philosophy—the person was defined *as truly human* by her efforts to pursue moral aims in the wider world. Thus, the intellectual leaders of East European dissent did not so much transform phenomenology into a social program as draw out its steady, long-standing convictions.

In the face of modern crises, this program took the form of a defense of persons against encroachment by impersonal authority and a defense of communities against technocratic leveling—by the state above all, but also by anonymous economic dictates, scientific laws, and rationalist formulae. Rejecting both the false wholeness of totalitarianism and the isolation of modern individualism, dissidents hoped to nurture their fellow citizens in new communities of hope and purpose. Solidarity, not laissez-faire; community-oriented personalism, not self-possessed individualism—these were their mantras. And instead of the liberal privatization of personality and morality, they proposed a kind of ethical and spiritual stewardship, a distant oversight by moral and intellectual leaders who guided men toward the good and fostered worldly engagement with others. Culture not politics was their favored domain of influence, and Husserl's philosopher-functionary stood as a distinctly pedagogical herald of their work, steering societies toward the steady polestars of truth and goodness.

For some, this smacked of elitism—a self-absolution designed to exalt an ethical vanguard, flush with pretensions to moral and cultural leadership, above the banal everydayness of ordinary men. The concern is not without merit. Today, in an age that has digested postmodern teaching, the phenomenologists' strong notions of intuitive truth cannot but evoke skepticism, as well as doubt about the democratic openness of their aims. At the extreme, dissident phenomenology could encourage contempt for the opinions and experiences of average men.[4] In communist Eastern Europe, Gil Eyal and Jiřína Šiklová have argued, "dreamy idealism" transformed dissident intellectuals into self-styled crusaders against evil and indifference, masking the advantages enjoyed by cultural elites under the old regime.[5] The post-1989 legacy of former dissidents highlights still further quandaries: Does an emphasis on moral solidarity stifle the partisan debate needed for democratic life? Does it ignore the pedestrian concerns of political strategy and alignment? Tactical disinterest was surely part of phenomenology's bequest. With the partial exception of some Polish dissidents, Husserl's followers were generally more taken with transcendent principles than with daily pragmatics. Calls for the rescue of a fallen humanity were rarely followed by precise directions on how this was to be accomplished. Of necessity, the 'antipoliticians' of Charter 77 and the tacticians of Solidarity confronted the challenges of political strategy and community building more directly than their German forebears had done, but they too exhibited a preference for distant aspiration over the near world of imperfect compromise, for the pieties of hope and moral renewal over the day-to-day impurities of politics—a disdain that sparked some of the internal battles noted among Czech activists.[6] While some phenomenologists challenged this aloofness—Kolnai and Hartmann in print, Havel, Wojtyła, and Tischner through action—their worries rarely led to a concrete political agenda. Phenomenology is, of course, hardly the only social philosophy to fall short in this regard—Marx's tactical silence famously forced disciples to fill in the blanks—but the limitation nonetheless hobbled social activists working within phenomenological premises.

The charge of elitism also grows from problems associated with a perceptual ethic of truth, with the notion that one can arrive at an essential and indubitable reality by purifying experience and stripping away interpretive tradition. Despite acknowledgement that insights must be confirmed by others, the notion of intuitive verification sometimes licensed overly peremptory declarations about human nature and social interaction; at other times, the attempt to accommodate empirical variety led to truth-claims that were so general as to be nearly empty. To be sure, phenomenologists after Brentano came to believe that intuition was not exclusive, that it depended upon intersubjective awareness and communication, just as logical and discursive statements must be evaluated by others. Nonetheless, phenomenology's own immense internal variance, noted in the introduction and canvassed throughout this book, shows the difficulty of converging on shared intuitive convictions even among a community of like-minded philosophers. While phenomenology was more committed to otherness and hybridity than many critics allow, there is little doubt that the pervasive rhetoric of truth poses particular problems within the realm of social thought and does not square comfortably with the political openness endorsed by many of phenomenology's East European votaries.

Phenomenology's elitist tendencies also gave rise to a Eurocentrism that is particularly troubling in a global age. Its program for modern renewal generally called for return to an ancient European culture defined as Hellenic in origin and Christian in evolution. This focus involved two sorts of blindness: First, despite the Jewish background of many leading phenomenologists, it tended to equate Europe's heritage with classical Greece and early Christianity alone, ignoring Hebraic and Islamic influences.[7] Second, despite the early spread of phenomenology to East Asia, phenomenologists tended to posit European humanity as a model for humanity as a whole. There were some counter-examples, noted in earlier chapters: Husserl's passing interest in East Asian philosophy; Scheler's cultural functionalization; Patočka's espousal of a post-European world. With the possible exception of Scheler, however, these nods to the value of other cultures were only brief forays in oeuvres otherwise preoccupied with Europe.

To this cultural elitism can be added a religious and political conservatism. Religious experience, as we have seen, was a central focus of phenomenological investigation, and phenomenologists shared with believers a conviction in the importance of absolute values. While Husserl feared that religiosity could compromise philosophical rigor, many of his disciples endorsed Christian and especially Catholic values, insisting on the necessity of faith for human dignity and fullness. Prior to its postwar enlistment in the dissident battles against communism, phenomenology's most direct political engagement was in Catholic anti-Nazi activism, an association that lent it solid credentials in the battle against totalitarianism but also aligned it with conservative authoritarians such as Austria's Dollfuß, raising anew the specter of elite stewardship found in Husserl's philosopher-functionary and Brentano's trained psychognost.

To dismiss early phenomenological social thought as authoritarian, however, would be a mistake. Not only does it ignore the range and variety of its pronouncements—as Kolnai's condemnation of Hildebrand shows, not all phenomenologists were ready to sanction authoritarianism—but it occludes the ties that postwar democratic parties, such as Germany's Christian Democratic Union, had to the Catholic strain of phenomenology represented by Scheler and Hildebrand. For even as phenomenologists indulged tendencies toward elitism and ex cathedra pronouncement, they also consistently defended human pluralism and openness. These commitments sometimes produced tensions in their thought. For example, phenomenologists sought to preserve both the objectivity of truth and the objectivity of experience, without reducing one to the other. To treat truth as mere perception, they argued, was to relativize it improperly; yet to deny the experiential validity of a perception—even a scrambled perception—was equally problematic, for it demeaned a person by dismissing his subjective view. The subjective experience was, objectively, a real experience with its own structure and essence, a pathway to a "real reality." This dual defense, however, also set up ambiguities, for the proper balance was rarely clear. Equally challenging to reconcile was the phenomenological defense of both human persons and social communities, for a strong emphasis on the one could threaten the viability of the other. Yet these twin fidelities may also have had a moderating effect, helping to inoculate some phenomenologists against the excesses of both extreme liberal individualism and totalitarian collectivism.

The dissident progeny of early German phenomenologists, as we have seen, set themselves against both liberal and Marxist versions of modernity. To be sure, most of them considered the liberal West more open and livable than the communist East. But they also deemed the Marxist critique a just execration of capitalist wrongs. In trying to redress these failings, however, communist leaders had exacerbated the technocratic oppression that spawned crisis in the first place, turning Central Europe into an infirmary of modern political ills. Interwar phenomenologists foresaw this danger in totalitarian ideologies that suppressed creativity and neglected the spiritual bases of freedom. For them, Communism and Nazism were the outer extremes of the hubristic modern conquest of earth and man, a contemporary nihilism gone horribly wrong. It is somewhat ironic, therefore, that the postwar fate of phenomenological social theory became bound up with the Soviet ideology it abhorred—its 1960s rehabilitation championed by reform socialists seeking to humanize Eastern societies; and its post–Cold War marginalization part of the broad neglect of collectivist social theories in the king tide of the liberal era. Even the dissidents themselves, as Slavoj Žižek remarked of Havel, seemed unaware that their opposition was enabled "by the utopian dimension generated and sustained by Communist regimes."[8] After the euphoria of 1989, dissident philosophy, and the phenomenological social thought on which it was based, became a largely defunct legacy of collective aspirations jettisoned in the new-world rush to liberal aggrandizement.

The disappearance of this tradition has implications that extend beyond a proper understanding of Eastern European. Since the 1980s, our social and political vision has narrowed considerably, with a righteous liberalism the only widely available social and political discourse. East European dissidents, selectively misunderstood, have been conscripted as agents of this liberal triumph. They would have shuddered at the role. Only by neglecting their urgent warnings against Western technocracy and economism could Patočka or Wojtyła be turned into a liberal vanguard. Their social and ethical views, as this book has argued, derived from an independent tradition of phenomenological social thought, one that offered a personalist and communitarian social vision distinct from both liberalism and totalitarianism. The recovery of this tradition, with all its strengths and weaknesses, can enrich contemporary social debates that are starved for novel visions of collective purpose. The same might be said of today's ethical discourse, which increasingly privatizes morality—in either individual or religious form—to the detriment of any collective sense of identity and responsibility. In this denuded landscape, the renewal of a worldly phenomenology retrieves a valuable heritage that few know outside of Central Europe. It is high time for phenomenology to take its place among the leading social and ethical philosophies of the twentieth century.

Notes

INTRODUCTION

1. See, e.g., Robert Sokolowski, *Introduction to Phenomenology* (Cambridge: Cambridge University Press, 1999), 203–4. Marxist phenomenologists such as Enzo Paci, Trần Đức Thảo, and Maurice Merleau-Ponty, whose counterparts in Eastern Europe are discussed later in this book, are important exceptions to this rule.

2. See, e.g., Kevin Thompson and Lester Embree, eds., *Phenomenology of the Political* (Dordrecht: Kluwer, 2000); John J. Drummond and Lester Embree, eds., *Phenomenological Approaches to Moral Philosophy* (Dordrecht: Kluwer, 2002).

3. Meticulous experiential description itself consumed pages. For useful dictionaries of Husserlian thought, see John J. Drummond, *Historical Dictionary of Husserl's Philosophy* (Lanham, MD: Scarecrow Press, 2008); Dermot Moran and Joseph Cohen, *The Husserl Dictionary* (London: Continuum:, 2012).

4. Jacques Maritain, *Moral Philosophy: An Historical and Critical Survey of the Great Systems* (New York: Scribner, 1964), 261.

5. The most prominent expression of this crisis mentality was, of course, Oswald Spengler's *The Decline of the West* (1918–23; *Der Untergang des Abendlandes*). For an excellent review of interwar crisis perception, see Jerry Z. Muller, *The Other God That Failed: Hans Freyer and the Deradicalization of German Conservatism* (Princeton, NJ: Princeton University Press, 1987). For a history of the concept of crisis that includes brief mention of Husserl, see Reinhart Kosellek, "Crisis," *Journal of the History of Ideas* 76, no. 2 (April 2006): 357–400. The neglect of phenomenology is being rectified in some recent works, especially in the French context. See Samuel Moyn, *The Origins of the Other: Emmanuel Levinas between Revelation and Ethics* (Ithaca, NY: Cornell University Press, 2005), 57–87; Ethan Kleinberg, *Generation Existential: Heidegger's Philosophy in France, 1927–1961* (Ithaca, NY: Cornell University Press, 2007); Stefanos Geroulanos, *An Atheism That Is Not Humanist Emerges in French Thought* (Stanford, CA: Stanford University Press, 2010), 100–130; and Edward Baring, *The Young Derrida and French Philosophy* (Cambridge: Cambridge University Press, 2011). On

German phenomenology, see Peter Gordon, *Continental Divide: Heidegger, Cassirer, Davos* (Cambridge, MA: Harvard University Press, 2010).

6. Where available, English sources are cited in the text and notes. I also cite English titles in the text, with the original given in parentheses on first appearance. In cases where the English title distorts the original, I have indicated a more proper translation in the notes. When no English translation exists, I cite the original with an unitalicized English translation immediately following the first appearance. For Czech or Polish, I cite original sources in the notes only where there is no translation into the more widely-known languages of English, German, or French; where existing translations are problematic; or where the original wording is necessary.

7. Theodor Adorno, *Against Epistemology: A Metacritique* (Cambridge, MA: MIT Press, 1983).

8. On the Heidegger controversy, see Víctor Farías, *Heidegger and Nazism* (1987; Philadelphia: Temple University Press, 1989); Richard Wolin, *The Heidegger Controversy: A Critical Reader* (Cambridge, MA: MIT Press, 1992); and Tom Rockmore, *On Heidegger's Nazism and Philosophy* (Berkeley, CA: University of California Press, 1992). The most recent and radical attack is Emmanuel Faye, *Heidegger: The Introduction of Nazism into Philosophy in Light of the Unpublished Seminars of 1933–1935* (New Haven, CT: Yale University Press, 2009). For a stringent critique of Faye and of the prosecutorial approach to intellectual history, see Peter E. Gordon's review in *Notre Dame Philosophical Reviews* (http://ndpr.nd.edu/news/24316-heidegger-the-introduction-of-nazism-into-philosophy-in-light-of-the-unpublished-seminars-of-1933-1935/).

9. Marvin Farber, "Max Scheler," *Encyclopedia Americana, International Edition*, vol. 24 (1965), 365; V. J. McGill, "Scheler's Theory of Sympathy and Love," *Philosophy and Phenomenological Research* 2, no. 3 (March 1942): 273–76.

10. Herbert Spiegelberg, *The Phenomenological Movement: A Historical Introduction* (1960; 3rd ed., The Hague: Nijhoff, 1984); Dermot Moran, *Introduction to Phenomenology* (London: Routledge, 2000).

11. Gordon, *Continental Divide*, 3–4.

12. Ludwig Landgrebe, "The World as a Phenomenological Problem," in id., *The Phenomenology of Edmund Husserl* (Ithaca, NY: Cornell University Press, 1981), 134.

13. Karl Schuhmann, "'Phänomenologie': Eine begriffsgeschichtliche Reflexion," in id., *Selected Papers on Phenomenology* (Dordrecht: Kluwer, 2004), 1–33, surveys some of the equivocations of the term's genealogy.

14. See, e.g., Steven Crowell, "Husserlian Phenomenology," in Hubert L. Dreyfus and Mark A. Wrathall, eds., *A Companion to Phenomenology and Existentialism* (Malden, MA: Wiley Blackwell, 2006), 9–30. Emmanuel Lévinas and Maurice Merleau-Ponty similarly characterized phenomenology as an attempt to recapture meaning, both as philosophical category and modern lived experience. See Lévinas, *The Theory of Intuition in Husserl's Phenomenology* (Evanston, IL:

Northwestern University Press, 1995); Merleau-Ponty, *The Visible and the Invisible* (Evanston, IL: Northwestern University Press, 1968).

15. Max Scheler, *On the Eternal in Man* (New Brunswick, NJ: Transaction, 2010), 250–51.

16. Spiegelberg's marginalization of the phenomenological trend to conversion is not convincing. See his note in *The Phenomenological Movement: A Historical Introduction*, 2nd ed. (The Hague: Nijhoff, 1971), 1: 172–73. Husserl, it seems, did not view all forms of religiosity as equal to his chosen Protestantism. Though born Jewish, the founder, reported his student Hans Jonas, scorned Jewish piety for detracting from philosophical autonomy; he similarly disparaged Stein's Catholicism. Jonas, *Memoirs* (Waltham, MA: Brandeis University Press, 2008), 43; Husserl, *Briefe an Roman Ingarden* (The Hague: Nijhoff, 1968), 22. For a recent study of Husserl's philosophy of God, see Emmanuel Housset, *Husserl et l'idée de Dieu* (Paris: Cerf, 2010).

17. Scheler, *On the Eternal in Man*, 35.

18. Hedwig Conrad-Martius, "Meine Freundin Edith Stein," in Weltraud Herbstrich, ed., *Denken im Dialog. Zur Philosophie Edith Steins* (Tübingen: Attempto, 1991), 177.

19. Scheler's term "world-open" (*weltoffen*) was adopted by philosophical anthropologists.

20. On French atheism, see Geroulanos, *An Atheism That Is Not Humanist*.

21. John Connelly, *From Enemy to Brother: The Revolution in Catholic Teaching on the Jews, 1933–1965* (Cambridge, MA: Harvard University Press, 2012), 96.

22. For the original slogan "zu den Sachen selbst," see Husserl, *Logical Investigations*, vol. 2, trans. J. N. Findlay (New York: Routledge, 1970), 252. It was repeated by many students.

23. Helmuth Plessner, *Husserl in Göttingen* (New York: Garland, 1980), 9–10.

24. To be clear, the *noema* and *noemata* were both aspects of subjective experience. The *noema* designated the subjective act of perception, *noemata* the object as perceived by the subject.

25. For our purposes, it is also the most important cleavage. Better-known schisms—for instance, the break between Husserl and Heidegger, or between phenomenology and existentialism—fall beyond the scope of this work.

26. Jürgen Habermas, e.g., offers an extended analysis of the lifeworld in *The Theory of Communicative Action*, vol. 2: *Lifeworld and System: A Critique of Functionalist Reason* (Boston: Beacon Press, 1987).

27. For many phenomenologists, community groups stamped by a shared cultural and moral disposition, or *habitus*, could also be called collective persons.

28. Martin Kusch, *Psychologism: A Case Study in the Sociology of Philosophical Knowledge* (London: Routledge, 1995), 211–71, attributes phenomenology's Weimar German ascendency as much to Scheler as to Husserl.

29. Eva Kantůrková in H. Gordon Skilling and Paul Wilson, eds., *Civic Freedom in Central Europe: Voices from Czechoslovakia* (New York: St. Martin's Press, 1991), 79.

30. Franz Brentano, *The Origin of Our Knowledge of Right and Wrong* (London: Routledge, 1969), 35.

CHAPTER 1

1. Franz Brentano, *Psychology from an Empirical Standpoint* (London: Routledge 1973), 22.

2. Ibid., 21, 24–5.

3. Brentano, *The Foundation and Construction of Ethics* (London: Routledge, 1973), 4.

4. Ibid., 279–80.

5. In *The Phenomenological Movement: A Historical Introduction* (1960; 3rd ed., The Hague: Nijhoff, 1984), 40, Herbert Spiegelberg describes ethics as the "[o]ne area in which Brentano's ideas influenced the Phenomenological Movement without Husserl's mediation." For Brentano's condemnation of modern thought, see his *Die Vier Phasen der Philosophie und ihr augenblicklicher Stand* (1895; Leipzig: Meiner, 1926) and *Über die Zukunft der Philosophie* (1893; Leipzig: Meiner, 1929).

6. As an indication of Brentano's influence, Martin Heidegger credited him with leading him to the question of Being. See Heidegger's Preface to William J. Richardson, *Heidegger: Through Phenomenology to Thought* (The Hague: Nijhoff, 1963), xi, 631. Despite this legacy, Brentano's contributions to modern Continental thought have been underappreciated—in contrast to his acknowledged impact on Anglo-American analytic philosophy and cognitive science, where the concept of intentionality revolutionized the understanding of cognition. His ethics in particular has been widely ignored. Howard Eaton's study, *The Austrian Philosophy of Values* (Norman: University of Oklahoma Press, 1930), contains a chapter on it. Barry Smith, *Austrian Philosophy: The Legacy of Franz Brentano* (Chicago: Open Court, 1994) examines Brentano's influence on value theory in philosophy and economics, but only touches on ethics. Otherwise, it remains the subject of specialist monographs, e.g., Linda McAlister, *The Development of Franz Brentano's Ethics* (Amsterdam: Rodopi, 1982); Alfred G. Scharwath, *Tradition, Aufbau, und Fortbildung der Tugendlehre Franz Brentanos* (Meisenheim am Glan: Hain, 1967); Hans Margolius, *Die Ethik Franz Brentanos* (Leipzig: Meiner, 1929); Otto Most, *Die Ethik Franz Brentanos und ihre geschichtlichen Grundlagen* (Münster: Helios, 1931); and Roderick M. Chisholm, *Brentano and Intrinsic Value* (Cambridge: Cambridge University Press, 1986).

7. In the public disputation that accompanied his *Habilitation*, Brentano defended a set of propositions regarding philosophical inquiry, the most famous of which, "Vera philosophiae methodus nulla alia nisi scientiae naturalis est" (The true method of philosophy is none other than that of the natural sciences), leaves no doubt about his empiricist allegiances. On Brentano's empiricism, see McAlister, *The Development of Franz Brentano's Ethics*, 11–18; Theodore de Boer, *The Development of Husserl's Thought* (The Hague: Nijhoff, 1978), 212–13. For discussions of nineteenth-century empiricism and psychology, see Mitchell Ash, *Gestalt Psychology in German Culture, 1890–1967: Holism and the Quest for Objectivity* (Cambridge: Cambridge University Press, 1995); Judith Ryan, *The Vanishing Subject: Early Psychology and Literary Modernism.* (Chicago: University of Chicago Press, 1991); and David Lindenfeld, *The Transformation of Positivism: Alexius Meinong and European Thought, 1880–1920* (Berkeley: University of California Press, 1980).

8. For general studies of Brentano, see Linda McAlister, ed., *The Philosophy of Franz Brentano* (London: Duckworth, 1976); Antos Rancurello, *A Study of Franz Brentano: His Psychological Standpoint and His Significance in the History of Psychology* (New York: Academic Press, 1968); Liliana Albertazzi, Massimo Libardi, and Robert Poli, eds., *The School of Franz Brentano* (Dordrecht: Kluwer, 1996); Barry Smith, *Austrian Philosophy: The Legacy of Franz Brentano* (Chicago: Open Court, 1994); R. M. Chisholm and R. Haller, eds., *Die Philosophie Franz Brentanos* (Amsterdam: Rodopi, 1978); Alfred Kastil, *Die Philosophie Franz Brentanos: Eine Einführung in seine Lehre* (Bern: Franke, 1951); Roberto Poli, ed., *The Brentano Puzzle* (Aldershot: Ashgate, 1998); Oskar Kraus, *Franz Brentano's Stellung zur Phänomenologie und Gegenstandstheorie* (Leipzig: F. Meiner, 1924); and Robin D. Rollinger, *Husserl's Position in the School of Brentano* (Dordrecht: Kluwer, 1999).

9. Some of these ideas may be traced to Brentano's professor in Berlin, Adolf Trendelenburg, best known today for his attack on Kant's doctrine of the ideality of time and space and his public dispute with the Kantian philosopher Kuno Fischer in the late 1860s. Published sixty years before the more famous phenomenological text of the same name, Trendelenburg's *Logische Untersuchungen* anticipated Brentano in its linkage of thought and being, subject and object. "In the point of contact where the appearances are born in sense perception," he wrote, "subject and object enter into a relation" (3rd ed. [Leipzig: Hirzel, 1870], 2: 523–24). There was no pure thought, no consciousness without objects. "Only the things can decide," he insisted (ibid., 2nd ed. (Leipzig: Hirzel, 1862), 2: 492), in an apothegm worthy of comparison to the phenomenological slogan "Zu den Sachen selbst!" For accounts of Trendelenburg's influence, see Gershon George Rosenstock, *F. A. Trendelenburg: Forerunner to John Dewey* (Carbondale: Southern Illinois University Press, 1964); Klaus Sachs-Hombach,

Philosophische Psychologie im 19. Jahrhundert (Freiburg: Karl Alber, 1993), 183–93; and Klaus Köhnke, *The Rise of Neo-Kantianism: German Academic Philosophy between Idealism and Positivism* (Cambridge: Cambridge University Press, 1991), 11–35, 167–78.

10. Brentano, *Descriptive Psychology* (London: Routledge, 1995), 23. On the ancient and medieval background to Brentano's doctrine, see Richard Sorabji, "From Aristotle to Brentano: The Development of the Concept of Intentionality," in Julia Annas, ed., *Aristotle and the Later Tradition*, Oxford Studies in Ancient Philosophy, suppl. vol. (Oxford: Oxford University Press, 1991), 227–59; and Herbert Spiegelberg, "'Intention' and 'Intentionality' in the Scholastics, Brentano and Husserl," in McAlister, ed., *Philosophy of Franz Brentano*, 108–27. On the modern concept of intentionality, see J. N. Mohanty, *The Concept of Intentionality* (St. Louis: Warren H. Green, 1972).

11. Brentano, *Psychology from an Empirical Standpoint*, 88.

12. Ibid., 79–80.

13. Ibid., 88–91.

14. To support an account of inexistent objects as signs pointing to external things, much as a word refers to a thing without taking its form internally, some interpreters have used scattered hints in Brentano's corpus. "The phenomena of light, sound, heat, spatial location, and locomotion," he wrote, "are signs of something real [*Zeichen von etwas Wirklichem*], which, through its causal activity, produces presentations of them" (ibid., 19). See, e.g., Ausonio Marras, "Scholastic Roots of Brentano's Conception of Intentionality," in McAlister, ed., *The Philosophy of Franz Brentano*, 128–139. Other statements, however, suggest a view closer to Kantian noumenality, despite Brentano's general disdain for the Königsberg sage. "We have no right," he said in 1874, "to believe that the objects of so-called external perception really exist as they appear to us." Moreover, "[w]e have no experience of that which truly exists, in and of itself, and that which we do experience is not true" (*Psychology from an Empirical Standpoint*, 10, 19). Still, Brentano refused to abandon the external world completely. The "relative truth" of "physical phenomena," he maintained, assured us that something exists to cause our sensations; mental impressions serve as "signs of something real." We could assume "a world which resembles one that has three dimensional extension in space and flows in one direction in time, and which influences our sense organs." The likely correspondence of perceptual and worldly paraphernalia, he concluded, formed the basis of a natural science (ibid., 98–99). This probabilistic ontology also allowed indirect access to the mental lives of others through their language and behavior (ibid., 37–40).

15. Brentano, *Psychology from an Empirical Standpoint*, 91–92.

16. Ibid., 30.

17. Brentano's method of inner perception had the following steps: The psychognost had to experience a wealth of facts about human consciousness; notice the component parts that make up these experiences; and fix the components in memory so that they could be communicated and compared. He generalized from these components in order to discern the laws of consciousness. Brentano, *Descriptive Psychology*, 31–79.

18. Brentano, *Foundation and Construction of Ethics*, 14–15.

19. Brentano, *The True and the Evident* (London: Routledge, 1966), 24–25. The phenomenologist Roman Ingarden, discussed later, criticized Brentano's translation of individual intuition into a more general postulate of objectivity. See Ingarden, "Le concept de philosophie chez Franz Brentano," pt. 1, *Archives de Philosophie* 32 (1969): 458–75.

20. Brentano, *Foundation and Construction of Ethics*, 122. Brentano's discussion here reflected the strong influence of Aristotle's concept of intuition in *Nichomachean Ethics*, bk. 6.

21. Husserl was only the most prominent of Brentano's protégés to point out this ambiguity. See inter alia *Logical Investigations*, vol. 2, trans. J. N. Findlay (New York: Routledge, 1970), 552–60. Brentano's oft-remarked *Immanenzkrise* of 1905, after which he adopted an austere reism that ascribed intentional objectivity only to concrete things, not concepts or qualities, suggests that even he never satisfied his own meticulous definitional standards. See Roderick Chisholm, Introduction to Brentano, *Descriptive Psychology* (London: Routledge, 1995), xxii. See also *The Cambridge Companion to Brentano*, ed. Dale Jacquette (Cambridge: Cambridge University Press, 2004), especially the articles by Dale Jacquette (98–103), Joseph Margolis (131–148), and Arkadiusz Chrudzimski and Barry Smith (197–219). On Brentano's inconsistent immanentism, see Oskar Kraus's Introduction to the 1924 edition of the *Psychologie*, reprinted in the English translation, 369–408; and Smith, *Austrian Philosophy*, 35–60.

22. Brentano, *Versuch über die Erkenntnis* (Leipzig: Meiner, 1925), 80–82.

23. In his lectures on ethics, Brentano made the same distinction: an evident judgment cited either the facts of inner perception or general laws derived immediately from those facts. *Foundation*, 15.

24. Brentano quoted in Roderick Chisholm, "Brentano's Descriptive Psychology," in McAlister, ed., *Philosophy of Franz Brentano*, 97. See also Victor Velarde-Mayol, *On Brentano* (Belmont, CA: Wadsworth, 2000), 24–25.

25. Brentano, "Von der Erkenntnis des Guten und Schlechten," quoted in Scharwath, *Tradition, Aufbau, und Fortbildung*, 76–77.

26. Brentano qualified this verdict for pain that is necessary to achieve a greater good. Clearly he put no stock in phenomena such as masochism, which interested his contemporary Leopold von Sacher-Masoch.

27. Roderick Chisholm, "Brentano's Theory of Correct and Incorrect Emotion," in McAlister, ed., *Philosophy of Franz Brentano*, 162.

28. Brentano, from a letter published in *Die Abkehr von Nichtrealen*, quoted in Chisholm, *Brentano and Intrinsic Value*, 49.

29. For an overview of mental structure according to Brentano, see Smith, *Austrian Philosophy*, 45–51.

30. Brentano, "Loving and Hating," in id., *The Origin of Our Knowledge of Right and Wrong*, ed. Roderick M. Chisholm, trans. Chisholm and Elizabeth H. Schneewind (New York: Humanities Press, 1969), 142.

31. Brentano, *Foundation and Construction of Ethics*, 38–66.

32. Brentano in Scharwath, *Tradition, Aufbau, und Fortbildung*, 76–77

33. Brentano, *Foundation and Construction of Ethics*, 130–32.

34. Unfortunately, the volume provides a somewhat unreliable representation of Brentano's early views because its editors removed inconsistencies by incorporating later, significantly altered opinions. I refer to it, therefore, only for general support.

35. Brentano, *Foundation and Construction of Ethics*, 138.

36. Ibid., 52.

37. Ibid., 136.

38. Ibid., 136.

39. Brentano also condemned Kant's categorical imperative, arguing that it lacked empirical self-evidence and logical consistency. He claimed, for example, that the imperative would call for submission to bribery. "For if the contrary maxim were to become a universal law, then people would no longer attempt bribery. Therefore the law could not be put into effect since there would be no instances to which it applied, and therefore it would nullify itself" (Brentano, *Origin of Our Knowledge*, ed. Chisholm, 49–50; *Foundation and Construction of Ethics*, 30–37). Outside a small circle of dedicated Brentanians, most commentators find this an extrapolation *ad absurdum*.

40. Brentano, "Loving and Hating," in id., *Origin of Our Knowledge*, ed. Chisholm, 146, 155. On psychologism, see Martin Kusch, *Psychologism: A Case Study in the Sociology of Philosophical Knowledge* (London: Routledge, 1995). Husserl never accused Brentano of psychologism as he did Lipps. Yet in the eyes of many contemporaries, Brentano's insistence on the primacy of psychology and his emphasis on describing the facts of consciousness opened him to the charge.

41. Brentano, "Loving and Hating," in id., *Origin of Our Knowledge*, ed. Chisholm, 147. The standard translation of *Vorstellen* as 'contemplation' masks the link between emotion and presentation (a more exact translation), two of Brentano's three modes of the mental apprehension.

42. Brentano, "Loving and Hating," in id., *Origin of Our Knowledge*, ed. Chisholm, 147–48.

43. Kant acknowledged a kind of ethical emotion in his emphasis on respect for the moral law, though it was nowhere near as broad as Brentano's—and later phenomenologists'—emotionalism.

44. Brentano, *Psychology from an Empirical Standpoint*, 236–37. He makes a similar point about the sensitive and active aspects of his third psychological category in *Foundation and Construction of Ethics*, 201. See Chisholm, *Brentano and Intrinsic Value*, 22–24, for a discussion of Brentano's linking of desire and will within the psychological categories of love and hate. Kant, by contrast, distinguished feelings of pleasure and pain from the practical, active faculty of will. See Kant, "The Metaphysics of Morals," in Mary J. Gregor, ed., *Immanuel Kant: Practical Philosophy* (Cambridge: Cambridge University Press, 1996), 373–76.

45. Brentano, *The True and the Evident*, 22.

46. Ibid., 23.

47. The lecture *Vom Ursprung sittlicher Erkenntnis* was framed as a refutation of the historicist legal scholar Rudolf von Jhering's 1884 speech *Ueber die Entstehung des Rechtsgefühles* (Naples: Jovene Editore, 1986), which argued that man's sense of justice was a product of history. Brentano distinguished his own account of ethical relativity, which acknowledged that intermediate goods vary depending upon the ends sought, from historicism and ethical relativism, which argued that there were no absolutely valid and fundamental moral precepts. He condemned the latter for undermining the philosophical commitment to truth and empirical science. Brentano, *Origin of Our Knowledge*, ed. Chisholm, 35–36.

48. Brentano, *Origin of Our Knowledge*, ed. Chisholm, 20.

49. "Truth speaks," Brentano declared, employing a different sense analogy, "and whoever is of the truth hears its voice" (ibid., 35).

50. Ibid., 9.

51. Ibid., 22. "To ask why we prefer knowledge to error would seem as absurd as asking why we would rather experience pleasure than suffer pain," Brentano writes in *Foundation and Construction of Ethics*, 168.

52. Brentano, *Origin of Our Knowledge*, ed. Chisholm, 22.

53. McAlister, *Development of Franz Brentano's Ethics*, 108–40. And see Brentano, *Foundation and Construction of Ethics*, 331–76. In McAlister's view, Brentano's practical ethics was far weaker than his theoretical insights. It should be noted that Brentano's advocacy of marriage came at personal cost. When he chose to marry in 1880, an Austrian law barring matrimony for anyone who had taken priestly vows forced him to relinquish his state professorship. He spent the rest of his career in Vienna working as a *Privatdozent*.

54. "[T]he sphere of the highest practical good is the whole area that is affected by our rational activities insofar as anything good can be brought about within it. Thus one must consider not only oneself, but also one's family, the city, the state, every living thing upon the earth, and one must consider not only the

immediate present but also the distant future. . . . To further the good throughout this great whole so far as possible—this is clearly the correct end of life and all our actions should be centred around it. It is the one supreme imperative on which all others depend." Brentano, *Origin of Our Knowledge*, ed. Chisholm, 32.

55. See Brentano, *Foundation and Construction of Ethics*, 307–36.

56. Brentano, *Psychology from an Empirical Standpoint*, 21, 24–5.

57. Brentano presents his cyclical history of philosophy in *Vier Phasen der Philosophie*.

58. On this comparison, see Jan Patočka's essay "Masaryk's and Husserl's Conception of the Spiritual Crisis of European Humanity," in Erazim Kohák, *Jan Patočka: Philosophy and Selected Writings* (Chicago: University of Chicago Press, 1989), 145–56.

59. J. N. Findlay, *Axiological Ethics* (London: Macmillan, 1970), 24. Findlay acknowledges that Brentano helped to revive a concern for value theory in ethics.

60. See the lectures collected in Brentano, *On the Existence of God* (Dordrecht: Kluwer, 1987).

61. "Duty is what the average among the best men will do." Brentano, *Foundation and Construction of Ethics*, 297.

62. Howard Eaton, "The Validity of Axiological Ethics," *International Journal of Ethics* 43, no. 3 (April 1933): 260.

63. Brentano, "Loving and Hating," in id., *Origin of Our Knowledge*, ed. Chisholm, 148.

64. Brentano, *Psychology from an Empirical Standpoint*, 40–42.

65. G. E. Moore, "Review of The Origin of the Knowledge of Right and Wrong," *International Journal of Ethics* 14, no. 1 (October 1903): 115–23.

66. G. E. Moore, "Preface" to *Principia Ethica* (New York: Dover, 2004), vi–vii. On Moore, see Mary Warnock, *Ethics since 1900* (London: Oxford University Press, 1960), 11–38; Alasdair MacIntyre, *A Short History of Ethics* (New York: Macmillan, 1968), 249–53. Moore's praise was not unalloyed. He accused Brentano of misconstruing the nature of value and overestimating the insight granted by emotion. These discrepancies suggest a deeper divergence: Moore took the fundamental question of philosophical ethics to be ontological, not practical: identifying the proper object of ethical thought and exorcising false idols. Brentano felt that ethics must culminate in practical insights and tied it to a program of renewal. For a longer discussion of Moore's review, see Michael Gubser, "Franz Brentano's Ethics of Social Renewal," *Philosophical Forum* 40, no. 3 (Fall 2009): 339–66.

67. By Husserl's account, deficient development accounted for many of Brentano's ambiguities—for example, the failure to distinguish the sundry aspects of ethical perception: the noetic (mental) judgment from the ontic (object) value. During the early period of static phenomenology, Husserl worked out tables and

hierarchies of formal and practical values in what grew into an ever more complex taxonomy. Husserl, *Vorlesungen über Ethik und Wertlehre, 1908–1914*, Husserliana, vol. 28 (Dordrecht: Kluwer, 1988), 90, and *Einleitung in die Ethik: Vorlesungen Sommersemester 1920 und 1924*, Husserliana, vol. 27 (Dordrecht: Kluwer, 2004), 15.

68. At the same time, Scheler attacked Brentano's doctrine of the infallibility of inner perception, accused him of overrationalization, and condemned him for betraying the social promise of descriptive psychology by neglecting its external applications. See Max Scheler, "The Idols of Self-Knowledge," in id., *Selected Philosophical Essays* (Evanston, IL: Northwestern University Press, 1973); and *Formalism in Ethics and Non-Formal Ethics of Values*, trans. Manfred S. Frings and Roger L. Funk (Evanston, IL: Northwestern University Press, 1973), 82. For a fuller discussion, see Gubser, "Franz Brentano's Ethics of Social Renewal."

69. The phrase "ghosts of Brentano" is from Nicolas de Warren, *Husserl and the Promise of Time* (Cambridge: Cambridge University Press, 2009).

CHAPTER 2

1. Jan Patočka, *An Introduction to Husserl's Phenomenology*, trans. Erazim Kohák (Chicago: Open Court, 1996), 135. Patočka's paraphrase is credited to "the thinker," a sobriquet he often reserved for Heidegger, but the remark here is clearly embedded in a discussion of Husserl that makes the attribution obvious.

2. Jan Patočka, *Body, Community, Language, World*, trans. Erazim Kohák (Chicago: Open Court, 1998), 36, 103.

3. Merleau-Ponty, too, saw in Husserl's corporeal phenomenology a strategy for exploring the "far-off reaches" of the world, in which culture and nature, subject and object, coexist. Maurice Merleau-Ponty, *The Visible and the Invisible* (Evanston, IL: Northwestern University Press, 1968), 188.

4. Anthony J. Steinbock, *Home and Beyond: Generative Phenomenology after Husserl* (Evanston, IL: Northwestern University Press, 1995), 115; Husserl, *Ideas Pertaining to a Pure Phenomenology and to a Phenomenological Philosophy*, Second Book (hereafter called *Ideas II*) (Dordrecht: Kluwer, [1952] 1989), 165–66. The discovery might be dated even earlier, to the winter lectures of 1910–/11, published in English as *The Basic Problems of Phenomenology: From the Lectures, Winter Semester, 1910–1911* (Dordrecht: Springer, 2006), where Husserl first introduced the "natural world concept," adapted from the positivist philosopher Richard Avenarius. On Avenarius's influence, see Rochus Sowa's Introduction to Edmund Husserl, *Die Lebenswelt: Auslegungen der Vorgegebenen Welt und ihrer Konstitution*, Husserliana, vol. 39 (Dordrecht: Springer, 2008), xxix–xxxiv. Some scholars trace Husserl's insights into corporeality and worldliness to his 1907 introduction of the phenomenological *epoché*, the reduction from the natural

assumption of external reality to an immediate experience that preserves worldly attributes without affirming their existence. See, e.g., Emmanuel Housset, *Husserl et l'énigme du monde* (Paris: Seuil, 2000).

5. As Dorion Cairns reports, the late Husserl insisted on the importance of phenomenological ethics. See Cairns, *Conversations with Husserl and Fink* (The Hague: Nijhoff, 1976), 50–60. Recent scholarship has concurred, departing from the largely epistemological focus of earlier interpreters. See Ulrich Melle, "Husserl's Personalist Ethics," *Husserl Studies* 23 (2007): 1–15; R. Philip Buckley, *Husserl, Heidegger, and the Crisis of Philosophical Responsibility* (Dordrecht: Kluwer, 1992); Dan Zahavi, *Husserl and Transcendental Intersubjectivity* (Columbus: Ohio University Press, 2001); Janet Donohoe, *Husserl on Ethics and Intersubjectivity: From Static to Genetic Phenomenology* (Amherst, NY: Humanity Books, 2004); James G. Hart, *The Person and the Common Life: Studies in a Husserlian Social Ethics* (Dordrecht: Kluwer, 1992); Steven Galt Crowell, *Husserl, Heidegger, and the Space of Meaning: Paths toward transcendental Phenomenology* (Evanston, IL: Northwestern University Press, 2001); Donn Welton, *The Other Husserl: The Horizons of Transcendental Phenomenology* (Bloomington: Indiana University Press, 2000); Welton, ed., *The New Husserl: A Critical Reader* (Bloomington: Indiana University Press, 2003); Steinbock, *Home and Beyond*. An older summary is Alois Roth, *Edmund Husserls ethische Untersuchungen* (The Hague: Nijhoff, 1960). For a concise distillation, see Nicolas de Warren, "Husserl and Phenomenological Ethics," in Sacha Golob and Jens Timmermann, eds., *Cambridge History of Moral Philosophy* (Cambridge: Cambridge University Press, 2014).

6. For a compelling discussion of Brentano's influence in Husserl's philosophy of time, see Nicolas de Warren's excellent *Husserl and the Promise of Time* (Cambridge: Cambridge University Press, 2009), which addresses not only time consciousness but also the radical philosophical "renewal" sought by Husserl in his transcendental phenomenology. On Brentano's influence, see also Maria Brück, *Über das Verhältnis E. Husserls zu F. Brentano vornehmlich mit Rücksicht auf Brentanos Psychologie* (Würzburg: Triltsch, 1933); Michael Gubser, "An Image of a Higher World: Franz Brentano and Edmund Husserl on Ethics and Renewal," *Santalka* 17, no. 3 (2009): 39–49.

7. Husserl, *Vorlesungen über Ethik und Wertlehre, 1908–1914*, Husserliana, vol. 28 (Dordrecht: Kluwer, 1988), 90–101. See also Ulrich Melle's helpful introduction to these lectures.

8. Ibid., 90; Husserl, *Einleitung in die Ethik: Vorlesungen Sommersemester 1920 und 1924*, Husserliana vol. 27 (Dordrecht: Kluwer, 2004), 15.

9. For a summary of the early ethics, see J. N. Mohanty, *The Philosophy of Edmund Husserl: A Historical Development* (New Haven, CT: Yale University Press, 2008), 288–305. Its companion volume is Mohanty, *Edmund Husserl's Freiburg Years, 1916–1938* (New Haven, CT: Yale University Press, 2011).

10. The most recent Husserliana publication, vol. 39, *Die Lebenswelt: Auslegungen der vorgegebenen Welt und ihrer Konstitution: Texte aus dem Nachlass (1916–1937)*, ed. Rochus Sowa (Dordrecht: Springer, 2008), for example, demonstrates Husserl's concern for the lifeworld thematic, normally associated with his final stage, as early as 1907.

11. "Up to the time of the war," Dorion Cairns reports Husserl as saying, "he was *theoretisch eingestellt* [set in a theoretical attitude], but since that time 'existential' problems have been of primary interest to him too" (Cairns, *Conversations with Husserl and Fink* [The Hague: Nijhoff, 1976], 60). There is a longstanding debate among Husserl scholars as to whether his work is best understood in terms of successive phases (early and late; static, genetic, generative; epistemological, Cartesian, worldly), or as a continuous unfolding of themes present from the start. While World War I was an important watershed in Husserl's ethical thought, many of his postwar preoccupations were adumbrated in earlier writings, and some of the prewar terminology persisted. All the same, Husserl's interwar publications exhibited a clear trend toward greater worldliness. Husserl noted it himself: in a 1919 letter to the young philosopher Arnold Metzger, he remarked that in his early career he had "no eyes for practical and cultural realities" (*Philosophical Forum* 21 [1963]: 56).

12. Husserl, "Fünf Aufsätze über Erneuerung," in id., *Aufsätze und Vorträge, 1922–1937*, Husserliana, vol. 27 (Dordrecht: Kluwer, 1989), 5. In a 1920 letter to the American philosopher William Hocking, he said that the war revealed "mankind's indescribable misery, which is not only moral and religious but philosophical." Husserl, *Briefwechsel*, vol. 2: *Die Göttinger Schule* (Dordrecht: Kluwer, 1994), 163, cited in Virginia López-Domínguez, "Body and Intersubjectivity: The Doctrine of Science and Husserl's Cartesian Meditations," in Violetta L. Waibel, Daniel Breazeale, and Tom Rockmore, eds.,, *Fichte and the Phenomenological Tradition* (Berlin: De Gruyter, 2010), 192n5.

13. Husserl, "Philosophy as Rigorous Science," in *Phenomenology and the Crisis of Philosophy* (New York: Harper, 1965), 71–147.

14. "We could not be persons for others," he wrote in 1912, "if a common surrounding world did not stand there for us in a community, in an intentional linkage of our lives" (Husserl, *Ideas II*, 201).

15. See Husserl to Roman Ingarden, July 8, 1917, in Husserl, *Briefe an Roman Ingarden*, 6–7. Husserl was not alone in his concern for cultural renewal in Germany and the West. For an intriguing parallel, see his praise for Albert Schweitzer's essay "The Decay and the Restoration of Civilization," (in Schweitzer, *The Philosophy of Civilization* [1923; reprint, Buffalo, NY: Prometheus, 1980]). Husserl commended his own *Kaizo* essays from the same year to Schweitzer. See "Husserl an Schweitzer, 28. VII. 1923," in Husserl, *Briefwechsel*, vol. 7 (Dordrecht: Kluwer, 1994), 253.

16. Husserl, "Fichtes Menschheitsideal," in *Aufsätze und Vorträge, 1911–1921*, Husserliana, vol. 25 (Dordrecht: Kluwer, 1987), 268. These lectures were not Husserl's earliest examination of Fichte. In 1903 and again during the war, he taught university seminars on *The Vocation of Humanity* and other Fichtean tracts. Fichte offered Husserl a model of philosophy lending significance to life by revealing a moral world order. Indeed, it is not hard to see in Husserl's lamentations for the present age a reiteration of Fichte's characterization of his era as an epoch of "absolute sinfulness." See, e.g., Fichte's *Addresses to the German Nation* (Chicago: Open Court, 1922). For analyses of Fichte's influence on Husserl, see Hart, *Person and the Common Life*; Waibel, et al., eds., *Fichte and the Phenomenological Tradition*; Hans Tietjen, *Fichte und Husserl. Letztbegründung, Subjektivität und praktische Vernunft im transzendentalen Idealismus* (Frankfurt: Vittorio Klostermann, 1980); Thérèse Pentzopoulou-Valalas, "Fichte et Husserl: Un lecture parallèle," in Wolfgang H. Schrader, ed., *Fichte im 20. Jahrhundert*, Fichte-Studien 13 (1997): 65–76. See also Andrzej Gniazdowski, "Phänomenologie und Politik: Husserl's These von der Erneuerung der Menschheit," in Paweł Dybel and Hans Jörg Sandkühler, eds., *Der Begriff des Subjekts in der modernen und postmodernen Philosophie* (Frankfurt: Lang, 2004), 67–79.

17. Husserl, "Fünf Aufsätze," in id., *Aufsätze und Vorträge, 1922–1937*, 35. Husserl occasionally wrote of "die Gottesidee," the infinite potential contained within men, though never attained in life.

18. Ibid., 33. Again the "absolute ought" is a Fichtean formulation.

19. The earliest publication of *Cartesian Meditations*, based on two lectures delivered in Paris, was the French translation of Emmanuel Lévinas and Gabrielle Pfeiffer. Dissatisfied with its analysis, Husserl abandoned the project of releasing a German edition. A German version first appeared in 1950, long after his death.

20. The personalist attitude appears most prominently in Husserl, *Ideas II*, esp. 181–222. For discussions, see Alfred Schutz, "Edmund Husserl's Ideas, Volume II," in Schutz, *Collected Papers III: Studies in Phenomenological Philosophy* (The Hague: Nijhoff, 1970), 27–36; Thomas Nenon, "'Umwelt' in Husserl and Heidegger" (paper presented at the conference "Judgment, Responsibility and the Life-world," Prague, May 2012).

21. See, e.g., Husserl, "Universal Teleology," *Telos* 4 (Fall 1969): 176–80, and "The World of the Living Present and the Constitution of the Surrounding World That Is Outside the Flesh," in Maurice Merleau-Ponty, *Husserl at the Limits of Phenomenology* (Evanston, IL: Northwestern University Press, 2002), 118, 132–33. In Husserl, "Foundational Investigations of the Phenomenological Origin of the Spatiality of Nature: The Originary Ark, the Earth, Does Not Move," ibid., 121), worldhood is experienced by individuals as a constant call: "I can

always go farther on my earth-ground and . . . always experience its 'corporeal' being more fully. . . . . I can always experience more of it"

22. Quoted in James G. Hart, "I, We, and God: Ingredients of Husserl's Theory of Community," in *Husserl-Ausgabe und Husserl-Forschung*, ed. Samuel IJsseling (Dordrecht: Kluwer, 1990), 136. Cf. Husserl, "Gemeingeist I.—Person, Personale Ganze, Personale Wirkungsgemeinschaften. Gemeinschaft—Gesellschaft," in *Zur Phänomenologie der Intersubjektivität: Zweiter Teil: 1921–1928* (The Hague: Nijhoff, 1973), 172, 174. Many late sketches are available in this volume and the *Dritter Teil (1929–1935)* (also The Hague: Nijhoff, 1973).

23. The 8 August 1922 inquiry letter from T. Akita also noted contributions from Karl Kautsky and Eduard Bernstein. See Husserl, *Briefwechsel: Institutionelle Schreiben*, vol. 8, ed. Karl Schuhmann (Dordrecht: Kluwer, 1994), 273. Husserl's occasional interactions with the Japanese prompted some of his more intriguing social speculations. His 1925 review of Karl Eugen Neumann's translation of Buddhist maxims, for example, celebrated a wholly non-European religious system whose assimilation, he believed, could invigorate an ailing *abendländische Kultur*. The Buddha and his votaries, averred Husserl, had defined a "method of *seelischer* purification and gratification of the highest dignity," a "novel type of human 'holiness'" that could help to spark the "ethical, religious, and philosophical renewal" for which he yearned (Husserl, *Aufsätze und Vorträge, 1922–1937*, Husserliana vol. 27, 126). To be sure, Husserl's attention to Eastern thought was superficial and Eurocentric, attitudes captured in his description of Japan as a "young, fresh, green branch of 'European' culture" (ibid., 95) Nonetheless, the flirtation with Eastern thought, both in print and through his Japanese students, suggests an awareness of traditions beyond his own. The Japanese embrace of phenomenology was one of the earliest steps in its internationalization. On Japanese phenomenology, see the entry on "Japan" by Hiroshi Kojima in Lester Embree et al., eds., *Encyclopedia of Phenomenology* (Dordrecht: Kluwer, 1997), 367–371; Anthony J. Steinbock, ed., *Phenomenology in Japan* (Dordrecht: Kluwer, 1998); and Yoshihiro Nitta, Hirotaka Tatematsu, and Eiichi Shimomissē, "Phenomenology and Philosophy in Japan," in *Analecta Husserliana*, vol. 8, Yoshihiro Nitta and Hirotaka Tatematsu, eds., *Japanese Phenomenology: Phenomenology as the Trans-cultural Philosophical Approach* (Dordrecht: Riedel, 1979), 3–20; and the volume *Japanese and Continental Philosophy: Conversations with the Kyoto School*, eds. Bret W. Davis, Brian Schroeder, and Jason Wirth (Bloomington: Indiana University Press, 2011).

24. For recent interpretations of these articles, see Welton, *Other Husserl*, and Steinbock, *Home and Beyond*.

25. Husserl, "Fünf Aufsätze," in id., *Aufsätze und Vorträge, 1922–1937*, 3.

26. Ibid., 5.

27. Husserl, "Philosophy as Rigorous Science." See also "The Dilthey-Husserl Correspondence," in *Husserl: Shorter Works*, ed. Peter McCormick and Frederick Elliston (Notre Dame, IN: University of Notre Dame Press, 1981), 198–209.

28. Husserl, "Fünf Aufsätze," in id., *Aufsätze und Vorträge, 1922–1937*, 5.

29. Ibid., 7.

30. Ibid., 14, 16.

31. Ibid., 20.

32. James G. Hart has called this turn the "ethical reduction." See Hart, *Person and the Common Life*; Hart, "The Absolute Ought and the Unique Individual," *Husserl Studies* 22 (2006): 223–40). It is also found in the ethics courses of 1920 and 1924 (Husserl, *Einleitung in die Ethik*). Other documents from the early 1920s attest to this new phenomenological sociality as well. See, e.g., Husserl, *Erste Philosophie (1923/24): Zweiter Teil: Theorie der phänomenologischen Reduktion*, Husserliana, vol. 8 (The Hague: Nijhoff, 1959), 296–97.

33. Husserl, "Fünf Aufsätze," in id., *Aufsätze und Vorträge, 1922–1937*, 36.

34. Here, of course, Husserl the Protestant convert echoed the old Protestant ideal of the calling, famously analyzed by Max Weber.

35. Patočka, too, would highlight the liberating value of a dissatisfaction that rejected factual earthly bounds. See his 1950s essay "Negative Platonism," in Erazim Kohák, ed., *Jan Patočka: Philosophy and Selected Writings* (Chicago: University of Chicago Press, 1989), 193.

36. Husserl, "Fünf Aufsätze," in id., *Aufsätze und Vorträge, 1922–1937*, 32.

37. "[T]he truly human life, a life of never-ending self-development," Husserl wrote, "is, so to say, a life of 'method,' the method for the ideal humanity [*Humanität*]"(ibid., 38).

38. Ibid., 39.

39. Ibid.,45.

40. Ibid.,22. Husserl himself did not use the Greek-cum-Heideggerian term *ethos*, though his notion of an individual and communal *seelischer Habitus* (ibid., 23) bore similarities to it. For Heidegger's famous invocation of the term, see Heidegger, "Letter on Humanism," in id., *Basic Writings* (New York: HarperCollins, 1993), 256–57. The term appeared prominently and contemporaneously in Scheler.

41. Husserl, "Fünf Aufsätze," in id., *Aufsätze und Vorträge, 1922–1937*, 48.

42. Ibid.,52.

43. Ibid.,57.

44. "The humanity of higher human nature or reason," he later wrote "requires . . . a genuine philosophy." Husserl, *The Crisis of European Sciences and Transcendental Phenomenology* (Evanston, IL: Northwestern University Press, 1970), 291; *Die Krisis der europäischen Wissenschaften und die transzendentale Phänomenologie*

(1936; The Hague: Nijhoff, 1952; texts from 1934–37), Husserliana, vol. 6 (Dordrecht, 1976): 338.

45. Husserl, "Fünf Aufsätze," in id., *Aufsätze und Vorträge, 1922–1937*, 58.

46. Hart, "I, We, and God," in *Husserl-Ausgabe*, ed. Ijsseling, 126. This conception of humanity as an outward ethical movement also infused Czech phenomenology through the writings of Jan Patočka.

47. Husserl, "Fünf Aufsätze," in id., *Aufsätze und Vorträge, 1922–1937*, 86. Cf. Patočka, *Plato and Europe*, trans. Petr Lom (Stanford, CA: Stanford University Press, 2002).

48. In numerous essays, Hart and Buckley try to extrapolate political positions from Husserl's pronouncements. For other explorations of the political leanings of Husserl's philosophy, see Karl Schuhmann, *Husserls Staatsphilosophie* (Freiburg: Karl Alber, 1988); Kevin Thompson and Lester Embree, eds. *Phenomenology of the Political* (Dordrecht: Kluwer, 2000.)

49. Husserl, "The Vienna Lecture," in *The Crisis of European Sciences*, 287–88.

50. By this time, of course, Husserl had already broached the topic of intersubjectivity in the 1910–11 lectures, *The Basic Problems of Phenomenology*. The most significant recent discussion of Husserl's alter ego remains Michael Theunissen, *The Other: Studies in the Social Ontology of Husserl, Heidegger, Sartre, and Buber* (Cambridge, MA: MIT Press, [1977] 1984), 13–163.

51. Welton, *Other Husserl*, 319.

52. Several recent works have challenged the traditional focus on empathy as the crux of Husserlian intersubjectivity, showing instead that Husserl's late and incomplete "generative" phenomenology took a novel tack regarding questions of world and community. See Steinbock, *Home and Beyond*; Welton, *Other Husserl*. For an earlier work that makes similar claims regarding Husserl's analysis of history, see David Carr, *Phenomenology and the Problem of History: A Study of Husserl's Transcendental Philosophy* (Evanston, IL: Northwestern University Press, 1974).

53. Husserl's later work grappled with the nexus between a primordial rational subject and an *equally* primordial affective sociability, between intersubjective reason and a prerational system of drives.

54. Christ, Husserl said, was the embodiment of this ethics. ("Gemeingeist I," 171, 174, 175–84).

55. See especially the extensive lectures and notes, dating from 1905, in the three Husserliana series volumes (vols. 13–15) published as *Zur Phänomenologie der Intersubjektivität*. Volumes 14 and 15 are contemporary with or later than the *Kaizo* essays.

56. Alfred Schutz, "Husserl's *Crisis of Western Science*," in Schutz, *Collected Papers*, vol. 4 (Dordrecht: Kluwer, 1996), 177–86; Aron Gurwitsch, "The Last Work of Edmund Husserl," pts. 1 and 2, *Philosophy and Phenomenological*

Research 16, no. 3 and 17, no. 3 (March 1956–March 1957): 388–99 and 370–98; Maximilien Beck, "The Last Phase of Husserl's Phenomenology: An Exposition and Criticism," *Philosophy and Phenomenological Research* 1, no. 4 (June 1941): 479–91; Roman Ingarden, "What's New in Husserl's 'Crisis,'" *Analecta Husserliana* 2 (1972): 23–47.

57. As Dermot Moran shows, Nazi ideologues used Husserl to exemplify the ills of Jewish universalist philosophy. Moran, "'Even the Papuan is a Man and not a Beast': Husserl on Universalism and the Relativity of Cultures," *Journal of the History of Philosophy* 49, no. 4 (2011): 472–76.

58. Prague in particular afforded the chance to renew ties with Landgrebe and Patočka in the land of his "first teacher," Tomáš Masaryk, who fulfilled the "spirit of international humanity" that Husserl's philosophy endorsed. Letter to the Austrian legal philosopher Felix Kaufmann, May 5, 1936, in Husserl, *Briefwechsel*, vol. 4: *Die Freiburger Schüler* (Dordrecht: Kluwer, 1994), 224–25. Husserl's family also suffered from the Nazi race laws. His son, a World War I veteran, lost his post as a jurisprudence professor, and his daughter was unable to secure domestic help. Husserl to Landgrebe, December 19, 1935, and to the Dutch philosopher Hendrik J. Pos, January 17, 1935; both ibid., 343, 448.

59. Husserl to Felix Kaufmann, January 5, 1934 ibid., 201.

60. Husserl, *Crisis of European Sciences*, 11.

61. Husserl, "Philosophy and the Crisis of European Man" in Quentin Lauer, ed., *Phenomenology and the Crisis of Philosophy* (New York: Harper, 1965), 192.

62. As Guy von Kerckhoven has noted, the term *Lebenswelt*, or "lifeworld" (in some manuscripts separated into home- and alien-worlds), first surfaced in *Ideen II*, though it was not carefully elaborated until the end of his life. See von Kerckhoven, "Zur Genese des Begriffs 'Lebenswelt' bei Edmund Husserl," *Archiv für Begriffsgeschichte* 29 (1985): 182–203.

63. Husserl may, of course, have presumed that the problem had already been dealt with by this stage in his career, yet even so there are tensions between the worldliness of the *Crisis of European Sciences* and the egology of the *Cartesian Meditations*. As Steinbock argues, the Cartesian approach to intersubjectivity retained an egological core, for the Other always appeared as a second and subordinate self. Steinbock, *Home and Beyond*, 49–78.

64. On the relation between Husserl and Heidegger, see Steven Galt Crowell, *Husserl, Heidegger, and the Space of Meaning*.

65. A joint student of Husserl and Heidegger, Eugen Fink spent a career arguing that the transcendental origin of the world was the *Grundproblem* of Husserl's phenomenology as early as the *Logical Investigations*. See his "Die Spätphilosophie Husserls in der Freiburger Zeit," *Phaenomenologica* 4 (1960; from a 1959 lecture): 99–115, and *Die Phänomenologische Philosophie Edmund Husserls in der gegenwärtigen Kritik* (Berlin: Pan-Verlagsgesellschaft, 1934). On Fink, Husserl,

and Heidegger, see Ronald Bruzina, *Edmund Husserl and Eugen Fink: Beginnings and Ends in Phenomenology* (New Haven, CT: Yale University Press, 2004).

66. Husserl, *Crisis of European Sciences*, 21–57. Cf. id., "The Origin of Geometry," ibid., 353–78.

67. Husserl, *Crisis of European Sciences*, 59.

68. Husserl, "Universale Teleologie. Der Intersubjektive, Alle und jede subjekte umspannende Trieb transzendental Gesehen. Sein der monadischen Totalität," in *Zur Phänomenologie der Intersubjektivität*, pt. 3 (The Hague: Nijhoff, 1973), 594. For a recent study of Husserl's social phenomenology, see Laurent Perreau, *Le monde social selon Husserl* (Dordrecht: Springer, 2013).

69. Husserl, "Foundational Investigations," in Merleau-Ponty, *Husserl at the Limits*.

70. Husserl, "World of the Living Present," in Merleau-Ponty, *Husserl at the Limits*, 118, 132–33.

71. Husserl, "Foundational Investigations," in Merleau-Ponty, *Husserl at the Limits*, 121.

72. Husserl, "World of the Living Present," in Merleau-Ponty, *Husserl at the Limits*, 153.

73. Husserl, *Crisis of European Sciences*, 15.

74. The term "distancing abstention" comes from Bernhard Waldenfels, "Experience of the Alien in Husserl's Phenomenology," *Research in Phenomenology* 20 (1990): 19. For an example of Husserl's continued desire for worldly abstention—his goal of becoming a "non-participating onlooker," a "mere spectator, or observing ego," an "impartial observer" of the "life-process in reduced form"—see the "The Amsterdam Lectures (on) Phenomenological Psychology" in Husserl, *Psychological and Transcendental Phenomenology and the Confrontation with Heidegger (1927–1931)* (Dordrecht: Kluwer, 1997), 222–24. Husserl spoke of the epochal I as occupying a position "above" givenness and pregivenness in *The Crisis of European Sciences* too (150).

I do not mean to sweep aside Husserl's frequent resort to primal subjectivity, most famously articulated in the *Crisis of European Sciences*, pt. 3, §54, on the *Ur-Ich*. But there was, as James Dodd puts it, a fruitful "tension between, on the one hand, Husserl's development of the theme of history [as a basis of extrasubjective worldliness] and, on the other, his unrelenting focus on the personal dimension of philosophical life." See Dodd's thought-provoking *Crisis and Reflection: An Essay on Husserl's Crisis of the European Sciences* (Dordrecht: Kluwer, 2004), 67. The tension lent the *Crisis* a greater suppleness than many critics allow. For example, Husserl may have already foreseen the danger of excessive subjectivity articulated in Adorno's later complaint that "[t]he 'absolutely other,' which should arise within the phenomenological ἐποχή is . . . nothing other than the reified performance of the subject radically alienated from its own origin." Theodor Adorno, *Against Epistemology: A Metacritique* (Cambridge, MA: MIT Press, 1983), 163. Dodd interprets the *Ur-Ich*, not as an individual subjectivity *in* the world, but as the subjectivity *of* the world, a world subjectivity. For a thoughtful discussion of the primal I, see Luis Niel, "Temporality, Stream of Consciousness, and the I in the Bernau Manuscripts," in Dietmar Lohmar, *On Time: New Contributions to the Husserlian Phenomenology of Time* (Springer: Dordrecht, 2010), 213–30.

75. "[W]orld is a validity which has sprung up within subjectivity, indeed ... within my subjectivity," Husserl wrote in the *Crisis of European Sciences* (96). His disciples would reject this configuration.

76. Ibid., 8.

77. Ibid.,8. See Patočka, *Plato and Europe*, for the next generation of this argument. Klaus Held maintained that Husserl's commitment to philosophical responsibility was rooted in his vision of the Greek tradition. At its origins, Held writes, Attic philosophy grew from two intellectual commitments: *theoría* (an organized sense of human wonder and curiosity); and *lógon didónai*, a responsibility to explain or account for things (in words). See Held, "Husserls These von der Europäisierung der Menschheit," in *Phänomenologie im Widerstreit: Zum 50. Todestag Edmund Husserls*, ed. Christoph Jamme and Otto Pöggeler (Frankfurt: Suhrkamp, 1989), 13–39.

78. Husserl, *Crisis of European Sciences*, 9.

79. Ibid.,17.

CHAPTER 3

1. As an example of the early influence, see Johannes Daubert's lecture from 1902, "Remarks on the Psychology of Apperception and Judgment," *The New Yearbook for Phenomenology and Phenomenological Philosophy* 2 (2002): 344–65. Husserl's analysis of judgment, which went beyond Brentano's existential theory of judgment by relating the ideal content of a judgment to the judging act, was also appreciated.

2. Moritz Geiger, "Alexander Pfänders methodische Stellung," in E. Heller and F. Löw, eds., in *Neue Münchener Philosophische Abhandlungen* (Leipzig: Johann Ambrosius Barth, 1933), 4. On Geiger, see also Alexandre Métraux, "Edmund Husserl und Moritz Geiger," in Helmut Kuhn, Eberhard Avé-Lallement, and Reinhold Gladiator, *Die Münchener Phänomenologie: Vorträge des Internationalen Kongresses in München 13.-18. April 1971* (The Hague: Nijhoff, 1975), 139–57.

3. The classic history of the movement is Herbert Spiegelberg, *The Phenomenological Movement: A Historical Introduction* (1960; 3rd ed. (The Hague: Nijhoff, 1984). Its different editions contain slightly different material, with the

most thorough being the third revised and enlarged edition. For a brief, standard account, see Eberhard Avé-Lallement, "Die phänomenologische Bewegung: Ursprung, Anfänge und Ausblick," in Hans Rainer Sepp, ed., *Edmund Husserl und die phänomenologische Bewegung: Zeugnisse in Text und Bild* (Freiburg: Karl Alber, 1988), 61–75. Sepp's anthology offers a general overview with photographs. See also the essays in Karl Schuhmann, *Selected Papers on Phenomenology* (Dordrecht: Kluwer, 2004), and Elisabeth Endres, *Edith Stein: Christliche Philosophin und jüdische Märtyrerin* (Munich: Piper, 1987), 77–109. On Daubert, see Reinhold N. Smid, "An Early Interpretation of Husserl's Phenomenology: Johannes Daubert and the Logical Investigations," *Husserl Studies* 2 (1985): 267–90. Daubert went unpublished in his lifetime.

4. The Greek phrase is quoted in Husserl's 1911 "Philosophy as Rigorous Science," in Quentin Lauer, *Phenomenology and the Crisis of Philosophy* (New York: Harper, 1965), 146.

5. Edith Stein, *Life in a Jewish Family, 1891–1916* (Washington, DC: ICS Publications, 1986), 250; Klaus Held, "Edmund Husserl (1859–1938)," in Otfried Höffe, ed., *Klassiker der Philosophie*, vol. 2: *Von Immanuel Kant bis Jean-Paul Sartre* (Munich: Beck, 1995), 278.

6. Quoted in Safranski, *Martin Heidegger: Between Good and Evil* (Cambridge, MA: Harvard University Press, 1998), 72. Stein echoed this sentiment in her memoir, *Life in a Jewish Family*.

7. Eberhard Avé-Lallement and Karl Schuhmann, "Ein Zeitzeuge über die Anfänge der phänomenologischen Bewegung: Theodor Conrads Bericht aus dem Jahre 1954," *Husserl Studies* 9 (1992): 82. The recollection belonged to Theodor Conrad, a contemporary of Daubert, Geiger, and Stein, who later married Hedwig Conrad-Martius (née Martius).

8. Theodor Lipps's discussion of empathy in "Das Wissen von fremden Ichen," in id., ed., *Psychologische Untersuchungen* (Leipzig: Wilhelm Engelmann, 1907), 694–722, was, as we have seen, particularly important for Husserl's later analysis of the Other in the Fifth Cartesian Meditation.

9. Adolf Reinach to Theodor Conrad, January 31, 1903, quoted in Avé-Lallemant and Schuhmann, "Zeitzeuge," 77. Cf. Melchior Palágyi, *Der Streit der Psychologisten und Formalisten in der modernen Logik* (Leipzig: Wilhelm Engelmann, 1902).

10. Smid, "Early Interpretation," 268–71. Kimberly Baltzer-Jaray, ed., *Selected Papers on the Early Phenomenology: Munich and Göttingen, Quaestiones Disputatae* 3, no. 1 (2012): 110, finds a Lippsian and a post-Lippsian phase in the Husserl reception.

11. Geiger, "Alexander Pfänders methodische Stellung," 5.

12. Adolf Reinach, "Concerning Phenomenology," in Dermot Moran and Timothy Mooney, eds., *The Phenomenology Reader* (London: Routledge, 2002), 194, 182.

13. Quoted in Karl Schuhmann, "The Development of Speech Act Theory in Munich Phenomenology," in *The New Yearbook for Phenomenology and Phenomenological Philosophy* 2 (2002): 84. Cf. Karl Schuhmann and Barry Smith, "Questions: An Essay in Daubertian Phenomenology," *Philosophy and Phenomenological Research* 43, no. 3 (1987): 353–84. For an analysis that builds (critically) on Daubert's reflections on questioning, see John Bruin, *Homo Interrogans: Questioning and the Intentional Structure of Cognition* (Ottawa: University of Ottawa Press, 2001).

14. Quoted in Smid, "Early Interpretation," 286; Schuhmann, "The Development of Speech Act Theory," 78; and Barry Smith, "Towards a History of Speech Act Theory," in Armin Burkhardt, ed., *Speech Acts, Meaning and Intentions: Critical Approaches to the Philosophy of John R. Searle* (Berlin: De Gruyter, 1990), 39. See also Kimberly Baltzer-Jaray, *Doorway to the World of Essences: Adolf Reinach and the Early Phenomenological Movement* (Saarbrücken: Müller, 2009), 118–27.

15. Husserl, *Logische Untersuchungen*, vol. 2, pt. 2 (4th ed., Tübingen: Max Niemeyer, 1968), 218. The phrase *einsamen Seelenleben* is rendered as "solitary mental life" in *Logical Investigations*, trans. J. N. Findlay (New York: Routledge, 1970), 2: 848.

16. The original editors were Geiger, Pfänder, Reinach, and Scheler. See Eberhard Avé-Lallement, "Die Antithese Freiburg-München in der Geschichte der Phänomenologie," in Kuhn et al., eds., *Münchener Phänomenologie*, 19–38.

17. Avé-Lallement and Schuhmann, "Zeitzeuge," 83.

18. Theodor Celms, *Der phänomenologische Idealismus Husserls* (Riga: Walters & Rapa, 1928) argued that Husserl's transcendentalism violated his own phenomenological principles by passing existential judgment on that which transcended consciousness—a thesis that was reluctantly endorsed by Alexander Pfänder in his review in the *Deutsche Literaturzeitung* 43 (1929): 2048–50. On Celms, see Ella Buceniece, "Teodors Celms, Kurt Stavenhagen and Phenomenology in Latvia," *Phenomenology World-Wide* 80 (2003): 312–16; and Uldis Vēgners, "Theodor Celms's Critique of Husserl's Transcendental Phenomenology," in Baltzer-Jaray, ed., *Selected Papers*, 48–64.

19. For a defense of the continuity of Husserl's development against the charges of followers, see J. N. Mohanty, *Phenomenology: Between Essentialism and Transcendental Philosophy* (Evanston, IL: Northwestern University Press, 1997).

20. Quoted in Avé-Lallement, "Die Antithese Freiburg München," 27. Husserl's former assistant Ludwig Landgrebe counterargues that the explorations leading to the transcendental ego can be read not so much as the loss but the discovery of the world as the "general thesis" or background assumption of every perception; it was this general thesis that the reduction was designed to suspend. See "The World as a Phenomenological Problem," in Landgrebe, *The Phenomenology of Edmund Husserl: Six Essays* (Ithaca, NY: Cornell University Press, 1981), 122–28.

21. This standard criticism was reported, e.g., in Jean Héring, "La phénoménologie d'Edmund Husserl il y a trente ans," *Revue internationale de philosophie* 2 (1939): 366–73. I tracked down the reference in Robert Denoon Cumming, *Phenomenology and Deconstruction*, vol. 3: *Breakdown in Communication* (Chicago: University of Chicago Press, 2001), 20.

22. On Reinach's importance for analytic philosophy, see Barry Smith, "Towards a History of Speech Act Theory"; Karl Schuhmann, "The Development of Speech Act Theory"; and the essays collected in Kevin Mulligan, ed., *Speech Act and Sachverhalt: Reinach and the Foundations of Realist Phenomenology* (Dordrecht: Nijhoff, 1987). For recent efforts to place Reinach in the history of phenomenology, see James M. DuBois, *Judgment and Sachverhalt: An Introduction to Adolf Reinach's Phenomenological Realism* (Dordrecht: Kluwer, 1995); and Kimberly Baltzer-Jaray, *Doorway to the World of Essences*.

23. Spiegelberg, *Phenomenological Movement*, 3rd ed., 191–21; Stein, *Life in a Jewish Family*, 247; Roman Ingarden "Meine Erinnerungen an Edmund Husserl," in Husserl, *Briefe an Roman Ingarden* (The Hague: Nijhoff, 1968), 113–14. Many early phenomenologists found Husserl distant and closed—an indifferent teacher—in contrast to the rakish and captivating Scheler and the sterling pedagogue Reinach. As Alice von Hildebrand piquantly recalled, her husband viewed Husserl's *Logical Investigations* as "greater than the man" (Alice von Hildebrand, "Dietrich von Hildebrand's Acquaintance with Early Phenomenology," in Baltzer-Jaray, ed., *Selected Papers*, 12).

24. Reinach, "Concerning Phenomenology," in Moran and Mooney, eds., *Phenomenology Reader*, 193.

25. Barry Smith, "Introduction to Reinach's Theory of Negative Judgment," in *Parts and Moments: Studies in Logic and Formal Ontology* (Munich: Philosophia, 1982), 297.

26. Reinach, "Concerning Phenomenology," in Moran and Mooney, eds., *Phenomenology Reader*, 190, 11.

27. Adolf Reinach, "Die Überlegung: Ihre ethische und rechtliche Bedeutung," pt. 1, *Zeitschrift für Philosophie und philosophische Kritik* 148 (1913): 182.

28. Adolf Reinach, "Die Überlegung: Ihre ethische und rechtliche Bedeutung," pt. 2, *Zeitschrift für Philosophie und philosophische Kritik* 149 (1913): 42, 33, 36, 37, 40.

29. Reinach, "The Apriori Foundations of the Civil Law," *Aletheia* 3 (1983): 19–20.

30. Ibid., 36, 19.

31. Ibid., 109.

32. The distinction is hard to render in English, because the German word *Recht* means both 'right' and 'law.' Moreover, Reinach's concept seems to invoke an older understanding of *Recht* as justice rather than legality—that is,

a contemplative and ideal awareness that did not necessarily align with any particular codification. On the early modern split between *Recht* and *Gesetz*, *ius* and *lex*, see Roger Berkowitz, *The Gift of Science: Leibniz and the Modern Legal Tradition* (Cambridge, MA: Harvard University Press, 2005). I thank Kimberly Baltzer-Jaray for this citation.

33. Reinach, "Apriori Foundations," 139. Commentators such as Josef Seifert and Stanley L. Paulsen complain that this restriction limited the jurisprudential impact of his seminal analysis. Josef Seifert, "Is Reinach's 'Apriorische Rechtslehre' More Important for Positive Law Than Reinach Himself Thinks?" *Aletheia* 3 (1983): 197–230; Stanley L. Paulsen, "Demystifying Reinach's Legal Theory," in Mulligan, ed., *Speech Act and Sachverhalt*, 133–54.

34. Reinach, "Apriori Foundations," 45.

35. The lecture was delivered before the Munich *Verein*. A sequel lecture on the person as a bearer of value was canceled by Reinach's temporary move to Tübingen. See Schuhmann, "Adolf Reinachs Vortrag über die Grundbegriffe der Ethik," in Mulligan, ed., *Speech Act and Sachverhalt*, 277. Schuhmann's article, based on notes by Daubert and Pfänder, conveys the excitement surrounding the *Verein's* Friday meetings.

36. Reinach, "Apriori Foundations," 11, 102. Reinach also introduced the concept of juristic and collective persons, the latter of which played a substantial role in the Husserl's later sketches.

37. John F. Crosby, "Adolf Reinach's Discovery of Social Acts," *Aletheia* 3 (1993): 143–94; James M. DuBois, *Judgment and Sachverhalt*, 154–57. Both men see Wojtyła as the ultimate cultivator of Reinach's germinal personalism. Schuhmann, "Adolf Reinachs Vortrag," 281–82, sees Dietrich von Hildebrand as the more direct inheritor.

38. Karl Schuhmann and Barry Smith, "Adolf Reinach: An Intellectual Biography," in Mulligan, ed., *Speech Act and Sachverhalt*, 24. For a recent discussion of the vexed relation between the two schools, see Peter E. Gordon, *Continental Divide: Heidegger, Cassirer, Davos* (Cambridge, MA: Harvard University Press, 2010), 43–86.

39. Reinach, "Concerning Phenomenology," in Moran and Mooney, eds., *Phenomenology Reader*, 180, 181. For a contrasting view of color, see Ludwig Wittgenstein's *Remarks on Colour* (Berkeley: University of California Press, 1977).

40. Reinach, "Concerning Phenomenology," in Moran and Mooney, eds., *Phenomenology Reader*, 186, 196.

41. Ibid., 184.

42. Alexander Pfänder, *Phenomenology of Willing and Motivation and Other Phaenomenologica*, ed. Herbert Spiegelberg (Evanston, IL: Northwestern University Press, 1967), 7. The work built on a similarly themed dissertation. In fact, Pfänder's use of the term *Phänomenologie* (phenomenology) predated Husserl's. For an archaeology of his early work, see Karl Schuhmann, "Bewußtseinsinhalte:

Die Frühphänomenologie Alexander Pfänders," in id., *Selected Papers in Phenomenology* (Dordrecht: Kluwer, 2004), 219–37. On Pfänder's career more generally, see Herbert Spiegelberg, *Alexander Pfänders Phänomenologie* (The Hague: Nijhoff, 1963).

43. Alexander Pfänder, *Die Seele des Menschen: Versuch einer verstehenden Psychologie* (Halle: Max Niemeyer, 1933).

44. Alexander Pfänder, "Grundprobleme der Charakterologie," *Jahrbuch der Charakterologie* 1 (1924): 289–355; id., *Philosophie der Lebensziele* (Göttingen: Vandenhoeck & Ruprecht, 1948). He described the object of characterology as "the peculiar essential nature of the whole human soul" ("Charakterologie," 295).

45. Alexander Pfänder, *Ethik in kurzer Darstellung: Ethische Wertlehre und Ethische Sollenslehre* (Munich: Wilhelm Fink, 1973). Spiegelberg himself, best known as the movement's historian, elaborated an ethics on Pfänderian terms in which he attempted to relate moral practice to the discernment of absolute values. He aspired to a practical "deontology" based not on formal laws or categorical imperatives but rather on the intuitive ascertainment, description, and analysis of an "ethical order" (*ethische Ordnung*). The project appeared primarily in three manuscripts from the 1930s. Herbert Spiegelberg, *Gesetz und Sittengesetz: Strukturanalytische und historische Vorstudien zu einer gesetzfreien Ethik* (Zürich: Max Niehans, 1935); *Antirelativismus* (Zürich: Max Niehans, 1935); *Sollen und Dürfen: Philosophische Grundlagen der ethischen Rechte und Pflichten* (Dordrecht: Kluwer, 1989). For English excerpts, see Spiegelberg, "What Makes Good Things Good? An Inquiry into the Grounds of Value," *Philosophy and Phenomenological Research* 7, no. 4 (1947): 578–611; and "Rules and Order: Toward a Phenomenology of Order," in Paul Kuntz, ed., *The Concept of Order: The Grinnell Symposium* (Seattle: University of Washington Press, 1968), 290–308. For a discussion of Spiegelberg's ethics, see Fred Kersten, "Herbert Spiegelberg: Phenomenology in Ethics," in John J. Drummond and Lester Embree, eds., *Phenomenological Approaches to Moral Philosophy* (Dordrecht: Kluwer, 2002), 437–49.

46. Pfänder, *Ethik in kurzer Darstellung*, 30.

47. Ibid., 49, 41.

48. Ibid., 40, 48. The recognition of ubiquitous value itself took on a kind of moral worth as a marker of someone who was not deadened into mechanical apathy.

49. Ibid., 140. He also called it the nomological perception, or perception of laws.

50. Pfänder, *Seele des Menschen*; *Philosophie der Lebensziele*. Nonetheless, Harald Delius is correct in saying that Pfänder never succeeded in fully appraising our mundane duty to others. Delius, "Alexander Pfänders Ethische Wert- und Sollenslehre," in Herbert Spiegelberg and Eberhard Avé-Lallemant, eds., *Pfänder-Studien* (The Hague: Nijhoff, 1982), 35–50.

51. Alexander Pfänder, "Zur Psychologie der Gesinnungen," pts. 1 and 2, *Jahrbuch für Philosophie und phänomenologische Forschung* 1 and 3 (1913–16): 325–404 and 1–125. For a brief summary, see Spiegelberg, *Alexander Pfänders Phänomenologie*, 23–25. The translation of *Gesinnung* as 'directed sentiment' follows Herbert Spiegelberg, *The Phenomenological Movement: A Historical Introduction*, 3rd ed. (The Hague: Nijhoff, 1984), 1: 181. Hatred, too, was a directed sentiment, but instead of uniting with its object, it rejected the object and denied its warrant to exist (*Daseinsermächtigung*).

52. Also worthy of mention is Hans Reiner, initially a disciple of Pfänder, Husserl, and Hildebrand, who wrote his first book on freedom of the will and then fell under the spell of Heidegger. Compare the ethically focused phenomenological analysis of *Freiheit, Wollen, und Aktivität: Phänomenologische Untersuchungen in Richtung auf das Problem der Willensfreiheit* (Halle: Max Niemeyer, 1927) with the Heideggerian analysis of belief in *Das Phänomen das Glaubens* (Halle: Max Niemeyer, 1934). Reiner soured on Heidegger after World War II, and his postwar ethics included an explicit rejoinder to the tainted sage. See *Die Grundlagen der Sittlichkeit* (Meisenheim am Glan: Anton Hain, [1951] 1974). On Reiner, see Spiegelberg, *Phenomenological Movement*, 3rd ed., 1: 250; Irene Eberhard, "Das philosophische Werk Hans Reiners. Zu seinem 75. Geburtstag," *Zeitschrift für philosophische Forschung* 25, no. 4 (October–December 1971): 615–18.

53. This work lay incomplete at Beck's death in 1950. For the proposed layout, see the table of contents of Beck, *Wesen und Wert: Grundlegung einer Philosophie des Daseins* (Berlin: Konrad Grethlein, 1925).

54. Maximilian Beck, "The Proper Object of Psychology," *Philosophy and Phenomenological Research* 13, no. 3 (March 1953), begins with rare praise from a phenomenologist for Freud's theory of the unconscious. Geiger and Nicolai Hartmann also explored the unconscious. On the latter, see Michael Landmann, "Nicolai Hartmann and Phenomenology," *Philosophy and Phenomenological Research* 3, no. 4 (1943): 414–15.

55. See Maximilian Beck, "On Typical Misinterpretations of the Religious and Moral Experience," *Review of Religion* 4, no. 4 (May 1940): 416–30, which treats religion as a unique and valid type of experience.

56. Maximilian Beck, *Psychologie: Wesen und Wirklichkeit der Seele* (Leiden: A. W. Sijthoff, 1938), 262; Beck, *Philosophie und Politik* (Zürich: Europa, 1938), 107.

57. Beck, *Philosophie und Politik*, 106–9; Maximilian Beck, "Der Geiz als Wurzel der faustisch-dynamischen Kultur (Ein Intermezzo des erkenntnistheoretischen Dialogs)," *Philosophische Hefte* 3, nos. 1–2 (1931): 779–99.

58. Gerda Walther, "Zur Ontologie der sozialen Gemeinschaften," *Jahrbuch für Philosophie und phänomenologische Forschung* 6 (1923): 20. For a summary of Walther's career, see Linda Lopez McAlister, "Gerda Walther (1897–1977)," in Mary Ellen Waithe, ed., *A History of Women Philosophers*, vol. 4 (Dordrecht:

Kluwer, 1995), 189–206. Walther's autobiography, *Zum anderen Ufer: Vom Marxismus und Atheismus zum Christentum* (Remagen: Otto Reichl, 1960), is also available.

59. Walther embraced Catholicism in the last years of Nazi rule.

60. Gerda Walther, *Phänomenologie der Mystik* (Olten: Walter, 1923). Her contribution to Pfänder's sixtieth birthday *Festschrift*, an article entitled "The Phenomenology of Telepathy," was rejected. If Walther represented the outer reaches of phenomenological exploration, it should be noted that a concern for mysticism was not completely unknown: the Catholic Max Scheler posited a cosmic experiential stream existing prior to individuation. Edith Stein and Karol Wojtyła both wrote significant works on mystical experience.

61. Reinach, "Concerning Phenomenology," in Moran and Mooney, eds., *Phenomenology Reader*, 191, 185. Kantian formalism, which identified the prerequisites of thought rather than the nature of things, was the obvious target here.

62. See Spiegelberg, *Phenomenological Movement*, 3rd ed., 206; Moritz Geiger, *Die Wirklichkeit der Wissenschaften und die Metaphysik* (1930; Hildesheim: Georg Olms, 1966).

63. Moritz Geiger, "Alexander Pfänders methodische Stellung," in E. Heller and F. Löw, eds., *Neue Münchener Philosophische Abhandlungen* (Leipzig: Johann Ambrosius Barth, 1933), 12.

64. Hedwig Conrad-Martius, from the postwar manuscript "Die transzendentale und die ontologische Phänomenologie," in Conrad-Martius, *Schriften zur Philosophie*, vol. 3 (Munich: Kösel, 1965), 397. The term "real reality" had wide currency in Munich: first used by Lipps, it came to designate a reality independent of human perception (whether essential or material) as opposed to intended reality. For a discussion of three early female phenomenologists—Hedwig Conrad-Martius, Edith Stein, and Gerda Walther—as pioneers of a feminine philosophy, see Angela Ales-Bello, "Unterwegs zu einer weiblichen Philosophie: Hedwig Conrad-Martius, Edith Stein, Gerda Walther," *Edith Stein Jahrbuch* 2 (1996): 165–74; as well as her book on the same theme: *Fenomenologia dell'essere umano: Lineamenti di una filosofia al femminile* (Rome: Città nuova, 1992). Barred as a woman from an academic career, Conrad-Martius lived primarily on the earnings of a fruit farm run by her husband, the phenomenologist Theodor Conrad.

65. Hedwig Conrad-Martius, "Zur Ontologie und Erscheinungslehre der realen Außenwelt," *Jahrbuch für Philosophie und phänomenologische Forschung* 3 (1916): 351.

66. Avé-Lallement, "Hedwig Conrad-Martius (1888–1966): Phenomenology and Reality," in Spiegelberg, *Phenomenological Movement*, 3rd ed., 216.

67. Conrad-Martius, "Zur Ontologie," 447, and *Schriften zur Philosophie*, 3: 325; quoted in Spiegelberg, *Phenomenological Movement*, 3rd ed., 216.

68. Hedwig Conrad-Martius, "Realontologie," *Jahrbuch für Philosophie und phänomenologische Forschung* 6 (1923): 159–60. For a thorough analysis of this process in the context of her overall philosophy, see Alexandra Elisabeth Pfeiffer, *Hedwig Conrad-Martius: Eine phänomenologische Sicht auf Natur und Welt* (Würzburg: Königshausen & Neumann, 2005); and James G. Hart's doctoral dissertation "Hedwig Conrad-Martius' Ontological Phenomenology" (Ph.D. diss., University of Chicago, 1972). My analysis here limits itself to the interwar period, but Conrad-Martius continued her elaboration of ontological phenomenology after World War II, notably in the book *Das Sein* (Munich: Kösel, 1957).

69. Conrad-Martius called the form of being that carried its essence or whatness (*Sosein*; *Washeit*) in itself the *hypokeimenon*, using a Scholastic term for metaphysical substrate or *subjectum*. Conrad-Martius, "Realontologie," 167–68, 179–80.

70. J. N. Mohanty, "Nicolai Hartmann und die Phänomenologie," in *Symposium zum Gedenken an Nicolai Hartmann (1882–1950)* (Göttingen: Vandenhoek & Ruprecht, 1982), 13–23. On Hartmann's relation to phenomenology, see Landmann, "Nicolai Hartmann and Phenomenology" and Johannes Thyssen, "Zur Neubegründung des Realismus in Auseinandersetzung mit Husserl," *Zeitschrift für philosophische Forschung* 7, no. 2 (1953): 145–70.

71. Hartmann also turned against the Kantianism of his youth for privileging consciousness over Being. For a critical analysis of Hartmann's views on Kant by a prominent midcentury Kantian, see Lewis White Beck, "Nicolai Hartmann's Criticism of Kant's Theory of Knowledge," *Philosophy and Phenomenological Research* 2, no. 4 (1942): 472–500.

72. Nicolai Hartmann, *Grundzüge einer Metaphysik der Erkenntnis*, 5th ed. (Berlin: De Gruyter, 1921). Hartmann's oeuvre was, as J. N. Findlay puts it in *Axiological Ethics* (London: Macmillan, 1970), 58, a Teutonic Valhalla rather than a Greek Olympus. For good accounts of Hartmann's ontology, see W. H. Werkmeister, *Nicolai Hartmann's New Ontology* (Tallahassee: Florida State University Press, 1990); Helmut Kuhn, "Nicolai Hartmann's Ontology," *Philosophical Quarterly* 1, no. 4 (1951): 289–318; Roberto Poli, Carlo Scognamiglio, and Frederic Trembley, eds., *The Philosophy of Nicolai Hartmann* (Berlin: De Gruyter, 2011); and the essays collected in a special Hartmann edition of the journal *Axiomathes* 12 (2001). For summaries of the errors of the "old ontology," see Werkmeister, xiv; Peter Cicovacki, "New Ways of Ontology—The Ways of Interaction," *Axiomathes* 12 (2001): 160; Hartmann, *Das Problem des geistigen Seins* (Berlin: De Gruyter, 1933), 99.

73. Nicolai Hartmann, *Grundzüge einer Metaphysik der Erkenntnis*, 30. In a 1939 essay, he noted that the critique of psychologism might allow for the recovery of the ancient concept of *eidos* and a return to things. See "Zur Lehre vom Eidos bei Platon und Aristoteles," in Hartmann, *Kleinere Schriften*, vol. 2 (Berlin: De Gruyter, 1957), 129.

74. Hartmann, *Zur Grundlegung der Ontologie* (Berlin: De Gruyter, 1935), 53. "Diesseits von Idealismus und Realismus," a phrase used in numerous works to summarize his ontological position, became the title of a 1924 *Kant-Studien* article, now anthologized in Hartmann, *Kleinere Schriften*, 2: 278–322.

75. Landmann, "Nicolai Hartmann and Phenomenology," 396. The most notable characteristic of Hartmann's Being was its infinite multiplicity, stratified into a lower material and organismic realm supporting higher mental and spiritual realities. The higher depended on the lower, but also enjoyed an intrinsic autonomy and richness—it was only the higher beings that could introduce novelty—a relationship carried over, as we will see in chapter 5, into Hartmann's value hierarchy.

76. Hartmann, *Zur Grundlegung der Ontologie* (1935; 4th ed., Berlin: De Gruyter, 1965), 52.

77. Roman Ingarden, "The Letter to Husserl about the VI [Logical] Investigation and 'Idealism,'" *Analecta Husserliana* 4 (1976), 419–38; Ingarden, "Bemerkungen zum Problem Idealismus-Realismus," *Jahrbuch für Philosophie und phänomenologische Forschung, Ergänzungsband: Festschrift, Edmund Husserl zum 70. Geburtstag gewidmet* (1929), 159–90; Ingarden, *Spór o istnienie Świata*, 2 vols. (Kraków, 1947–48); vol. 1 trans. Arthur Szylewicz as *The Controversy over the Existence of the World* (Frankfurt: Peter Land, 2013). For recent monographs on Ingarden, see Jeff Mitscherling, *Roman Ingarden's Ontology and Aesthetics* (Ottawa: University of Ottawa Press, 1997); Arkadiusz Chrudzimski, ed., *Existence, Culture, and Persons: The Ontology of Roman Ingarden* (Frankfurt: Ontos, 2005); and Gregor Haefliger, *Über Existenz: Die Ontologie Roman Ingardens* (Dordrecht: Kluwer, 1994).

78. Husserl quoted in Roman Ingarden, "Letter to Husserl about the VI," 423.

79. Roman Ingarden, *On the Motives Which Led Husserl to Transcendental Idealism* (The Hague: Nijhoff, 1975), 1. The dispute between Husserl and Ingarden has provoked considerable heat in the philosophical literature. Starting in the 1970s, as more of Husserl's manuscripts became available, Husserlians started attacking Ingarden's project as a misinterpretation and arguing against the view that Husserl was a metaphysical idealist. Richard H. Holmes, "Is Transcendental Phenomenology Committed to Idealism?" *The Monist* 59, no. 1 (1975): 98–114, argued that Husserl was "epistemologically idealistic but metaphysically neutral" (98). Karl Ameriks, "Husserl's Realism," *The Philosophical Review* 86, no. 4 (1977): 498–519, claimed that Husserl's idealism was embedded in a wider argument for metaphysical realism. Harrison Hall, "Was Husserl a Realist or Idealist?" in Hubert L. Dreyfus and Harrison Hall, eds., *Husserl, Intentionality and Cognitive Science* (Cambridge, MA: MIT Press, 1984), 196–90, dismissed the very question of realism-idealism as misplaced. And Ingrid Wallner, "In Defense of Husserl's Transcendental Idealism: Roman Ingarden's Critique Re-examined,"

Husserl Studies 4 (1987): 3–43, argues that Ingarden systematically misrepresented Husserl's position. Mitscherling, in contrast, defends Ingarden, arguing that his critics shield Husserl from the charge of Berkeleyan idealism (whereby the world is only a construct of the mind), but ignore his quasi-Kantian idealism, in which "the only world of which we can have certain knowledge is that constituted by consciousness" (Mitscherling, *Roman Ingarden's Ontology*, 47).

80. Ingarden, "Letter to Husserl about the VI," 424. Ingarden later came to doubt the radical distinction between consciousness and world. Roman Ingarden, *Controversy over the Existence of the World*, vol. 1 (Frankfurt: Peter Lang, 2013 [1947–48]), 32–45.

81. Ingarden, "Letter to Husserl about the VI," 429.

82. Artworks, in contrast, were constituted by the intending mind, and their ontology was not that of the real world. Ingarden undertook the analysis of literature in his most famous work, *The Literary Work of Art* (Evanston, IL: Northwestern University Press, 1973). For a discussion, see Mitscherling, *Roman Ingarden's Ontology*, 123–62.

83. Roman Ingarden, "Le concept de philosophie chez Franz Brentano (fin)," *Archives de philosophie* 32, no. 4 (October–December 1969): 622, 638; the first part of the article appeared in ibid., no. 3 (July–September 1969): 458–75.

84. Roman Ingarden, "Über die Gefahr einer Petitio Principii in der Erkenntnistheorie," *Jahrbuch für Philosophie und phänomenologische Forschung* 4 (1921): 545–68. The fallacy of petitio principii—begging the question, or assuming rather than proving an initial point—prevented one from of placing knowledge on a secure epistemological foundation. For Ingarden, it plagued the history of philosophy.

85. Ibid., 563.

86. Ibid., 564.

87. Roman Ingarden, *Über die Stellung der Erkenntnistheorie im System der Philosophie* (Halle: Max Niemeyer, 1926).

88. Roman Ingarden, "Bemerkungen zum Problem Idealismus-Realismus." Ingarden reports having begun sketches for the essay as early as 1918. See his "Erläuterungen," in Husserl, *Briefe an Roman Ingarden*, 142.

89. For a review of these categories as elaborated in the *Controversy*, see Mitscherling, *Roman Ingarden's Ontology*, 86–110.

90. Ingarden, "Bemerkungen zum Problem Idealismus-Realismus," 165–66.

91. Ibid., 168. Once these existential regions had been mapped, an ontologist could use eidetic analyses to identify formal structures and material elements that might fit under them.

92. Ingarden, *Controversy over the Existence of the World*, vol. 1, 77. The volumes published during his lifetime dealt only with ontology.

93. See Ingarden's "Erläuterungen" in Husserl, *Briefe an Roman Ingarden*, 166. For a more thorough discussion of Ingarden's epistemology than can be offered

here, see Guido Küng, "Zum Lebenswerk von Roman Ingarden: Ontologie, Erkenntnistheorie und Metaphysik," in Kuhn et al., eds., *Münchener Phänomenologie*, 158–73.

94. Ingarden, "Bemerkungen zum Problem Idealismus-Realismus," 187–88.

95. Ingarden's student Anna-Teresa Tymieniecka contends that he never managed to link the human being and the real world because of a failure to consider fully "the pre-conscious life conditions of man and the world" (Tymieniecka, "Beyond Ingarden's Idealism/Realism Controversy with Husserl—The New Contextual Phase of Phenomenology," *Analecta Husserliana* 4 [1976]: 245). She sees in his late work on ethics and freedom (and might have seen in his early conception of intuition as *Durchleben*) an opening to a more active and interconnected vision of phenomenological reality. For "it is not only by conceiving man as transcending his founding functions in their mere operations but in their *operative reach*—that is, as transcending the limits of the transcendental *lifeworld*—that we could speak about reaching the gate to an epistemological realism" (360). This criticism is shrewd, even if it was mounted primarily to clear the way for her more amorphous project of contextual (and, later, cosmological and ontopoietic) analysis.

CHAPTER 4

1. Edmund Husserl, "Fichtes Menschheitsideal," in id., *Aufsätze und Vorträge, 1911–1921*, Husserliana vol. 25 (Dordrecht: Kluwer, 1987), 288–89.

2. Ulrich Melle, in "Schelersche Motive in Husserls Freiburger Ethik," in Gerhard Pfafferott, ed., *Vom Umsturz der Werte in der modernen Gesellschaft: II. Internationales Kolloquium der Max-Scheler-Gesellschaft* (Bonn: Bouvier, 1997), speculates that Husserl's concepts of a *Liebesgemeinschaft* (community of love) and of personalities of a higher order may have been influenced by Scheler.

3. Martin Heidegger, "In Memory of Max Scheler," in Thomas Sheehan, ed., *Heidegger: The Man and the Thinker* (Chicago: Precedent, 1981), 159.

4. For a piquant recollection of Scheler's "demonic" presence (as well as Husserl's "explicit discomfort" with him), see Hans-Georg Gadamer, "Max Scheler—der Verschwender," in Paul Good, ed., *Max Scheler im Gegenwartsgeschehen der Philosophie* (Bern: Francke, 1975), 11–18.

5. Cited in Melle, "Schelersche Motive," 204.

6. Husserl, *Briefe an Roman Ingarden* (The Hague: Nijhoff, 1968), 67.

7. These comments are from eulogies printed after Scheler's death. José Ortega y Gasset, "Max Scheler," in *Neue Schweizer Rundschau* 21, no. 10 (October 1928): 728, 729; Dietrich von Hildebrand, "The Personality of Max Scheler," *American Catholic Philosophical Quarterly* 79, no. 1 (2005): 48; Nicolai Hartmann, "Max Scheler," *Kantstudien* 33(1928): xiv. Roman Ingarden leveled similar

charges in the 1950s: Scheler had "no patience," "insufficient inner calm," and jumped "too quickly to results." Ingarden, "Ueber der Gegenwaertigen Aufgaben der Phaenomenologie," *Il compito della fenomenologia* 1–2 (1957): 239. The philosopher Joachim Ritter sees in Scheler's claims an "absolutization of one's own subjectivity." Ritter, *Über den Sinn und die Grenze der Lehre vom Menschen* (Potsdam: Alfred Protte, 1933), 28. As ever, Alfred Schutz's summaries are clear and cogent. See "Scheler's Theory of Intersubjectivity and the General Thesis of the Alter Ego," in Schutz, *Collected Papers*, vol. 1: *The Problem of Social Reality* (The Hague: Nijhoff, 1971), 150–79; "Max Scheler's Philosophy," and "Max Scheler's Epistemology and Ethics," ibid., vol. 3: *Studies in Phenomenological Philosophy* (The Hague: Nijhoff, 1970), 133–78.

8. See especially the Husserlian Marvin Farber, "Max Scheler," Encyclopedia Americana, International edition, vol. 24 (1965), 365. See also Farber, "Max Scheler on the Place of Man in the Cosmos," *Philosophy and Phenomenological Research* 14, no. 3 (March, 1954): 393–99; V. J. McGill, "Scheler's Theory of Sympathy and Love," *Philosophy and Phenomenological Research* 2, no. 3 (March 1942): 273–91; and Ernst Bloch, *Heritage of our Times* (Berkeley: University of California Press, 1990), 277–80. On Scheler's English-language reception, see Manfred Frings, *The Mind of Max Scheler: The First Comprehensive Guide Based on the Complete Works* (Milwaukee: Marquette University Press, 1997), 12–18; and Wilfried Hartmann, "Max Scheler and the English-Speaking World," *Philosophy Today* 12, no. 1 (Spring 1968): 31–41. Scheler's admirer Aurel Kolnai expressed a similar worry, cataloging his wartime writings with what he saw as a general German hypernationalism. Kolnai, *The War against the West* (Viking: New York, 1931), 421–22.

9. They have succeeded in blunting the charge of fascism: Scheler was, after all, one of the few prominent German scholars to warn against National Socialism. See Frings, *The Mind of Max Scheler*, 11. Frings, Scheler's most devoted English-language proponent, took over the editorship of Scheler's *Gesammelte Werke* from his widow, Maria Scheler. The obvious starting points for Scheler study are Frings, *Max Scheler: A Concise Introduction into the World of a Great Thinker* (Pittsburgh: Duquesne University Press, 1965), and *The Mind of Max Scheler*. John Raphael Staude, *Max Scheler, 1874–1928: An Intellectual Portrait* (New York: Free Press, 1967) is also valuable. Maurice Dupuy, *La philosophie de Max Scheler: Son évolution et son unité* (Paris: Presses universitaires de France, 1959), offers a thorough reconstruction of his work with the aim of demonstrating its inner coherence. Eugene Kelly—*Max Scheler* (Boston: Twayne, 1997) and *Structure and Diversity: Studies in the Phenomenological Philosophy of Max Scheler* (Dordrecht: Kluwer, 1997)—has contributed to the more recent rehabilitation, as has Stephen Schneck, whose *Person and Polis: Max Scheler's Personalism as Political Theory* (Albany: State University of New York Press, 1987) attempts to recover

Scheler's personalism for political theory. Still more recently, see Hans Joas, *The Genesis of Values* (Chicago: University of Chicago Press, 2000), 84 -102, and Peter H. Spader, *Scheler's Ethical Personalism: Its Logic, Development, and Promise* (New York: Fordham University Press, 2002).

10. James Chappel, "Slaying the Leviathan: Catholicism and the Rebirth of European Conservatism, 1920–1950" (Ph.D. diss., Columbia University, 2012).

11. Max Scheler, "Phenomenology and the Theory of Cognition," in id., *Selected Philosophical Essays* (Evanston, IL: Northwestern University Press, 1973), 137.

12. See Scheler, *Gesammelte Werke*, vol. 7: *Die Deutsche Philosophie der Gegenwart* (Bern: Francke, 1973), 308. Scheler had worked at the University of Jena under the philosopher Rudolf Eucken, who promoted a sturdy morality and renewed spirituality in a series of widely read essays, which, he hoped, would prompt "the rebirth of culture" (Eucken, *The Meaning and Value of Life* [London: Black, 1916)] v; cf. Meyrick Booth, ed., *Collected Essays of Rudolf Eucken* [London: T. Fisher Unwin, 1914], 35–100). The 1908 Nobel laureate in literature, Eucken was an influential thinker in his time, but is little known today and survives chiefly as a minor protagonist in several German dramas of the fin-de-siècle: the demise of psychologism, the rise of cultural holism, and the decline of academic mandarins. See Martin Kusch, *Psychologism: A Case Study in the Sociology of Philosophical Knowledge* (London: Routledge, 1995); Mitchell Ash, *Gestalt Psychology in German Culture, 1890–1967: Holism and the Quest for Objectivity* (Cambridge: Cambridge University Press, 1995); and Fritz Ringer, *The Decline of the German Mandarins: The German Academic Community, 1890–1933* (Cambridge, MA: Harvard University Press, 1969). Scheler retained many of Eucken's themes and concerns.

13. Husserl's phenomenological reduction, which suspended reality and provided the gateway to the transcendental realm, came in for particular anathema—even though at times Scheler advanced an alternate reduction as a spiritual *Technik* for revealing the realm of essences. For a discussion, see Eberhard Avé-Lallemant, "Die phänomenologische Reduktion in der Philosophie Max Schelers," in Good, ed., *Max Scheler im Gegenwartsgeschehen der Philosophie*, 159–78.

14. For discussions of his ambivalent position in phenomenology, see Kelly, *Max Scheler*, and Herbert Spiegelberg, *The Phenomenological Movement: A Historical Introduction*, pt. 1 (1960; 3rd ed., The Hague: Nijhoff, 1984), 268–305.

15. Max Scheler, "Phenomenology and the Theory of Cognition," in id., *Selected Philosophical Essays* (Evanston, IL: Northwestern University Press, 1973), 138.

16. Ibid., 141, 143.

17. Ibid.,154, 177–78.

18. Max Scheler, "The Idols of Self-Knowledge," in id., *Selected Philosophical Essays*, 76.

19. Scheler, "The Theory of the Three Facts," in id., *Selected Philosophical Essays*, 202–87.

20. Scheler, "Phenomenology and the Theory of Cognition," 155. *Malgré* Scheler, Husserl acknowledged this problem in 1901: "[T]here is a well-justified distinction between evident and non-evident, or between infallible and fallible perception. But, if one understands by outer perception (as one naturally does, and as Brentano also does) the perception of physical things, properties, events etc., and classes all other perceptions as inner perceptions, then such a division will not coincide at all with the division previously given. For not every perception of the ego, nor every perception of a psychic state referred to the ego, is certainly evident" (Husserl, *Logical Investigations*, trans. J. N. Findlay [New York: Routledge, 1970], 859).

21. Scheler, "Idols of Self-Knowledge," 3.

22. Scheler, "Idols of Self-Knowledge," 14–15.

23. Scheler, "Phenomenology and the Theory of Cognition," 148–49.

24. Scheler, *On the Eternal in Man* (New Brunswick, NJ: Transaction, 2010), 198.

25. Scheler, "Idols of Self-Knowledge," 38.

26. Scheler, "Ordo Amoris," in id., *Selected Philosophical Essays*, 102–3.

27. Scheler, *On the Eternal in Man*, 209.

28. Ibid., 205, 208.

29. See Graham McAleer's Introduction to Scheler, *The Nature of Sympathy* (New Brunswick, NJ: Transaction, 2008), as well as chaps. 5 and 6. Scheler's attitude toward Indian thought evolved over his career. At first he denigrated it in comparison to Western Christianity, but by the 1920s, he had come to see Buddhism as a valuable corrective to the West's go-getting individualism and exploitation of nature. See Scheler, "The Meaning of Suffering," in id., *On Feeling, Knowing, and Valuing* (Chicago: University of Chicago Press, 1992), 99–105.

30. Patočka, "Max Scheler—Versuch einer Gesamtcharakteristik," in Ludger Hagedorn and Hans Rainer Sepp, eds., *Jan Patočka: Texte, Dokumente, Bibliographie* (Freiburg: Karl Alber, 1999), 379.

31. Scheler confronted Kant directly rather than taking on the latter-day Neo-Kantians. On Neo-Kantianism, see Klaus Köhnke, *The Rise of Neo-Kantianism* (Cambridge: Cambridge University Press, 1991); Thomas E. Willey, *Back to Kant: The Revival of Kantianism in German Social and Historical Thought, 1860–1914* (Detroit: Wayne State University Press, 1978).

32. Max Scheler, *Formalism in Ethics and Non-Formal Ethics of Values*, trans. Manfred S. Frings and Roger L. Funk (Evanston, IL: Northwestern University Press, 1973), 6.

33. Ibid., 214.

34. In Scheler's view, it was Luther who launched the modern descent to individualism and materialism. Subjectivism was a "child of Protestantism." Scheler, *On the Eternal in Man*, 283, 363.

35. Scheler, *Formalism in Ethics and Non-Formal Ethics of Values*, 63. See Pascal's *Pensées*, §IV, 277: "Le cœur a ses raisons, que la raison ne connaît point" (The heart has its reasons, which reason does not know).

36. Scheler, *Formalism in Ethics and Non-Formal Ethics of Values*, 14–15.

37. Ibid., 256, 258.

38. Ibid., 260.

39. Ibid., 68.

40. Ibid., 201.

41. Scheler, "Ordo Amoris," 100.

42. Scheler, *Formalism in Ethics and Non-Formal Ethics of Values*, 247.

43. Ibid., 328–44. He distinguished higher values from lower by their greater endurance, indivisibility, foundational quality, capacity for offering deep contentment, and absoluteness.

44. Ibid., 42. The emphasis on movement foreshadowed Patočka.

45. Lewis Coser, "Max Scheler: An Introduction," in Scheler, *Ressentiment* (New York: Schocken Books, 1972), 14; Scheler, *Formalism in Ethics and Non-Formal Ethics of Values*, 142.

46. Scheler, *Formalism in Ethics and Non-Formal Ethics of Values*, 270.

47. Ibid., 305, 349.

48. Ibid., 361, 359.

49. Ibid., 372–73.

50. Ibid., 383, 371.

51. Ibid., 390, 428–29.

52. Ibid., 289. Scheler used many metaphors to describe man's liminality: a boundary, a transition, a between, a moving-through, a crossing-over, a pioneer, a being who is tired of being man, a being who becomes. Scheler, "On the Idea of Man," 192, 194, 195, 197; *Formalism*, 292.

53. Scheler, *Formalism in Ethics and Non-Formal Ethics of Values*, 420, 394.

54. Ibid., 385.

55. Ibid., 488.

56. Ibid., 490, 495.

57. Ibid., 509.

58. Ibid., 495.

59. Ibid., 505.

60. Ibid., 509; and the 1912–14 essay "Exemplars of Person and Leaders," in Scheler, *Person and Self-Value*, (Dordrecht: Nijhoff, 1987), 127–98.

61. Scheler, *Problems of a Sociology of Knowledge* (London: Routledge, 1980), 67.

62. Scheler, *The Nature of Sympathy*, 235.

63. Scheler, *Formalism in Ethics and Non-Formal Ethics of Values*, 533.
64. Scheler, *The Nature of Sympathy*, 254, 256.
65. Ibid., 10. Cf. Husserl, *Logical Investigations*, 278: "Common sense credits us with percepts even of other people's inner experiences; we 'see' their anger, their pain etc. Such talk is quite correct."
66. Scheler, *The Nature of Sympathy*, 46.
67. Ibid., 246.
68. Cf. "Idols of Self-Knowledge," 20–21.
69. Scheler, *The Nature of Sympathy*, 250.
70. These formulations enabled Scheler's designation of man as a transition toward divinity. Embellishing a key phenomenological principle that each act must have its correlate object, Scheler claimed that the innate human "movement" of transcendence presupposed "the quality of the divine, or the quality of the holy, that is given in an infinite fullness of being" (Scheler, *Formalism in Ethics and Non-Formal Ethics of Values*, 292). Phenomenological insight thus assured the ascendancy of being and divinity. God was an ocean, men were rivers, said the Catholic convert. From their source, "the rivers already sense the ocean ahead, toward which they flow" (Scheler, "On the Idea of Man," 192). Man is a God-seeker, the living X that yearns for the divine, even an appearance of God in the stream of life. In this regard, Scheler also rehabilitated Christian virtues such as humility, which "open[ed] the spiritual eyes for all the values in the world"; reverence, which brought to clarity "the depth and fullness of the world and ourselves"; and shame, which protected the values of the person against public exploitation and prurient abuse. See "Zur Rehabilitierung der Tugend," in *Vom Umsturz der Werte: Abhandlungen und Aufsätze* (Bern: Francke, 1955), 21, 27; Scheler, "Shame and Feelings of Modesty," in id., *Person and Self-Value*, 1–85.
71. Scheler, *Nature of Sympathy*, 161.
72. Scheler, *Formalism in Ethics and Non-Formal Ethics of Values*, 488, 113. As we will see, however, Scheler disdained humanitarianism as a false love.
73. Scheler, *The Nature of Sympathy*, 128. Thomas Aquinas defined knowledge as the participation of the knower in the known, an epistemology that is quite distinct from either the grasp of a priori forms or the correlation with empirical reality. Kenneth W. Stikkers's Introduction to Scheler's *Problems of a Sociology of Knowledge* is helpful on this point.
74. Scheler, *Formalism in Ethics and Non-Formal Ethics of Values*, 305, 496–98. Scheler's notion of solidarity was informed partly by his reception of the French fin-de-siècle solidarism of Léon Bourgeois and Émile Durkheim, a connection noted in Chappel, "Slaying the Leviathan," 103–4.
75. For a discussion of Scheler's critique of capitalism, see Schneck, *Person and Polis*, 90–94.

76. Scheler, *Ressentiment*, 45–46. The full title of the original volume, *Das Ressentiment im Aufbau der Moralen* (*Ressentiment in the Construction of Morals*), highlights Scheler's ethical preoccupations.

77. Ibid., 50.

78. Ibid., 68.

79. Ibid., 59.

80. Scheler, *Formalism in Ethics and Non-Formal Ethics of Values*, 268.

81. Scheler, *Ressentiment*, 67. Cf. Scheler, "Idealism and Realism," in id., *Selected Philosophical Essays*, 295.

82. Scheler, *Ressentiment*, 69, 60.

83. Maurice Merleau-Ponty, "Christianity and Ressentiment," *Review of Existential Psychology and Psychiatry* 9 (Winter 1968): 12.

84. Scheler, *Ressentiment*, 121, 116.

85. Ibid., 121–23.

86. Scheler, *On the Eternal in Man*, 367–71. Erich Voegelin, himself indebted to Scheler's philosophical anthropology, famously complained of this tendency in modern thought.

87. Scheler, *Ressentiment*, 96.

88. Ibid., 89, 143.

89. Ibid., 90–91.

90. Ibid., 94.

91. Ibid., 90–91.

92. Ibid., 102.

93. Scheler, *Formalism in Ethics and Non-Formal Ethics of Values*, 533. For essays on Scheler's social philosophy, see Ralf Becker, Christian Bermes, and Heinz Leonardy, *Die Bildung der Gesellschaft: Schelers Sozialphilosophie im Kontext* (Würzburg: Königshausen & Neumann, 2007). This volume is one of several that the Max Scheler Gesellschaft has organized to apply Scheler to contemporary themes.

94. Stefanos Geroulanos, *An Atheism That Is Not Humanist Emerges in French Thought* (Stanford, CA: Stanford University Press, 2010), 115.

95. Scheler, *Ressentiment*, 118–19, 170.

96. Scheler, *Formalism in Ethics and Non-Formal Ethics of Values*, 525.

97. Roland N. Stromberg highlights Scheler's bellicosity in *Redemption by War: The Intellectuals and 1914* (Lawrence: Regents Press of Kansas, 1982). Kusch, *Psychologism*, 216–19, also reviews Scheler's propaganda.

98. The epigraph to *Der Genius des Krieges und der Deutsche Krieg* is a couplet from Friedrich Schiller's *Die Braut von Messina* (1803): "Aber der Krieg auch hat seine Ehre, / der Beweger des Menschengeschicks" ("War too has its honor, / the mover of man's fate"). In Scheler, *Gesammelte Werke*, vol. 4: *Politisch-Pädagogische Schriften*, (Bern: Francke, 1982).

99. Ibid., 12, 68.

100. Ibid., 108. Scheler's vision was a virulent expression of a wider nineteenth-century transformation from the view of warfare as a legal procedure to be deployed and contained by sovereign combatants to a vision of war as a "Handmaiden of History" (258) and national destiny, uncontained and limitless precisely because it was bound to supposedly millennial struggles over justice, morality, and right. See James Q. Whitman, *The Verdict of Battle: The Law of Victory and the Making of Modern War* (Cambridge, MA: Harvard University Press, 2012).

101. Scheler, "Europa und der Krieg," in id., *Politisch-Pädagogische Schriften*, 253.

102. Scheler, "Der Krieg als Gesamterlebnis," in id., *Politisch-Pädagogische Schriften*, 282; and "Soziologische Neuorientierung und die Aufgabe der deutschen Katholiken nach dem Krieg," ibid., 373–472.

103. Scheler, *On the Eternal in Man*, 361.

104. Ibid., 373, 375.

105. Ibid., 379.

106. Ibid., 379, 383.

107. Ibid., 384–86.

108. Ibid., 387–88.

109. Ibid., 389–90.

110. Ibid., 416. For a modern Catholic application of Scheler's notion of co-responsibility, see John F. Crosby, "Max Scheler's Principle of Moral and Religious Solidarity," *Communio Viatorum* 24, no. 1 (1997): 110–27.

111. Scheler, *On the Eternal in Man*, 421, 429.

112. Scheler, "The Meaning of Suffering," 113.

113. Scheler, *On the Eternal in Man*, 363, 116–17. On pantheism in interwar Germany, see Benjamin Lazier, *God Interrupted: Heresy and the European Imagination between the World Wars* (Princeton, NJ: Princeton University Press, 2008).

114. See John R. White, "Exemplary Persons and Ethics: The Significance of St. Francis for the Philosophy of Max Scheler," *American Catholic Philosophical Quarterly* 70, no. 1 (Winter 2005): 59–90. As opposed to pantheism, panentheism did not reduce God to the natural world, but saw the world as imbued with a God who nonetheless maintained his heavenly berth.

115. Scheler, *On the Eternal in Man*, 38.

116. Ibid., 42, 46.

117. Ibid., 57–8. For a later essay in the phenomenological tradition that employs the concept of repentance and change of heart to explain interpersonal forgiveness, see Aurel Kolnai, "Forgiveness," in *Ethics, Value, and Reality: Selected Papers of Aurel Kolnai* (Indianapolis: Hackett, 1978), 211–24.

118. Scheler, *On the Eternal in Man*, 59.

119. Ibid., 109.

120. Ibid., 120.

121. Ibid., 160–62. Scheler cited Rudolf Otto's *The Idea of the Holy* (1917; *Das Heilige: Über das Irrationale in der Idee des Göttlichen und sein Verhältnis zum Rationalen*) as a good example of phenomenology of religion.

122. Scheler, *On the Eternal in Man*, 304.

123. Ibid., 250–51.

124. Ibid., 263–64.

125. Ibid., 250–51, 254.

126. Ibid., 251. The Latin should properly read 'Inquietum est cor nostrum . . . " but the 'est' is missing from Scheler's text. For a review of Scheler's corpus that places special emphasis on his call for religious renewal, see Karl Löwith, "Max Scheler und das Problem einer philosophischen Anthropologie," *Theologische Rundschau* 7 (Winter 1935): 349–72.

127. Scheler, *On the Eternal in Man*, 269. This point would later become important for Karol Wojtyła.

128. Ibid., 267.

129. The end of Scheler's second marriage was prompted by an affair he had with a student, who later became his third wife.

130. Anthropology occupied Scheler long before his later so-called anthropological phase. See the opening statement of his 1915 essay "On the Idea of Man," *Journal of the British Society for Phenomenology* 9, no. 3 (October 1978): 184–98: "In a certain sense all of the central problems of philosophy can be said to lead us back to the questions of what man is and what the metaphysical position and status is which he occupies within the totality of being, world and God" (184). On philosophical anthropology, see Peter E. Gordon, *Continental Divide: Heidegger, Cassirer, Davos* (Cambridge, MA: Harvard University Press, 2010), 69–77; Axel Honneth and Hans Joas, *Social Action and Human Nature* (Cambridge: Cambridge University Press, 1989); Joachim Fischer, *Philosophische Anthropologie: Eine Denkrichtung der 20. Jahrhundert* (Freiburg: Karl Alber, 2008); Karl-Siegbert Rehberg, "Philosophische Anthropologie und die 'Soziologisierung' des Wissens vom Menschen," *Kölner Zeitschrift für Soziologie und Sozialpsychologie* 23 (1981): 160–98; Jürgen Habermas, "Philosophische Anthropologie (ein Lexikonartikel) 1958," in id., *Kultur und Kritik: Verstreute Aufsätze* (Frankfurt: Suhrkamp, 1973), 87–111.

131. Scheler, "The Forms of Knowledge and Culture," in id., *Philosophical Perspectives*, (Boston: Beacon Press, 1958), 42.

132. Ibid., 43.

133. For Scheler on feminism, see "Concerning the Meaning of the Feminist Movement" (1913), *Philosophical Forum* 9, no. 1 (1978): 42–54. A comment by Hilde Hein follows the essay.

134. Scheler, "Man in the Era of Adjustment," in id., *Philosophical Perspectives*, 107, 112.

135. Ibid., 115, 122.

136. Scheler, *Problems of a Sociology of Knowledge*, 182. A more literal translation of "Der Mohr hat seine Schuldigkeit getan" would read "The Moor has done his duty," but the version cited appears in the English translation of Scheler's text.

137. Scheler, "Man in the Era of Adjustment," 101–2.

138. Scheler, *The Human Place in the Cosmos* (Evanston, IL: Northwestern University Press, 2009), 51. For an appreciative but critical appraisal of this work, see Ernst Cassirer, "'Spirit' and 'Life' in Contemporary Philosophy," in Paul Arthur Schilpp, ed., *The Philosophy of Ernst Cassirer* (Evanston, IL: Library of Living Philosophers, 1949), 857–80.

139. Scheler, *Human Place*, 47.

140. Ibid., 66.

141. Ibid., 28.

142. Scheler, "Man and History," 65; "The Philosopher's Outlook," 11, both in id., *Philosophical Perspectives*.

CHAPTER 5

1. Helmuth Plessner, *Husserl in Göttingen* (New York: Garland, 1980), 6, 9.

2. Ibid., 10.

3. Helmuth Plessner, *Die Stufen des Organischen und der Mensch: Einleitung in die philosophische Anthropologie* (1928; 2nd ed., Berlin: De Gruyter, 1965), 29.

4. Plessner, *Husserl in Göttingen*, 9.

5. In his Foreword to *Stufen des Organischen*, Plessner insisted that Scheler remained a phenomenologist to the end, disputing those who saw Scheler's late phase as a deviation from his original agenda.

6. Nicolai Hartmann, *Ethics*, vol. 1: *Moral Phenomena* (London: Allen & Unwin, 1967), 15–16, 168–72, 177–78, 183, 204. For a recent analysis of Hartmann's ethics, see Eugene Kelly, *Material Ethics of Value: Max Scheler and Nicolai Hartmann* (Dordrecht: Springer, 2011).

7. Hartmann, *Ethics*, 1: 16–17, 60–61. On Hartmann's Platonism, see Eva Hauel Cadwallader, *Searchlight on Values: Nicolai Hartmann's Twentieth-Century Value Platonism* (Lanham, MD: University Press of America, 1984); Andreas Kinneging, "Hartmann's Platonic Ethics," in Roberto Poli, Carlo Scognamiglio, and Frederic Trembley, eds., *The Philosophy of Nicolai Hartmann* (Berlin: De Gruyter, 2011), 195–220.

8. Hartmann, *Ethics*, 1: 67.

9. Ibid., 177.

10. Ibid., 185.

11. Ibid., 218.
12. Ibid., 265, 261. In Hartmann, *Ethics*, vol. 3: *Moral Freedom* (New Brunswick, NJ: Transaction, 2004), freedom is thus examined as an intrinsically moral distinction.
13. Hartmann, *Ethics*, 1: 272–73.
14. Ibid., 268. On Hartmann's personalism, see Helen James, "Nicolai Hartmann's Study of Human Personality," *The New Scholasticism* 34 (1960): 204–33.
15. Hartmann, *Ethics*, vol. 2: *Moral Values* (New Brunswick, NJ: Transaction, 2003), 65.
16. Ibid., 52–3.
17. Presaging Patočka, Hartmann invoked Heraclitus's *polemos* to describe the antagonisms of the value sphere. Ibid., 94.
18. Leszek Kołakowski, who appears in a subsequent chapter, adopted a similarly sober "ethics without a moral code." Kołakowski, "Ethics without a Moral Code," *TriQuarterly* 22 (Fall 1971): 153–82.
19. Hartmann, *Ethics*, 2: 189. The phrase, as we know, was Scheler's, borrowed from Pascal.
20. Ibid., 373.
21. Ibid., 357.
22. Ibid., 210.
23. Hartmann, *Ethics*, 1: 290; *Ethics*, 2: 147
24. Hartmann, *Ethics*, 2: 463.
25. Ibid., 144, 385. Cadwallader, *Searchlight on Values*, 89–102. Her metaphor distills the following passage from Hartmann: "In the revolution of the ethos, the values themselves do not shift. Their nature is super-temporal, super-historical. But the consciousness of them shifts. From the whole realm it cuts out, for the time being, a little circle of something seen. And this little circle 'wanders about' on the ideal plane of values" (*Ethics*, 1: 88–89)
26. Hartmann, *Ethics*, 1: 36.
27. Ibid., 45.
28. Ibid., 42.
29. See Ernst Wenisch's introduction to Dietrich von Hildebrand, *Memoiren und Aufsätze gegen den Nationalsozialismus, 1933–1938* (Mainz: Matthias Grünewald, 1994), 15–16. Like other realists, Hildebrand observed "with great pain" Husserl's transcendental violation of reality (ibid., 15).
30. For favorable takes on Hildebrand, see Balduin V. Schwarz, ed., *The Human Person and the World of Values: A Tribute to Dietrich von Hildebrand by His Friends in Philosophy* (New York: Fordham University Press, 1960); and Alice von Hildebrand, *The Soul of a Lion: Dietrich von Hildebrand* (San Francisco: Ignatius, 2000). For a review of his early ethics, see Karla Mertens, "Hinweise auf Dietrich v. Hildebrands Ethisches Werk," the afterword to the 1969 German edition of Hildebrand's *Die Idee der sittlichen Handlung/Sittlichkeit und ethische*

Werterkenntnis (Darmstadt: Wissenschaftliche Buchgesellschaft, 1969), 269–78. On the relation between personalism and resistance, see Josef Seifert, "Personalistische Philosophie und der Widerstand gegen Hitler," in Seifert, ed., *Dietrich von Hildebrand's Kampf gegen den Nationalsozialismus* (Heidelberg: C. Winter, 1998), 107–63.

31. For a brief account of Hildebrand's early philosophical mentors and friends, see Alice von Hildebrand, "Dietrich von Hildebrand's Acquaintance with Early Phenomenology," in Kimberly Baltzer-Jaray, ed., *Selected Papers on the Early Phenomenology: Munich and Göttingen, Quaestiones Disputatae* 3, no. 1 (2012): 7–19.

32. Dietrich von Hildebrand, "Die Idee der sittlichen Handlung," *Jahrbuch für Philosophie und phänomenologische Forschung* 3 (1916): 126–251. On Husserl's appreciation, see Karl Schuhmann, "Husserl und Hildebrand," *Aletheia* 5 (1992): 6–33.

33. On the spontaneity of *Stellungnahme*, whose most basic form was "for or against," see Hildebrand, "Idee," 138. The concept came from Reinach (ibid., 140), but Husserl had also anticipated it in his 1914 ethics lectures.

34. Dietrich von Hildebrand, *Fundamental Moral Attitudes* (Freeport, NY: Books for Libraries Press, 1950), 3.

35. On the *Wertantwort*, see Josef Seifert, "Dietrich von Hildebrands Philosophische Entdeckung der 'Wertantwort' und die Grundlegung der Ethik," *Aletheia* 5 (1992): 34–58.

36. Hildebrand, "Idee," 154. On the Schelerian centrality of feeling, see Hildebrand, "Sittlichkeit und ethische Werterkenntnis," *Jahrbuch für Philosophie und phänomenologische Forschung* 5 (1922): 463–602. Hildebrand's student Balduin Schwarz, in "Dietrich von Hildebrand on Value," *Thought* 24 (1949): 655–76, points out that all values, as per Scheler, stood in a hierarchy leading to the divine.

37. On the history of the *Sachverhalt* concept, see Kimberly Baltzer-Jaray, *Doorway to the World of Essences: Adolf Reinach and the Early Phenomenological Movement* (Saarbrücken: Müller, 2009), 41–66.

38. Hildebrand, "Idee," 214.

39. Hildebrand, "Sittlichkeit und ethische Werterkenntnis," 548.

40. Ibid., 587.

41. Dietrich von Hildebrand, *In Defense of Purity: An Analysis of the Catholic Ideals of Purity and Virginity* (Baltimore: Helicon, 1962); Hildebrand, *Marriage: The Mystery of Faithful Love* (Manchester, NH: Sophia Institute, 1984). See also id., *Liturgy and Personality: The Healing Power of Formal Prayer* (1933; New York: Longmans, Green, 1943), a book that defended Catholic liturgy as an essential element of worship. Husserl too, we may recall, took the *Liebesgemeinschaft* as a communal ideal.

42. Dietrich von Hildebrand, *Die Metaphysik der Gemeinschaft* (Regensburg: Josef Habbel, 1955), 304.

43. Ibid., 9.
44. Ibid., 118
45. Ibid., 185, 397.
46. Hildebrand, "Die korporative Idee und die natürlichen Gemeinschaften," *Der katholische Gedanke* 6 (1933): 48–58. "The higher the domain of value," he continued, "the deeper the stratum in the person to which it beckons, and the more it addresses itself not only to the individual, but rather to the community" (56). The passages are cited in James Chappel's "Slaying the Leviathan: Catholicism and the Rebirth of European Conservatism, 1920–1950" (Ph.D. diss., Columbia University, 2012), 224.
47. On a 1921 trip to Paris, Hildebrand had condemned German nationalism and blamed his country for launching the Great War. His resistance to German patriotism during World War I stood in marked contrast to the attitudes of Husserl, Scheler, Reinach, and other contemporary phenomenologists. On Hildebrand's battle against Nazism, see Ernst Wenisch's introduction to *Memoiren und Aufsätze*, as well as a concluding essay by Balduin Schwarz; and the essays collected in Seifert, ed., *Dietrich von Hildebrand's Kampf*. On Hildebrand's remark about World War I, see John Connelly, *From Enemy to Brother: The Revolution in Catholic Teaching on the Jews, 1933–1965* (Cambridge, MA: Harvard University Press, 2012), 109, which contains a longer discussion of Hildebrand and the Jew-turned-Catholic priest Johannes Österreicher in chapter 4 (94–146). After his flight to the United States, Österreicher profiled the frequent conversion of philosophers—including the four phenomenologists Husserl, Reinach, Scheler, and Stein—from Judaism to Christianity in *Walls Are Crumbling: Seven Jewish Philosophers Discover Christ* (New York: Devin-Adair, 1953). He helped to draft Vatican II's renunciation of anti-Semitism in the declaration *Nostra Aetate*.
48. Chappel, "Slaying the Leviathan," 200–246; Chappel, "The Catholic Origins of Totalitarianism Theory in Interwar Europe," *Modern Intellectual History* 8, no. 3 (2011).
49. Rudolf Ebneth has written an excellent monograph on Hildebrand's Austrian journal, entitled *Die österreichische Wochenschrift "Der christliche Ständestaat": Deutsche Emigration in Österreich, 1933–1938* (Mainz: Matthias Grünewald, 1976).
50. Elke Seefried, *Reich und Stände: Ideen und Wirken des deutschen politischen Exils in Österreich, 1933–1938* (Düsseldorf: Droste, 2006), 251. Quoted in Chappel, "Slaying the Leviathan," 205.
51. Hildebrand, *Memoiren und Aufsätze*, 166.
52. Ibid., 168, 191; *Menschheit am Scheideweg*, 288. "The individual is not a citizen in the first instance," Hildebrand wrote in 1929. Quoted in Chappel, "Catholic Origins," 573.
53. Hildebrand, *Memoiren und Aufsätze*, 318. Man's highest aim, Hildebrand argued, is likeness to God and orientation toward the divine (232).

54. Ibid., 168, 236–37.

55. Hildebrand, "The World Crisis and Human Personality," *Thought* 16 (1941): 457–72; id., *Memoiren und Aufsätze*, 198.

56. Hildebrand, *Memoiren und Aufsätze*, 171. Hildebrand was fond of emphasizing, in phenomenological fashion, that his criticism concerned not simply the *activities* of Nazism, but its ideological essence.

57. Hildebrand, "Das Chaos der Zeit und die Rangordnung der Werte," in id., *Memoiren und Aufsätze*, 185.

58. Hildebrand, *Memoiren und Aufsätze*, 205.

59. Connelly, *From Enemy to Brother*, 130–33; Hildebrand, "Die Juden und das christliche Abendland," in id., *Memoiren und Aufsätze*, 340–58. Hildebrand himself had a Jewish grandmother.

60. A. G. Kraus, "Der religiöse Antisemitismus im Lichte des Katholischen Dogmas," *Der Christliche Ständestaat* 8 (April 1934): 5–6. On Kraus, see Connelly, *From Enemy to Brother*, 113–15; and Gerhard Rexin, "Kraus, Annie," in *Biographisch-bibliographisches Kirchenlexicon*, vol. 30 (Nordhausen: Bautz, 2009), 810–14.

61. On Gurian, see esp. Chappel, "Catholic Origins" and "Slaying the Leviathan."

62. Quoted in Francis Dunlop, *The Life and Thought of Aurel Kolnai* (Aldershot, UK: Ashgate, 2002), 137.

63. Ibid., 147.

64. Because it falls outside the scope of this brief discussion, I do not examine here Kolnai's most famous essay, "On Disgust," published in Husserl's *Jahrbuch* in 1929. One of three essays on negative feelings, it provides a phenomenology of an emotion that reveals disvalue, namely, the potentially dangerous threat of formless life verging on death. Kolnai, *On Disgust* (Chicago: Open Court, 2004). For a recent book inspired by Kolnai's analysis, see Colin McGinn, *The Meaning of Disgust* (Oxford: Oxford University Press, 2011).

65. On Kolnai, see Francis Dunlop, *The Life and Thought of Aurel Kolnai*; Lee Congdon, *Exile and Social Thought: Hungarian Intellectuals in Germany and Austria, 1919–1933* (Princeton, NJ: Princeton University Press, 1991), 233–53; Zoltán Balázs and Francis Dunlop, eds., *Exploring the World of Human Practice: Readings in and about the Philosophy of Aurel Kolnai* (Budapest: Central European University, 2004).

66. Aurel Kolnai, *Political Memoirs* (Lanham, MD: Lexington Books, 1999), 126. By his account, it was a course by the psychologist Karl Bühler that first stimulated his interest in Husserl and Brentano (ibid., 129).

67. Kolnai, "Ethical Value and Reality," in Dunlop, ed., *Early Ethical Writings of Aurel Kolnai* (Aldershot, UK: Ashgate, 2002), 26.

68. Aurel Kolnai, *Sexual Ethics: The Meaning and Foundations of Sexual Morality* (Aldershot, UK: Ashgate, 2005), 2–3. Echoing Hildebrand and presaging Wojtyła, the book presents sexuality as central to a loving marriage, not simply a means of reproduction.

69. Kolnai, *Early Ethical Writings*, xi–xiv. "Ethical Value and Reality" was published in 1927.

70. Kolnai, "Ethical Value and Reality," in id., *Early Ethical Writings*, 4.

71. Ibid., 12.

72. Ibid., 3, 27.

73. Ibid., 59.

74. Ibid., 62.

75. Ibid., 136–37.

76. Ibid., 59.

77. Ibid., 43, 105.

78. Ibid., 157–58.

79. Kolnai's descriptors are abundant: the person is "an axiological 'manifold,'" a "conjunction of experiences and acts . . . laid around an ethical core," responsible and willing "to take on obligations" (ibid., 21, 147, 155).

80. Kolnai, "Duty, Inclination, and 'Moral-Mindedness'" (1928) in id., *Early Ethical Writings*, 191; id., "Ethical Value and Reality," 156.

81. Kolnai, "Ethical Value and Reality," 56.

82. Ibid., 158; id., "Duty, Inclination, and 'Moral-Mindedness,'" 190.

83. Kolnai, "The Structure of Moral Intention" (1928), in id., *Early Ethical Writings*, 169–81.

84. Kolnai, "Ethical Value and Reality," 94.

85. Ibid., 34. At the same time, more far-ranging ethical concerns and responsibilities could reveal "a calling of solitary dignity" (ibid., 144). There was simply no formula.

86. Kolnai, "Fascismus und Bolschewismus," *Der deutsche Volkswirt* 1, no. 7 (1926): 206–13; "Rechts und Links in der Politik," ibid. 23, no. 2 (1927): 665–71; and *The War against the West* (New York: Viking, 1938), 19. The best review of Kolnai's Vienna journalism is in Congdon, *Exile and Social Thought*, 241–53.

87. Aurel Kolnai, "Die Ideologie des sozialen Fortschritts," *Der deutsche Volkswirt* 1, no. 30 (1927): 933–36; "Kritik des sozialen Fortschritts," ibid., no. 31 (1927): 965–69.

88. Kolnai seconded G. K. Chesterton's condemnation of the servile capitalist state in which property is plutocratically concentrated. Kolnai, "Der Abbau des Kapitalismus: Die Soziallehren G. K. Chestertons," *Der deutsche Volkswirt* 1, no. 44 (1927): 1382–86.

89. Kolnai, "Fascismus und Bolschewismus," 213.

90. Aurel Kolnai, "Gegenrevolution," pts. 1 and 2, *Kölner Vierteljahrshefte für Soziologie* 10, nos. 2 and 3 (1931–32): 171–99, 295–319. On Nazism as counterrevolution, see also Kolnai, *War against the West*, 672.

91. Aurel Kolnai, "What Is Politics About?" in Balázs and Dunlop, eds., *Exploring the World of Human Practice*, 31, 34. Carl Schmitt's 1927 classic, revised and republished in 1932, is *The Concept of the Political* (Chicago: University of Chicago Press, 1996). For a recent summary of it, see Martin Jay, *The Virtues of Mendacity: On Lying in Politics* (Charlottesville: University of Virginia Press, 2010), 86–9.

92. See, e.g., Aurel Kolnai, "Persönlichkeit und Massenherrschaft," *Der österreichische Volkswirt* 26, no. 1 (1933–34): 444.

93. Aurel Kolnai, "Die Aufgabe des Konservatismus," *Der österreichische Volkswirt* 26, no. 2 (1934): 944.

94. Aurel Kolnai, "Katholizismus und Demokratie," *Der österreichische Volkswirt* 26, no. 1 (1933–34): 319; Kolnai, "Persönlichkeit und Massenherrschaft," 442. In her Introduction to Kolnai, *Political Memoirs*, xi, Francesca Murphy identifies constitutional monarchy—at once conservative and democratic—as his ideal.

95. Kolnai also expressed guarded concern with the Catholic embrace of corporatism in the 1931 encyclical *Quadragesimo Anno*. See Aurel Kolnai, "Quadragesimo Anno," *Der österreichische Volkswirt* 23, no. 2 (1931): 892.

96. Kolnai, *Political Memoirs*, 140–41.

97. Wiggins and Williams co-introduced a volume of Kolnai's later essays entitled *Ethics, Value, and Reality* (Indianapolis: Hackett, 1978), ix–xxv. Pierre Manent admired Kolnai's anti-utopian thought, most famously articulated in "The Utopian Mind," in Dunlop, ed., *The Utopian Mind and Other Papers* (London: Athlone, 1995), 1–129. See David Wiggins, "Aurel Kolnai and Utopia," and Manent, "Aurel Kolnai: A Political Philosopher Confronts the Scourge of Our Epoch," in Balázs and Dunlop, eds., *Exploring the World of Human Practice*, 219–30, 207–18.

98. Quoted in Hedwig Conrad-Martius, introduction to Adolf Reinach, *Gesammelte Schriften* (Halle: Max Niemeyer, 1921), xxxvii. Edith Stein edited the collection with Conrad-Martius.

99. These fragments are collected in Adolf Reinach, *Sämtliche Werke*, vol.1, ed. Karl Schuhmann and Barry Smith (Munich: Philosophia, 1989), 589–611.

100. After Reinach's death, his widow, who had joined him in Protestant conversion, converted finally to Catholicism. For Stein, the final nudge came from a 1921 reading of Teresa of Avila's autobiography while she was staying in Conrad-Martius's country home.

101. Predictably, Stein has attracted significant scholarly interest. The most widely regarded biography is Waltraud Herbstrich, *Edith Stein: A Biography* (San

Francisco: Harper & Row, 1985). For excellent interpretations of her thought, see Marianne Sawicki, *Body, Text, and Science: The Literacy of Investigative Practices and the Phenomenology of Edith Stein* (Dordrecht: Kluwer, 1997), and Alasdair MacIntyre, *Edith Stein: A Philosophical Prologue, 1913–1922* (Lanham, MD: Rowman & Littlefield, 2006). Other useful introductions are Elisabeth Endres, *Edith Stein: Christliche Philosophin und jüdische Märtyrerin* (Munich: Piper, 1987), Mary Catherine Baseheart, *Person in the World: Introduction to the Philosophy of Edith Stein* (Dordrecht: Kluwer, 1997), and Sarah Borden, *Edith Stein* (London: Continuum, 2003). For a review of the literature on Stein through the late 1990s, see Sawicki, *Body, Text, and Science*, 184–221.

On Wilhelm Stern's psychologistic personalism, see James T. Lamiell, *Beyond Individual and Group Differences: Human Individuality, Scientific Psychology, and William Stern's Critical Personalism* (Thousand Oaks, CA: Sage, 2003), and *William Stern (1871–1938): A Brief Introduction to His Life and Works* (Lengerich, Germany: Pabst Science Publishers, 2010). Stern's 1897 essay "Mental Presence-Time" (in Burt Hopkins and Steven Galt Crowell, eds., *The New Yearbook for Phenomenology and Phenomenological Philosophy* [Seattle: Noesis, 2005], 325–51) influenced Husserl's analysis of time consciousness, and Stern's son Günther became a Husserl student in Freiburg (Nicolas de Warren, *Husserl and the Promise of Time* [Cambridge: Cambridge University Press, 2009], 92–96).

102. See John Paul II, "Pope's Remarks about Edith Stein [at her beatification]," *Carmelite Studies* 4 (1987): 295–309, and *L'Osservatore Romano*, weekly English ed., 14 October 1998, 1, on her canonization.

103. Although she was not credited with authorship in the 1952 publication, many of the manuscripts were in such disarray that her contribution was necessarily extensive. Her involvement in the sections on the body and empathy, the topic of her dissertation, was probably quite substantial and has led to questions about the accuracy of *Ideas II* as a reflection of Husserl's thought. For a description of his tortured working style and a defense of Stein's heavy redaction, see Roman Ingarden and Edith Stein, "Edith Stein on Her Activity as an Assistant of Edmund Husserl," *Philosophy and Phenomenological Research* 23, no. 2 (December 1962): 155–75. The most detailed reconstruction of her involvement is in Sawicki, *Body, Text, and Science*, 153–65.

104. Edith Stein, *On the Problem of Empathy* (Washington, DC: Institute of Carmelite Studies, 1989), 3. Her friend and colleague Roman Ingarden felt that she was drawn to this topic due to her inner need for community and her positive experience of it in Göttingen, an experience that her friend Hedwig Conrad-Martius recalled as a new "birth in a common spirit" of Husserlian thought and research. Ingarden, "Über die philosophichen Forschungen Edith Steins," *Freiburger Zeitschrift für Philosophie und Theologie* 2–3 (1979): 472–73. Ingarden's remarks, it bears note, were delivered in 1968 as part of an invited lecture

in Cracow organized by Archbishop Karol Wojtyła. See also Conrad-Martius, "Meine Freundin Edith Stein," in Weltraud Herbstrich, ed., *Denken im Dialog: Zur Philosophie Edith Steins* (Tübingen: Attempto, 1991), 176–77.

105. Adolf Reinach, "Einleitung in die Philosophie," in id., *Sämtliche Werke*, vol. 1 (Munich: Philosophia, 1989), 369–513.

106. Stein, *On the Problem of Empathy*, 10.

107. Ibid., 17, 43.

108. Ibid., 56.

109. Ibid., 64.

110. Ibid., 108.

111. Ibid., 118. Her call was taken up by Kurt Stavenhagen, *Absolute Stellungnahme: Eine ontologische Untersuchung über das Wesen der Religion* (Erlangen: Philosophischen Akademie, 1925), and Jean Héring, *Phénoménologie et philosophie religieuse: Étude sur la théorie de la connaissance religieuse* (Paris: Félix Alcan, 1926).

112. Edith Stein, *Philosophy of Psychology and the Humanities* (Washington, DC: Institute of Carmelite Studies, 1989). While praising her work, Husserl recommended Stein for an academic post only if the profession were open to women, which it was not.

113. Tönnies's distinction, of course, is usually anglicized as community and society.

114. Motivation was, following Pfänder, Stein's form of "sentient causality," linking acts into meaningful wholes (Stein, *Philosophy of Psychology and the Humanities*, 44). The claim against collective personhood was muddied in her subsequent work on the state, but even there she insisted that legislation required free persons and that the state did not constitute an independently acting whole. See Edith Stein, *An Investigation Concerning the State* (Washington, DC: Institute of Carmelite Studies, 2006), 46–52.

115. Stein, *Philosophy of Psychology and the Humanities*, 172.

116. Ibid., 187.

117. Even the demagogue, a pure "association man" seeking to use others to achieve power, postured himself as a "community man." Ibid., 131.

118. Ibid., 203.

119. Ibid., 275.

120. Ibid., 214.

121. Ibid., 226–27.

122. Ibid., 230, 238. Conrad-Martius's *Metaphysische Gespräche* (Halle: Max Niemeyer, 1921), 26–86, is a book-length dialogue between two imagined philosophers, a genre that Stein later adopted for her dialogue between Thomas and Husserl.

123. Stein, *Philosophy of Psychology and the Humanities*, 275.

124. Ibid., 309. Stein delivered a series of lectures between 1928 and 1932 that ascribed the personalist attitude most particularly to women. While women embraced the "living, personal, and whole," men tended toward the abstract. Women had a "singular sensitivity to moral values and an abhorrence for all which is low and mean." Incorporating women into the work world, she concluded, would not only help them combat a tendency toward the subjective; it would also help society as a whole to overcome the "inner disunion" of the age, the tendency toward "one-sided professional work," by restoring an original personal and communitarian harmony. Through an innate "motherliness," women contribute to healing "contemporary sickness" and making humans moral again. Women's redemptive calling was "to bring true humanity in oneself and in others." Edith Stein, *Woman* (Washington, DC: Institute of Carmelite Studies, 1996), 45, 78, 259, 264.

125. Edith Stein, *An Investigation Concerning the State* (Washington, DC: Institute of Carmelite Studies, 2006), 10.

126. Ibid., 40–1, 58–59, 61. "Governing" was Stein's term for the executive or command function of a state. Like Kolnai's, her view contrasted with Carl Schmitt's contemporaneous characterization of the state as primarily the executor of foreign policy, defined in terms of friend-foe relationships.

127. Ibid., 31–32. The need for executors—political, military, legal, and cultural state stewards— is particularly evident in her discussion of social hierarchy, where she even allowed for the possibility of establishing of a class of Platonic state guardians (134–40).

128. Ibid., 50.

129. Ibid., 87, 142.

130. Ibid., 39, 48.

131. Ibid., 150.

132. Ibid., 51, 67, 86–87.

133. Ibid., 50.

134. Ibid., 191.

135. Ibid., 159. The text was completed in 1921, though not published until 1925. Stein was baptized in 1922.

136. Edith Stein, *Life in a Jewish Family, 1891–1916* (Washington, DC: Institute of Carmelite Studies, 2000), 250. Elisabeth de Miribel, *Edith Stein, 1891–1942* (Paris: Seuil, 1954), 73, reports on a 1935 conversation in which Husserl said that phenomenology "converges toward Thomism and prolongs Thomism," indeed that it might someday help the Church surpass neo-Thomism.

137. For an article that finds a similar end in Husserl, see Stephan Strasser, "History, Teleology, and God in the Philosophy of Husserl," *Analecta Husserliana* 9 (1979): 317–33. Regarding Husserl's influence on religious philosophy, see also Jean Héring, "La phenomenology d'Edmund Husserl il y a trente ans: Souvenirs

et réflexions d'un étudiant de 1909," *Revue internationale de philosophie* 1, no. 2 (1939): 366–73.

138. Stein's close friend Fritz Kaufmann felt so betrayed that he cut off correspondence for years, resuming friendship only after fleeing from the Nazis; he ultimately helped to spread her name in the United States. Husserl himself feared that Stein had lost her intellectual autonomy in converting to Catholicism (Husserl, *Briefe an Roman Ingarden*, 22). And her friend Roman Ingarden, while sympathetic to her new endeavors, worried that Stein's embrace of traditional religious premises violated the phenomenological ban on all prior theses in favor of the testimony of pure evidence (Ingarden, "Über die philosophischen Forschungen Edith Steins," 468). As Alasdair MacIntyre shows, Stein's 1931 translation of Aquinas's *Quaestiones disputatae de veritate*, undertaken at the request of the theologian Erich Przywara, elicited complaints from Thomists for miscasting the spiritual master in phenomenological guise (MacIntyre, *Edith Stein*, 177–78). Przywara himself was influenced by the phenomenology of Scheler, Stein, Husserl, and Heidegger, as demonstrated in his formidable 1932 opus *Analogia Entis: Metaphysik; Ur-Struktur und All-Rhythmus* (Munich: Kösel & Pustet, 1932).

139. Edith Stein, *Potency and Act* (Washington, DC: Institute of Carmelite Studies, 2005), 3. The essays "Die weltanschauliche Bedeutung der Phänomenologie," and "Zwei Betrachtungen zu Edmund Husserl" appeared in the 1930s. They are reprinted in Stein, *Welt und Person: Beitrag zum christliche Wahrheitsstreben* (Louvain: Nauwelaerts; Freiburg: Herder, 1962), 1–18, 33–38.

140. The imagined dialogue was later rewritten in essay form at the request of Martin Heidegger, its editor. The two versions appear side by side in Edith Stein, *Knowledge and Faith* (Washington, DC: Institute of Carmelite Studies, 2000), 1–63.

141. Stein, "Husserl and Aquinas: A Comparison," in *Knowledge and Faith*, 27.

142. Ibid., 39.

143. Stein, *Potency and Act*, 121.

144. Edith Stein, *Finite and Eternal Beings* (Washington, DC: Institute of Carmelite Studies, 2005), 11–12, xxix. Her final work, *The Science of the Cross* (Washington, DC: Institute of Carmelite Studies, 2002), also treats its subject, St. John of the Cross, as a personal unity who cannot be reduced to biography or doctrine. Several years later, before Stein's work appeared in print, Karol Wojtyła interpreted the same mystic in similarly personalist tones.

145. Karl-Siegbert Rehberg has dubbed their trajectory "the 'sociologization' of philosophical reflection" on man. Rehberg, "Philosophische Anthropologie und die 'Soziologisierung' des Wissens vom Menschen," *Kölner Zeitschrift für Soziologie und Sozialpsychologie* 23 (1981): 162.

146. Plessner, *Stufen des Organischen*, 27.

147. Ibid., 291. Plessner also discussed "political anthropology" in *Macht und menschliche Natur: Ein Versuch zur Anthropologie der geschichtlichen Weltansicht* (Berlin: Junker & Dünnhaupt, 1931).

148. Honneth and Joas, *Social Action and Human Nature*, 75.

149. Helmuth Plessner, *The Limits of Community: A Critique of Social Radicalism* (Amherst, NY: Humanity Books, 1999), 65, 41. Andrew Wallace's introduction to this volume provides a useful overview of the thinker. Plessner identified two types of worrisome communal aspiration: the community of blood and the community of the ideal. He would likely have questioned Husserl's *Liebesgemeinschaft* as an example of the latter.

150. In *Cool Conduct: The Culture of Distance in Weimar Germany* (Berkeley: University of California Press, 2002), Helmut Lethen places Plessner's "doctrine of distance" (54) within the wider pale of a Weimar culture of objectivity. For his discussion of Plessner, see 52–69.

151. Plessner, *The Limits of Community*, 78; cf. Lethen, *Cool Conduct*, 66–67.

152. As Lethen shows, Plessner embraced the anti-liberal political analysis of the controversial legal theorist Carl Schmitt, whose agonistic vision of politics he cited favorably in 1931's *Macht und menschliche Natur*. See Lethen, *Cool Conduct*, 88–95. Their career trajectories diverged sharply, of course, with Schmitt espousing Nazism while Plessner decamped to the Netherlands.

153. For an account of Gehlen's career and deradicalization, see Jerry Muller, *The Other God That Failed: Hans Freyer and the Deradicalization of German Conservatism* (Princeton, NJ: Princeton University Press, 1987), 395–99. The Nazi ideologue Alfred Rosenberg is cited in the first edition of Gehlen's *Der Mensch: Seine Natur und seine Stellung in der Welt* (1940; *Man: His Nature and Place in the World*), but the reference disappeared from the 1944 second edition. That phenomenological study provided no inoculation against Nazi sentiments is also revealed by Husserl students such as the philosopher of science and mathematics Oskar Becker and the anthropologist Ludwig Ferdinand Clauss, both discussed in Dermot Moran, "'Even the Papuan is a Man and not a Beast': Husserl on Universalism and the Relativity of Cultures," *Journal of the History of Philosophy* 49, no. 4 (2011): 469–72.

154. Arnold Gehlen, "An Anthropological Model," *Human Context* 1 (1968–69): 12. Gehlen too likened phenomenology to the impressionist revolution in painting.

155. The improvisatory process resembled the mastery of language. See Gehlen, *Man: His Nature and Place in the World* (New York: Columbia University Press, 1988). Karl-Siegbert Rehberg's Introduction is insightful.

156. Gehlen became known after the war for his conservative defense of social institutions weakened by modern acceleration. See Gehlen, *Man in the Age of Technology* (1957; New York: Columbia University Press, 1980).

157. Ilja Srubar, "On the Origin of 'Phenomenological' Sociology," *Human Studies* 7, no. 2 (1984): 163–89. On the sociological dividends of Husserl's thought, see also René Toulement, *L'essence de la société selon Husserl* (Paris: Presses universitaires de France, 1962); Stephan Strasser, "Grundgedanken der Soziolontologie Edmund Husserls," *Zeitschrift für philosophische Forschung* 29 (1975): 3–33; Strasser, *Welt im Widerspruch: Gedanken zu einer Phänomenologie als ethischer Fundamentalphilosophie* (Dordrecht: Kluwer, 1991). For current applications, see Jürgen Raab, Michaela Pfadenhauer, Petr Stegmaier, Jochen Dreher, and Brent Schnettler, eds., *Phänomenologie und Soziologie: Theoretische Positionen, aktuelle Problemfelder und empirische Umsetzungen* (Wiesbaden: Verlag für Sozialwissenschaften, 2008).

158. Quentin Lauer, *Phenomenology: Its Genesis and Prospect* (New York: Harper, 1958), 77. I found the citation in Martin Jay, "Phenomenology and Lived Experience," in *Essays from the Edge: Parerga and Paralipomena* (Charlottesville: University of Virginia Press, 2011), 104.

159. Theodor Litt, *Individuum und Gesellschaft: Grundfragen der sozialen Theorie und Ethik* (Leipzig: Teubner, 1919); Siegfried Kracauer, *Soziologie als Wissenschaft: Eine erkenntnistheoretische Untersuchung* (Dresden: IM Sibyllen-Verlag, 1922); Fritz Schreier, *Grundbegriffe und Grundformen des Rechts: Entwurf einer phänomenologisch begründeten formalen Rechts- und Staatslehre* (Vienna: Wiener staatswissenschaftliche Studien, 1924); Alfred Vierkandt, *Gesellschaftslehre: Hauptprobleme der philosophischen Soziologie* (Stuttgart: Enke, 1933); Tomoo Otaka, *Grundlegung der Lehre vom sozialen Verband* (Vienna: J. Springer, 1932); Gerhart Husserl, *Rechtskraft und Rechtsgeltung: Eine Rechtsdogmatische Untersuchung* (Berlin: J. Springer, 1925); and *Rechtsgegenstand: Rechtslogische Studien zu einer reine Theorie des Eigentums* (Berlin: J. Springer, 1933). On Kracauer's early phenomenological flirtations, see Vierkandt, "S. Kracauer, Soziologie als Wissenschaft," *Kant-Studien* 30 (1925): 220–22; Gertrud Koch, *Siegfried Kracauer: An Introduction* (Princeton, NJ: Princeton University Press, 2000), 11–25.

160. Schutz, *The Phenomenology of the Social World* (Evanston, IL: Northwestern University Press, 1967), 43.

161. For Schutz's discussions of Husserl's relevance to sociology, see Schutz, "Husserl's Importance for the Social Sciences," in Schutz, *Collected Papers*, vol. 1: *The Problem of Social Reality*, 3rd ed. (The Hague: Nijhoff, 1971), 140–49. For the critique of Husserl's transcendentalism, see "Edmund Husserl's Ideas, Volume II," and "The Problem of Transcendental Intersubjectivity in Husserl," ibid., vol. 3: *Studies in Phenomenological Philosophy* (The Hague: Nijhoff, 1970), 15–39, 51–83. For an epistolary defense of the *Crisis* written to his friend Eric Voegelin, see "Husserl's *Crisis of Western Sciences*," ibid., vol. 4 [untitled] (Dordrecht: Kluwer, 1996), 177–86.

162. Schutz, *Phenomenology of the Social World*, 222–23.

163. Ibid., 203.
164. Ibid., 193.
165. Ibid., 191.
166. Both Schutz and Kaufmann were students of Hans Kelsen, whose Pure Theory of Law, based on the concept of binding norms that were segregated from both human conduct and moral evaluation, exerted wide influence on twentieth-century jurisprudence.
167. Felix Kaufmann, *Logik und Rechtswissenschaft: Grundriss eines Systems der reinen Rechtslehre* (Tübingen: J. C. B. Mohr, 1924), 1. It followed that "methodological coherence ... [was] substantive coherence." Kaufmann, *Die Kriterien des Rechts: Eine Untersuchung über die Prinzipien der juristischen Methodenlehre* (Tübingen: J. C. B. Mohr, 1924), 4.
168. Kaufmann, *Logik und Rechtswissenschaft*, 103.
169. Felix Kaufmann, "Die philosophischen Grundprobleme der Lehre von der Strafrechtsschuld," *Wiener Staats- und Rechtswissenschaftliche Studien*, vol. 11 (1929): iii–v, 1–138. This view contravened both Scheler's reified value sphere and Hans Kelsen's strict divide between norms (the ought) and human behavior (the is).
170. This was Alfred Schutz's verdict in the encomium "In Memory of Felix Kaufmann," in Harry P. Reeder, *The Work of Felix Kaufmann* (Washington, DC: University Press of America, 1991), xi. Reeder's synopsis of Kaufmann's thought is a useful though quite general English-language introduction. Kaufmann's summative work *Methodenlehre der Sozialwissenschaft* (Vienna: Julius Springer, 1936) was not overtly phenomenological.
171. Aron Gurwitsch, *Human Encounters in the Social World* (Pittsburgh: Duquesne University Press, 1979), 152–53. First published in 1977, the work had limited interwar impact.
172. On Heidegger's French reception, see Ethan Kleinberg, *Generation Existential: Heidegger's Philosophy in France, 1927–1961* (Ithaca, NY: Cornell University Press, 2005).
173. In this conviction, it should be noted, Heidegger reflected some of the concerns raised by Munich phenomenologists. He was—though he might have balked at the characterization—a potent anthropologist.
174. Kleinberg, *Generation Existential*, 11–17
175. Joanna Hodge, *Heidegger and Ethics* (London: Routledge, 1995), discusses Heidegger's tendency to muddy his own analysis of *Mitsein* by condemning public conformity in favor of an isolated quest for authenticity.
176. Surprisingly, Heidegger's Nazism, so scandalous in France and the United States, provoked little concern in the geographic epicenter of German and Soviet crimes, the bloodlands of Eastern Europe, as defined by Timothy Snyder, *Bloodlands: Europe between Hitler and Stalin* (New York: Basic Books, 2010). As Marci

Shore has shown in "Can We See Ideas? On Evocation, Experience, and Empathy," in Darrin M. McMahon and Samuel Moyn, eds., *Rethinking Modern European Intellectual History* (Oxford: Oxford University Press, 2014), 199–200, Jan Patočka even rationalized Heidegger's 1933 enlistment in the Nazi Party as a decision taken before the horror of that movement could be known, likening it to Husserl's World War I nationalism.

177. For the most seminal texts, see Jean-Paul Sartre, *The Transcendence of the Ego: An Existentialist Theory of Consciousness* (New York: Noonday Press, 1957), and Emmanuel Lévinas, *Totality and Infinity: An Essay on Exteriority* (Pittsburgh: Duquesne University Press, 1969).

178. To the Lithuanian Lévinas can be added Aron Gurwitsch and the Russians Alexandre Koyré, Alexandre Kojève, and Georges Gurvitsch. Bernhard Waldenfels noted the infusion of Eastern philosophers in *Phänomenologie in Frankreich* (Frankfurt: Suhrkamp, 1983). For a more recent reminder, see Stefanos Geroulanos, "Russian Exiles, New Scientific Movements, and Phenomenology: A History of Philosophical Immigrations in 1930s France," *New German Critique* 113 (Summer 2011): 89–128.

INTERLUDE

1. Edmund Husserl, *The Crisis of European Sciences and Transcendental Phenomenology* (Evanston, IL: Northwestern University Press, 1970). Milan Kundera, *The Art of the Novel* (1986; New York: Grove Press, 1988), 3–20. Translated from French, Kundera's opening essay first appeared under the title "The Novel and Europe," *New York Review of Books,* 19 July 1984: 15–18.

2. For debates on Eurocentrism and Russophobia incited by Kundera's "The Tragedy of Central Europe," see Milan Šimečka, "Another Civilization? An Other Civilization?" *East European Reporter* 1, no. 2 (1985): 37–39, and Mihály Vajda, "Who Excluded Russia from Europe?" ibid., no. 4 (1986): 45–49.

3. For examples of those who saw 1989 as a return to the ideals of 1789, see Ralf Dahrendorf, *Reflections on the Revolution in Europe: In a Letter Intended to Have Been Sent to a Gentleman in Warsaw* (New York: Times Books, 1990); Bruce Ackerman, *The Future of Liberal Revolution* (New Haven, CT: Yale University Press, 1992); Ken Jowitt, "The Leninist Extinction," in Daniel Chirot, ed., *The Crisis of Leninism and the Decline of the Left: The Revolutions of 1989* (Seattle: University of Washington Press, 1991), 77. Others see the dissidents as theoretical innovators but pay little attention to phenomenology: see Barbara J. Falk, *The Dilemmas of Dissidence in East-Central Europe: Citizen Intellectuals and Philosopher Kings* (Budapest: Central European University Press, 2003); Delia Popescu, *Political*

Action in Václav Havel's Thought: The Responsibility of Resistance (Lanham, MD: Lexington Books, 2012).

4. For analyses of the Russian reception of phenomenology, see Alexander Haardt, *Husserl in Rußland: Phänomenologie der Sprache und Kunst bei Gustav Špet und Aleksej Losev* (Munich: Fink, 1993), 23–63; Thomas Seifrid, *The Word Made Self: Russian Writings on Language, 1860–1930* (Ithaca, NY: Cornell University Press, 2005), 130–201; and Leonid Ionin, "Sozialphänomenologische Themen in der sowjetischen Soziologie und Sozialpsychologie," in Richard Grathoff and Bernhard Waldenfels, eds., *Sozialität und Intersubjektivität: Phänomenologische Perspektiven der Sozialwissenschaften im Umkreis von Aron Gurwitsch und Alfred Schütz* (Munich: Wilhelm Fink, 1983), 369–71. On Shpet, see also Galin Tihanov, ed., *Gustav Shpet's Contribution to Philosophy and Cultural Theory* (West Lafayette, IN: Purdue University Press, 2009); and the introductory essays by Thomas Nemeth and Alexander Haardt in Shpet, *Appearance and Sense: Phenomenology as the Fundamental Science and Its Problems* (Dordrecht: Kluwer, 1991). The philosopher Aleksei Losev, Shpet's student, also drew on Husserl in his writings on music, language, and myth. On Losev, see Alexander Haardt, Thomas Seifrid, and Vladimir Marchenkov's Introduction to Aleksei Losev, *The Dialectics of Myth* (London: Routledge, 2003), 3–65. The Russian Jewish Lev Shestov deserves mention as well; his encounter with Husserl and Heidegger while in French exile—including a collegial friendship with Husserl—galvanized his own thinking about philosophical method and the dangers of scientific absolutism. Shestov's 1926 critique of Husserlian rationalism is "Memento Mori," in Shestov, *Potestas Clavium* (Athens: Ohio University Press, 1968), 287–359.

5. For an essay that recognizes this scope, see Zdzisław Krasnodębski, "Longing for Community: Phenomenological Philosophy of Politics and the Dilemmas of European Culture," *International Sociology* 8, no. 3 (1993): 339–53.

6. On the young Lukács, see Lee Congdon, *The Young Lukács* (Chapel Hill: University of North Carolina Press, 1983). For Lukács's later consideration of Hartmann, see the posthumously published *Zur Ontologie des gesellschaftlichen Seins*, pt. 1 (Darmstadt: Hermann Luchterhand, 1984), 421–67.

7. Wolfgang Harich's Hartmann project was mostly unknown before his death. It has since appeared in Harich, *Nicolai Hartmann: Leben, Werk, Wirkung* (Würzburg: Königshausen & Neumann, 2000), and *Nicolai Hartmann—Größe und Grenzen: Versuch einer marxistischen Selbstverständigung* (Würzburg: Königshausen & Neumann, 2004). On Harich's arrest and sentencing—accused in part of relations to Lukács and the anti-communist Petöfi Circle in Budapest—see John Connelly, *Captive University: The Sovietization of East German, Czech, and Polish Higher Education, 1945–1956* (Chapel Hill: University of North Carolina Press, 2000), 196–98.

8. Wolfgang Harich, *Ahnenpass: Versuch einer Autobiographie* (Berlin: Schwarzkopf & Schwarzkopf, 1999), 169.

9. For overviews of phenomenological Marxism, see Paul Piccone's essay "Phenomenological Marxism," in *Confronting the Crisis: Writings of Paul Piccone* (New York: Telos, 2008), 29–61; and Bernhard Waldenfels, "Sozialphilosophie im Spannungsfeld von Phänomenologie und Marxismus," in G. Fløistad, ed., *Contemporary Philosophy: A New Survey*, vol. 3 (The Hague: Nijhoff, 1982), 219–42. In the English-speaking world, Piccone's journal *Telos*, founded in 1968, two years before Husserl's *Crisis* appeared in English translation, was crucial in disseminating phenomenological Marxism. On Marxist humanism more generally, see James H. Satterwhite, *Varieties of Marxist Humanism: Philosophical Revision in Postwar Eastern Europe* (Pittsburgh: University of Pittsburgh Press, 1992).

10. Mihály Vajda, *Zárójelbe tett tudomány: a husserli fenomenológia tudományfelfogásának bírálatához* (Budapest: Akadémiai Kiadó, 1968); *A mítosz és a ráció határán: Edmund Husserl fenomenológiája* (Budapest, Gondolat Kiadó: 1969); "Marxism, Existentialism, Phenomenology: A Dialogue," *Telos* 7 (Spring 1971): 3–29; "Lukács' and Husserl's Critique of Science," *Telos* 38 (Winter 1978–79): 104–18. Vajda's Husserlian critique of Europe's imperial *ratio*, as embodied in Soviet communism, is also evident in the post-1989 essay "Central Europe—One Europe: Past, Present, Future," *East European Reporter* 4, no. 3 (Autumn–Winter 1990): 51–54—in which he praised Husserl, Heidegger, and Scheler for their appraisals of modern culture.

11. See Gajo Petrović, *Marx in the Mid-Twentieth Century* (Garden City, NY: Anchor Books, 1967), 76, 86, 183–89. Not all reform Marxists found in phenomenology a useful reagent. Mihailo Marković, also of *Praxis*, considered it inherently incapable of addressing historical or social questions. See his "Reason and Social Practice," in Gerson S. Sher, ed., *Marxist Humanism and Praxis* (Buffalo: Prometheus, 1978), 19–20. On *Praxis*, see Sher, *Praxis: Marxist Criticism and Dissent in Socialist Yugoslavia* (Bloomington: Indiana University Press, 1977).

12. Zdzisław Krasnodębski cited its influence in faraway Poland. Krasnodębski, "Phänomenologie und Soziologie in Polen: Der Anfang eines Dialogs," in Richard Grathoff and Bernhard Waldenfels, eds., *Sozialität und Intersubjektivität: Phänomenologische Perspektiven der Sozialwissenschaften im Umkreis von Aron Gurwitsch und Alfred Schütz* (Munich: Fink, 1983), 363. For essays from the workshop, see Bernhard Waldenfels, Jan M. Broekman, and Ante Pažanin, eds., *Phenomenology and Marxism* (London: Routledge & Kegan Paul, 1984).

13. See Cristian Ciocan, "Philosophy without Freedom: Constantin Noica and Alexandru Dragomir," in *Phenomenology 2005*, vol. 3: *Selected Essays from the Euro-Mediterranean Area* (Bucharest: Zeta, 2007), 63–79. On Noica's influence, see the fascinating book by Gabriel Liiceanu, *The Păltiniş Diary: A Paideic Model in Humanist Culture* (Budapest: Central European University Press, 2000)—first published in the Romanian underground in 1983. Noica's *Six Maladies of the Contemporary Spirit*

(1978; Plymouth, UK: University of Plymouth, 2009) and *Becoming with Being* (1981; Milwaukee: Marquette University Press, 2009) have both appeared in English. On Dragomir, see *Studia Phænomenologica* 4, nos. 3–4 (2004), *The Ocean of Forgetting— Alexandru Dragomir: A Romanian Phenomenologist, 1916–2002.*

14. Jonathan Bolton, *Worlds of Dissent: Charter 77, the Plastic People of the Universe, and Czech Culture under Communism* (Cambridge, MA: Harvard University Press, 2012), 17.

15. Václav Havel, *Letters to Olga* (New York: Henry Holt, 1988), 119.

CHAPTER 6

1. Jan Patočka, *Éternité et historicité* (Lagrasse: Verdier, 2011), 15.

2. I borrow the term "anti-foundational" from Stefanos Geroulanos, *An Atheism That Is Not Humanist Emerges in French Thought* (Stanford, CA: Stanford University Press, 2010). The Czech reception of phenomenology differed markedly from the anti-humanist French reading that he chronicled, 3. Husserl to Felix Kaufmann, 5 May 1936, in Husserl, *Briefwechsel*, vol. 4: *Die Freiburger Schüler* (Dordrecht: Kluwer, 1994), 224–25, and to František Jančik, 21 August 1936, ibid., vol. 8: *Institutionelle Schreiben* (Dordrecht: Kluwer, 1994), 57. The second letter exists only in a Czech translation; the original German letter has been lost. For a detailed reconstruction of Husserl's relation to Masaryk, see Karl Schuhmann, "Husserl and Masaryk," in Josef Novák, ed., *On Masaryk* (Amsterdam: Rodopi, 1988), 129–56.

4. Husserl to Masaryk, 3 January 1935, Husserl, *Briefwechsel*, vol. 1: *Die Brentanoschule*, 120.

5. Husserl to Masaryk, 2 March 1922, ibid., 114.

6. Aurel Kolnai, *The War against the West* (New York: Viking, 1938), 223.

7. Jan Patočka, "An Attempt at Czech National Philosophy and Its Future" (1976) in Milič Čapek and Karel Hrubý, eds., *T. G. Masaryk in Perspective: Comments and Criticism* (Ann Arbor, MI: SVU Press, 1981), 3.

8. On Masaryk's relation to the school, see Josef Novák, "Masaryk and the Brentano School," in Novák, ed., *On Masaryk*, 27–38, and Józef Zumr and Thomas Binder, eds., *T. G. Masaryk und die Brentano Schule: Beiträge zur gleichnamigen Symposium vom 15.–17. October 1991* (Prague: Filosofický ústav Československé akademie věd, 1992). Erazim Kohák, Patočka's premier interpreter in English, stretches a bit in describing Masaryk's analysis of Marx as "social phenomenology" and "eidetic description" ("Editor's Preface," in Kohák, ed., *Masaryk on Marx* [Lewisburg, PA: Bucknell University Press, 1972], 10).

9. In an intermittent correspondence, the two men professed admiration for one another in precisely those domains where they did not overlap: Husserl

praised his old friend's political work, Masaryk his younger colleague's theoretical advances, which he had no time to follow. For their surviving correspondence, see Husserl, *Briefwechsel*, vol. 1: *Die Brentanoschule* (Dordrecht: Kluwer, 1994), 99–120.

10. Interpreters such as Emanuel Rádl and Milič Čapek have contested this diminishment of Masaryk. For Husserl's reference to Masaryk's conversations with Karel Čapek, see Husserl, *Briefe an Roman Ingarden* (The Hague: Nijhoff, 1968), 101. For Brentano's opinion of Masaryk, see Novák, "Preface," in *On Masaryk*, 9; Milič Čapek, "The Presence of Masaryk's Thought," in Čapek and Hrubý, eds., *T. G. Masaryk in Perspective*, 23; Patočka, "Erinnerungen an Husserl" in *Die Welt der Menschen—Die Welt der Philosophie* (The Hague: Nijhoff, 1976), xv. Patočka's description of Masaryk as a man of action appears in numerous essays. For a collection of Patočka's Masaryk essays in French, see *La crise du sens*, 2 vols. (Brussels: Ousia, 1985–86). Masaryk himself cultivated the image of a practical man. See his 1922 letter to Husserl, quoted in Schuhmann, "Husserl and Masaryk," 153.

11. I have found the following surveys of Masaryk's thought useful: W. Preston Warren's *Masaryk's Democracy: A Philosophy of Scientific and Moral Culture* (Chapel Hill: University of North Carolina Press, 1941) is a celebratory synthesis. Later and more measured are Antonie van den Beld, *Humanity: The Political and Social Philosophy of Thomas G. Masaryk* (The Hague: Mouton, 1975); Roman Szporluk, *The Political Thought of Thomas G. Masaryk* (Boulder, CO: East European Monographs, 1981); Hanus J. Hajek, *T. G. Masaryk Revisited: A Critical Assessment* (Boulder, CO: East European Monographs, 1983). There are also several collections that gather East European views, including Čapek and Hrubý, eds., *T. G. Masaryk in Perspective*; Novák, ed., *On Masaryk*; Stanley B. Winters, ed., *T. G. Masaryk, 1850–1937: Thinker and Politician* (New York: St. Martin's Press, 1990); Robert B. Pynsent, ed., *T. G. Masaryk (1850–1937): Thinker and Critic* (New York: St. Martin's Press, 1989); and Harry Hanak, ed., *T. G. Masaryk (1850–1937): Statesman and Cultural Force* (New York: St. Martin's Press, 1990). Recent literature has highlighted the personality cult surrounding Masaryk and his interwar democracy. On Masaryk's image as propaganda, see Andrea Orzoff, "The Husbandman: Tomáš Masaryk's Leader Cult in Interwar Czechoslovakia," *Austrian History Yearbook* 39 (2008): 121–37.

12. T. G. Masaryk, *Suicide and the Meaning of Civilization* (Chicago: University of Chicago Press, 1970).

13. T. G. Masaryk, *Modern Man and Religion* (Freeport, NY: Books for Libraries Press, 1938), 32.

14. Ibid., 226, 45, 37–8. Musset, of course, referred to a nineteenth-century *mal du siècle*, which Masaryk extended to the twentieth. For a contemporary application of the concept of titanism to literary analysis, see Václav Černý, *Essai*

sur le Titanisme dans la Poésie Romantique Occidentale entre 1815 et 1850 (Prague: Orbis, 1935).

15. Ján Pavlík, "Brentano und Masaryks Auffassung der Ethik," in Zumr and Binder, eds., *T. G. Masaryk und die Brentano Schule*, 82–93.

16. On this theme, see the beginning of Masaryk's *Versuch einer konkreten Logik: Klassifikation und Organisation der Wissenschaften* (1885; Vienna: Karl Konegen, 1887), 1–10. Regarding the treacheries of modern thought, see Masaryk, "The Ideals of Humanity," in id., *The Ideals of Humanity and How to Work* (London: Allen & Unwin, 1938), 13–98.

17. Masaryk, *Suicide*, 159, 161.

18. Religion, Masaryk remarked to Karel Čapek, was "a personal relation," but one with profound social impact. Masaryk, *On Thought and Life: Conversations with Karel Čapek* (Freeport, NY: Books for Libraries Press, 1938), 143. Small wonder that he traced the font of modern Czech history to the fifteenth-century Hussite Reformation, a movement, he believed, that stamped a uniquely Protestant and democratic character in the heart of Europe. This nationalist tale was contested by the Czech historian Josef Pekař. Masaryk, *The Meaning of Czech History* (Chapel Hill: University of North Carolina Press, 1974).

19. Andrea Orzoff, *Battle for the Castle: The Myth of Czechoslovakia in Europe, 1914–1948* (New York: Oxford University Press, 2009), 8, 30–32. Like many of his generation, Masaryk feared ochlocracy (mob rule) as much as dictatorship. As Jan Patočka noticed, democracy for Masaryk was "not only a state form, but that theistic metaphysics which responds to the moral value of human reality." Patočka, "An Attempt at Czech National Philosophy," 8.

20. See esp. "How to Work," in Masaryk, *The Ideals of Humanity*, 101–91. According to Masaryk, revolutions, whether Marxist or liberal, promoted violence and destroyed unity. They generally targeted external material structures but failed to reach man's spiritual core. Revolution was, in other words, *less* radical than humanitarian reform—a position similar to Kolnai's. See *Masaryk on Marx* and Masaryk, *The Spirit of Russia: Studies in History, Literature, and Philosophy* (London: Allen & Unwin, 1911), 2: 528–52, for his critique of revolution.

21. Masaryk, *Spirit of Russia*, 2: 510.

22. Ibid., 514.

23. T. G. Masaryk, *The Making of a State* (New York: Frederick A. Stokes, 1927), 439; Masaryk, *The New Europe: The Slav Standpoint* (London: Eyre & Spottiswoode, 1918), 21. He later dubbed this person-centered philosophy "concretism"—the view that "[e]very man is a whole world, a microcosm" (Masaryk, *On Thought and Life*, 14–15).

24. T. G. Masaryk, *The Spirit of Russia*, vol. 3 (London: Allen & Unwin, 1967), 111. Masaryk's "small-scale work" had an anticipation in the nineteenth-century Warsaw Positivist movement, which called on Polish gentry and recently

emancipated peasants in the Russian empire to build a popular national base through "work at the foundations" (*praca u podstaw*). In articles coining the phrase, Alexander Świętochowski and Leopold Mikulski rejected the Romantic suffering and heroism associated with earlier Polish nationalism in favor of dedication to the everyday work of nation-building. On this topic, see Stanislaus Blejwas, *Realism in Polish Politics: Warsaw Positivism and National Survival in Nineteenth Century Poland* (New Haven, CT: Yale University Press, 1984), 88–94.

25. Husserl's *Crisis of European Sciences and Transcendental Phenomenology* (1936) was finally translated into Czech in 1971–72, becoming available just in time for disconsolate regime critics after the Soviet invasion.

26. In December 1934, Husserl bequeathed to Patočka the gift of a small lectern that Masaryk had given him sixty years earlier upon his departure from Leipzig.

27. For a report on the Congress, see Ernest Nagel, "The Eighth International Congress of Philosophy," *Journal of Philosophy* 31, no. 22 (1934): 589–601. See also "Achter Internationaler Kongreß für Philosophie in Prag," in Ludger Hagedorn and Hans Rainer Sepp, eds., *Jan Patočka: Texte, Dokumente, Bibliographie* (Freiburg: Karl Alber, 1999), 176–87.

28. Translated as Edmund Husserl, *Experience and Judgment: Investigations in a Genealogy of Logic* (Evanston, IL: Northwestern University Press, 1973), with Ludwig Landgrebe's useful 1948 introduction.

29. On these dramatic events, including the successful effort by the Belgian friar Herman Leo van Breda to smuggle Husserl's papers from Prague, see "Patočka und der Cercle philosophique de Prague" in Ludger Hagedorn and Hans Rainer Sepp, eds., *Jan Patočka: Texte, Dokumente, Bibliographie* (Freiburg: Karl Alber, 1999), 188–257. Patočka described these activities in his 1967 interview with József Zumr, translated as "Entretien avec Jan Patočka sur la philosophie et les philosophes," in Étienne Tassin and Marc Richir, eds., *Jan Patočka: Philosophie, phénoménologie, politique* (Grenoble: Millon, 1992), 7–36.

30. Emil Utitz, *Die Sendung der Philosophie in unserer Zeit* (Leiden: Sijthoff, 1935), 156. Utitz's view of philosophers as "missionaries" owed itself partly to his encounters with Brentano, whose zeal for the philosophical renewal of modern humanity he recalled in "Erinnerungen an Franz Brentano," *Zeitschrift für philosophische Forschung* 13, no. 1 (1959): 102–10.

31. Ladislav Rieger, *Idea filosofie* (Prague: Nákladem Filosofické Fakulty, University Karlovy, 1939), 17, 350.

32. J. L. Hromádka, *Don Quijote České Filosofie* (1943; Brno: L. Marek, 2005).

33. Emmanuel Rádl, "Trost der Philosophie," in Ludger Hagedorn, ed., *Tschechische Philosophen im 20. Jahrhundert: Klíma, Rádl, Patočka, Havel, Kosík* (Stuttgart: Deutsche-Verlags-Anstalt, 2002), 180. On Rádl, see Hagedorn's essay in

the same volume, 425–35; Erazim Kohák, *Hearth and Horizon: Cultural Identity and Global Humanity in Czech Philosophy* (Prague: Filosofia, 2008), 128–33; and Shimona Löwenstein, *Emanuel Rádl: Philosoph und Moralist, 1873–1942* (Frankfurt: Peter Lang, 1995). Hagedorn and Kohák disagree on the relative significance within his overall oeuvre of Rádl's final period, and hence of "Trost der Philosophie." The philosopher and Charter 77 signatory Ladislav Hejdánek, however, calls the book his main "philosophical bequest" (*Tschechische Philosophen*, 432).

34. Rádl, "Trost," 203–4.

35. Ibid., 103. The truth, or "true reality [*pravá skutečnost*]," simply is, and the struggle for true reality is moral in that it does not seek to instrumentalize knowledge by subordinating it to a human agenda ("Trost," 180–85).

36. Bradley Abrams, *The Struggle for the Soul of a Nation* (Lanham, MD: Rowman & Littlefield, 2004), 118–38.

37. Author interview with Patočka's colleague Józef Zumr, Prague, 15 May 2012.

38. Zumr, "Entretien avec Jan Patočka," 24, 27. The original Czech interview was published in a 1967 issue of *Filosofický časopis* dedicated to Patočka on his sixtieth birthday.

39. Though widely translated in his heyday, Kosík is now largely overlooked, a casualty of the Soviet invasion as well as the post–Cold War disdain for any sort of socialism. On Kosík, see Hagedorn, *Tschechische Philosophen*, 449–55; Kohák, *Hearth and Horizon*, 159–62. On his path, with many of his generation, from 1950s Stalinism to 1960s reform, see Marci Shore, "Engineering in the Age of Innocence: A Genealogy of Discourse inside the Czechoslovak Writers' Union, 1949–76," *East European Politics and Societies* 12 (1998): 397–441. Kosík's main English-language champion was Paul Piccone, who considered the Czech philosopher "[t]he most important figure who has attempted to articulate the phenomenological basis of Marxism" and published him liberally in his journal *Telos*. Paul Piccone, "Phenomenological Marxism" (1971) in Piccone, *Confronting the Crisis: The Writings of Paul Piccone* (New York: Telos, 2008), 42. On Kosík's influence during the Prague Spring, see Vladimir Kusin, *The Intellectual Origins of the Prague Spring: The Development of Reformist Ideas in Czechoslovakia* (Cambridge: Cambridge University Press, 1971).

40. Karel Kosík, *Dialectics of the Concrete* (Dordrecht: Reidel, 1976), 1, 2, 4, 11.

41. Ibid., 11, 57–60, 53.

42. Ibid., 14–15, 30.

43. "Care is the world in the subject," Kosík asserted (ibid., 37–38).

44. Ibid., 152.

45. Ibid., 49. For a discussion of Adorno's critique of authenticity, including the phenomenological quest for a direct relation with objects, see Martin Jay, "Taking on the Stigma of Authenticity: Adorno's Critique of Genuineness," in

Jay, *Essays from the Edge: Parerga and Paralipomena* (Charlottesville: University of Virginia Press, 2011), 9–21.

46. Karel Kosík, "Our Current Crisis," in id., *The Crisis of Modernity: Essays and Observations from the 1968 Era* (Lanham, MD: Rowman & Littlefield, 1995), 24–25.

47. Ibid., 40–41; "The Dialectics of Morality and the Morality of Dialectics," ibid., 74.

48. Kosík, "Socialism and the Crisis of Modern Man," ibid., 54–55, 58.

49. After the Velvet Revolution a quarter-century later, a rejuvenated Kosík, still oppositional after years of isolation, disparaged Havel's post-partisan governance for its lack of higher purpose and transcendental goals. The year 1989, he rued, never achieved the aspirations of 1968, succumbing instead, with Left and Right parties, to a "politics of the cave." Kosík, "The Third Munich," *Telos* 94 (Winter 1993–94): 154.

50. Ivan Sviták, *Man and the World: A Marxist Interpretation* (1968; New York: Delta, 1970), 136, 161; id., *The Czechoslovak Experiment* (New York: Columbia University Press, 1971), 212.

51. Robert Kalivoda, *Der Marxismus und die moderne geistige Wirklichkeit* (1968; Frankfurt: Suhrkamp, 1970), 10.

52. Antonín Mokrejš, *Fenomenologie a problém intersubjektivity* (Prague: Svoboda, 1969). The book appeared soon after the Soviet invasion.

53. Józef Zumr, "K filosofovým šedesátinám. S Janem Patockou o filosofii a filosofech," *Filosofický casopis* 15, no. 5 (1967): 585–98; Jaroslav Kohout, "Konstanty a proměny Patočkovy filosofie," ibid.: 599–608; Ivan Dubský, "Svět, domov a cesta u Jana Patočky," ibid.: 609–24; Ladislav Major, "Sebeuvědomení a čas. K Patočkově interpretaci Hegelovy estetiky," ibid.: 625–35; Radim Palouš, "Pedagogické teorie a jejich antropologické předpoklady," ibid.: 641–45. Dubský, also a reform Marxist, praised the renewed timeliness of Patočka's *Natural World as a Philosophical Problem* (Prague: Ústřední nakladatelství a knihkupectví učitelstva československého, 1936).

54. Kohák, *Hearth and Horizon*, 166; and see Patočka, "Unser Nationalprogramm und die heutige Zeit" (1969), in Klaus Nellen, Petr Pithart, and Miloš Pojar, eds., *Schriften zur tschechischen Kultur und Geschichte* (Stuttgart: Klett-Cotta, 1992), 24.

CHAPTER 7

1. In the minds of many of his Czech acolytes, Patočka's late activism clearly aligned with his philosophy. The case for a strong link between the two is made in Aviezer Tucker, *The Philosophy and Politics of Czech Dissidence from Patočka to Havel* (Pittsburgh: University of Pittsburgh Press, 2000); and Alexandra

Laignel-Lavastine, *Jan Patočka: L'esprit de la dissidence* (Paris: Michalon, 1998) and *Esprits d'Europe: Autour de Czeslaw Milosz, Jan Patočka, István Bibó* (Paris: Calmann-Lévy, 2005). For a summary of Patočka's personal and moral influence, see Helena Sedlačkova-Gibbs, "Moral Politics and Its Others: The Charter 77 Dissident Movement in Czechoslovakia (1977–1989)" (Ph.D. diss., New York University, 2003), 70–115.

2. For a myth-debunking account of Patočka's death and the martyrdom that followed, see Jonathan Bolton, *Worlds of Dissent: Charter 77, the Plastic People of the Universe, and Czech Culture under Communism* (Cambridge, MA: Harvard University Press, 2012), 155–60.

3. Patočka's English translator Erazim Kohák notes the centrality of ethics in his thought. See "Jan Patočka: A Philosophical Biography," in Kohák, ed., *Jan Patočka: Philosophy and Selected Writings* (Chicago: University of Chicago Press, 1989), 52.

4. See Paul Ricœur, "Hommage an Jan Patočka" (1992), in Ludger Hagedorn and Hans Rainer Sepp, eds., *Jan Patočka: Texte—Dokumente—Bibliographie* (Freiburg: Karl Alber, 1999), 41–9; Ricœur , "Preface" to Jan Patočka, *Heretical Essays on the Philosophy of History* (Chicago: Open Court, 1996), vii–xvi; Jacques Derrida, *The Gift of Death* (Chicago: University of Chicago Press, 1995). Havel frequently cited Patočka's influence on his life. For a particularly poignant remembrance, see "Last Conversation, 1 May 1977," in H. Gordon Skilling, ed., *Charter 77 and Human Rights in Czechoslovakia* (London: Allen & Unwin, 1981), 242–44. The earliest celebrity homage after Patočka's death came from his fellow Czech Roman Jakobson, "Jan Patočka: From the Curriculum Vitae of a Czech Philosopher," *New Republic* 176 (7 May 1977): 26–28. See also Ludwig Landgrebe's encomium, "Jan Patocka," *Philosophy and Phenomenological Research* 38, no. 2 (December 1977): 287–90; and the eulogy by Zdeněk Pinc, "Odvaha k smyslu života," *Svědectví* 14, no. 54 (1977): 185–92.

5. In English, the starting point is Kohák, ed., *Jan Patočka*. See also Tucker, *Philosophy and Politics of Czech Dissidence*; Edward F. Findlay, *Caring for the Soul in a Postmodern Age: Politics and Phenomenology in the Thought of Jan Patočka* (Albany: State University of New York Press, 2002); and the essays of Ivan Chvatík, head of the Jan Patočka Archive in Prague, cited below. Rodolphe Gasché, *Europe, or the Infinite Task* (Stanford, CA: Stanford University Press, 2009) situates Patočka in the wider phenomenological arc of thinkers conceptualizing Europe's destiny. There is a substantial literature in French, German, and Czech, much of it cited below. The French, in particular, recognized Patočka's importance quite early. See, e.g., Etienne Tassin and Marc Richir, eds., *Jan Patočka: Philosophie, Phénoménologie, Politique* (Grenoble: Millon, 1992). One of the preoccupations of the secondary literature has been to unravel the

Husserlian and Heideggerian strands of Patočka's thought. Kohák and Tucker favor the Husserlian; Richard Rorty privileges the Heideggerian in "The Seer of Prague: Influence of Czechoslovakian Philosopher Jan Patočka," *New Republic*, 1 July 1991, repr. in Hagedorn and Sepp, eds., *Jan Patočka*, 50–58. Findlay challenges the good-Patočka (democratic, Husserlian), bad-Patočka (dark, violent, Heideggerian) narrative of the Czech philosopher's earliest English publicists in the Appendix to *Caring for the Soul in a Postmodern Age*, 185–205.

6. Patočka interacted mostly with Husserl's assistant Eugen Fink, whose influence can be felt in Patočka's later asubjective phenomenology. See Fink and Patočka, *Briefe und Dokumente, 1933–1977*, ed. Michael Heitz and Bernhard Nessler (Freiburg: Karl Alber, 1999).

7. See Ivan Chvatík "Jan Patočka and His Concept of an 'A-Subjective' Phenomenology," in *Phenomenology 2005: Selected Essays from Northern Europe*, vol. 4, pt. 1 (Bucharest: Zeta, 2007), 197–215.

8. See, e.g., Jan Patočka, *Body, Community, Language, World*, trans. Erazim Kohák (Chicago: Open Court, 1998), 123ff. Patočka made this criticism despite his awareness of Husserl's incomplete lifeworld project and his unpublished manuscripts from the 1930s, which he cited in his 1936 *Habilitationsschrift* and again in the 1970s. See Patočka, *Le monde naturel comme problème philosophique* (The Hague: Nijhoff, 1976), 90.

9. Patočka, "Briefe an Krzysztof Michalski," *Studia Phænomenologica* 7 (2007): 113. Nonetheless, Heidegger was, he told Michalski, the "thinker of our late European epoch," of our "time of catastrophes" (110). Somewhat conversely, Patočka also detected a lingering subjectivism in Heidegger, notably in the conception of *Dasein* as a being that projects its ownmost possibilities. Contra Heidegger, "I do not open my possibilities, but my situation in light of possibilities is disclosed," he wrote in "Leib, Möglichkeiten, Welt, Erscheinungsfeld," a manuscript from the early 1970s, in Patočka, *Vom Erscheinen als solchem: Texte aus dem Nachlass* (Freiburg: Karl Alber, 2000), 93. Cf. Patočka's 1974 brief "Heidegger," Center for Theoretical Study Working Paper, 98–06 (July 1998), trans. Edward Findlay.

10. Patočka, "Edmund Husserl zum Gedächtnis," in Hagedorn and Sepp, eds., *Jan Patočka*, 268–69.

11. Patočka, *An Introduction to Husserl's Phenomenology* (Chicago: Open Court, 1996), 167.

12. Patočka, "Equilibre et amplitude dans la vie," in id., *Liberté et sacrifice*, 27–39. Émilie Tardivel's *La liberté au principe: Essai sur la philosophie de Patočka* (Paris: Librairie philosophique J. Vrin, 2011) makes a compelling case for viewing liberty as the guiding thread of Patočka's work—from an early transcendental concept of liberty to an existential version elaborated during 1950s and 1960s in dialogue with Heidegger, and culminating in a historico-phenomenological account of liberty that moved beyond ontology.

13. Patočka, *Introduction to Husserl's Phenomenology*, 172.
14. Kohák, ed., *Jan Patočka*, 83.
15. Patočka, *Introduction to Husserl's Phenomenology*, 1.
16. Ibid., 14–17.
17. Patočka thought Husserl's career was tainted by the failure fully to escape Brentano's Cartesian empiricism. See Patočka, "Le subjectivisme de la phénoménologie husserlienne et la possibilité d'une phénoménologie 'asubjective,'" in id., *Qu'est-ce que la phénoménologie?* (Grenoble: Millon, 1988), 191. Balázs M. Mezei, in "Brentano, Cartesianism and Jan Patočka," *Brentano Studien* 5 (1994): 69–87, defends Brentano against Patočka's criticism.
18. Patočka, *Introduction to Husserl's Phenomenology*, 135
19. See Patočka's 1976 essay "Cartesianism and Phenomenology," in Kohák, ed., *Jan Patočka*, 285–326.
20. Patočka, "Negative Platonism," in Erazim Kohák, ed., *Jan Patočka: Philosophy and Selected Writings* (Chicago: University of Chicago Press, 1989), 196.
21. Patočka, *Introduction to Husserl's Phenomenology*, 159.
22. Ibid., 104–6. *Ekstasis* is a Heideggerian term indicating that beings in time are always 'outside themselves.'
23. Ibid., 141–42, 144.
24. Ibid., 137.
25. Ibid., 160.
26. Patočka, "Filosofie výchovy," in id., *Peče o duši*, vol. 1 (Prague: Oikoymenh, 1996), 435. Cf. Findlay, *Caring for the Soul*, 104.
27. Originally quoted in Czech translation, the passage appears in Patočka, *Introduction to Husserl's Phenomenology*, 167.
28. Patočka, "Das Innere und die Welt," *Studia Phænomenologica* 7 (2007): 36. See also Patočka, *Body, Community, Language, World*, 134.
29. Patočka, "Edmund Husserl's Philosophy of the Crisis of Science and His Conception of a Phenomenology of the 'Life-World,'" in Kohák, ed., *Jan Patočka*, 235.
30. Patočka, "Réflexion sur l'Europe," 196.
31. Patočka, *Le monde naturel comme problème philosophique*, trans. Jaromir Danek and Henri Declève (The Hague: M. Nijhoff, 1976), 79–81. An English translation is in preparation.
32. Ibid., 81–83, 86–88. As we will see, this argument is similar to one made decades later by Józef Tischner in Poland.
33. Patočka, *Le monde naturel et le mouvement de l'existence humaine* (Dordrecht: Kluwer, 1988), 56.
34. Patočka, *Le monde naturel comme problème philosophique*, 164–66. In a 1976 Postface to the French translation, Patočka politicized its analysis by issuing a rousing cry not to dismiss man as an epiphenomenon of objective forces (ibid., 181).

35. Patočka, *Body, Community, Language, World*, 5, 27.

36. Ibid., 5, 178. Corporeity, of course, was also an originally Husserlian insight, but one that he seemed to ignore when he divorced transcendental subjectivity from the thetic world.

37. Ibid., 13, 80, 103.

38. "Movement is that which allows things to be, that which allows at the same time that their being is alive, that it is a something in the order of life, a unity, a comprehensible sense, a path 'toward . . . ' Movement is thus the origin and the reason for the comprehensibility of the world, for its sense potency [*teneur de sens*]." Patočka, "La conception aristotélienne du mouvement: Signification philosophique et recherches historiques," in id., *Le monde naturel et le mouvement de l'existence humaine*, 129.

39. Its first adumbration appeared the journal *Tvář* in 1965. In French, see "Notes sur la préhistoire de la science du mouvement: Le monde, la terre, le ciel et la movement de la vie humaine," in Patočka, *Le monde naturel et le mouvement de l'existence humaine*, 3–12. German and Italian translations have since also appeared.

40. Patočka, *Heretical Essays*, 15. Though the book title is unnamed, the reference is to Hannah Arendt's *The Human Condition* (Chicago: University of Chicago Press, 1958).

41. Patočka, *Body, Community, Language, World*, 151; *Heretical Essays*, 74, cited in Marc Crépon, *Altérités de l'Europe* (Paris: Galilée, 2006), 156.

42. For the earth-sky metaphor, see Patočka, "Notes sur la préhistoire de la science du mouvement," 7. For Patočka the concepts of "earth" and "world" were antithetical. Whereas "earth" designated those forces that bound humans to life and restricted freedom, "world" named the open horizon of striving to break free from mere necessity.

43. Gasché, *Europe*, 225; in general, 211–62.

44. Patočka, *Plato and Europe,* trans. Petr Lom (Stanford, CA: Stanford University Press, 2002), 35.

45. Ibid.,13. On this theme, see Filip Karfík, *Unendlichwerden durch die Endlichkeit: Eine Lektüre der Philosophie Jan Patočkas* (Würzburg: Königshausen & Neumann, 2008).

46. The term is Gasché's. For the theme, see Patočka, *Plato and Europe*, 36.

47. The juncture was the body context, which formed the "sympathetic unity of a living being." Patočka, *Body, Community, Language, World*, 84, 133, 141

48. Ibid., 179.

49. Ibid., 177.

50. Ibid., 139.

51. Patočka, "Filosofie výchovy," 435, quoted in Findlay, *Caring for the Soul*, 151.

52. Patočka, *Heretical Essays*, 99. Indeed, "[t]here is nothing distinctive about the human ability to . . . accumulate power and might," he remarked in *Body, Community, Language, World* (170).

53. Patočka, *Body, Community, Language, World*, 178.

54. Ibid., 139.

55. Ibid., 36.

56. Ibid., 46, 48.

57. Ibid., 57.

58. Ibid., 65, 46.

59. On Patočka's conception of Europe, see Gasché, *Europe*; Crépon, *Altérités de l'Europe*; Armin Homp and Markus Sedlaczek, *Jan Patočka und die Idee von Europa* (Berlin: MitOst: 2003); and Denis Guénoun, *About Europe: Philosophical Hypotheses* (Stanford, CA: Stanford University Press, 2013). 'Normalization' (*normalizace*) refers to the period following the Prague Spring when Soviet authority and Communist Party control were restored in Czechoslovakia under the leadership of Gustáv Husák.

60. Patočka, "Quelques remarques sur les concepts d'histoire et d'historiographie," in id., *L'Europe après l'Europe* (Lagrasse, France: Verdier, 2007), 145.

61. Ibid., 150.

62. Patočka, "Quelques remarques sur le concept d'histoire universelle," in id., *Europe après l'Europe*, 155–71, 165. On Patočka's philosophy of history, see Ivan Chvatík, "Jan Patočka," in Aviezer Tucker, ed., *A Companion to the Philosophy of History and Historiography* (Malden, MA: Wiley-Blackwell, 2009), 518–28.

63. Patočka, "An Attempt at Czech National Philosophy and its Future," in Milič Čapek and Karel Hrubý, eds., *T. G. Masaryk in Perspective: Comments and Criticism* (Ann Arbor, MI: SVU Press, 1981), 1.

64. Patočka, *Heretical Essays*, 15.

65. Ibid., 39–40.

66. Ibid., 35, 38, 39. On Patočka's wide-ranging appropriation of the Greeks, see Jean-Louis Poirier, "Patočka et le Grecs ou Philosopher au fond de la caverne?" *Cahiers philosophiques* 50 (1992): 167–200.

67. Patočka, "La surcivilisation et son conflit interne," in id., *Liberté et sacrifice*, 103–4.

68. Ibid., 120, 141, 150–51. Patočka thought that one measure of this impotence was the modern lack of heroes. See ibid., 174, and, also in *Liberté et sacrifice*, "Remarques sur la position de la philosophie dans et dehors de monde" (1934), 34; "Les fondements spirituels de la vie contemporaine" (1970s), 234; and "Les heros de notre temps," 325–30.

69. Patočka, "Surcivilisation," 126.

70. Ibid., 163–64.

71. Patočka, "L'epique et le dramatique, l'epos et le drame," *Revue de métaphysique et de morale* 90, no. 2 (1985): 180.

72. Patočka, "Surcivilisation," 163–65.

73. Ibid., 156.

74. Ibid., 133; id., "Fondements spirituels," 217.

75. Patočka, "Surcivilisation," 123, 126–29. Nazism was a different beast, a challenger to the challenger that aimed to discipline a slothful West and break Eastern radicalism (149).

76. Ibid., 167. Metaphysically speaking, Heidegger warned in 1953, "Russia and America are the same." Heidegger, *An Introduction to Metaphysics* (New Haven, CT: Yale University Press, 1959) , 37.

77. Patočka, "Réflexion sur l'Europe," 184–85.

78. Patočka, "Europa und Nach-Europa: Die nacheuropäische Epoche und ihre geistigen Probleme," in id., *Ketzerische Essais zur Philosophie der Geschichte und ergänzende Schriften* (Vienna: Klett-Cotta, 1984), 217–18; id., "Surcivilisation," 201–3. This argument bears comparison with Theodor Adorno and Max Horkheimer's well-known *Dialectic of the Enlightenment*.

79. Patočka, "Die Epochen der Geschichte" in Patočka, *Ketzerische Essais*, 183–203. Patočka's notion of *aletheia* as openness and unveiling derives from Heidegger.

80. Patočka, "Europa und Nach-Europa," 210–11.

81. Patočka, "Surcivilisation," 169, 172, 175; "Réflexion sur l'Europe," 211. Tomaš Masaryk, we recall, introduced the term "titanism" as a critique of modern moral subjectivism. While Patočka was not so contemptuous of modern titans in a 1936 essay ("Titanism," in Kohák, ed., *Jan Patočka*, 139–44), seeing in them an emancipatory heroism, the 1950s reference echoed Masaryk's mistrust.

82. Patočka, "Réflexion sur l'Europe," 197.

83. Ibid., 212.

84. Patočka, "Europa und Nach-Europa," 211. On this theme, see Gasché.

85. Patočka, "Europa und Nach-Europa," 232.

86. Ibid., 215, 218, 221. It is worth noting that Patočka's distinction of Europe from non-Western societies, while naïve and often patronizing, was a far cry from Husserl's earlier description of Japan as a green branch of Occidental culture. Citing Karl Jaspers' thesis of an axial age, Patočka even suggested the possibility of pre-Socratic "kinship . . . between Greek philosophy and the Oriental philosophical beginnings" ("Negative Platonism," 181). Kwok-Ying Lau, one of the few scholars to address Patočka's post-European vision, argues that he largely escaped Husserl's Eurocentrism. See Lau, "Patočka's Concept of Europe: An Intercultural Consideration," in Ivan Chvatík and Erika Abrams, eds., *Jan Patočka and the Heritage of Phenomenology* (Dordrecht: Springer, 2011), 229–44.

87. Patočka, "Europa und Nach-Europa," 218–19; id., *Heretical Essays*, 132–33. See also Crépon, *Altérités de l'Europe*, chap. 5 (113–51), on the threats to the European idea.

88. Patočka, "Europa und Nach-Europa," 223.
89. Ibid., 225, 228, 230.
90. Ibid., 232–38.
91. Ibid., 226, 230.
92. Patočka, *Plato and Europe*, 221.
93. Ibid., 54.

94. The phrase τῆς ψυχῆς ἐπιμελεῖσθαι appears in Plato's "Apology," where Socrates explains: "For I do nothing but go about persuading you all, old and young alike, not to take thought for your persons or your properties, but first and chiefly to care about the greatest improvement of the soul" (quoted in Tucker, *Philosophy and Politics of Czech Dissidence*, 31, with a useful genealogy of Patočka's concept, 31–33).

95. For summaries of Plato's unwritten doctrine and debates over its relevance, see the Tübingen School representative Konrad Gaiser, "Plato's Enigmatic Lecture 'On the Good,'" *Phronesis* 25, no. 1 (1980): 5–37; Hans-Georg Gadamer, "Plato's Unwritten Dialectic," in *Dialogue and Dialectic: Eight Hermeneutical Studies on Plato* (New Haven, CT: Yale University Press, 1980), 124–55; and Giovanni Reale, *Toward a New Interpretation of Plato* (Washington, DC: Catholic University of America Press, 1997). On Patočka's relation to the ancients, see Philippe S. Merlier's excellent *Patočka: Le soin de l'âme at l'Europe* (Paris: Harmattan, 2009).

96. Plato, "Letters: VII," in Edith Hamilton and Huntington Cairns, eds., *The Collected Dialogues of Plato Including the Letters* (Princeton, NJ: Princeton University Press, 1961), 1589.

97. Patočka, *Plato and Europe*, 102.

98. Patočka, "Negative Platonism," in Kohák, ed. *Jan Patočka*, 198–99. On this theme, see Renaud Barbaras, *Le mouvement de l'existence: Études sur la phénoménologie de Jan Patočka* (Chatou, France: La Transparence, 2007), 7–28. Heidegger, for whom the *chōrismos* set up the metaphysical gap between real being and mere appearance, may be the initial source for this analysis, as Findlay (*Caring for the Soul*, 74–75) notes. See Heidegger, *An Introduction to Metaphysics* (New Haven, CT: Yale University Press, 1959), 106. The problem of the gap between Ideas and human reality in Plato was first broached by Aristotle in the *Nichomachean Ethics*, book 1, and its resolution came in his theory of potency or entelechy.

99. In an important postwar essay, Patočka distinguished ideas, which appeal to "our most personal inner core" and draw men to higher ethical pursuits, from ideologies, which "grasp" and "seize" men and subordinate them to a singular program. See Patočka, "Ideology and Life in the Idea," *Studia Phænomenologica* 7 (2007): 90.

100. Patočka, "Negative Platonism," 204.

101. Patočka, *Plato and Europe*, 2–3. As Marc Crépon points out, Patočka's project may be understood in response to Nietzsche as an effort to revive the

relationship with truth and eternity in post-metaphysical terms. Crépon, *Altérités de l'Europe*, 156.

102. Patočka, *Plato and Europe*, 19.

103. Ibid., 26. In a very different vein, Jürgen Habermas, in *The Philosophical Discourse of Modernity* (Cambridge, MA: MIT Press, 1990), included phenomenology under his criticism of subject-centered philosophies.

104. Patočka, "Le subjectivisme de la phénoménologie husserlienne et la possibilité d'une phénoménologie 'asubjective'" (1970) and "Le subjectivisme de la phénoménologie husserlienne et l'exigence d'une phénoménologie asubjective" (1971), in Patočka, *Qu'est-ce que la phénoménologie?* 189–216, 217–248. On asubjective phenomenology, see Chvatík "Jan Patočka and His Concept of an 'A-Subjective' Phenomenology"; Renaud Barbaras, "L'être et la manifestation—Sur la phénoménologie de Jan Patočka," *Revue de métaphysique et de morale* 4 (2006): 484–94; and Saulius Geniusas, "The Question of the Subject: Jan Patočka's Phenomenological Contribution," *Analecta Husserliana* 110, pt. 2 (2011): 599–612.

105. Contra Heidegger, Patočka viewed showing as prior to Being (*Plato and Europe*, 165).

106. Patočka, "Negative Platonism," 188. See Gasché, *Europe*, 229–31. The phrase "integral humanism" is likely a reference to Jacques Maritain's famous book.

107. For a discussion of Heidegger's negative anthropology in the "Letter on Humanism," see Geroulanos, *Atheism That Is Not Humanist*, 229–50.

108. Patočka, *Plato and Europe*, 27.

109. Patočka, "Leib, Möglichkeiten, Welt, Erscheinungsfeld," in *Vom Erscheinen als solchem: Texte aus dem Nachlaß* (Freiburg: Karl Alber, 2000), 97. For a fascinating analysis of the topic, see Karel Novotný, "L'ouverture du champ phenomenal: La donation ou l'interpretation? Sur le problème de l'apparaître comme tel chez Jan Patočka," in Hans Rainer Sepp and Ion Copoeru, eds., *Phenomenology 2005: Selected Essays from Northern Europe*, pt. 2 (Bucharest: Zeta Books, 2007), 545–72.

110. Gasché, *Europe*, 232.

111. Patočka, "Europa und Nach-Europa," 268.

112. Patočka, *Plato and Europe*, 13, 27, 41.

113. Ibid., 97.

114. Patočka, "Europa und Nach-Europa," 270–81; id., *Plato and Europe*, 109–30.

115. Patočka, *Plato and Europe*, 111.

116. Ibid., 36.

117. Ibid., 85, 105, 124.

118. Patočka, "Europa und Nach-Europa," 287; *Plato and Europe*, 36.

119. Patočka, *Plato and Europe*, 138.

120. Ibid., 45, 92.

121. Ibid., 23.

122. Ibid., 41, 180–98. Where Plato's care was vertical, aimed at a heavenly ideal, Aristotle's was horizon(t)al, earthly, directed toward the world. On Patočka's account of the historical "interplay of metaphysical and anti-metaphysical" thought, see Johann Arnason, "The Idea of Negative Platonism: Jan Patočka's Critique and Recovery of Metaphysics," *Thesis Eleven* 90, no. 6 (2007): 6–26.

123. The *Heretical Essays* have attracted particular interest among Patočka scholars. Ivan Chvatík's analyses, published as Working Papers of the Center for Theoretical Studies in Prague, remain touchstones: "The Heretical Conception of the European Legacy in the Late Essays of Jan Patočka," CTS-03–14 (2003); "Prolegomena to a Phenomenology of the Meaning of Human Life in the Late Essays of Jan Patočka," CTS-04–18 (2004); and "The Responsibility of the 'Shaken': Jan Patočka and his 'Care for the Soul' in a 'Post-European World,'" CTS-09–06. See also Derrida's appropriative but influential reading of the Fifth Heretical Essay in *The Gift of Death*.

124. Patočka, *Heretical Essays*, 41, 43. The relevant fragments from Heraclitus are §80, "It is necessary to know that war [πόλεμον] is common and right is strife and that all things happen by strife and necessity," and §53 "War is the father of all and king of all, and some he shows as gods, others as men; some he makes slaves, others free" (G. F. Kirk, J. E. Raven, and M. Schofield, *The Presocratic Philosophers: A Critical Edition with a Selection of Texts*, 2nd ed. [Cambridge: Cambridge University Press, 1983], 193–94). Patočka's *polemos* and his invocation of the front-line experiences of Ernst Jünger and Pierre Teilhard de Chardin have discomfited some interpreters. In a benign reading, we could say that *polemos* characterizes the constant turmoil of the world and the risky exposure of those who renounce comforting myths to struggle for truth. Yet Patočka also used the term to characterize Europe's heroic defensive battle against the non-European East, a battle, he said, that helped give rise to the ancient polis. For critical interpretations, see Erazim Kohák and Aviezer Tucker. As usual with Patočka, the transmission of the Heraclitean *polemos* likely came through Heidegger, who read it as the conflict that "first caused the realm of being to separate into opposites" (Heidegger, *Introduction to Metaphysics*, 61–62). As we have seen, Nicolai Hartmann also invoked the term to describe the conflict among values.

125. Patočka, *Heretical Essays*, 75, 62, 46.

126. Ibid., 115.

127. Ibid., 61.

128. Ibid., 103.

129. Ibid., 111.

130. Ibid., 134–36.

131. Patočka, *Plato and Europe*, 26.

132. Patočka, *Heretical Essays*, 118.

133. Patočka, "Quelques remarques sur les concepts d'histoire et d'historiographie," 152.

134. Patočka, "The Obligation to Resist Injustice," in Kohák, ed., *Jan Patočka*, 342.

135. "This conviction," Patočka went on, "is present in individuals as well, as the ground for living up to their obligations in private life, at work, and in public. The only genuine guarantee that humans will act not only out of greed and fear but freely, willingly, responsibly, lies in this conviction" (ibid., 341).

136. For an essay that briefly examines this tension, see James R. Mensch, "Patočka's Conception of the Subject of Human Rights," *Idealistic Studies* 41, nos. 1–2 (2011): 1–10. The vocabulary of rights, used during Patočka's final months and now closely associated with his name, did not appear elsewhere in his corpus. Earlier manuscripts, as we saw, characterized Western rights-based liberalism as an inessential political complement to modern rational civilization, a useful framework for protecting "the rights of rationality," but not a necessary partner. Against those who see the dissidents as freedom fighters spearheading Western liberalism, it is important to note that a phenomenology of human openness and self-transcendence need not have taken a human rights format. On human rights as a recent utopia, see Samuel Moyn, *The Last Utopia: Human Rights in History* (Cambridge, MA: Harvard University Press, 2010). On human rights in socialist Czechoslovakia, see Celia Donert, "Charter 77 and the Roma: Human Rights and Dissent in Socialist Czechoslovakia," in Stefan-Ludwig Hoffman, ed., *Human Rights in the Twentieth Century* (Cambridge: Cambridge University Press, 2011), 191–211. For a brief but thoughtful analysis of Patočka's philosophy and dissidence, see Richard Kearny, "Poetics and the Right to Resist: Patočka's Testimony," *International Journal of Philosophical Studies* 2, no. 1 (1994): 31–44.

CHAPTER 8

1. For an excellent recent reconstruction, see Jonathan Bolton, *Worlds of Dissent: Charter 77, the Plastic People of the Universe, and Czech Culture under Communism* (Cambridge, MA: Harvard University Press, 2012). The most granular account of the first four years remains H. Gordon Skilling, ed., *Charter 77 and Human Rights in Czechoslovakia* (London: Allen & Unwin, 1981). On the background of Charter 77, see Vladimir Kusin, *From Dubček to Charter 77* (Edinburgh: Q Press, 1978). The other necessary sourcebook is Vilém Prečan, *Charta 77, 1977–1989: Od morální k demokratické revoluci* (Bratislava: Archa, 1990). For the broader impact of the Helsinki Accords in fostering East European dissent, see Daniel Thomas, *The Helsinki Effect: International Norms, Human Rights, and*

the Demise of Communism (Princeton, NJ: Princeton University Press, 2001); and Sarah B. Snyder, *Human Rights Activism and the End of the Cold War: A Transnational History of the Helsinki Network* (Cambridge: Cambridge University Press, 2011).

2. See Aviezer Tucker, *The Philosophy and Politics of Czech Dissidence from Patočka to Havel* (Pittsburgh: University of Pittsburgh Press, 2000); Edward F. Findlay, *Caring for the Soul in a Postmodern Age: Politics and Phenomenology in the Thought of Jan Patočka* (Albany: State University of New York Press, 2002); and Alexandra Laignel-Lavastine, *Jan Patočka: L'esprit de la dissidence* (Paris: Michalon, 1998).

3. This chapter benefited greatly from conversations with Erazim Kohák, Józef Zumr, and Ivan Havel in Prague, May 2012.

4. The descriptor "binding agent" is Václav Havel's. For a discussion of Patočka's unifying influence, see Helena Sedláčková-Gibbs, "Moral Politics and Its Others: The Charter 77 Dissident Movement in Czechoslovakia (1977–1989)" (Ph.D. diss., New York University, 2003), 70–115. For portraits of and selections from Patočka printed soon after his death, see the underground volumes listed in Skilling, *Charter 77*, 36–37.

5. Václav Havel, *Disturbing the Peace* (New York: Vintage Books, 1990), 136. Cf. Havel's recollection of Patočka delivered at a centenary conference in Prague, 23 April 2007, in Ivan Chvatík and Erika Abrams, eds., *Jan Patočka and the Heritage of Phenomenology* (Dordrecht: Springer, 2011), xv–xvi.

6. Patočka, "Two Charter 77 Texts," in Erazim Kohák, ed., *Jan Patočka: Philosophy and Selected Writings* (Chicago: University of Chicago Press, 1989), 340–47.

7. For Benda, Patočka's death meant that an abstract moral stance alone would no longer suffice. Having established itself as a leader of Czechoslovak countersociety, Charter 77 had to move toward tactical support for independent cultural and social initiatives beyond the reach of the state. Václav Benda, "The Parallel 'Polis,'" in Skilling and Paul Wilson, eds., *Civic Freedom in Central Europe: Voices from Czechoslovakia* (New York: St. Martin's Press, 1991), 35–41. Cf. Martin Palouš, "Jan Patočka versus Václav Benda," in the same volume, which argues that Benda reoriented Patočka's inward-directed freedom toward the public sphere; and id., "The Parallel Polis after Twelve Years," *Uncaptive Minds* 2, no. 5 (1989): 36–40.

8. Ladislav Hejdánek, *Wahrheit und Widerstand: Prager Briefe* (Munich: Kirchheim, 1988), 29, 31; Ludvík Vaculík, "Mortal Illness," in Skilling, ed., *Charter 77*, 240. See also eulogies from the former Prague Spring foreign minister Jiří Hajek, the literary theorist Václav Černý, and the writer Ludvík Vaculík in Skilling, ed., *Charter 77*, 235–44.

9. Though active in cultural circles in the 1960s and 1970s, Mandler refused to sign the Charter. For his critique of Patočka, see Emanuel Mandler,

"Intelektuálové na cestě k nepolitické politice: Dva fragmenty," *Soudobé dějiny* 2, no. 1 (1995): 65–92. Sedláčková-Gibbs discusses his critique in her chapter on Patočka.

10. Milan Šimečka, "Speaking My Mind," in Mary Kaldor, ed., *Europe from Below: An East-West Dialogue* (London: Verso, 1991), 77–81.

11. Petr Uhl, "The Alternative Community as Revolutionary Avant-garde," in Václav Havel et al., *The Power of the Powerless: Citizens against the State in Central-Eastern Europe* (New York: M. E. Sharpe, 1985), 193–94.

12. For Bělohradský, Machiavelli was as much the culprit as Husserl's Galileo.

13. Elsewhere he described this as the replacement of truth by necessity. Václav Bělohradský, "La précession de la légalité, or l'Empire d'Autriche comme métaphore," *Le Cahier* 6 (October 1988), 156–59.

14. Václav Bělohradský, "Krize eschatologie neosobnosti," in *Přirozený svět jako politický problém: Eseje o člověku pozdní doby* (Prague: Edice Orientace, 1991), 98. For the Italian translation, see Belohradsky, *Il mondo della vita: Un problema politico: L'eredità europea nel dissenso a in Charta 77* (Milan: Jaca, 1980).

15. Bělohradský, "Krize eschatologie neosobnosti," 63–64.

16. The enfant terrible of recent Czech literature, Ludvík Vaculík, for example, disclaimed any familiarity with phenomenological arguments, although his demurral seems somewhat exaggerated: see Skilling, ed., *Charter 77*, 239; and from Vaculík, *A Cup of Coffee with My Interrogator* (London: Readers International, 1987), 36. On samizdat, see Skilling, *Samizdat and Independent Society in Central and Eastern Europe* (Columbus: Ohio State University Press, 1989). The term "unbooks" described the unofficial transcripts, often copied and circulated by hand, through which Czechoslovak philosophy and belles-lettres survived under normalization.

17. Ladislav Hejdánek, "The Conception of Truth and Its Meontological Preconditions" (1985), in Marketa Goetz-Stankiewicz, ed., *Good-bye, Samizdat: Twenty Years of Czechoslovak Underground Writing* (Evanston, IL: Northwestern University Press, 1992), 250. On Hejdánek's biography, see the brief essay by translator Milan Walter at the end of Hejdánek, *Wahrheit und Widerstand*, 276–79.

18. Ladislav Hejdánek, "Prospects for Democracy and Socialism in Eastern Europe," in Havel et al., *Power of the Powerless*, 148, 144.

19. Ivan Havel, "Modes of Cognition" (1985), in Goetz-Stankiewicz, ed., *Good-bye, Samizdat*, 231, 227.

20. Václav Malý in Skilling and Wilson, eds., *Civic Freedom*, 86; Benda in Havel et al., *Power of the Powerless*, 112.

21. Skilling and Wilson, eds., *Civic Freedom*, 116. It is worth noting the linguistic echo of Karel Kosík, who in 1968 worried about the *Gleichschaltung*, or

enforced conformity, imposed by modern states. See Karel Kosík, "Our Current Crisis," in id., *The Crisis of Modernity: Essays and Observations from the 1968 Era* (Lanham, MD: Rowman & Littlefield, 1995), 39–40. *Gleichschaltung* was, of course, the Nazi term for the forced coordination of Reich and Land governments. Czech critics used it in mordant comparison of Nazi and communist control.

22. Rudolf Battěk, "Spiritual Values, Independent Initiatives and Values," in Havel et al., *Power of the Powerless*, 97–98.

23. Ibid., 102. "In the past," Battěk continued, "people never dreamed that humanity itself would one day become the divine agent threatening the destruction of the world, as if the crisis of today had sprung from humanity's own indifference toward itself."

24. Uhl, "Alternative Community," in Havel et al., *Power of the Powerless*, 188. This was straight Kosík, who wrote in 1968: "[H]umanist socialism is the negation of both capitalism and Stalinism." Kosík, *Crisis of Modernity*, 55.

25. We have already noted Patočka's respect for Marxist thought. Havel too appreciated its importance: In 1978, he signed a declaration protesting normalization in the name of a Czech tradition of democratic socialism. See "100 Years of Czech Socialism," *Labour Focus on Eastern Europe* 2, no. 2 (1978): 11–12.

26. For critics such as Emmanuel Mandler, this association tarnished Chartism and turned it into a hideout for unapologetic leftists. See Mandler, "O hrdinech a o těch druhých," *Kritická Příloha* 8 (1997): 218–31.

27. Tomáš Halík, "Ego Dormio (A Meditation on the Night Path of Knowledge)," (1985), in Goetz-Stankiewicz, ed., *Good-bye, Samizdat*, 280. Halík was influenced by Poland's Józef Tischner, discussed in chapter 10.

28. Hejdánek, "Conception of Truth," in Goetz-Stankiewicz, ed., *Good-bye, Samizdat*, 248.

29. Martin Palouš, "Philosophy as Personal Experience and the Others," in Goetz-Stankiewicz, ed., *Good-bye, Samizdat*, 261.

30. Ibid., 262, 265.

31. Josef Zvěřina, "On Not Living in Hatred," in Havel et al., *Power of the Powerless*, 212–13. The term *ressentiment* is Hejdánek's (echoing Nietzsche and Scheler), used to describe the regime-friendly anti-Chartists. Hejdánek, *Wahrheit und Widerstand*, 123.

32. Skilling and Wilson, eds., *Civic Freedom*, 70.

33. Ibid., 117.

34. Václav Černý, "On the Question of Chartism," in Havel et al., *Power of the Powerless*, 132–33. In the late 1940s, based on a popular lecture series, Černý wrote two tracts on existentialism that assured his familiarity with the phenomenological family tree. See Černý, *První a druhý sešit o existencialismu* (Prague: Mladá fronta, 1992). On Černý, see Bolton, *Worlds of Dissent*, 67–68.

35. Vilém Prečan, quoted in John Keane, *Václav Havel: A Political Tragedy in Six Acts* (New York: Basic Books, 2000), 247.

36. The quotation is from Malý in Skilling and Wilson, eds., *Civic Freedom*, 86; but see also Hejdánek and Zvěřina in the volume for representative statements; cf. Hejdánek, *Wahrheit und Widerstand*, 54–55.

37. Radim Palouš, "'My' Philosophy," in Goetz-Stankiewicz, ed., *Good-bye Samizdat*, 267–74.

38. Eva Kantůrková in Skilling and Wilson, eds., *Civic Freedom*, 79.

39. Malý, in ibid., 86.

40. Halík, "Ego Dormio," in Goetz-Stankiewicz, ed., *Good-bye Samizdat*, 275–84. For some of Patočka's complex reflections on God and modern godlessness, see his private letters to Miloslava Holubová in Holubová, *Necestou cestou* (Torst: Prague, 1998).

41. Václav Benda, "Catholicism and Politics," in Havel et al., *Power of the Powerless*, 110–24; Cf. the Protestant Hejdánek, *Wahrheit und Widerstand*, 83.

42. Skilling, ed., *Charter 77*, 287.

43. Kantůrková, in Skilling and Wilson, eds., *Civic Freedom*, 79.

44. Patočka, "Two Charta 77 Texts," in Kohák, ed., *Jan Patočka*, 342.

45. Havel, "Politics and Conscience"; George Konrad, *Antipolitics: An Essay* (San Diego: Harcourt, Brace, Jovanovich, 1984).

46. Palouš, "'My' Philosophy," in Goetz-Stankiewicz, ed., *Good-bye Samizdat*, 273. This perspective evoked Masaryk as well as Husserl, Erazim Kohák reminds us in "Czech Philosophy in Samizdat: An Introduction" (ibid., 217–21).

47. Hejdánek, *Wahrheit und Widerstand*, 162, 168.

48. Konrad, *Antipolitics*, 223. For the earlier view, see George Konrad and Ivan Szelényi, *The Intellectuals on the Road to Class Power: A Sociological Study of the Role of the Intelligentsia in Socialism* (New York: Harcourt Brace Jovanovich, 1979). Konrad's new aristocracy was intended as a more distant social and political guide than the communist nomenklatura. For an analysis of the "new class" of intellectuals globally written during the same era, see Alvin Gouldner, *The Future of Intellectuals and the Rise of the New Class* (New York: Seabury, 1979). The term "new class," of course, dates back to the Yugoslav Milovan Djilas's famous critique, *The New Class: An Analysis of the Communist System* (New York: Praeger, 1957).

49. Gil Eyal, *The Origins of Postcommunist Elites: From Prague Spring to the Breakup of Czechoslovakia* (Minneapolis: University of Minnesota Press, 2003).

50. Hejdánek, *Wahrheit und Widerstand*, 58. For a well-known early exchange about the elitism of Charter 77, see the Vaculík-Havel debate translated as "Discussion within the Charter—The Ethics of Opposition," *Labour Focus on Eastern*

Europe 2, no. 3 (1979): 16–18. Emanuel Mandler, Havel's 1960s antagonist on the board of *Tvář* literary magazine, picked up Vaculík's charge of "showy heroism" and made it a centerpiece of his postcommunist critique of the Charter in "O hrdinech a o těch druhých." Both Helena Sedláčková-Gibbs and Gil Eyal agree that the charge holds some validity. For an anthropological account of the gulf between dissidents and the majority of their countrymen, see Ladislav Holý, *The Little Czech and the Great Czech Nation* (Cambridge: Cambridge University Press, 1996), 27–33. For an intriguing account of the lives of ordinary Czechoslovaks—Havel's greengrocers—during the era of normalization, see Paulina Bren, *The Greengrocer and His TV: The Culture of Communism after the Prague Spring* (Ithaca, NY: Cornell University Press, 2010).

51. Miroslav Kusý, "Chartism and 'real socialism,'" in Havel et al., *Power of the Powerless*, 173.

52. Jiřina Šiklová and Gerald Turner, "Courage, Heroism, and the Postmodern Paradox," *Social Research* 71, no. 1 (Spring 2004): 135–48. As Slavoj Žižek remarks, Havel's power of the powerless applied only in late communist societies that made it "possible for the dissidents to assume the heroic position of the tragic victim" in relative physical safety. It was untenable under ferocious Stalinist regimes. Žižek, *Did Somebody Say Totalitarianism? Five Interventions in the (Mis)use of a Notion* (London: Verso, 1996), 96.

53. On Havel, see Keane, *Václav Havel*; Eda Kriseová, *Václav Havel: The Authorized Biography* (New York: St. Martin's Press 1993); Marketa Goetz-Stankiewicz and Phyllis Carey, eds., *Critical Essays on Václav Havel* (New York: G. K. Hall, 1999); James F. Pontuso, *Václav Havel: Civic Responsibility in the Postmodern Age* (Lanham, MD: Rowman & Littlefield, 2004); Delia Popescu, *Political Action in Václav Havel's Thought: The Responsibility of Resistance* (Lanham, MD: Lexington, 2012); and Martin Matuštík, *Postnational Identity: Critical Theory and Existential Politics in Habermas, Kierkegaard, and Havel* (New York: Guilford Press, 1993). On Havel the playwright, see Carol Rocamora, *Acts of Courage: Václav Havel's Life in the Theater* (Hanover, NH: Smith & Kraus, 2005).

54. Havel wrote "The Power of the Powerless" for a joint Czechoslovak-Polish collection whose Polish half never appeared. Regarding Havel's influence in Poland, the factory organizer Zbigniew Bujak's remark that Havel's essay restored confidence in Polish grassroots activity is widely cited. See Paul Wilson's introduction to "The Power of the Powerless," in Havel, *Open Letters: Selected Writings, 1965–1990* (New York: Vintage Books, 1992), 125–26. Adam Michnik and Stanisław Barańczak also confirm Havel's popularity in Poland: Michnik, "Letter from the Gdańsk Prison," in *Letters from Prison and Other Essays* (Berkeley: University of California Press, 1985), 91; Barańczak, "The Absolute Horizon," in *Breathing under Water and Other East European Essays* (Cambridge, MA: Harvard University Press, 1990), 54.

55. Havel's admission is in *Letters to Olga* (New York: Henry Holt, 1988), 147. Ladislav Hejdánek affirms this assessment in Havel, *Living in Truth* (London: Faber & Faber, 1987), 226.

56. Havel, "Remembering Jan Patočka," in *Jan Patočka and the Heritage of Phenomenology*, xv–xvi; "Last Conversation," in Skilling, ed., *Charter 77*, 242–44.

57. Havel, *Letters to Olga*, 119.

58. Ibid., 371.

59. Ibid., 268.

60. Ibid., 294–5.

61. Ibid., 232.

62. Ibid., 332–33.

63. Ibid., 319.

64. Ibid., 311–15. Paul Berman uncharitably describes Havel as another "befuddled left-wing reader of Martin Heidegger." Berman, *A Tale of Two Utopias: The Political Journey of the Generation of 1968* (New York: Norton, 1996), 226. Cf. Aviezer Tucker, "Václav Havel's Heideggerianism," *Telos* 85 (1990): 63–78.

65. Havel, *Letters to Olga*, 363, 365.

66. Havel, "Politics and Conscience," in id., *Open Letters*, 250, 254, 260.

67. Ibid., 263.

68. Ibid., 269, 271. In a 1987 interview, Havel insisted that too much was made of the term "antipolitics." "Doing without Utopias: An Interview with Vaclav Havel," *Times Literary Supplement*, no. 4373 (23 January 1987): 81.

69. The self-deprecating image of the *malý český človĕk* is discussed in Holý, *Little Czech and the Great*.

70. Havel, "Power of the Powerless," in id., *Open Letters*, 141.

71. For the difference between post-totalitarian power and classical dictatorship, see ibid., 127–32.

72. Ibid., 143.

73. The authorities "behave as if the ideological kingdom of real socialism existed in 'what we have here now,' as if they had, in all earnestness, convinced the nation of its existence; the nation behaves as if it believed it, as if it were convinced that it lived in accordance with this real socialism." Kusý, "Chartism and 'real socialism,'" in Havel et al., *Power of the Powerless*, 164.

74. Havel, "Power of the Powerless," in id., *Open Letters*, 153–54, 131.

75. Ibid., 152–53, 207–9. The phrase "live in truth," of course, came from Patočka. The philosopher and Patočka student Petr Rezek has argued that the concept of living in truth—which, through Havel, became the slogan of the Czech dissident movement—was unsuited to political action and hence to the dissident engagement it purportedly justified. According to Rezek, Patočka's living in truth required a Heideggerian abandonment of worldliness in favor of life "at the summit [*na vrcholu*]." See Rezek, "Život disidentův jako 'život v pravdĕ'?"

and "Životní pohyb pravdy a život v pravdě u Jana Patočky," in *Filosofia a politika kýče* (Prague: Oikoymenh, 1991), 45–78. Cf. Rezek, *Jan Patočka a věc fenomenologie* (Prague: Oikoymenh, 1993). Rezek's position is considered too extreme by most former dissidents and Patočka students. On Rezek, see Tucker, *Philosophy and Politics of Czech Dissidence*, 116–23; Bren, *The Greengrocer and His TV*, 102, 205–6.

76. We have already seen that Havel signed the declaration entitled "100 Years of Czech Socialism." For a debate over the values of 1968, see Havel, "Český úděl," in id., *O lidskou identitu* (Prague: Rozmluvy, 1990), 187–200; Karel Kosík, "The Weight of Words, in id., *Crisis of Modernity*, 113–16.

77. Havel, "Power of the Powerless," in id., *Open Letters*, 161. During the 1960s thaw, Havel called for a democratic opposition party, a position he later discounted as simplistic. See "On the Theme of an Opposition," ibid., 25–35.

78. Havel, "Power of the Powerless," in id., *Open Letters*, 209.

79. Ibid., 176–81.

80. Ibid., 209–14. On an economics oriented to individuals, see Havel, *Disturbing the Peace*, 13–14.

81. Havel, "Power of the Powerless," in id., *Open Letters*, 210. Havel's ideas, said the dissident writer Milan Šimečka in 1989, bore "the stamp of detachment from the people." Šimečka, "Speaking my Mind," in *Europe from Below: An East-West Dialogue* (London: Verso, 1991), 78. This opinion differs markedly from Richard Rorty's call to exchange Lenin and Bolshevism for Havel and Charter 77 in the leftist imaginary, the latter an example of the "groundless hope" and "social poetry" that Rorty prized. Rorty, "The End of Leninism, Havel, and Social Hope," in id., *Truth and Progress: Philosophical Papers 3* (Cambridge: Cambridge University Press, 1998), 228–43.

82. Stanislaw Baranczak notes this practical bent in Havel's plays. See Baranczak, "All the President's Plays," in Carey and Goetz-Stankiewicz, eds., *Critical Essays on Václav Havel*, 53. By his own account, Havel pursued theater because it was a social art, and his colleagues recall him as a vibrant organizer—a characterization I heard in conversations with Ivan Havel and Józef Zumr in Prague in May 2012.

83. Havel also came closer to a religious characterization of Being than did his philosopher-mentors. He said he used the term 'Supreme Being' rather than 'God' because he had never experienced a personal revelation himself.

84. Skilling and Wilson, eds., *Civic Freedom*, 79.

CHAPTER 9

1. Karol Wojtyła, "The Intentional Act and the Human Act, That Is, Act and Experience," *Analecta Husserliana* 5 (1976): 278.

2. Robert F. Harvanek, "The Philosophical Foundations of the Thought of John Paul II," in John McDermott, ed., *The Thought of John Paul II* (Rome: Pontificia Università Gregoriana, 1993), 8. Ingarden was an examiner of Wojtyła's *Habilitationsschrift* along with the lay Catholic philosopher Stefan Swieżawski and the theologian Władysław Wicher.

3. Kazimierz Twardowski, *On the Content and Object of Presentations* (The Hague: Nijhoff, 1977). Cf. Dariusz Łukasiewicz, "Polish Metaphysics and the Brentanian Tradition," in Sandra LaPointe, Jan Woleński, Mathieu Marion, and Wiletta Miskeiwicz, eds., *The Golden Age of Polish Philosophy: Kazimierz Twardowski's Philosophical Legacy* (Dordrecht: Springer, 2009), 19–31; Barry Smith, *Austrian Philosophy: The Legacy of Brentano* (Chicago: Open Court, 1994), 155–91.

4. Quoted in Smith, *Austrian Philosophy*, 159.

5. Jan Łukasiewicz, "Teza Husserla o stosunku logiki do psychologii," *Przegląd Filozoficzny* 4 (1904): 476–77; Władysław Tatarkiewicz, *Szkoła fenomenologów, Ruch Filozoficzny* 3, no. 10 (1913): 257–63. In his book *Husserl und die Polen* (Würzburg: Königshausen & Neumann, 2011), the Katowice philosopher Czesław Głombik examines a clutch of young Polish thinkers who joined Ingarden in Göttingen and took interest in Husserl's ideas. In addition to those indicated, he discusses Aleksandr Rozenblum and Stefan Błachowski. For a shorter summary, see Głombik, "Die Polen und die Göttinger phänomenologische Bewegung," *Husserl Studies* 21, no. 1 (2005): 1–15.

6. For the standard history, see Jan Wolenski, *Logic and Philosophy in the Lvov-Warsaw School* (Dordrecht: Kluwer, 1989). Along with its theories of logic and language, several philosophers in the Lvov-Warsaw tradition elaborated theories of value. See Czesław Porębski, *Polish Value Theory* (Kraków: Kraków Academy of Economics and Jagiellonian University, Dialogikon series, 1996); Janina Makota, "Value as Considered by Some 20th Century Polish Philosophers," in Jochen Bloss, Władysław Stróżewski, and Józef Zumr, eds., *Intentionalität, Werte, Kunst: Husserl, Ingarden, Patočka* (Prague: Filosofia, 1995), 119–27.

7. Like many Polish philosophers, Swieżawski knew both analytic and neo-Thomist traditions, and his 1965 rallying cry—"There is no true philosophy and no philosophical truth outside of realism"—might have recalled either. Jerzy Kalinowski and Stefan Swieżawski, *La philosophie à l'heure du Concile* (Paris: Société d'Éditions internationales, 1965), 45. The revolutionary personalist Emmanuel Mounier also exerted considerable sway in interwar Polish Catholic circles, a link demonstrated by Piotr Kosicki, "L'avènement des intellectuals catholiques: La mensuel *Więź* et les conséquences polonaises du personalisme mounierien," *Vingtième Siècle: Revue d'histoire* 102 (April–June 2009): 31–47. For an introduction to interwar French Catholic circles, see Joseph Amato, *Mounier and Maritain: A French Catholic Understanding of the Modern World* (Tuscaloosa: University of Alabama Press, 1975).

8. Husserl did appear to the interwar Polish avant-garde in the writings of the painter, philosopher, and novelist Stanisław Ignacy Witkiewicz (a.k.a. Witkacy). A character in Witkiewicz's novel *Insatiability* (Evanston, IL: Northwestern University Press, 1996) calls him "a truly inspired madman whose mistakes are worth a hundred times more than all the correct assertions of academic pseudoprobes too squeamish for introspection in psychology" (193). Witkiewicz also discussed Husserl in two articles on art. See Marek Bartelik, *Early Polish Modern Art: Unity in Multiplicity* (Manchester: Manchester University Press, 2005), 69, 88n31. Though he achieved posthumous renown, Witkacy was little known in his lifetime, and his praise of Husserl did not betoken widespread appreciation of the latter among Poland's literati.

9. Husserl, *Ideas*, 361–62. In two manuscripts from the 1890s (published in *Husserliana*, vol. 22: *Aufsätze und Rezensionen (1890-1910)* (The Hague: Nijhoff, 1979), 307–11, 349–56), Husserl rejected Twardowski's distinction for duplicating the intended object by splitting it into two categories. For a brief discussion, see Dermot Moran, *Edmund Husserl: Founder of Phenomenology* (Cambridge: Polity Press, 2005), 21–2. For an extended analysis of the two Brentanians, see Jens Cavallin, *Content and Object: Husserl, Twardowski and Psychologism* (Dordrecht: Kluwer, 1997).

10. See John Connelly, *Captive University: The Sovietization of East German, Czech, and Polish Higher Education, 1945–1956* (Chapel Hill: North Carolina, 2000).

11. Czesław Miłosz, *Native Realm: A Search for Self-Definition* (New York: Farrar, Straus & Giroux, 1968), 258–300.

12. Tadeusz Kroński, "Filozofia i świat naiwny (rec. Jan Patočka, Přirozený svět jako filosofický problem,") *Ateneum* 1 (1939): 130, 131.

13. Tadeusz Kroński, "Świat w klamrach ontologii," *Myśl filozoficzna* 1 (1952): 318. Excerpts of the thirteen-page review are translated in Józef Tischner, *Marxism and Christianity* (Washington, DC: Georgetown University Press, 1981), 23–25. Kroński joined Adam Schaff's Institute for Training Scientific Cadres (later the Institute of Social Sciences), created to indoctrinate social scientists in Marxism-Leninism. See Connelly, *Captive University*, 156–57.

14. Kroński, "Świat w klamrach ontologii," 318–20. The story is unattributed.

15. Ibid., 330–31. Scheler was, in Kroński's estimation, "a lecher and a drunk ... and an intellectual precursor to Hitlerism" (331). Husserl, he conceded, did not go this far.

16. Ibid., 331. Credit where it is due: Kroński's complaint (323) that Ingarden never provided the promised metaphysical voucher for his ontological claims is accurate.

17. "Ingarden," wrote the First Secretary of the Polish Communist Party, "is committed to idealism and is an enemy of materialism. He is one of the foremost

representatives of so-called Husserlism." Quoted in Jeff Mitscherling, *Roman Ingarden's Ontology and Aesthetics* (Ottawa: University of Ottawa Press, 1996), 33, 111–13. On these attacks, see also Zdzisław Krasnodębski, "Phänomenologie und Soziologie in Polen: Der Anfang eines Dialogs," in Richard Grathoff and Bernhard Waldenfels, eds., *Sozialität und Intersubjektivität: Phänomenologische Perspektiven der Sozialwissenschaften im Umkreis von Aron Gurwitsch und Alfred Schütz* (Munich: Fink, 1983), 361.

18. The growing influence was partly due to reputation: Ingarden was "one of the true symbols at the time of an unblemished ethical position in the Jagiellonian University," Tischner writes in *Marxism and Christianity*, 90.

19. Ingarden claimed a lifelong interest in the topic, having originally proposed a dissertation on the person, which Husserl discouraged as too time-consuming.

20. For English translations, see Roman Ingarden, *Man and Value* (Washington, DC: Catholic University of America Press, 1983). This contains the short version of "On Responsibility" that appeared in the Polish edition, not the lengthier German study *Über die Verantwortung: Ihre ontische Fundamente* (Stuttgart: Philipp Reclam, 1970). The 1961 seminar lectures are collected and published in Ingarden, *Wykłady z etyki* (Warsaw: Państwowe Wydawnictwo Naukowe, 1989). One of them, "An Analysis of Moral Values," also appears in *Man and Value*, 165–78.

21. Ingarden, *Man and Value*, 24.

22. Ibid., 25, 30.

23. Ibid., 80, 85.

24. Ingarden, "On Responsibility: Its Ontic Foundations," in ibid., 53–117.

25. Karol Wojtyła (Pope John Paul II), *Osoba i czyn* (Kraków: Polskie Towarzystwo Teologiczne, 1969), trans. as *The Acting Person* (Dordrecht: D. Reidel, 1979). "Person and Act" would be more accurate.

26. George Hunston Williams, *The Mind of John Paul II: Origins of His Thought and Action* (New York: Seabury Press, 1981), 193–94. On Ingarden's similarity to Wojtyła, see Tadeusz Styczeń, "O metodzie antropolgii filozoficznej na marginesie Osoby i czynu K. Wojtyły oraz Książeczki o człowieku R. Ingardena" (On the Method of Philosophical Anthropology at the Margins of K. Wojtyła's *Person and Act* and R. Ingarden's *A Little Book on the Human Being*), *Roczniki Filozoficzne* 21, no. 2 (1973): 105–114.

27. See, e.g., the conference papers on Wojtyła's volume delivered at the Catholic University of Lublin and gathered together as "Z zagadnień filozoficznych—Dyskusja nad dziełem kardynała Karola Wojtyły ‚Osoba i czyn'" (Philosophical Problems—A Discussion of the Publication "Person and Act" by Cardinal Karol Wojtyła), *Analecta Cracoviensia* 5–6 (1973–74): 49–297. See also Józef Tischner, J. M. Życiński, and George F. McLean, eds., *The Philosophy of Person: Solidarity and Cultural Creativity* (Washington, D.C.: Paideia Press; Council for Research

in Values and Philosophy, 1994); Karol Wojtyła, Andrzej Szostek, and Tadeusz Styczeń, eds., *Der Streit um den Menschen: Personaler Anspruch des Sittlichen* (Kevelaer, Germany: Butzon & Bercker, 1979).

28. For a wide-ranging history of the concept of solidarity, see Steinar Stjernø, *Solidarity in Europe: The History of an Idea* (Cambridge: Cambridge University Press, 2009).

29. The indispensable guide to Wojtyła's thought is Rocco Buttiglione, *Karol Wojtyła: The Thought of the Man Who Became Pope John Paul II* (Grand Rapids, MI: Eerdmans, 1997). For the details of Wojtyła's intellectual biography, Williams, *Mind of John Paul II* is also useful. In addition, see Kenneth L. Schmitz, *At the Center of the Human Drama: The Philosophical Anthropology of Karol Wojtyła/John Paul II* (Washington, DC: Catholic University of America Press, 1993); Andrew N. Woznicki, *A Christian Humanism: Karol Wojtyła's Existential Personalism* (New Britain, CT: Mariel, 1980), by a second-generation Lublin Schooler and Wojtyła student; and Josef Seifert, "Karol Cardinal Wojtyla (Pope John Paul II) as a Philosopher and the Cracow/Lublin School of Philosophy," *Aletheia* 2 (1981): 130–99, and "Truth and Transcendence of the Person in the Philosophical Thought of Karol Wojtyła," in Rocco Buttiglione, Carlo Fedeli, and Angelo Scola, eds., *Karol Wojtyla: Filosofo, teologo, poeta : atti del 1° Colloquio internazionale del pensiero cristiano* (Vatican City: Libreria Editrice Vaticana, 1984), 93–106. George Weigel's bestselling biography is *Witness to Hope: The Biography of Pope John Paul II* (New York: Cliff Street Books, 1999). For a useful chronology of his life (through the early papacy) in Polish, see Adam Boniecki, ed., *Kalendarium życia Karola Wojtyły* (Kraków: Społeczny Instytut Widawniczy Znak, 1983).

30. For the label "existential personalism," see Woznicki, *Christian Humanism*.

31. On this theme, see Samuel Moyn, "Personalism, Community, and the Origins of Human Rights," in Stefan-Ludwig Hoffmann, *Human Rights in the Twentieth Century* (Cambridge: Cambridge University Press, 2010), 85–106.

32. See Jacques Maritain, *Existence and the Existent* (New York: Image, 1948). For surveys of modern Thomism, see Gerald McCool, *Nineteenth-Century Scholasticism: The Search for a Unitary Method* (New York: Fordham University Press, 1989); *From Unity to Pluralism: The Internal Evolution of Thomism* (New York: Fordham University Press, 1989); and *The Neo-Thomists* (Milwaukee: Marquette University Press, 1994).

33. See Jacques Maritain, *Integral Humanism: Temporal and Spiritual Problems of a New Christendom* (Notre Dame, IN: University of Notre Dame Press, 1973). On Maritain's early personalism, see Moyn, "Jacques Maritain: Le origini dei diritti umani e il pensiero politico cristiano," in Luigi Bonanate and Roberto Papini, eds., *Dialogo interculturale e diritti umani: La Dichiarazione Universale dei Diritti Umani, genesi, evoluzione, e problemi odierni (1948–2008)* (Bologna: Il Mulino, 2008), 97–124.

34. For the account of his sojourn to France to study new missionary methods of mingling with workers—a strategy Wojtyła later encouraged in Poland—see Wojtyła, "Mission de France" (1949) in *En esprit et en vérité: Recueil de textes, 1949–78* (Paris: Centurion, 1978), 9–17. Cf. Williams, *Mind of John Paul II*, 110–13. Piotr Kosicki provides background to the worker-priest movement in "Between Catechism and Revolution: Poland, France, and the Story of Catholicism and Socialism in Europe, 1878–1958" (Ph.D. diss., Princeton University, 2011), 189–96.

35. Wojtyła defended the use of philosophical frameworks for interpreting the Gospels—what he called speculative theology or theological ethics—as requisite to reveal their significance. While the Bible was complete in itself, he averred, its truths sometimes required elucidation. Thomistic metaphysics was the noblest hermeneutic framework, but modern philosophy could also afford insight into eternal verities as long as it did not violate scriptural revelation. Wojtyła, "Ethics and Moral Theology," 101, 103–4; "The Personal Structure of Self-Determination," 187; and "Thomistic Personalism," 165ff., all in id., *Person and Community: Selected Essays* (New York: Peter Lang, 1993).

36. Wojtyła, "Ethics and Moral Theology," 104.

37. See esp. Wojtyła's essay "Thomistic Personalism," originally published in the Polish Catholic journal *Znak* in 1961, in id., *Person and Community*. See also in the same volume, "The Problem of the Separation of Experience from the Act in Ethics in the Philosophy of Immanuel Kant and Max Scheler," 24. Avery Cardinal Dulles notes these doubts in "John Paul II and the Mystery of the Human Person," in *Church and Society: The Laurence McGinley Lectures, 1988–2007* (New York: Fordham University Press, 2008), 414–15. They have even led some to deny that Wojtyła was a Thomist at all. See the remark from his friend Krzysztof Kozłowski, quoted in Kosicki, "Between Catechism and Revolution," 252n55.

38. Wojtyła, *Acting Person*, 78; *Osoba i czyn*, 81. Cf. "The Transcendence of the Person in Action and Man's Teleology," *Analecta Husserliana* 9 (1979): 204.

39. "Où va la nouvelle théologie?" asked Reginald Garrigou-Lagrange. "Elle revient au modernisme." His best-known attack came in "La nouvelle théologie où va-t-elle?" *Angelicum* 23 (1946): 126–45. The most prominent modernist was Maurice Blondel, whose 1893 essay *Action: Essay on a Critique of Life and Science of Practice* (Notre Dame, IN: University of Notre Dame Press, 1984, 2003) launched a new strain of Catholic thought that was vigorously condemned by Pius X. For a recent treatment of the political implications, see Peter J. Bernardi, *Maurice Blondel, Social Catholicism, and Action française* (Washington, D.C.: Catholic University of America Press, 2009).

40. The dissertation described God as a "person rather than a 'divine object,'" Garrigou-Lagrange complained. See Weigel, *Witness to Hope*, 86. Wojtyła's dissertation has been translated into English as *Faith according to St. John of the Cross* (San Francisco: Ignatius Press, 1981).

41. Buttiglione, *Karol Wojtyła*, 54; Williams, *Mind of John Paul II*, 115. Wojtyła noted that Scheler's work had attracted Catholic moralists such as Fritz Tillman and Hermann Schmidt. Wojtyła, "Über die Möglichkeit, eine christliche Ethik in Ahnlehnung an Max Scheler zu schaffen" in id., *Primat des Geistes: Philosophische Schriften* (Stuttgart: Seewald, 1979), 38.

42. Wojtyła, "On the Metaphysical and Phenomenological Basis of the Moral Norm in the Philosophy of Thomas Aquinas and Max Scheler," in id., *Person and Community*, 73. For a brief on Woroniecki, see Edward Nieznański, "Polen," in Emerich Coreth, Walter M. Neidl, and Georg Pfligersdorffer, eds., *Christliche Philosophie im katholischen Denken des 19. und 20. Jahrhunderts*, vol. 2 (Graz: Styria, 1988), 812.

43. For a comparison of Wojtyła and Stein, see Andrzej Półtawski, "Personalismus in phänomenologischer Sicht (Edith Stein und Karol Wojtyla)," *Schriften der Wiener Katholischen Akademie* 9 (Vienna: Wiener Katholische Akademie, 1995). By the late 1960s, Wojtyła clearly knew Stein's work—Ingarden delivered a lecture on Stein at one of Wojtyła's gatherings—but it seems likely that he knew her long before this time as well.

44. Wojtyła, "Über die Möglichkeit," in id., *Primat des Geistes*, 193–97.

45. Ibid., 43. Wojtyła may have seen the battle between realism and idealism in phenomenology partly as a struggle over Brentano's legacy. While intentionality afforded a basis for realism by linking consciousness with objects, it also, in Brentano's formulation, divided mental phenomena from material, a gulf that betokened the turn to consciousness. Indeed, Wojtyła sometimes traced Scheler's thought back to the Aristotelian Brentano, identifying a realist, Catholic, and Thomist pedigree for phenomenology to combat Husserl's seductive countermodel. On Brentano as the origin of realist phenomenology, see "The Problem of the Separation of Experience" and "In Search of the Basis of Perfectionism in Ethics," both in Wojtyła, *Person and Community*, 23–44, 45–56. See also the lectures on ethics at the Catholic University of Lublin, published as *Lubliner Vorlesungen* (Stuttgart: Seewald, 1981).

46. Wojtyła, "Über die Möglichkeit," in id., *Primat des Geistes*, 80–84.

47. Wojtyła, "Problem of the Separation of Experience," in id., *Person and Community*, 41.

48. Wojtyła, "Über die Möglichkeit," in id., *Primat des Geistes*, 85.

49. Wojtyła, "On the Metaphysical and Phenomenological Basis," in id., *Person and Community*, 90.

50. Wojtyła, "Über die Möglichkeit," in id., *Primat des Geistes*, 126.

51. Ibid., 189, 173; id., *Lubliner Vorlesungen*, 45.

52. Wojtyła, "Über die Möglichkeit" in id., *Primat des Geistes*, 122–25.

53. Ibid., 125.

54. Wojtyła, "On the Metaphysical and Phenomenological Basis," in id., *Person and Community*, 83.

55. Wojtyła, "Über die Möglichkeit," in id., *Primat des Geistes*, 102–3, 91.
56. Ibid., 114–15.
57. Ibid., 116, 118.
58. Wojtyła, *Lubliner Vorlesungen*, 41.
59. Wojtyła, "Über die Möglichkeit," in id., *Primat des Geistes*, 149.
60. Ibid., 98.
61. Ibid., 93–94, 140; Wojtyła, "On the Metaphysical and Phenomenological Basis," in id., *Person and Community*, 83.
62. Wojtyła, "Über die Möglichkeit," in id., *Primat des Geistes*, 150–53.
63. Ibid., 140, 146–47, 176–79.
64. Ibid., 161–62, 185. Wojtyła, "Die Prinzip der Nachahmung im Evangelium anhand der Quellen der Offenbarung und das philosophische System von Max Scheler," in id., *Primat des Geistes*, 279.
65. Wojtyła, "Prinzip der Nachahmung," in id., *Primat des Geistes*, 277.
66. Wojtyła, "Problem of the Separation of Experience," in id., *Person and Community*, 39.
67. Karol Wojtyła, *Love and Responsibility* (San Francisco: Ignatius Press, 1993). Buttiglione describes *Love and Responsibility*, a bit prematurely, as "an organic synthesis of ontology and phenomenology" (*Karol Wojtyła*, 83).
68. Wojtyła, *Love and Responsibility*, 65, 126. Wojtyła attacked two main errors in sexual ethics: Against rigorism, the view that sex should serve only for procreation, he underscored the importance of physical enjoyment. Against libidinism, or libertinism, he argued that thwarting procreation denied the natural purpose of intercourse. The sexual act had to be embraced as a whole. He later extended the role of interpersonal self-giving, placing it at the foundation not only of family, but also of community, especially the community, or communion, of the Church.
69. Williams, *Mind of John Paul II*, 164–85. Wojtyła and the Polish delegation also demanded a strong condemnation of systematic atheism as a violation of fundamental religious freedom, and they expressed skepticism about proposals that Church officials negotiate with Communist authorities. For the full Council proceedings, see *Acta Synodalia Sacrosancti Concilii Oecumenici Vaticani II* (Vatican City: Polyglot, 1970–96); and the five-volume *History of Vatican II*, ed. Giuseppe Alberigo; English ed. Joseph A. Komonchak (Maryknoll, NY: Orbis, 1995–2006). We also have some sense of Wojtyła's extracameral conversations, recorded by his colleague Mieczysław Maliński, in which he praised the effort to forge Christian unity by bridging not only recent disputes between traditional and *nouvelle* theologians, but also the millennial battles between Catholicism, Protestantism, and Orthodoxy. Malinski, *Pope John Paul II: The Life of Karol Wojtyla* (New York: Seabury, 1979), 162–90.
70. Walter M. Abbott, ed., *The Documents of Vatican II* (New York: Guild Press, 1966), 201. The Latin original reads: "Hominis enim persona salvanda est humanaque societas instauranda."

71. Wojtyła, *Sources of Renewal: The Implementation of the Second Vatican Council* (San Francisco: Harper Collins, 1980), 293.

72. Ibid., 77, 69, 15.

73. Ibid., 18, 263, 279, 118–19, 178, 185–87.

74. Karol Wojtyła, *The Acting Person*, Analecta Husserliana 10 (Dordrecht: D. Reidel, 1979). The book has a fraught translation history. The English edition, published a decade after the Polish original and presented as "the definitive version," was substantially revised under the supervision of the Polish-American phenomenologist Anna-Teresa Tymieniecka, an Ingarden student. The first six chapters were revised in concert with Wojtyła, but the seventh was completed without his involvement after he became pope. John Paul II approved of the edition, but the scholarly consensus is that Tymieniecka distorted Wojtyła's text by exaggerating its phenomenological leanings and hiding the Thomistic. Among the errors, the translation anglicizes Scholastic terms of art, such as *suppositum*, that appear in Latin in the Polish original. For an account of the dispute, see Williams, *Mind of John Paul II*, chap. 8, "From *Osoba i czyn* to *The Acting Person*." Tymieniecka's account of the process can be found in "Feature Study," *Phenomenology Information Bulletin* 3 (October 1979): 2–52. For the earliest attack on her translation, see Alfred Bloch, "Phenomenology and the Pope: An 'Incredible Misreading,'" *New York Times*, 24 December 1978. In light of these difficulties, I cite the English and Polish texts jointly throughout this chapter and include the Polish terms for key Wojtyłian concepts. Where it is accurate, I quote the English edition, with occasional alterations to match the Polish original. All of these alterations are indicated in notes. The French and German editions are more faithful to the Polish at the sentence level, though they adhere to the structure of the English version.

75. Emmanuel Lévinas, writing in 1980, expressed surprise at the strictly philosophical language of the analysis. Lévinas, "La filosofia di Karol Wojtyla," *Vita e pensiero* 58 (April 1980): 30.

76. Quoted in Henri de Lubac's fascinating memoir *At the Service of the Church: Henri de Lubac Reflects on the Circumstances That Occasioned His Writings* (San Francisco: Ignatius Press, 1993), 171–72. Like many postwar Catholic thinkers and the prewar Scheler, Lubac had written extensively on the tragedy and bankruptcy of atheism, notably in *Le drame de l'humanisme athée* (The Drama of Atheist Humanism) (Paris: Éditions Spes, 1945). For a discussion, see Geroulanos, *Atheism That Is Not Humanist*, 252–53.

77. Wojtyła, *Acting Person* 98–99, 9. The English translation misrepresents Wojtyła by stifling the Latin *fieri*, Wojtyła's term for human becoming or bringing into being; it suggests a more purely experiential and passive notion than he intended. "The becoming of man," he wrote, "the human *fieri* [L.: to become or cause to be] in a moral regard, a *fieri* tightly linked to the person, decides the real

character of goodness and badness themselves, of the moral values themselves" (my translation). The combination of Polish [*stawanie się*] and Latin [*fieri*] in the original highlights Wojtyła's vision of becoming as both experiential and metaphysical.

78. The relevant discussion, which appears in *The Acting Person*, 31–33, has been significantly altered from the Polish original, where it appears on pp. 36–37. Jean-Luc Marion argues that Wojtyła replaced intentionality with action, stressing an internal transcendence of self-determination that was distinct from the Brentanian and Husserlian linkage of intentionality with self-transcendent objects. See Marion, "L'autotranscendence de l'homme: Signe de contradiction dans le pensée de Karol Wojtyła," in Buttiglione et al., eds., *Karol Wojtyła*, 53–70.

79. Wojtyła, *Acting Person*, 14–18; *Osoba i czyn*, 17–23. See also "The Problem of Experience in Ethics," in id., *Person and Community*, 113–14, where manifestation, à la Patočka, is described as the very heart of experience. On the distinction between "thematic" and "operational," see Eugen Fink, "Operative Begriffe in Husserls Phänomenologie," in Fink, *Nähe und Distanz: Phänomenologische Vorträge und Aufsätze* (Freiburg: Karl Alber, 1976), 180–204.

80. For the analysis in these sentences, see Wojtyła, *Acting Person*, 41–45; *Osoba i czyn*, 44–47.

81. Wojtyła, *Acting Person*, 13–14; *Osoba i czyn*, 17.

82. Wojtyła, "Problem of Experience," in id., *Person and Community*, 116–17.

83. Wojtyła, "The Problem of the Theory of Morality," in id., *Person and Community*, 134.

84. Ibid., 134–35.

85. Turning to contemporary science for support, Wojtyła appealed to the psychologies of Narziß Ach (1871–1946) and his Polish followers, who identified the will as an independent human faculty. The most thorough among several references is Wojtyła, "The Problem of the Will in the Analysis of the Ethical Act," in id., *Person and Community*, 3–22. Nineteenth-century thinkers tended to join the will with other human faculties; Brentano, it will be recalled, collapsed emotion and will into the single faculty of "interest." Ach's most influential work was *Über den Willensakt und das Temperament* (Leipzig: Quelle & Meyer, 1910). In 1933, Ach enrolled his ideas in the service of the new Nazi regime, favorably citing Hitler's dictum that "the will is everything." Mitchell Ash, *Gestalt Psychology in German Culture, 1890–1967: Holism and the Quest for Objectivity* (Cambridge: Cambridge University Press, 1995), 342. The leading Polish psychologist of will was Mieczysław Dybowski.

86. Wojtyła, *Acting Person*, 100, 106, 70, 119; *Osoba i czyn*, 105–6, 110, 72, 123–24. Cf. Wojtyła, *Love and Responsibility*, 115.

87. Wojtyła, "The Degrees of Being from the Point of View of the Phenomenology of Action," *Analecta Husserliana* 11 (1979): 127.

88. Wojtyła, *Acting Person*, 105; *Osoba i czyn*, 109.

89. Wojtyła, *Acting Person*, 112, 149; *Osoba i czyn*, 116, 157. For a consideration of the relation between these two transcendences, see Marion, "Autotranscendence de l'homme," in Buttiglione et al., eds., *Karol Wojtyła*.

90. Wojtyła, *Acting Person*, 151; *Osoba i czyn*, 159. Translation altered to reflect the Polish original.

91. Wojtyła, *Acting Person*, 121, 131; *Osoba i czyn*, 126, 137.

92. Wojtyła, *Acting Person*, 159; *Osoba i czyn*, 166–67. Translation altered to reflect the Polish original.

93. Wojtyła, *Acting Person*, 127, 156; *Osoba i czyn*, 133, 163; id., "Problem of the Theory of Morality," in id., *Person and Community*, 152.

94. Wojtyła, *Acting Person*, 162; *Osoba i czyn*, 169–70.

95. Wojtyła, *Acting Person*, 165–66; *Osoba i czyn*, 172–73.

96. Wojtyła, *Acting Person*, 166–68; *Osoba i czyn*, 173–76.

97. Wojtyła, "Problem of the Theory of Morality," in id., *Person and Community*, 155.

98. Wojtyła, *Acting Person*, 179–86; *Osoba i czyn*, 187–96. Cf. "The Intentional Act and the Human Act, That is, Act and Experience," *Analecta Husserliana* 5 (1976): 269–80.

99. Because Wojtyła, by then John Paul II, was unable to review Tymieniecka's redaction, the chapter appears twice, in revised and unrevised forms, in the English translation. In keeping with my preference for the original, my English citations refer to the unrevised chapter 7.

100. Wojtyła, *Acting Person*, 325; *Osoba i czyn*, 294. For a reflection on the Husserlian bases of Wojtyła's concept of participation, see Peter Costello, "Pope John Paul II's 'Participation' in the 'Neighborhood' of Phenomenology," in Nancy Mardas Billias, Agnes B. Curry, and George F. McLean, eds., *Karol Wojtyła's Philosophical Legacy* (Washington, DC: Council for Research in Values and Philosophy, 2008), 45–59.

101. Wojtyła, "Participation or Alienation?" in id., *Person and Community*, 200.

102. Wojtyła, *Acting Person*, 337–51; *Osoba i czyn*, 306–10, 319–22.

103. Wojtyła, *Acting Person*, 351; *Osoba i czyn*, 322.

104. Wojtyła, *Acting Person*, 354; *Osoba i czyn*, 325.

105. Wojtyła, *Acting Person*, 332; *Osoba i czyn*, 301.

106. These essays appeared mostly in Tymieniecka's journal *Analecta Husserliana*, and their phenomenological drift may owe something to her influence.

107. Wojtyła, "The Person: Subject and Community," in id., *Person and Community*, 225, 227.

108. Wojtyła, "Subjectivity and the Irreducible in the Human Being," in id., *Person and Community*, 213.

320 Notes

109. Ibid., 215. As John Paul II later noted, "With the phenomenological method . . . we can study experiences of morality, religion, or simply what it is to be human, and draw from them a significant enrichment of our knowledge. Yet we must not forget that all these analyses implicitly presuppose the reality of the Absolute Being and also the reality of being human, that is, being a creature. If we do not set out from such 'realist' presuppositions, we end up in a vacuum." John Paul II, *Memory and Identity: Conversations at the Dawn of the Millennium* (New York: Rizzoli, 2005), 12. For an essay that highlights the conformity between Thomism and phenomenology, see Wojtyła, "The Degrees of Being from the Point of View of the Phenomenology of Action," *Analecta Husserliana* 11 (1979): 125–30.

110. Wojtyła, "Intentional Act," 278. All the same, Wojtyła described his phenomenological position as situated between Scheler's narrow emotive personalism and Husserl's restrictive rationalism. (270–72)

111. Wojtyła, "Subjectivity and the Irreducible," in id., *Person and Community*, 215. Cf. Wojtyła, "Transcendence of the Person in Action." In a footnote, he credited Schelerian phenomenology as well as its elaboration by Nicolai Hartmann and Dietrich von Hildebrand.

112. Wojtyła, "The Person," in id., *Person and Community*, 234.

113. Wojtyła, "The Constitution of Nature through Human Praxis" (1977), in id., *Person and Community*, 267, 269.

114. Wojtyła, "The Person," in id., *Person and Community*, 240.

115. Ibid., 252–57. Critics have noted that his papacy, by contrast, often emphasized centralization.

116. John Paul II, *Redemptor Hominis*, in *The Encyclicals of John Paul II*, ed. J. Michael Miller (Huntington, ID: Our Sunday Visitor, 1996), 56–57.

117. Ibid., 72–73; *Sollicitudo Rei Socialis*, ibid., 462–64. The pope confronted what he saw as the decline of the modern moral sense directly in his 1993 encyclical *Veritatis Splendor*, which took as its central task the defense of a morality of absolute truth against several purportedly mistaken philosophies of the modern age.

118. John Paul II, *Laborem Exercens*, ibid., 175.

119. John Paul II, *Centesimus Annus*, ibid., 601, 605.

CHAPTER 10

1. It has long been tempting to view Poland's "resistance Church" as the spearhead of opposition to communism, with Wojtyła as its paladin. See, e.g., George Weigel, *The Final Revolution: The Resistance Church and the Collapse of Communism* (Oxford: Oxford University Press, 1992). The story was more complex: Poland's primate, Cardinal Stefan Wyszyński, maintained an uneasy truce with

the regime for much of the postwar era and occasionally found common cause around social questions. The best source for this is Piotr H. Kosicki's excellent "Between Catechism and Revolution: Poland, France, and the Story of Catholicism and Socialism in Europe, 1878–1958" (Ph.D. diss., Princeton University, 2011); see also Jonathan Luxmoore and Jolanta Babiuch, *The Vatican and the Red Flag: The Struggle for the Soul of Eastern Europe* (London: Geoffrey Chapman, 1999). Wojtyła, too, did not overtly back anti-regime agitators until well into the 1970s, almost a decade after his appointment as Cracow's archbishop and well after the upheavals of 1968 and 1970.

2. On this issue, see Luxmoore and Babiuch, *Vatican*, 176–254. There are many chronicles of the pope's Polish return. For these quotations, see *Return to Poland: The Collected Speeches of John Paul II* (London: Collins, 1979), 170, 22.

3. Timothy Garton Ash, *The Polish Revolution: Solidarity* (New Haven, CT: Yale University Press, 2002), 31; Adam Michnik, "A Lesson in Dignity" (1979), in Michnik, *The Church and the Left* (Chicago: University of Chicago Press, 1993), 223–31.

4. Józef Tischner lists some of Ingarden's disciples in *Marxism and Christianity* (Washington, DC: Georgetown University Press, 1981), 7. For a fuller discussion, see Antoni B. Stępien, "Fenomenologia w Polsce (w powojennym dwudziestoleciu)," *Studia Philosophiae Christianae* 2, no. 1 (1966): 29–47.

5. Stanisław Judycki, "Fenomenologia w Katolickim Uniwersytecie Lubelskim," *Zeszyty naukowe Katolickiego Uniwersytetu Lubelskiego* 45, bks. 3–4 (2002): 116–22. Antoni B. Stępień has chronicled this trend in "Byt—Człowiek—Świadomość: Lubelskie badania fenomenologiczne," in Adam Węgrzecki, ed., *Roman Ingarden a filozofia naszego czasu* (Kraków: Polskie Towarzystwo Filozoficzne, 1995), 311–19. For his analysis of the kinship between Thomism and phenomenology, see "Tomizm a Fenomenologia," *Znak* 26 (1974): 790–98.

6. Jerzy Kalinowski, *Initiation à la philosophie morale: À l'usage de l'homme d'action* (Paris: Société d'Éditions internationales: 1966), 21–2. Kalinowski singled out Husserl, Scheler, and Hartmann. Cf. Kalinowski, "La logique des normes d'Edmund Husserl," *Archives de philosophie du droit* 10 (1965): 107–16; *Querelle de la science normative: Une contribution à la théorie de la science* (Paris: R. Pichon & R. Durand-Auzias, 1969), 113–24; and *La logique des normes* (Paris: Presses universitaires de France, 1972). For his dialogue with Stefan Swieżawski on the Council, see Swieżawski and Kalinowski, *La philosophie à l'heure du Concile* (Paris: Société d'Éditions internationales, 1965).

7. Translations of Husserl's work appeared in the following order: *Ideas I* (1967), *Ideas II* (1975), *Cartesian Meditations* (1982), and *Crisis of European Sciences* (1987). A volume of Heidegger's selected essays, translated by Krzysztof Michalski, appeared in 1977, as did Scheler's *Ressentiment*. The following year brought Michalski's monograph *Heidegger i filozofia współczesna* (*Heidegger and Contemporary Philosophy*). Two further translations of Scheler appeared in 1980s.

8. Mieczysław Krąpiec, *I-Man: An Outline of Philosophical Anthropology* (1979; abridged ed., New Britain, CT: Mariel, 1985), 81–87; Krąpiec, *Person and Natural Law* (1975; New York: Peter Lang, 1993), 40. Ingarden too, per Krąpiec, failed to grasp the structures of existence. Krąpiec's students Władysław Stróżewski and Marian Jaworski worked to blend phenomenology and Thomism in their thought. See Edward Nieznański, "Polen," in Emerich Coreth, Walter M. Neidl, and Georg Pfligersdorffer, eds., *Christliche Philosophie im katholischen Denken des 19. und 20. Jahrhunderts*, vol. 2 (Graz: Styria, 1988), 815.

9. Leszek Kołakowski, *The Presence of Myth* (Chicago: University of Chicago Press, 1989), 13–14, 34, 40. Not all Marxists were charitable. For the philosopher and Party apologist Adam Schaff, Husserl and Heidegger reflected "the worst traditions of German pedantry and obscurity" (Schaff, *The Philosophy of Man* [New York: Monthly Review Press, 1963], 36). Schaff ultimately fell afoul of the regime in part because of his interest in existentialism as a tool for humanizing Soviet doctrine. See Schaff, *Philosophy of Man* and *Marxism and the Human Individual* (1965; New York: McGraw-Hill, 1970).

10. Leszek Kołakowski, *Husserl and the Search for Certitude* (Chicago: University of Chicago Press, 1987), 79. By this point, it should be noted, Kołakowski had traveled from one ideological pole to the other, from ardent young Stalinist in the early 1950s to papal supporter after 1978, when his friend Karol Wojtyła donned the vestments. For a brief biography of Kołakowski, see John Connelly. "Jester and Priest," *The Nation* (September 23, 2013), 27–34.

11. Jan Szewczyk, *O fenomenologii Edmunda Husserla* (Warsaw: Kolegium Otryckie, Wydział Propagandy Rady Naczelnej ZSP, 1987) was published posthumously. I thank Witold Płotka for this citation.

12. Zdzisław Krasnodębski, "Phänomenologie und Soziologie in Polen: Der Anfang eines Dialogs," in Richard Grathoff and Bernhard Waldenfels, eds., *Sozialität und Intersubjektivität: Phänomenologische Perspektiven der Sozialwissenschaften im Umkreis von Aron Gurwitsch und Alfred Schütz* (Munich: Fink, 1983), 360–67. For a eulogy that recounts Michalski's undertakings, see Timothy Snyder, "Krzysztof Michalski (1945–2013)," *New York Review of Books* 60, no. 5 (21 March 2013): 8.

13. On this topic and on Michalski's intellectual milieu, see Marci Shore, "Out of the Desert: A Heidegger for Poland," *Times Literary Supplement*, no. 5757 (2 August 2013): 14–15.

14. Marci Shore, "After Marzec: The *Komandosi* and the Search for Meaning after Marxism," in Glenn Dynner and Francois Guesnet, eds., *Warsaw: The History of a Jewish Metropolis* (Brill Academic Publishers, forthcoming). On Poland's dissident Marxists, including Michnik and Kuroń, see Raymond Taras, "Marxist Critiques of Political Crises in Poland," in id., ed., *The Road to Disillusion: from Critical Marxism to post-communism in Eastern Europe* (Armonk: M.E. Sharpe, 1992), 81–113.

15. I use the term 'renewal' advisedly in this chapter. Its Polish equivalent, *odnowienie*, was rejected by most dissidents because of its widespread use by the

regime. Adam Michnik, *Letters from Prison and Other Essays* (Berkeley: University of California Press, 1985), 13.

16. For accounts of KOR written by two of its founders, see Jan Józef Lipski, *KOR: A History of the Worker's Defense Committee in Poland, 1976–1981* (Berkeley: University of California Press, 1985); Jacek Kuroń, *Maintenant ou jamais* (Paris: Fayard, 1993). On Solidarity, in addition to Ash, *Polish Revolution*, see Jerzy Holzer, *Solidarität: Die Geschichte einer freien Gewerkschaft in Polen* (1984; Munich: Beck, 1985); and David Ost, *Solidarity and the Politics of Anti-Politics: Opposition and Reform in Poland since 1968* (Philadelphia: Temple University Press, 1990).

17. Michnik, "A New Evolutionism," in id., *Letters from Prison*, 147.

18. Michnik, *Church and the Left*, 170, 123, 193. The religious renaissance that contributed to Solidarity's success, he wrote in 1990, was "simply a collective return to issues of transcendence, to issues of whether there is any order that is absolutely hard and fast." Michnik, "The Moral and Spiritual Origins of Solidarity," in William Brinton and Alan Rinzler, eds., *Without Force or Lies: Voices from the Revolution of Central Europe in 1989–90* (San Francisco: Mercury House, 1990), 246.

19. Michnik, "Letter from the Gdansk Prison," in id., *Letters from Prison*, 93. For a Michnik biography, see Cyril Bouyeure, *L'invention du politique: Une biographie d'Adam Michnik* (Lausanne: Éditions Noir sur blanc, 2007).

20. Jacek Kuron and Karol Modzelewski, "An Open Letter to Communist Party Members," in *Revolutionary Marxist Students in Poland Speak Out* (New York: Pathfinder Press, 1972).

21. Jacek Kuroń, *La foi et la faute* (Paris: Fayard, 1991), 425–26. He claims to have read Husserl too late for it to shape his views.

22. Ibid., 435.

23. Ibid., 431, 439–40.

24. Ibid., 441.

25. Ibid., 446. Kuroń declared himself a Christian without God, for whom Christianity served as a system of values but not a religion. His fellow secularist Adam Michnik took a similar stance: "[B]y rejecting Christ's teachings of love for one's neighbor, one rejects the canonical foundation of European culture. By rejecting these teachings, we lose the foundation of our belief in the autonomous value of truth and human solidarity" (Michnik, *Church and the Left*, 123).

26. Jacek Kuroń, "Chrześcijanie bez Boga," in *Polityka i odpowiedzialność* (London: Aneks, 1984), 18. I thank Witold Płotka for his translation assistance with these passages.

27. Maryjane Osa, *Solidarity and Contention: Networks of Polish Opposition* (Minneapolis: University of Minnesota Press, 2003), 67.

28. These early writings only recently appeared in print as Tischner, *Studia z filozofii świadomości* (Kraków: Instytut Myśli Józefa Tischnera, 2006). The one full-length biography of Tischner is Wojciech Bonowicz, *Tischner* (Kraków: Znak,

2001). For a briefer biography in German, see Steffen Huber's introduction to Józef Tischner, *Der Streit um die Existenz des Menschen* (Berlin: Insel, 2010), 9–32. And for a review of Tischner's thought, see the summary by Aleksander Bobko, Tischner's longtime assistant: "Philosophical Anthropology as the Main Thread of Tischner's Work," *Tischner Institute Journal of Philosophy* 1 (2007): 11–27.

29. Józef Tischner, "Schyłek chrześcijaństwa tomistycznego," *Znak* 1 (1970): 1–26. Less well known are several articles on phenomenological themes drawn from his *Habilitationsschrift*: "Gnozeologiczny podmiot poznania [The Gnosiological Subject of Cognition]," *Analecta Cracoviensia* 1 (1969): 9–20; "Typowe odmiany pierwotności rsp. wtórności [The Typical Variants of Primordiality and Non-primordiality in the Domain of Consciousness]," *Analecta Cracoviensia* 2 (1970): 27–52; "Aksjologiczne podstawy doświadczenia 'ja' jako całości cielesno-przestrzennej [The Axiological Foundations of the Experience of the 'I' as a Corporeal-Spatial Totality]," *Logos i ethos: Rozprawy filozoficzne* (1971): 33–82.

30. Through Wojtyła's assistance, Tischner won a fellowship to study at the Husserl Archive in Leuven, Belgium.

31. The texts of this series have been published by Krzysztof Michalski through the Institute for Human Sciences in Vienna.

32. Józef Tischner, *Myślenie według wartości* (1982; Kraków: Znak, 1993), 10.

33. Ibid., 91.

34. Tischner's *Filozofia dramatu* appeared in France in Polish in 1990, and in Poland in 1998. *Spór o istnienie człowieka* also appeared in 1998. Both have subsequently been translated into German, with selections appearing in English. I cite the English where available.

35. Józef Tischner, "Phenomenology of the Encounter" (1978), *Tischner Institute Journal of Philosophy* 3 (2011): 45.

36. Bobko, "Philosophical Anthropology," 11.

37. "[O]ur world," Tischner insisted, "is a hierarchically ordered world and our thinking, a preferential thinking." Józef Tischner, "Thinking in Values," *Tischner Institute Journal of Philosophy* 2 (2008): 50. He praised Scheler for recognizing axiological shallows and depths. Tischner, *Der Streit um die Existenz des Menschen* (Berlin: Insel, 2010), 301.

38. Józef Tischner, "Axiological Pieces," *Tischner Institute Journal of Philosophy* 2 (2008): 35–37; *Das Menschliche Drama: Phänomenologische Studien zur Philosophie des Dramas* (Munich: Fink, 1989), 267; *Streit um die Existenz des Menschen*, 235.

39. The philosopher and translator Jacek Filek finds a tension between the phenomenological ethics of absolute value and dialogical ethics of responsibility to the other. See Filek, "Man Facing Values or Man Facing Man?" *Tischner Institute Journal of Philosophy* 2 (2008): 133–51.

40. Józef Tischner, *Myślenie według wartości* (Thinking in Values) (Kraków: Znak, 1982). Here Tischner set his theory against Scheler's, for whom tragedy

involved the clash of two higher goods in which one was perforce violated. Tischner, "Phenomenology of the Encounter," 45. Scheler's "On the Tragic," *Cross Currents* 4 (1954): 178–91, originally appeared in the essay collection *Vom Umsturz der Werte* (Leipzig: Der Neue Geist, 1919; 2nd rev. ed. 1923). The phrase 'thinking in values' comes from Heidegger's "Letter on Humanism," though Tischner inverted its meaning. For Heidegger, values-thinking perpetuated the forgetfulness and the subjectivizing of Being; for Tischner, values were man's essential content. On this, see Ingarden's disciple and Scheler's translator Adam Węgrzecki, "What Is Thinking in Values?" *Tischner Institute Journal of Philosophy* 2 (2008): 11–17.

41. Józef Tischner, "Axiological Pieces" (1970), *Tischner Institute Journal of Philosophy* 2 (2008): 38. At one point here, Tischner equates the axiological I with the transcendental ego, viewing both as unreal (ibid., 43n6). See also Tischner, *Streit um die Existenz des Menschen*, 241, 269; as well as two excerpts from *Filozofia dramatu*: "The Good," *Tischner Institute Journal of Philosophy* 2 (2008): 61, and "A Response to a Question, or: Reciprocity," ibid. 3 (2011): 108.

42. Tischner, "Phenomenology of the Encounter," 62.

43. Józef Tischner, "Wandering within the Heart of the Good," *Tischner Institute Journal of Philosophy* 2 (2008): 69–70, and "Evil in the Domain of Dialogue," ibid. 3 (2011): 121, both excerpted from *Filozofia dramatu*.

44. Józef Tischner, "Das Denken aus dem Innern der Metapher," *Phänomenologische Forschungen* 12 (1982): 129.

45. Tischner, *Menschliche Drama*, 32.

46. Ibid., 33, 31; "Evil in the Domain of Dialogue," 121.

47. "Observable, 'spectacular' freedom shows itself like a dance." Józef Tischner, "Freedom as a Manner of Existence of the Good [excerpt from the *Controversy over the Existence of Man*]," *The Tischner Institute Journal of Philosophy* 2 (2008): 94.

48. Tischner, "Freedom as the Manner of Existence of the Good," 93.

49. Józef Tischner, "For the Existence of Man: Ontological Argument" (excerpt from *Spór o istnienie człowieka*), *Tischner Institute Journal of Philosophy* 2 (2008): 80. Light, dance, face—Tischner's thought was expressly metaphorical. On the role of metaphors in philosophy, see Tischner, "Denken aus dem Innern der Metapher," 123–44.

50. Tischner, "Evil in the Domain of Dialogue," 112.

51. Ibid., 117–20.

52. In contrast, ontological evil—such as natural disasters that destroy life and property—is really only misfortune, an imperfection built into the essence of the world stage. Tischner, "Evil in the Domain of Dialogue," esp. 116–17. Cf. Karol Tarnowski, "Paths of Damnation, Paths of Salvation," *Tischner Institute Journal of Philosophy* 2 (2008): 18–32.

53. Tischner, "Thinking in Values," 59.
54. Tischner, *Streit um die Existenz des Menschen*, 65.
55. Tischner, "Thinking in Values," 48; "Freedom as a Manner of Existence of the Good," 94. Tischner praised Scheler and Hartmann over Heidegger on this point, for the latter's abandonment of ethics and aversion to public engagement not only ignored an essential human need; it also jeopardized moral freedom and the ability to combat evil.
56. Tischner, *Marxism and Christianity*, 50.
57. Ibid., 70.
58. Ibid., 81.
59. Józef Tischner, *Etyka solidarności* (Kraków: Znak, 1981). "Father Tischner's book," wrote Lech Wałęsa in an Afterword to the English translation, "recounts the basic concepts utilized during innumerable meetings, conventions, demonstrations, and discussions, and which we still use today in personal conversations and underground publications." *The Spirit of Solidarity* (San Francisco: Harper & Row, 1984), 105. "The Ethics of Solidarity" would be a more accurate translation of the title.
60. For discussions of Tischner's concept of solidarity, see Charles Taylor, "Several Reflections on the Theme of Solidarity," *Tischner Institute Journal of Philosophy* 1 (2007): 68–77; Dobrosław Kot, "Solidarity without Solidarity," ibid.: 96–106; Adam Workowski, "The Solidarity Community: A Phenomenological Analysis," ibid.: 107–19.
61. Tischner, *Spirit of Solidarity*, 9.
62. Ibid., 13.
63. Ibid., 2.
64. Wyszyński quoted in Luxmoore and Babiuch, *Vatican*, 226.
65. Tischner, *Spirit of Solidarity*, 9. "One who condones moral oppression tightens a noose over his or her own humanity" (24).
66. Ibid., 98.
67. Ibid., 53.
68. Ibid., 14.
69. Ibid., 20, 17.
70. Ibid., 28–29. Farming fell into this category of work. In a strongly Heideggerian passage, Tischner described farming as a spiritual activity linked to a common heritage and cultural homeland. Both privatization and nationalization (socialization) distort these essential links and alienate men from common agricultural fruits (60–65).
71. Ibid., 27. In a 1996 lecture, after the rapid privatization of the immediate postcommunist years, Tischner rued the decline of solidaristic values into consumerism and moralizing. "The Ethics of Solidarity Years Later," *Tischner Institute Journal of Philosophy* 1 (2007): 52–67.

72. Tischner, *Spirit of Solidarity*, 25–29, and *Streit um die Existenz des Menschen*, 68–69. Land, also a common human trust, suffered similar exploitation.
73. Tischner, *Spirit of Solidarity*, 49.
74. Ibid., 91.
75. Richard Grathoff makes the connection to Scheler in his introduction to Tischner, *Menschliche Drama*, 9–20. For Tischner's lectures on Scheler, see Józef Tischner, *Etyka a Historia Wykłady* (Kraków: Instytut J. Tischnera, 2008), 329–480. In a 1967 essay, Tischner also praised Husserl for the moral impulses of his *Crisis* work, which called forth a sense of philosophical responsibility. Józef Tischner, *Świat ludzkiej nadziei: Wybór szkiców filozoficznych, 1966–1975* (Kraków: Znak, 1994), 50.
76. Tischner, "Thinking in Values," 54.
77. Tischner singled out the modern schools of phenomenology and existentialism in *Marxism and Christianity* (75).
78. Michnik, "Letter from the Gdańsk Prison," 91, 93.
79. Weigel, *Witness to Hope*, 409.
80. Tischner, *Spirit of Solidarity*, 70.

CONCLUSION

1. For prominent examples of those who saw the 1989 revolutions as a renewal of the liberal tradition, see Ralf Dahrendorf, *Reflections on the Revolution in Europe: In a Letter Intended to Have Been Sent to a Gentleman in Warsaw* (New York: Times Books, 1990); Bruce Ackerman, *The Future of Liberal Revolution* (New Haven, CT: Yale University Press, 1992); Ken Jowitt, "The Leninist Extinction," in Daniel Chirot, ed., *The Crisis of Leninism and the Decline of the Left: The Revolutions of 1989* (Seattle: University of Washington Press, 1991), 77.
2. Francis Fukuyama, "The End of History?" *The National Interest* 16 (Summer 1989), 3–18; Fukuyama, *The End of History and the Last Man* (New York: Free Press, 1992).
3. Czechoslovakia's most famous liberal was Havel's nemesis Václav Klaus, who succeeded the dissident-playwright as president of the Czech Republic. Polish liberals have accused Solidarity of perpetuating a dangerously egalitarian ideology that impeded postcommunist social and economic progress. See Henryk Flakierski, "Solidarity and Egalitarianism," *Canadian Slavonic Papers* 25, no. 3 (September 1983): 380–91; Andrzej Walicki, "Liberalism in Poland," *Critical Review* 2, no. 1 (1988): 8–38; Jerzy Szacki and Elzbieta Matynia, "A Revival of Liberalism in Poland?" *Social Research* 57, no. 2 (Summer 1990): 463–91.
4. Václav Klaus is the most famous purveyor of this criticism.
5. Gil Eyal, *The Origins of Postcommunist Elites: From Prague Spring to the Breakup of Czechoslovakia* (Minneapolis: University of Minnesota Press, 2003);

Jiřína Šiklová and Gerald Turner, "Courage, Heroism, and the Postmodern Paradox," *Social Research* 71, no. 1 (Spring 2004): 135–48.

6. For an acute dissection of this complex and its political dangers, see Slavoj Žižek, "Attempts to Escape the Logic of Capitalism," *London Review of Books*, 28 October 1999, 3–7.

7. Rodolphe Gasché draws particular attention to this blindness among early phenomenologists such as Husserl and Heidegger in *Europe, or the Infinite Task* (Stanford, CA: Stanford University Press, 2009), 126–27, 339–47.

8. Žižek, "Attempts to Escape," 7.

Index

Ach, Narziß, 318n85
Adenauer, Konrad, 81
Adorno, Theodor, 18, 249–50n74, 291n45, 298n78
Ajdukiewicz, Kazimierz, 190, 192
Akita, T., 245n23
analytic philosophy (Lvov-Warsaw School), 188, 190, 192, 234n6
anthropology, philosophical, 3, 9, 11–12, 14, 20, 21, 39, 71, 82, 98–100, 101–2, 122–24, 129, 139, 147, 149, 155, 159, 168, 188, 189, 192–93, 195–96, 202–8, 210, 212, 216, 220, 233n19, 269n130
Arendt, Hannah, 4, 5, 81, 158, 161, 182, 296n40
Aristotle, 30, 40, 43, 53, 72, 112, 166, 170, 198, 237n20, 299n98, 301n122, 315n45
atheism, 13, 18, 96, 98, 104, 194, 202, 205, 316n69, 317n76
Augustine, 96, 97, 200, 207
Austin, J. L., 68
Avé-Lallement, Eberhard, 65

Baltzer-Jaray, Kimberly, 64
Battěk, Rudolf, 178
Beck, Maximilien, 56, 72
Becker, Oskar, 281n153
Bělohradský, Václav, 23, 276–77, 184
Benda, Václav, 175–76, 178, 180, 186, 214, 303n7
Bergson, Henri, 90, 125
Bernstein, Eduard, 245n23

Bierut, Bolesław, 192
body, 10, 44, 48, 59, 74, 84, 89, 118, 147, 155–56, 158, 183, 241n3, 241–42n4, 277n103, 296n36, 296n47
Bolton, Jonathan, 136
Bourgeois, Léon, 266n74
Brentano, Franz, 1, 2, 3, 6, 7, 8, 9, 11, 12, 13, 15, 19, 24, 29–43, 45, 46, 55, 58, 60, 71, 83, 88, 90, 105, 106, 112, 121, 127, 131, 140, 142, 143, 154, 167, 177, 179, 189, 197, 198, 206, 225, 227, 228, 315n45

Cadwallader, Eva Hauel, 105
Cairns, Dorion, 243n11
capitalism, 91, 99, 149, 162, 178, 220–21, 305n24
Catholic University of Lublin, 190, 212, 197
Celms, Theodor, 66, 134, 252n18
Černý, Václav, 179, 305n34
Chappel, James, 81, 109
Charter 77, 22–23, 54, 151, 159, 172–73, 174–81, 187, 189, 214, 226, 303n7, 306–7n50, 309n81
Chisholm, Roderick, 34
Christian Democracy, 81, 228
Civic Forum, 175
Clauss, Ludwig Ferdinand, 291n153
Cohen, Hermann, 102
collectivism, 95–97, 119, 134, 218–20, 229
community, 6, 9, 10, 11, 12, 18, 23, 49, 50, 53–56, 60, 61, 73, 84, 88, 89,

93–94, 95–96, 98, 104, 107–9, 113, 119–21, 123, 128, 147, 156, 166, 169, 176, 179, 183–84, 186, 196, 201, 207, 208–9, 218–20, 222, 225, 226, 228, 229, 233n27, 243n14, 247n52, 273n46, 279n124, 281n149, 316n68

communism (Soviet Bloc)/Bolshevism, 3, 81, 108–10, 111, 113, 115, 133, 135, 163, 177, 181, 220, 221, 227, 229, 320n1

Comte, Auguste, 142

Conrad, Theodor, 66, 251n7, 257n64

Conrad-Martius, Hedwig, 12, 62, 63, 66, 74, 120

corporatism, 81, 95, 108–9, 276n95

Coser, Lewis, 87

Cracow Synod, 202

crisis, 1, 2, 3, 7, 9, 10, 13, 18, 20, 21, 47, 55, 57–58, 110, 115, 117, 133, 135, 142–43, 146, 149, 150, 151, 176–78, 181, 183–84, 194, 196, 208, 214, 216, 219, 225, 228, 231n5, 305n23

Crosby, John, 69

Czeżowski, Tadeusz, 192

Daubert, Johannes, 63, 64, 65

Derrida, Jacques, 151

Descartes, Rene, 167, 218

Dilthey, Wilhelm, 125

dissidents, 3, 4, 5, 6, 9, 21–25, 54, 55, 57, 120, 129, 133–36, 140, 146, 147, 148, 150, 151, 159, 172–73, 174–87, 210, 211–23, 224–29, 302n136, 306–7n50, 307n52, 308–9n75, 309n81

Dollfuß, Engelbert, 108–9, 111, 116, 228

Dragomir, Alexandru, 135

DuBois, James, 69

Dubský, Ivan, 150

Durkheim, Émile, 266n74

Dybowski, Mieczysław, 318n83

eidetic analysis, 7–8, 15–16, 51, 66, 67, 69, 77, 82, 83, 91, 102, 125, 127, 134, 148, 171, 258n73, 260n91

Eliot, T. S., 57

empathy/sympathy, 3, 7, 21, 48, 55, 56, 58, 60, 65, 80, 88–91, 93, 118, 127, 143, 159

epoché (bracketing), 17, 74, 123, 128, 152, 154–55, 165, 169, 204, 241–42n4

Erdmann, Benno, 48

ethics, ethos, 54, 87, 95, 199–200, 202, 222, 246n40; good vs. evil, 96, 204–6, 217–19; practical ethics, 40, 51–54, 88, 105–15, 172–73, 184–85; values/axiology, 1, 3, 6, 11, 12, 14, 19, 21, 35–43, 46, 47, 67, 69, 71–72, 81, 83–87, 88, 91–94, 98–9, 102–5, 106–8, 110, 112–14, 118, 119, 120, 130, 145, 149, 178, 179–80, 190, 192–93, 197–200, 204–6, 208–9, 212, 213, 215–18, 217–20, 225, 229, 240n59, 240n66, 240–41n67, 255n45, 259n75, 265n43, 271n25, 273n46, 274n64, 279n124, 289n19, 310n6, 324n39, 324n37, 325–25n40, 325n41

ethos. See ethics

Eucken, Rudolf, 263n12

Europe/Europeanism, 13–14, 54, 57, 59–61, 84–85, 94–96, 98–100, 133, 140–42, 160–65, 170, 179, 180, 286n10, 293n5, 198n86, 301n124; Eurocentrism, 14, 61, 227, 245n23, 284n2, 298n86

existentialism, 1, 12, 130, 136, 182–83, 187, 193–96, 202, 204, 218, 221, 233n25, 305n34, 322n9, 327n77

Eyal, Gil, 181, 226

Farber, Marvin, 4

Fichte, Johann Gottlieb, 16, 47–48, 80, 155, 244n16

Fink, Eugen, 58, 203, 248n65, 294n6

Fischer, Kuno, 235n9

Francis of Assisi, 96

Freud, Sigmund, 30, 256n54

Friedrich, Carl, 81

Fromm, Erich, 149

Galileo, 54, 59, 146, 148

Garrigou-Lagrange, Reginald, 196–97
Gehlen, Arnold, 14, 21, 102, 122, 124
Geiger, Moritz, 62–65, 73–4, 78, 106, 127, 256n54
Geroulanos, Stefanos, 93
Gierek, Edvard, 211
Gilson, Étienne, 190, 194
Gordon, Peter E., 6
government. *See* politics
Gurian, Waldemar, 111
Gurwitsch, Aron, 56, 127–28, 284n178

Hajek, Jiří, 151, 174
Halík, Tomaš, 178, 180
Harich, Wolfgang, 135
Hart, James, 49, 54
Hartmann, Nicolai, 11, 21, 74–75, 81, 102–5, 112, 113, 124, 134–35, 205, 226, 256n54
Havel, Ivan, 177
Havel, Václav, 3, 12, 14, 22, 23, 129, 136, 151, 172, 174, 175, 176, 177, 178, 181, 182–87, 219, 221, 226, 229
Hegel, Georg Wilhelm Friedrich, 16, 172, 191, 215
Heidegger, Martin, 3, 4, 5, 11, 18, 21, 22, 57, 58, 80, 82, 102, 127, 128–32, 133, 134, 135, 145, 148, 152–53, 154, 157, 167, 168, 169, 172, 180, 182, 183, 184, 187, 213, 214, 217, 218
Hejdánek, Ladislav, 176, 177, 179, 180, 181, 291n33, 308n55
Held, Klaus, 63, 250n77
Helsinki Accords, 174
Heraclitus, 170, 271n17
Hildebrand, Dietrich von, 9, 12, 13, 21, 46, 66, 81, 91, 102, 105–10, 111–12, 113, 114, 116, 121, 130, 131, 200, 228
Honneth, Axel, 123
human rights, 172–72, 174, 175, 186, 209, 215
humanism, 7, 22, 23, 50, 129, 133, 135, 139–44, 145, 146, 147, 149, 150, 163, 168, 177, 194, 215, 287n2, 300n106
Husák, Gustav, 174, 187, 297n59

Husserl, Edmund, 1–25, 44–61, 31, 40, 41, 42–43, 62–66, 71, 73–74, 76–79, 80, 101–2, 117, 120–22, 124, 125–27, 128, 130, 131, 133, 140–42, 144–45, 152–56, 163, 165–66, 177–81, 188–89, 191–92, 216–17, 222; *Cartesian Meditations*, 48, 55, 58, 244n19, 248n63; *The Crisis of European Sciences and Transcendental Phenomenology*, 56–61; *Logical Investigations*, 2, 11, 16–17, 20, 45, 51, 62–64, 82, 121, 188; on renewal, 49–56
Husserl, Gerhart, 125
Hvížďala, Karel, 175

idealism-realism dispute, 6, 8, 11, 13, 16–18, 20, 31, 33, 38, 45, 56, 58, 60, 63–66, 73–79, 80, 82,, 83, 106, 112, 117, 118, 121, 122, 126, 127, 130, 131, 134, 135, 152, 154, 166, 188, 190, 191, 192, 193, 203, 213, 216–17, 218, 242n6, 248n65, 252n18, 259–60n79, 261n95, 263n13, 310n7, 311–12n17, 315n45, 320n109, 325n41
Indian thought, 85, 264n29
Ingarden, Roman, 20, 24, 56, 66, 69, 73–79, 91, 107, 117, 134, 136, 188, 189–93, 197, 212, 213, 216, 217
intentionality, 7, 8, 11–12, 15, 21, 30–37, 45–46, 65–68, 72, 74, 76, 78, 81, 86–87, 97, 114, 121–23, 125, 145, 148, 179, 191, 198, 200, 201, 203, 205–6, 213, 215, 217–19, 234n6, 237n21, 243n14, 315n45, 318n78
intersubjectivity, 3, 20, 48–49, 55–56, 58, 88, 89–91, 125, 127, 129, 150, 156, 207–9, 227, 247n52, 247n53, 248n63

Jahrbuch für Philosophie und phänomenologische Forschung, 66
James, William, 90
Japan, 47, 49, 99, 245n23
Jaworski, Marian, 322n8
Jhering, Rudolf von, 239n47

Jirous, Ivan, 179, 186
Joas, Hans, 123
John of the Cross, 197, 280n144
John XXIII, 201, 209
John Paul II. *See* Karol Wojtyła
Jonas, Hans, 233n16

Kaizo (Renewal), 49–56
Kalinowski, Jerzy, 213
Kalivoda, Robert, 149–50
Kant, Immanuel/Kantianism/neo-Kantianism, 31, 37, 38, 43, 45, 47, 49, 51, 52, 59, 61, 63, 70, 74, 78, 85, 87, 98, 102, 105, 125, 145, 198, 200, 201, 206
Kantůrková, Eva, 23, 180, 187
Kaufmann, Felix, 127
Kaufmann, Fritz, 280n138
Kautsky, Karl, 245n23
Kelsen, Hans, 283n166, 283n169
Klaus, Václav, 327n3, 327n4
Kleinberg, Ethan, 129
Kohák, Erazim, 150, 154
Kohout, Jaroslav, 150
Kołakowski, Leszek, 18, 213, 214
Kolnai, Aurel, 9, 12, 13, 21, 91, 102, 107, 111–16, 121, 130, 131, 134, 141, 200, 226, 228
Konrád, György, 181
Kosík, Karel, 22, 135, 147–49, 178
Kotarbiński, Tadeusz, 192
Koyré, Alexander, 66, 134
Kozák, Jan Blahoslav, 140, 145, 146, 176
Kracauer, Siegfried, 125
Krąpiec, Mieczysław, 213
Kraus, Annie, 111
Kraus, Karl, 108
Krońska, Irena, 214
Kroński, Tadeusz, 190–92, 214
Kundera, Milan, 14, 133, 179
Kuroń, Jacek, 14, 211, 214, 215–16
Kusý, Miroslav, 181–82, 185

Landgrebe, Ludwig, 10, 140, 145, 248n58, 252n20

Landmann, Michael, 75
Lauer, Quentin, 125
legal theory, 20, 67–69, 120–21, 127, 239n47, 253–54n32, 254n33, 268n100, 283n166
Lenin, Vladimir, 135, 162, 163
Leo XIII, 195, 196, 209, 220
Lévinas, Emmanuel, 4, 130, 182, 183, 217
liberalism, 3, 6, 9, 10, 17, 23, 81, 108–10, 113–15, 133, 136, 159, 162–63, 172–73, 177, 186, 209, 224–29, 302n136
lifeworld, 17, 20, 47, 57–59, 63, 125, 133, 147, 157, 176, 233n26, 243n10, 248n62, 294n8
Lipps, Theodor, 20, 48, 63, 64–65, 71, 106, 118
Litt, Theodor, 125
Losev, Alexei, 285n4
love, 35–40, 42, 43, 56, 72, 84–87, 90–91, 92–3, 94–98, 104, 107, 109, 199–201, 206–7, 215, 220, 222, 261n2, 323n25
Lubac, Henri de, 202
Lukács, György, 134–35
Łukasiewicz, Jan, 190

Major, Ladislav, 150
Malý, Václav, 178, 180
Manent, Pierre, 116
Mao Tse Tung, 164
Marcuse, Herbert, 5, 135, 149
Maritain, Jacques, 3, 190, 194, 300n106
Marković, Mihailo, 286n11
Marx, Karl/Marxism/socialism, 18, 22, 23, 73, 99, 108, 134–36, 140, 146–50, 162, 163, 164, 172, 174, 177, 178, 186, 190, 210, 212, 213, 214, 215, 216, 219–21, 224, 226, 228, 229
Masaryk, Tomáš, 22, 41, 140–44, 145, 146, 168
materialism, 94–95, 97, 110, 113–14, 148, 164, 191, 196, 210, 212, 219
McAleer, Graham, 85
McGill, V. J., 4
Meinong, Alexius, 29

Merleau-Ponty, Maurice, 4, 92, 130, 135, 232n14, 241n3
Michalski, Krzysztof, 152, 214
Michnik, Adam, 212, 214–25, 221, 222, 223
Mikulski, Leopold, 290n24
Miłosz, Czesław, 190–91
Mohanty, J. N., 74
Mokrejš, Antonín, 150
Moore, G. E., 42, 240n66
motivation, 20, 46, 65, 70–71, 119, 278n114
Mounier, Emmanuel, 310n7
Movement for the Defense of Human and Civic Rights (ROPCiO), 214
Musset, Alfred de, 142

National Socialism, 3, 4, 5, 9, 13, 21, 55, 57, 81, 102, 106, 107, 108–10, 111, 112, 115, 117, 124, 130, 131, 145, 227, 229, 248n57, 248n58, 262n9, 273n47, 274n56, 281n153, 283n176, 298n75, 306n21, 318n85
Natorp, Paul, 102
natural world, 17, 98, 101, 127, 150, 154, 156–57, 183–84, 241–42n4
Nietzsche, Friedrich, 18, 91, 92, 93, 99, 103, 125, 167, 299n101
Noica, Constantin, 135

Odrodzenie Group, 190
ontology, 13, 61, 73–75, 77–78, 102, 103, 117, 122, 124, 129–30, 134–35, 183, 189, 190, 193, 196, 236n14, 260n82
Ortega y Gasset, José, 81
Orzoff, Andrea, 143
Otaka, Tomoo, 125
Otto, Rudolf, 269n121

Paci, Enzo, 135
Palouš, Martin, 179
Palouš, Radim, 150, 180, 181
Pascal, Blaise, 86
Patočka, Jan, 2, 3, 4, 12, 13, 18, 22, 23, 44, 55, 85, 128, 129, 136, 139, 141, 142, 144, 145, 146, 147, 150, 151–73, 174–77, 178, 179, 180, 181, 182, 184, 187, 191, 205, 214, 218, 227, 229
Pavlík, Jan, 143
personalism, 3, 7, 8, 9, 10, 13, 14, 17–8, 20, 21, 23, 38, 47–49, 52–53, 56, 69, 72, 79, 82, 84, 85, 87–88, 89, 91, 93–94, 97–98, 103, 104, 106–10, 113–16, 117, 118, 119–20, 121, 123, 127, 129 , 139, 142, 144, 148, 160, 176–78, 179, 183–84, 186, 190, 193–96, 199, 200–10, 212, 214, 215, 216–23, 225, 228, 229, 233n27, 243n14, 254n36, 254n37, 273n46, 275,76, 279n124, 280n144, 289n23, 310n7, 312n19, 314n40
Petrović, Gajo, 135
Pfänder, Alexander, 20, 46, 63, 64, 65, 66, 70–2, 106, 119, 252n18, 278n114
phenomenology (definitions of), 11–19
Piccone, Paul, 135, 286n9, 291n39
Pius XI, Pope, 13, 194, 209
Plastic People of the Universe, 174, 179
Plato/Platonism, 11, 41, 54, 61, 68, 102, 153, 155, 159, 166–67, 170, 171, 207, 279n127, 199n94
Plessner, Helmuth, 14, 21, 101, 102, 122–24
politics/government/state, 2, 3, 4, 5, 6, 9, 10, 11, 14, 21–23, 24, 25, 26, 29, 40, 41, 45, 47, 50, 53, 54, 61, 72, 81, 98, 100, 105, 108–10, 111, 114–16, 120–21, 130, 133–36, 140–43, 147, 149, 151, 161–65, 170–73, 174–81, 183–87, 192, 193, 195, 196, 209–10, 211–12, 215, 219, 220, 221, 222, 224–29, 239–40n54, 247n48, 262–63n9, 278n114, 279n126, 279n127, 281n152, 292n49, 295n34, 302n136, 304–5n21, 306n48, 308–9n75
Prague Circle (Cercle philosophique de Prague pour les recherches sur l'entendement humain , 22, 145
Prague Spring -22, 146–50, 297n59
Prečan, Vilém, 179
Przywara, Erich, 280n138

psychology/psychologism, 16, 18, 19, 20, 29–34, 36, 37, 39, 40–41, 45, 46, 51, 59, 62, 63, 64, 71, 127, 139, 143, 189, 197, 238n40, 241n68, 258n73, 263n12

Rádl, Emanuel, 146, 288n10
realist phenomenology. *See* idealism-realism dispute
Reinach, Adolf, 3, 11, 12, 13, 20, 21, 63, 64, 65, 66–70, 73, 105, 106, 110, 116–17, 118, 120, 131
Reinach, Anna, 116–17, 276n100
Reiner, Hans, 256n52
religion, conversion, 12, 21, 82, 85, 92, 93, 97, 107, 111, 112, 117, 118, 121, 143, 171, 177, 180, 220, 221, 227, 233n16, 264n29, 280n138, 323n25; Buddhism, 90, 245n23, 264n29; Catholicism, 6, 12–13, 18, 21, 23, 30, 81, 82, 84, 86, 89, 92, 94–98, 107, 109, 111, 112, 113, 117, 118, 121, 143, 175, 178, 180, 188–89, 190, 193–210, 212, 214, 215, 216–23, 227, 228, 233n16, 257n59, 272n41, 273n47, 276n95, 276n100, 280n138, 310n7, 314n39, 315n41, 315n45, 317n76; Judaism, 13, 57, 82, 110, 111, 112, 117, 140, 227, 233n16, 248n57, 273n47, 274n59; Protestantism, 12, 18, 85, 86, 96, 107, 117, 143, 146, 177, 180, 233n16, 246n34, 265n34, 276n100, 289n18
renewal, 1–6, 8–10, 13, 19–20, 22, 24, 29, 41, 43, 47, 49–56, 60–61, 87, 89–91, 94–97, 100, 114, 121, 123, 130, 140–44, 152, 160–65, 170–72, 179–80, 183, 201, 202, 212, 214, 222, 224–29, 243n15, 245n23, 263n12, 290n30, 322n15
ressentiment, 21, 91–94, 99, 110, 111, 179, 222,
Rickert, Heinrich, 49
Ricoeur, Paul, 151
Rieger, Ladislav, 145, 146
Riegl, Alois, 30
Rorty, Richard, 309n81

Rosenberg, Alfred, 281n153
Różycki, Ignacy, 197
Russell, Bertrand, 49

Safranski, Rüdiger, 63
Said, Edward, 99
Saint-Simon, Comte de, 98
Sartre, Jean-Paul, 3, 4, 130, 194
Scheler, Max, 3, 4, 10, 11, 12, 13, 14, 17, 18, 20–1, 22, 23, 43, 48, 63, 64, 66, 67, 70, 71, 72, 80–100, 101, 102, 103, 104, 105, 106, 107, 110, 111, 112, 113, 118, 121, 124, 125, 127, 129, 130, 131, 134, 139, 145, 188, 189, 190, 191–92, 193, 194–95, 197–200, 201, 202, 204, 205, 206, 208, 213, 217, 222, 225, 227, 228
Schiller, Friedrich, 99–100
Schmidt, Hermann, 315n41
Schmitt, Carl, 115, 279n126, 297n152
Schreier, Fritz, 125
Schuhmann, Karl, 69
Schutz, Alfred, 21, 56, 102, 125–27, 131
Searle, John, 68
sexuality and marriage, 40, 107, 200–201, 239n53, 275n68
Shestov, Lev, 285n4
Shore, Marci, 214
Shpet, Gustav, 134
Šiklová, Jiřína, 182, 226
Šimečka, Milan, 176, 309n81
Smid, Reinhold, 64
social acts, 3, 20, 68–69, 110, 120
sociology, 21, 81, 84, 100, 125–28
Socrates, 112, 163, 166, 171
Solidarity (trade union), 22, 23, 24, 193, 214, 216, 223, 226, 327n3
solidarity (concept), 9, 18, 23, 73, 89, 90–91, 93–95, 119, 129, 172, 179, 186, 193, 207, 209, 214, 215, 218–23, 225, 226, 266n74, 323n18,m 323n25
solidarism, 266n74
Spengler, Oswald, 50, 91
Spiegelberg, Herbert, 6, 71, 255n45
state. *See* politics

Stavenhagen, Kurt, 134
Stein, Edith, 3, 12, 13, 21, 43, 48, 63, 66, 89, 102, 107, 112, 116–22, 125, 127, 131, 190, 197, 257n60, 315n43
Stępień, Antoni Bazyli, 212
Stern, Wilhelm, 117
Stoker, Bram, 112
Strożewski, Władysław, 322n8
subjectivity, 4, 7, 8, 13, 15, 16, 20, 30–31, 37, 41, 43, 44, 51, 53, 57–59, 61, 65, 69, 75, 78, 97–98, 115, 118, 121–22, 126, 142, 148, 152, 155–56, 158, 159, 163–69, 176, 177, 191, 195, 197–99, 203, 206, 208, 210, 213, 214, 218, 221–22, 228, 233m24, 249n53, 249–50n74
Sviták, Ivan, 149
Swieżawski, Stefan, 190, 194, 213
Świętochowski, Alexander, 290n24
Szewczyk, Jan, 213

Tatarkiewicz, Władysław, 190, 192
technology/technocracy, 8, 9, 10, 29, 83, 99, 129, 133, 140, 146, 148, 152, 162–65, 168, 171, 175, 176, 178, 180, 183, 184, 215, 225, 228, 229
Thao, Tran Duc, 135
Thomas Aquinas/Thomism/neo-Thomism, 12–13, 24, 74, 91, 112, 121–22, 190, 193–96, 199, 200, 201, 212, 213, 216, 266n73, 279n136, 280n138, 314n35, 314n37, 317n74, 322n8
Tillman, Fritz, 315n41
Tischner, Józef, 12, 23–24, 128, 206, 210, 215, 216–23, 226, 295n32, 305n27, 312n18
titanism, 141, 142, 164, 168, 288n14, 298n81
Tocqueville, Alexis de, 98
Tönnies, Friedrich, 91, 119
totalitarianism—9, 10, 24, 81, 108–9, 111, 113, 115, 116, 123, 124, 130, 173, 177, 184, 185–86, 194, 209, 219–20, 225, 228, 229

transcendental phenomenology. *See* idealism-realism dispute
Trendelenburg, Adolf, 235–36n9
Tübingen School classicists, 166
Twardowski, Kazimierz, 30, 189–90, 311n9
Tymieniecka, Anna-Teresa, 261n95, 317n74

Uhl, Petr, 176, 178
Utitz, Emil, 140, 145, 146

Vaculík, Ludvík, 176, 304n16, 306n50
Vajda, Mihály, 135
values (axiology). *See* ethics
Vatican II, 23, 195, 201–2, 209, 213, 222
Vierkandt, Alfred, 125
Voegelin, Erich, 267n86

Wałesa, Lech, 223, 326n59
Walther, Gerda, 72–3
Weber, Max, 125–26
Welton, Donn, 55
Wiggins, David, 116
Williams, Bernard, 116
Wojtyła, Karol (Pope John Paul II), 2, 3, 4, 12, 13, 18, 21, 22, 23, 24, 43, 46, 69, 79, 91, 107, 112, 113, 121, 136, 188–210, 215, 216, 217, 218, 220, 221, 222, 223, 226, 229; Pope John Paul II, 117, 178, 189, 209–10, 211–13, 214, 215
Wolff, Christian, 190
work/labor, 143–44, 208, 209–10, 211, 220–22, 289n24
Workers' Defense Committee (KOR), 211, 214
Woroniecki, Jacek, 197
Wust, Peter, 12
Wyszyński, Cardinal Stefan, 190, 220–21, 320n1

Žižek, Slavoj, 229, 307n52
Zumr, Josef, 147
Zvěřina, Josef, 178, 179, 180

Cultural Memory in the Present

Simona Forti, *The New Demons: Rethinking Power and Evil Today*
Joseph Vogl, *The Specter of Capital*
Hans Joas, *Faith as an Option*
Michael Gubser, *The Far Reaches: Phenomenology, Ethics, and Social Renewal in Central Europe*
Françoise Davoine, *Mother Folly: A Tale*
Knox Peden, *Spinoza Contra Phenomenology: French Rationalism from Cavaillès to Deleuze*
Elizabeth A. Pritchard, *Locke's Political Theology: Public Religion and Sacred Rights*
Ankhi Mukherjee, *What Is a Classic? Postcolonial Rewriting and Invention of the Canon*
Jean-Pierre Dupuy, *The Mark of the Sacred*
Henri Atlan, *Fraud: The World of Ona'ah*
Niklas Luhmann, *Theory of Society, Volume 2*
Ilit Ferber, *Philosophy and Melancholy: Benjamin's Early Reflections on Theater and Language*
Alexandre Lefebvre, *Human Rights as a Way of Life: On Bergson's Political Philosophy*
Theodore W. Jennings, Jr., *Outlaw Justice: The Messianic Politics of Paul*
Alexander Etkind, *Warped Mourning: Stories of the Undead in the Land of the Unburied*
Denis Guénoun, *About Europe: Philosophical Hypotheses*
Maria Boletsi, *Barbarism and its Discontents*
Sigrid Weigel, *Walter Benjamin: Images, the Creaturely, and the Holy*
Roberto Esposito, *Living Thought: The Origins and Actuality of Italian Philosophy*
Henri Atlan, *The Sparks of Randomness, Volume 2: The Atheism of Scripture*
Rüdiger Campe, *The Game of Probability: Literature and Calculation from Pascal to Kleist*
Niklas Luhmann, *A Systems Theory of Religion*
Jean-Luc Marion, *In the Self's Place: The Approach of Saint Augustine*
Rodolphe Gasché, *Georges Bataille: Phenomenology and Phantasmatology*

Niklas Luhmann, *Theory of Society, Volume 1*
Alessia Ricciardi, *After La Dolce Vita: A Cultural Prehistory of Berlusconi's Italy*
Daniel Innerarity, *The Future and Its Enemies: In Defense of Political Hope*
Patricia Pisters, *The Neuro-Image: A Deleuzian Film-Philosophy of Digital Screen Culture*
François-David Sebbah, *Testing the Limit: Derrida, Henry, Levinas, and the Phenomenological Tradition*
Erik Peterson, *Theological Tractates*, edited by Michael J. Hollerich
Feisal G. Mohamed, *Milton and the Post-Secular Present: Ethics, Politics, Terrorism*
Pierre Hadot, *The Present Alone Is Our Happiness, Second Edition: Conversations with Jeannie Carlier and Arnold I. Davidson*
Yasco Horsman, *Theaters of Justice: Judging, Staging, and Working Through in Arendt, Brecht, and Delbo*
Jacques Derrida, *Parages*, edited by John P. Leavey
Henri Atlan, *The Sparks of Randomness, Volume 1: Spermatic Knowledge*
Rebecca Comay, *Mourning Sickness: Hegel and the French Revolution*
Djelal Kadir, *Memos from the Besieged City: Lifelines for Cultural Sustainability*
Stanley Cavell, *Little Did I Know: Excerpts from Memory*
Jeffrey Mehlman, *Adventures in the French Trade: Fragments Toward a Life*
Jacob Rogozinski, *The Ego and the Flesh: An Introduction to Egoanalysis*
Marcel Hénaff, *The Price of Truth: Gift, Money, and Philosophy*
Paul Patton, *Deleuzian Concepts: Philosophy, Colonialization, Politics*
Michael Fagenblat, *A Covenant of Creatures: Levinas's Philosophy of Judaism*
Stefanos Geroulanos, *An Atheism That Is Not Humanist Emerges in French Thought*
Andrew Herscher, *Violence Taking Place: The Architecture of the Kosovo Conflict*
Hans-Jörg Rheinberger, *On Historicizing Epistemology: An Essay*
Jacob Taubes, *From Cult to Culture*, edited by Charlotte Fonrobert and Amir Engel
Peter Hitchcock, *The Long Space: Transnationalism and Postcolonial Form*
Lambert Wiesing, *Artificial Presence: Philosophical Studies in Image Theory*
Jacob Taubes, *Occidental Eschatology*
Freddie Rokem, *Philosophers and Thespians: Thinking Performance*
Roberto Esposito, *Communitas: The Origin and Destiny of Community*
Vilashini Cooppan, *Worlds Within: National Narratives and Global Connections in Postcolonial Writing*
Josef Früchtl, *The Impertinent Self: A Heroic History of Modernity*
Frank Ankersmit, Ewa Domanska, and Hans Kellner, eds., *Re-Figuring Hayden White*
Michael Rothberg, *Multidirectional Memory: Remembering the Holocaust in the Age of Decolonization*
Jean-François Lyotard, *Enthusiasm: The Kantian Critique of History*

Ernst van Alphen, Mieke Bal, and Carel Smith, eds., *The Rhetoric of Sincerity*
Stéphane Mosès, *The Angel of History: Rosenzweig, Benjamin, Scholem*
Pierre Hadot, *The Present Alone Is Our Happiness: Conversations with Jeannie Carlier and Arnold I. Davidson*
Alexandre Lefebvre, *The Image of the Law: Deleuze, Bergson, Spinoza*
Samira Haj, *Reconfiguring Islamic Tradition: Reform, Rationality, and Modernity*
Diane Perpich, *The Ethics of Emmanuel Levinas*
Marcel Detienne, *Comparing the Incomparable*
François Delaporte, *Anatomy of the Passions*
René Girard, *Mimesis and Theory: Essays on Literature and Criticism, 1959–2005*
Richard Baxstrom, *Houses in Motion: The Experience of Place and the Problem of Belief in Urban Malaysia*
Jennifer L. Culbert, *Dead Certainty: The Death Penalty and the Problem of Judgment*
Samantha Frost, *Lessons from a Materialist Thinker: Hobbesian Reflections on Ethics and Politics*
Regina Mara Schwartz, *Sacramental Poetics at the Dawn of Secularism: When God Left the World*
Gil Anidjar, *Semites: Race, Religion, Literature*
Ranjana Khanna, *Algeria Cuts: Women and Representation, 1830 to the Present*
Esther Peeren, *Intersubjectivities and Popular Culture: Bakhtin and Beyond*
Eyal Peretz, *Becoming Visionary: Brian De Palma's Cinematic Education of the Senses*
Diana Sorensen, *A Turbulent Decade Remembered: Scenes from the Latin American Sixties*
Hubert Damisch, *A Childhood Memory by Piero della Francesca*
José van Dijck, *Mediated Memories in the Digital Age*
Dana Hollander, *Exemplarity and Chosenness: Rosenzweig and Derrida on the Nation of Philosophy*
Asja Szafraniec, *Beckett, Derrida, and the Event of Literature*
Sara Guyer, *Romanticism After Auschwitz*
Alison Ross, *The Aesthetic Paths of Philosophy: Presentation in Kant, Heidegger, Lacoue-Labarthe, and Nancy*
Gerhard Richter, *Thought-Images: Frankfurt School Writers' Reflections from Damaged Life*
Bella Brodzki, *Can These Bones Live? Translation, Survival, and Cultural Memory*
Rodolphe Gasché, *The Honor of Thinking: Critique, Theory, Philosophy*
Brigitte Peucker, *The Material Image: Art and the Real in Film*
Natalie Melas, *All the Difference in the World: Postcoloniality and the Ends of Comparison*
Jonathan Culler, *The Literary in Theory*
Michael G. Levine, *The Belated Witness: Literature, Testimony, and the Question of Holocaust Survival*

Jennifer A. Jordan, *Structures of Memory: Understanding German Change in Berlin and Beyond*
Christoph Menke, *Reflections of Equality*
Marlène Zarader, *The Unthought Debt: Heidegger and the Hebraic Heritage*
Jan Assmann, *Religion and Cultural Memory: Ten Studies*
David Scott and Charles Hirschkind, *Powers of the Secular Modern: Talal Asad and His Interlocutors*
Gyanendra Pandey, *Routine Violence: Nations, Fragments, Histories*
James Siegel, *Naming the Witch*
J. M. Bernstein, *Against Voluptuous Bodies: Late Modernism and the Meaning of Painting*
Theodore W. Jennings Jr., *Reading Derrida / Thinking Paul: On Justice*
Richard Rorty and Eduardo Mendieta, *Take Care of Freedom and Truth Will Take Care of Itself: Interviews with Richard Rorty*
Jacques Derrida, *Paper Machine*
Renaud Barbaras, *Desire and Distance: Introduction to a Phenomenology of Perception*
Jill Bennett, *Empathic Vision: Affect, Trauma, and Contemporary Art*
Ban Wang, *Illuminations from the Past: Trauma, Memory, and History in Modern China*
James Phillips, *Heidegger's* Volk: *Between National Socialism and Poetry*
Frank Ankersmit, *Sublime Historical Experience*
István Rév, *Retroactive Justice: Prehistory of Post-Communism*
Paola Marrati, *Genesis and Trace: Derrida Reading Husserl and Heidegger*
Krzysztof Ziarek, *The Force of Art*
Marie-José Mondzain, *Image, Icon, Economy: The Byzantine Origins of the Contemporary Imaginary*
Cecilia Sjöholm, *The Antigone Complex: Ethics and the Invention of Feminine Desire*
Jacques Derrida and Elisabeth Roudinesco, *For What Tomorrow . . . : A Dialogue*
Elisabeth Weber, *Questioning Judaism: Interviews by Elisabeth Weber*
Jacques Derrida and Catherine Malabou, *Counterpath: Traveling with Jacques Derrida*
Martin Seel, *Aesthetics of Appearing*
Nanette Salomon, *Shifting Priorities: Gender and Genre in Seventeenth-Century Dutch Painting*
Jacob Taubes, *The Political Theology of Paul*
Jean-Luc Marion, *The Crossing of the Visible*
Eric Michaud, *The Cult of Art in Nazi Germany*
Anne Freadman, *The Machinery of Talk: Charles Peirce and the Sign Hypothesis*
Stanley Cavell, *Emerson's Transcendental Etudes*
Stuart McLean, *The Event and Its Terrors: Ireland, Famine, Modernity*
Beate Rössler, ed., *Privacies: Philosophical Evaluations*

Bernard Faure, *Double Exposure: Cutting Across Buddhist and Western Discourses*
Alessia Ricciardi, *The Ends of Mourning: Psychoanalysis, Literature, Film*
Alain Badiou, *Saint Paul: The Foundation of Universalism*
Gil Anidjar, *The Jew, the Arab: A History of the Enemy*
Jonathan Culler and Kevin Lamb, eds., *Just Being Difficult? Academic Writing in the Public Arena*
Jean-Luc Nancy, *A Finite Thinking*, edited by Simon Sparks
Theodor W. Adorno, *Can One Live after Auschwitz? A Philosophical Reader*, edited by Rolf Tiedemann
Patricia Pisters, *The Matrix of Visual Culture: Working with Deleuze in Film Theory*
Andreas Huyssen, *Present Pasts: Urban Palimpsests and the Politics of Memory*
Talal Asad, *Formations of the Secular: Christianity, Islam, Modernity*
Dorothea von Mücke, *The Rise of the Fantastic Tale*
Marc Redfield, *The Politics of Aesthetics: Nationalism, Gender, Romanticism*
Emmanuel Levinas, *On Escape*
Dan Zahavi, *Husserl's Phenomenology*
Rodolphe Gasché, *The Idea of Form: Rethinking Kant's Aesthetics*
Michael Naas, *Taking on the Tradition: Jacques Derrida and the Legacies of Deconstruction*
Herlinde Pauer-Studer, ed., *Constructions of Practical Reason: Interviews on Moral and Political Philosophy*
Jean-Luc Marion, *Being Given That: Toward a Phenomenology of Givenness*
Theodor W. Adorno and Max Horkheimer, *Dialectic of Enlightenment*
Ian Balfour, *The Rhetoric of Romantic Prophecy*
Martin Stokhof, *World and Life as One: Ethics and Ontology in Wittgenstein's Early Thought*
Gianni Vattimo, *Nietzsche: An Introduction*
Jacques Derrida, *Negotiations: Interventions and Interviews, 1971–1998*, edited by Elizabeth Rottenberg
Brett Levinson, *The Ends of Literature: The Latin American "Boom" in the Neoliberal Marketplace*
Timothy J. Reiss, *Against Autonomy: Cultural Instruments, Mutualities, and the Fictive Imagination*
Hent de Vries and Samuel Weber, eds., *Religion and Media*
Niklas Luhmann, *Theories of Distinction: Re-Describing the Descriptions of Modernity*, edited and introduced by William Rasch
Johannes Fabian, *Anthropology with an Attitude: Critical Essays*
Michel Henry, *I Am the Truth: Toward a Philosophy of Christianity*
Gil Anidjar, *"Our Place in Al-Andalus": Kabbalah, Philosophy, Literature in Arab-Jewish Letters*
Hélène Cixous and Jacques Derrida, *Veils*
F. R. Ankersmit, *Historical Representation*
F. R. Ankersmit, *Political Representation*

Elissa Marder, *Dead Time: Temporal Disorders in the Wake of Modernity (Baudelaire and Flaubert)*

Reinhart Koselleck, *The Practice of Conceptual History: Timing History, Spacing Concepts*

Niklas Luhmann, *The Reality of the Mass Media*

Hubert Damisch, *A Theory of /Cloud/: Toward a History of Painting*

Jean-Luc Nancy, *The Speculative Remark: (One of Hegel's bon mots)*

Jean-François Lyotard, *Soundproof Room: Malraux's Anti-Aesthetics*

Jan Patočka, *Plato and Europe*

Hubert Damisch, *Skyline: The Narcissistic City*

Isabel Hoving, *In Praise of New Travelers: Reading Caribbean Migrant Women Writers*

Richard Rand, ed., *Futures: Of Jacques Derrida*

William Rasch, *Niklas Luhmann's Modernity: The Paradoxes of Differentiation*

Jacques Derrida and Anne Dufourmantelle, *Of Hospitality*

Jean-François Lyotard, *The Confession of Augustine*

Kaja Silverman, *World Spectators*

Samuel Weber, *Institution and Interpretation: Expanded Edition*

Jeffrey S. Librett, *The Rhetoric of Cultural Dialogue: Jews and Germans in the Epoch of Emancipation*

Ulrich Baer, *Remnants of Song: Trauma and the Experience of Modernity in Charles Baudelaire and Paul Celan*

Samuel C. Wheeler III, *Deconstruction as Analytic Philosophy*

David S. Ferris, *Silent Urns: Romanticism, Hellenism, Modernity*

Rodolphe Gasché, *Of Minimal Things: Studies on the Notion of Relation*

Sarah Winter, *Freud and the Institution of Psychoanalytic Knowledge*

Samuel Weber, *The Legend of Freud: Expanded Edition*

Aris Fioretos, ed., *The Solid Letter: Readings of Friedrich Hölderlin*

J. Hillis Miller / Manuel Asensi, *Black Holes / J. Hillis Miller; or, Boustrophedonic Reading*

Miryam Sas, *Fault Lines: Cultural Memory and Japanese Surrealism*

Peter Schwenger, *Fantasm and Fiction: On Textual Envisioning*

Didier Maleuvre, *Museum Memories: History, Technology, Art*

Jacques Derrida, *Monolingualism of the Other; or, The Prosthesis of Origin*

Andrew Baruch Wachtel, *Making a Nation, Breaking a Nation: Literature and Cultural Politics in Yugoslavia*

Niklas Luhmann, *Love as Passion: The Codification of Intimacy*

Mieke Bal, ed., *The Practice of Cultural Analysis: Exposing Interdisciplinary Interpretation*

Jacques Derrida and Gianni Vattimo, eds., *Religion*

The authorized representative in the EU for product safety and compliance is:
Mare Nostrum Group
B.V Doelen 72
4831 GR Breda
The Netherlands

www.ingramcontent.com/pod-product-compliance
Lightning Source LLC
Chambersburg PA
CBHW030604230426
43661CB00053B/1842